WARSHIP
VOLUME III

Edited by John Roberts

Conway Maritime Press
Naval Institute Press

WARSHIP Volume III

Managing Editor Robert Gardiner
Editor John Roberts
Art Editor Geoff Hunt

© **Conway Maritime Press Ltd 1979**

Second Impression 1984

**All articles published in WARSHIP are strictly
copyright and may not be reproduced without
the written consent of the publisher**

Published in the UK by
Conway Maritime Press Limited
24 Bride Lane,
Fleet Street,
London EC4Y 8DR

**Published and distributed in the United States of
America by**
The Naval Institute Press,
Annapolis,
Maryland 21402

Library of Congress Catalog No 78-55455
UK ISBN 0 85177 204 8
USA ISBN 0-87021-977-4

Manufactured in the United Kingdom

Contents

The 16in Mk 1 guns of HMS *Nelson*'s 'X' turret, 1934

Editorial

After guiding *Warship* through its early years and seeing the magazine established as a leading journal Antony Preston has retired as editor of the magazine to follow up his many other interests in the field of naval journalism. Myself, as the new editor, and the other members of the staff of *Warship* wish him well with all his future projects.

This edition of *Warship* sees the introduction of a letters page; although this is not strictly a correct description. We have called it *A's and A's,* the abbreviation of *Alterations and Additions,* which was used by the Admiralty's design departments to describe general modifications carried out to warships during refits. This title is particularly appropriate as the column is intended primarily as a platform to provide additions and corrections to previously published material together with any information which is considered to be of general interest to our readers. The origin of this information is not restricted and may come from a reader's letter, an author (as demonstrated in this issue with Friedrich Prasky's additions to his article in *Warship 6*), the staff of *Warship* or any other source.

Friedrich Prasky's list of the faults of the *Viribus Unitis* class brought to mind the fact that adverse criticism of warship design, both past and present, has generally and often unfairly been directed at their designers.

The first British battlecruisers of the *Invincible* and *Indefatigable* classes for example have been described as 'bad designs' which gives the impression that the DNC's department was in some way incompetent. In fact the main faults of these ships were the result of a bad specification for which Admiral Fisher and the other members of the Board of Admiralty were responsible. The design department produced exactly what was asked of them and in this respect the ships can only be described as good designs.

Many other factors outside the warship designer's control can also affect the quality of the finished product, principally financial restrictions and the competence of the shipyard which constructs the ship. Both these latter combined to reduce the quality of the Austro-Hungarian dreadnought *Szent Istvan* which might otherwise have been a first class vessel. The *Viribus Unitis* class, to which she belonged, were smaller ships than the designer would have wished which, combined with a heavy main armament,meant their stability and speed were less than might have been provided. Limited funds also prevented the setting up of a programme of underwater protection experiments, as were carried out by the majority of the other naval powers, and the torpedo defence system of the class suffered in consequence. These faults together with poor quality riveting were major contributory factors in the loss of the *Szent Istvan* which capsized and sank after being torpedoed in 1918 (see *Warship 6*). As a result the designer, Siegfried Popper, was severely reprimanded which, considering the difficulties he had to overcome, was hardly fair. It is always best to consider all the possible origins of faults before hanging the designer from the nearest tree.

A more recent example of financial restriction can be found in this issue in Peter Hodges description of the *Tribal* class frigates, although in this case the author does not direct his criticisms at Bath – which says much for the author and makes a pleasant change.

John Roberts

FIGURE 1: **THE PARTS OF A WOODEN SHIP**

1. HANGING KNEE (when positioned diagonally – to avoid a gunport, for example – they were known as 'dagger knees')
2. LODGING KNEE
3. DECK CLAMP (In French practice this was often more substantial)
4. WATERWAY TIMBER (In French practice this was usually more substantial and often rebated down onto the beams)
5. DECK BEAM (Formed of two timbers scarphed together)
6. CARLINGS
2. LEDGES
8. KEEL
9. KEELSON
10. FALSE KEEL
11. A FRAME (or 'Framed Bend', made up of two sets of futtock timbers bolted side by side) The individual parts are as follows:
   a. half-floor
   b. floor-timber (The two floor-timbers of a frame, and the space between them and the next pair, is known as 'room-and-space' and is a crucial measurement of the lightness or heaviness of construction in any vessel)
   c. 1st futtock
   d. 2nd futtock
   e. 3rd futtock
   f. 4th futtock (obscured by the beam knees, but above the 2nd futtock)
   g. 5th futtock
   h. Top timbers
   i. Chock (The French used a simple butt-joint without a chock to connect the futtock timbers: this was not as sturdy)
12. FLOOR RIDERS (There were also riders higher up the hull sides known as 'futtock riders' and 'top riders')

FIGURE 2: **INTERIOR CONSTRUCTIONAL DETAILS**

1. UPPER DECK BEAM
2. HANGING KNEE
3. CHOCK IN THE THROAT OF KNEE
4. INTERCOSTAL PACKING
5. AIR SPACE TO VENTILATE TIMBERS
6. DECK CLAMP OR BEAM SHELF
7. INNER PLANKING
8. SPIRKETTING
9. WATERWAY
10. SECTION OF FRAME
11. LODGING KNEE
12. VENTILATION SPACE
13. DECK CLAMP
14. CEILING OR INNER PLANKING
16. SPIRKETTING
17. INTERCOSTAL PACKING
18. REVERSE HANGING KNEE OR STANDARD
19. ORLOP DECK BEAM (note no waterway on this deck)
20. FLOOR RIDER
21. BEAM CHOCK COMBINED WITH IRON BEAM KNEE BRACKET
22. IRON WEDGES TO TAKE UP TRANSVERSE MOVEMENT (ie racking stresses)
23. INTERCOSTAL PACKING
24. GUN DECK BEAMS
25. PART OF FRAME EXPOSED AT GUNPORT (note that not all small ships had ports on this deck)
26. MAINWALE
27. OUTER PLANKING

This drawing was based on Keith Hobbs' illustration in *Model Shipwright* 25 and was redrawn with his permission. 1-12 represents standard English practice in the period under discussion: 13 onwards was practice adopted in the Royal Navy towards the end of the eighteenth century. but in some ways compares with mid-century French practice. In both cases it was the result of shortages of the expensive 'grown' timber for proper knees, which affected the French Navy much earlier.

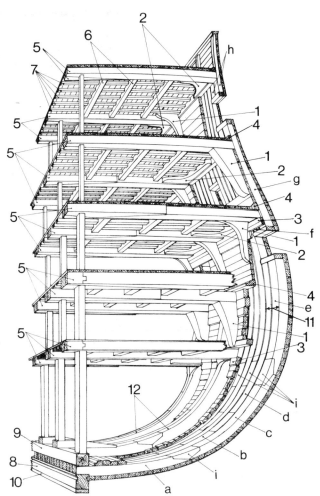

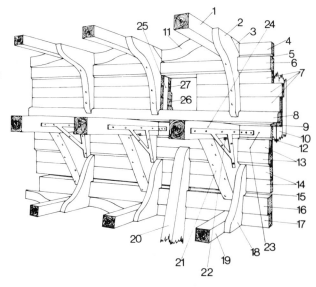

FRIGATE DESIGN
IN THE 18th CENTURY
PART 1
BY ROBERT GARDINER

It may come as a surprise to many to find that sailing warships can be treated in the same fashion as modern vessels – certainly very little of a technical nature has ever been published. However, ships-of-the-line and frigates were built in classes, the vessels of which differed very little from one another, just like modern warships, and their particulars, performance and development can be described in similar detail. The one major difference is that little of the design discussion has survived, if indeed it was ever written down. This is not to say that eighteenth century warships were not designed for specific functions, it was simply that what modern navies call 'staff requirements' did not change, were perfectly understood by all, and consequently were rarely even mentioned. This leaves the present-day historian with the difficult task of reconstructing the 'staff requirements' from an analysis of the characteristics of the vessels themselves.

While it would be possible to write about classes and their particulars, the ships themselves are not well-known to modern readers, and the following general study of the differences between British and French frigate design is felt to be of more interest. Everybody who has read any naval history knows that eighteenth century French design is supposed to be far superior, and that the chief means of improvement in the Royal Navy was copying captured vessels. The truth is very different, and as with contemporary ships, it only proves how misleading comparisons can be, and how meaningless are terms like 'better' and 'best' when applied to ship design. Ultimately it is a question of what requirements and restraints were placed on the designer and how well he overcame them.

Part 1 of this article covers the period of the 1744-48 war and is concerned principally with constructional practices; Part 2 deals with the Seven Years War (1756-63) and design differences and comparative sailing performances; while Part 3 is devoted to later vessels and the staff requirements of the two navies.

ENGLISH CRUISER DESIGN 1700–1744

After the innovations of the late seventeenth century when the English had adopted long, low hulls and fine lines, supposedly inspired by Dunkirk privateers, there was a reversal of policy. These so-called 'frigate-built' principles had been extended up the battle-order as far as third rates (60-70 gun ships) which started a tradition of complaint about crankness (ie instability) and lack of freeboard to the lower deck guns that lasted – with less and less justification – for more than half a century. It may have been that the English sacrificed other qualities for sheer speed: certainly these ships did not carry their guns well, were accused of decaying rapidly, and probably were less stable and seaworthy than their tactical usage required.

An attempt was made to remedy these faults with the first proper 'Establishment' in 1706. The Establishments were designed to standardise ships and shipbuilding by fixing the dimensions and scantlings (ie the sizes of structural timbers) for each rate. In 1706, 20 and 30 gun ships were not included but the first full Establishment was promulgated in 1719. England was at war with Spain and this probably provided the impetus towards improved and extended standardisation: it was certainly very thorough in its provisions and no other Establishment was ratified until England was again at war. The 1706 regulations had produced relatively beamier and hence more stable vessels, and the trend was continued in 1719. Judging by the details of the scantlings, robustness and seaworthiness seem to have been the requirements, which should have produced the durable, low-maintenance vessels that a peace-time administration would favour.

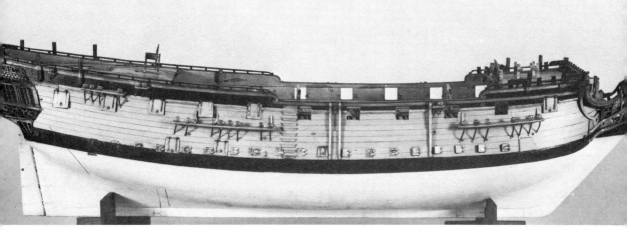

A model of a 1741 Establishment 20 gun ship. Note the oarports on the lower deck, the small ballast port amidships and the 2 gunports aft of amidships. The channels are below the upper deck ports. Earlier 20 gun ships could be distinguished by the lower deck gunports being further aft and more widely separated on 1733 ships, and on 1719 ships there were no gunports at all on the lower deck. *NMM*

The Establishments are always criticised for discouraging innovation, but the real reason for the slow rate of improvement in the 1720s and '30s was the absence of the incentive of war. Moreover, the Establishments laid down dimensions and scantlings and concerned themselves with the structure of the ships but allowed considerable leeway in designing the hull form. This was exploited particularly for small ships which in peace-time were the rates most frequently employed and whose relative cheapness would not discourage experiment.

Alterations to the Establishment were proposed in 1733, most ships having their beams increased to give all ships the same length-to-breadth ratio. Although not ratified most new vessels were built to these specifications and these were the newest vessels in service when war with Spain broke out in 1739. It was soon obvious that what had been adequate in 1719 was outclassed twenty years later. Warships of equivalent rates in Continental

navies had grown in size and possessed superior sailing qualities and, in the earlier years of the war, English cruisers had little success. As an interim measure, increased dimensions were proposed in 1741 and, although again not signed by the King in Council, were widely adopted. It was the first general increase *in length* since 1719 and, for the 60 gun ships since 1691! (Since speed and waterline length are related it is interesting that so many French frigates were captured by 60s or 64s – see Table 1 – relatively, the longest ships in the Navy.) Proportionally the 20 gun ships enjoyed the largest increase, indicating perhaps that they were most in need of it. Certainly they were much smaller than the next rate, the 40s, since the 30s proposed in 1719 were not built and thereafter the class lapsed.

However, it was not just size that was the problem with the sixth rates, since they were built to a clumsy two-decked design. The lower deck – for historical reasons called the 'Gun Deck' – only had ports for 2 guns a side, the remaining space being taken up with oar ports, but this deck had to be far enough above the waterline to allow the guns to be worked when the ship was heeling or rolling in a seaway. This meant that the 'Upper Deck' – in effect, the main gun deck – was even higher out of the water, with the resulting problems of stability and windage

caused by the relatively tall hull sides. This otherwise irrational disposition of armament had one advantage in that it allowed a few larger guns to be carried low down in small ships. The earlier English 24s sometimes carried a pair of 9pdrs on the Gun Deck to supplement their Upper Deck 6pdrs, and the French built a number of *demi-batterie* frigates of 28 to 36 guns with between 8 and 12 guns of 8 or 12pdr calibre on the Gun Deck beneath an Upper Deck armament of 6pdrs.

However, France also built smaller vessels with one gun deck, below which there was sometimes another complete deck clear of any ports. This deck was placed at or below the waterline which resulted in a hull with lower topsides and potentially greater stability. In 1744 France launched the first of these, *La Medée* of 26 guns, thus introducing what came to be accepted as the true 'frigate-form'. It was this type of vessel which opposed the obsolescent and inadequate English 20 and 24 gun ships when France entered the War of Austrian Succession in 1744.

FRENCH CRUISERS CAPTURED 1744-1748
During the course of the war a number of French cruisers corresponding in size to English fifth and sixth rates were captured and the more important of these are listed in Table 1. These vessels were

FRENCH FRIGATES CAPTURED 1744-48

TABLE 1

Name	Tonnage	Armament	Captured
A: PRIVATEERS			
LEOPARD	438	22 x 9pdr	27 Oct 1746 by
(*Margate*)		*22 x 9pdr, 2 x 4pdr*	*Windsor*, 60
			guns
DUC DE CHARTRES	354	32, calibre unknown	18 Jan 1976 by
(*Inverness*)		*20 x 9pdr, 2 x 3pdr*	*Edinburgh*, 64
TYGRE	576	26 x 9pdr	22 Feb 1747 by
(*not brought in*)			*Falkland*, 44
BELLONE	541	36, calibre unknown	2 Feb 1747 by
(*Bellona*)		*24 x 9pdr, 6 x 4pdr*	*Nottingham*, 60
DEUX COURONNES	639	24 x 9pdr	5 May 1747 by
(*Ranger*)		*24 x 9pdr, 6 x 4pdr*	*Gloucester*, 50
B: NATIONAL FRIGATES			
MEDÉE	670?	26 x 9pdr	4 April 1744 by
(*Boscawen*, privateer)		?	*Dreadnought*, 60
DAUPHIN	395	24, calibre unknown	Jan 1747 by
(*Richmond*)		?	Admiral
			Townsend's sqd.
FAVORETTE	744	30, calibre unknown	Jan 1747 by
(*Medway's Prize*)		?	*Medway*, 60
PANTHÈRE	481	20, calibre unknown	July 1747 by
(*Amazon*)		*24 x 6pdr*	*Monmouth*, 64
EMBUSCADE	746	40, calibre unknown	21 April 1746 by
(*Ambuscade*)		*26 x 12pdr, 14 x 6pdr*	*Defiance*, 60
SUBTILE	?	26, calibre unknown	19 Nov 1746 by
(*not brought in*)			*Portland*, 50
RENOMMÉE	669	30, calibre unknown	27 Sept 1747 by
(*Renown*)		*24 x 9pdr, 6 x 4pdr*	*Dover*, 44
CASTOR	605	26?	30 Oct 1747 by
(*not brought in*)			*Hampshire*, 50

Name and armament in italics is as borne in the Royal Navy. By way of comparison English 24 gun ships were 498 tons (1741 Establishment) or 508 tons (1745 Establishment) and mounted 22 x 9pdr and 2 x 3pdr. The earlier sixth rates of the 1733 Establishment measured 429 tons and carried 20 x 6pdr.

surveyed in detail and most of the surveys survive. In most cases a combination of the information from this source and from the Progress Books, which detail the extent, cost and duration of repairs and refits, gives a clear picture of the construction of these vessels. The most outstanding feature of the surveys, however, is the repetition of the same criticisms of all vessels. From the consistency of this critique, it becomes obvious that French and English styles of construction were radically different.

The surveyors' basic comments on French ships can be summarised as follows:
1. The internal arrangements were inadequate for Royal Navy warships. They had too few cabins, platforms in the hold, store rooms or magazines; some could not stow enough provisions and others did not have satisfactory messing arrangements.
2. They were too lightly built, with insufficient scantling and deck beams and frame timbers too far apart.
3. They were too lightly fastened, being short on structural members generally and beam knees (supporting brackets) in particular. Each frame, knee or beam had too few fastenings – either bolts, nails or treenails (oak pegs).
4. They were shoddily built of inferior timber and second-rate workmanship, crudely finished. Furthermore, instead of treenails

and bolts, too much use was made of iron nails which corroded and gave rise to the condition known as 'nail-sickness', a diagnosis frequently applied to ailing French warships.
5. This gave rise to the final accusation, that French ships were not built to last and consequently were costly to maintain.

Each of these assertions is worth a little more attention.

Internal Arrangements. To some extent this simply reflects different practices in the two navies, the Royal Navy, for example, preferring magazines aft where they were considered drier. However, the French Navy seems to have paid less attention to the requirements of long periods at sea and in particular the well-being of the crew.

Light Building. When taken with the accusation of light fastening, this is a criticism of central importance to the understanding of the French style of construction. All wooden ships' hulls distorted to some extent during their lives but the more lightly they were built the more rapidly this would occur and the more serious the resulting hogging, sagging or racking (transverse distortion). The essence of 'light' or 'heavy' building is the scantling of the frame timbers and the distance between them, which in shipwrights' terminology is known as 'room-and-space'. This also applied to deck beams and generally the lack of longitudinal strength was considered a hall-mark of French construction. The speed of many vessels was associated with this light style of building but paradoxically the better sailing qualities of such ships was quickly destroyed when the hull hogged and/or warped. Similarly, the stress on these delicate hulls must have been a major factor in the lack of duration also attributed to French frigates.

Light Fastening. Surveying officers were often ordered explicitly to take particular account of the fastening of French prizes and of the ironwork in general. The most fundamental problem was the French system of attaching the beams to the side of the ship, which employed a longitudinal deckclamp below the beam, a rebated waterway above and sometimes hanging (ie vertical) knees. The strength of the beam/hull side joint decided much of the ship's transverse rigidity and also decided the weight of armament a deck could carry and so the Royal Navy felt its system of substantial hanging and lodging (horizontal) knees was eminently superior. French hulls tended to suffer from the effects of their own gunfire and the strains of the masts and rigging. Therefore, French ships had fewer guns and less lofty masts and spars for a given tonnage than equivalent English vessels. Ironically, because of their robust construction which could stand the higher ratio of guns, English vessels have been regarded as over-gunned.

Shoddy Building. The Royal Dockyards set very high standards, they frequently criticised the English commercial shipbuilders – and there are frequent references in the surveys to the French use of poor materials (mainly softwoods) and inadequate seasoning, or dubious practices such as short scarph-joints. Many common French techniques, such as the butt-jointing of the futtock timbers in a frame (as opposed to the English use of scarphs and chocks) was considered shoddy. Nevertheless many of these reviled Gallic shortcomings were little more than further extensions of the desire to build a hull as lightly as possible, which goes to strengthen the feeling that light construction was a response to some officially sanctioned 'staff requirement'.

Lack of Duration. The surveys reiterate that because these ships are lightly built they will soon deteriorate and will either cost a lot to refit or will be very quickly rendered unserviceable. Certainly many of the French prizes enjoyed very short active careers by English standards – indeed, some as short as 5 years.

This, then, was the accepted view of French frigates among the Navy's administrators but it is not the one known to history. This is partly explained by the case of the French 30 gun frigate *Favorette*. In January 1745 *Favorette* surrendered to the

Medway, 60, and became known as the *Medway's Prize,* a common if unimaginative way of naming captured vessels. Her captor, Commodore Burnett, wrote to the Navy Board saying that she was a fine ship and although only mounting 30 guns, was a strong, well-built vessel which, with little expense, could be made into a proper (two-decked) 44 gun ship. Being on a foreign station (the West Indies) Burnett was not open to contradition but a survey carried out in September 1749 after *Medway's Prize* returned to England found her to be a weak ship, particularly in the upper works (she would never have carried the additional topsides necessary to make her a 44); with no platforms or storerooms in the fore hold, the beams only rebated into thick pieces of timber and the sheer much broken (ie the hull was badly hogged). Furthermore, the French reputation for poor durability and high maintenance costs led the surveyors to claim that the ship 'being a French bottom (ie hull), will require a middling if not a large repair'.

This case – which has innumerable parallels – clearly demonstrates why historians should be sceptical of claims made by captors about design, construction and sailing qualities. It was in the captor's interest to exaggerate the prize's performance, since this magnified his achievement in bringing her to battle and, knowing the Navy Board's concern with the material aspects of ship design, construction was always said to be strong and in healthy condition. The captor was also a salesman for his prize since he stood to earn far more if bought by the Navy than if sold to a commercial concern. This is also true of the distant commanders-in-chief who took a share of any prize-money made on their station and also had the power to 'buy in' any prizes they thought worthy. Whereas in England the surveying officers reported directly to a disinterested Navy Board, on foreign stations the surveyors were responsible to the local commander-in-chief who, consequently, could influence the

valuation. Naturally, to allay suspicion, the commanders always reported that the prizes were worth the money.

The Navy Board was not fooled and periodically complained to the Admiralty about the practice but there was no easy alternative and nothing was done. Unfortunately, most naval history concerns itself with either biography or the larger issues of tactics and strategy, and in both areas the correspondence of sea-officers is widely used. This tends to give a one-sided view of technical matters to a historian concerned with other aspects and a lack of understanding of the interest behind the sea-officers' praise has led to the widespread acceptance of the myth of over-whelming French design superiority throughout the eighteenth century. This is not to say that France did not build ships which found favour in England and the *Panthère* captured in July 1745 is a case in point. A full survey was not transmitted to the Admiralty but when their Lordships queried the twenty-four 6pdrs suggested by the Navy Board (the Admiralty wanted 9pdrs), the Navy Board quoted the survey assessment that *Amazon,* as she was renamed, was 'not so strong built as the English 24 gun ships, her masts being taunter (taller) in proportion' which would not stand the strain of 9pdrs without damage to the fabric of the hull and her performance under sail. Once again it is a case of the light construction of the French vessel preventing her being armed with the same weight of metal as an English ship of the same tonnage and the Navy Board, realising that the style of construction was an integral feature of the design, was reluctant to alter the balance of the design.

The largest frigate captured during the 1744-48 war was the *Embuscade,* 40 guns, taken by the *Defiance,* 60, on 21 April 1746. The survey of this vessel complained of the usual lack of beam knees and fastenings in the spirketting and clamps but, although the deck was planked with fir and the fastenings made too little use of treenails, the surveying officers concluded that 'the works are very well wrought'.

However, in her state of repair she seemed 2-3 years old whereas she was hardly more than a year from launching. Once again the Navy Board, anxious not to damage the qualities of the French ship, suggested an armament of twenty-six 9pdrs, ten 6pdrs on the quarterdeck and four more on the forecastle, 'as the said ship is not so strongly built as the English forty-four gun ships', the nearest equivalent in rating and tonnage, although not in armament. Consequently the Admiralty insisted on the substitution of 12pdrs for the 9pdrs.

Captain Powlett of the *Defiance,* not enjoying the lax surveying standards of a foreign station, had his prize valued at less than his own estimate and disputed the price. The ship was resurveyed and the second survey is worth quoting at some length because it is more explicit in its exposition of the differences between English and French practice.

The surveyors observed that 'there is a great difference in the manner of her building to the methods practiced in the English Navy, great deficiencies in the strength, and as we conceive, in the duration of ships built with foreign timber.' She suffered from the usual deficiencies of too great a distance between frames and insufficient beam knees, breast hooks, transom knees and fastenings. Five lower deck beams were not kneed at all and the rest had only one dagger knee with two bolts in each arm, 'which although they have a waterway pricked down (rebated), bolted through the sides and beams, it is not equal to our manner of having one hanging and one lodging knee to each end of the beam, bolted with ten bolts through the side and the beam. Spirketting, clamps and works in general are slightly fastened. The upper deck has not a sufficient number of knees and bolts. The quarterdeck has no knees to the beams, trusting to a 6in waterway let down on the beams and bolted through the side and to the beams, which we judge is not sufficient to carry a proper weight of metal as beams kneed in His Majesty's ships.' Furthermore, the

underwater planking was fastened with iron nails and the topsides were lower than HM ships, which would make her wetter in a seaway or on a wind. Apart from shoddy workmanship, all the other standard criticisms are expounded and at length.

La Subtile of 26 guns was taken by the *Portland,* 50, in December 1746. Although she was not very old there was considerable decay in her frames and she could only be fitted for 3-4 years' service without a Great Repair. Since they estimated that the necessary work would cost £7. 2s. 0d. per ton – more than a new 24 gun ship – they did not recomment purchase. However, they made an interesting suggestion: should the Admiralty want 'the preserving of her body' (that is, hull form) they proposed having a merchant yard replace the defective timbers, and keep strictly to the present scantlings, shape of the body, and dimensions of her masts, yards and sails.' This reveals an awareness that the Admiralty was on the look-out for a new model for a small cruiser-design. The attention to the details of scantling and spar dimensions also demonstrates that the Navy Board regarded a ship design as a physical entity – not just a hull shape but a hull of particular style of construction.

Probably the best known of all the small cruisers captured in this war was the *Renommé*, a 669 ton, 30 gun vessel of the new frigate form, taken on 27 September 1747 by the *Dover,* 44 guns. The survey, carried out with regard to having to make the fewest possible alterations, called attention to the lack of lodging knees and fastenings to the beams and to the distance between beams but on the other hand was favourably impressed by the frames: 'are all framed bends in the French manner, both timbers as joined are from 1ft 2in to 1ft 6in and in the room between from 4in to 7in' which was much closer than usual French cruiser practice. Furthermore, they found the ship 'well built' and having 'that appearance, and a very promising body for going, and common fame says she outsailed everything...'

Renown, as she was renamed, became a favourite cruiser having a longer career than any of the other frigates under discussion, finally being broken up in May 1771. This may appear to contradict the French reputation for lack of durability but *Renown's* upkeep was costly: in 1751 it was found that she wanted a 5-month Great Repair, whereas it only took 9-10 months to build a new frigate of that size, and for a while breaking her up was strongly considered. After the Great Repair of 1751 she was reported unfit for service again in 1755 but it was not until the beginning of the Seven Years War that she received the necessary attention, which took 12 months and cost as much as a new 32. Even so she required another large (that is, Great) repair in 1764 and a complete 18 month rebuild by 1770 when it was considered that the estimated £7000 might be better spent elsewhere. She was broken up at Woolwich.

One other frigate was captured but not purchased during the war. The *Castor* of 605 tons had been built at Quebec in 1744, with knees, breathooks and so forth of local timber, haughtily dismissed as 'a kind of pine'. However, the surveying officers found her 'well-built', although they qualified this with the somewhat supercilious 'in the French taste'. Unfortunately, she was reputed to have become a poor sailer, which was put down to having been built in North America since 'ships built in those countries are very uncertain in duration, many of them decaying soon'. It is rarely realised that a wooden ship's shape can alter considerably during her lifetime which usually affects her sailing performance adversely. Obviously the more slightly built and lightly fastened French ships were more prone to this than their stronger, more durable, English counterparts. Speed could be achieved at the expense of robustness but the design would have to accept a short optimum life for the hull.

'THE FRENCH INFLUENCE'
To fully appreciate the significance of the subsequent developments it is

necessary to digress at this point into naval administration. Essentially the Royal Navy was run by a permanent bureaucracy, the Navy Board, which looked after the design, construction, maintenance, victualling and manning of the ships. However, the Admiralty dictated overall policy and took the decisions (often advised by the Navy Board) which the Board was supposed to execute. Theoretically, the Admiralty was superior in authority but it was an ad hoc collection of politicians and senior sea officers appointed by the Government of the day, whereas the Navy Board, containing sea officers and civil servants, was a permanent professional body; and, with the contempt of the professional for the amateur, often set itself against its nominal masters. The ambiguity of the situation made the Navy Board sensitive to 'uninformed' criticism (real or imagined) and its dealings with the Admiralty were guarded at best and sometimes openly antagonist.

As far as ship design was concerned there was a division of 'feed-back', dockyard officials reporting to the Navy Board but sea-officers to the Admiralty. Bearing in mind that sea-officers often complained about their ships as an excuse for failure or covert praise of achievement, the Admiralty's view of a design could easily be at odds with that of the Navy Board. Furthermore the junior body had very little access to sea-officers' opinions, except at second-hand when passed on by the Admiralty, which was usually construed as criticism of the designer and his department. This is possibly the background to the setting up of the Sailing Quality Reports, which would give the Navy Board not only design information but reasonably objective evidence from sea-officers with which to counter complaints to the Admiralty.

However, by the mid-1740s the Admiralty had a corpus of opinion that pointed to inadequacies in English ships, despite the 1741 alterations. In February the Admiralty ordered the Navy Board to stop work on a number of recently laid down line-of-battle-ships and the senior body set up a commission to decide on a new Establishment, chaired by a technically minded Admiral, Sir John Norris. The Navy Board resented the usurpation of its authority and vigorously and successfully opposed some of the more radical proposals of the Admiralty. Possibly the Navy Board was kept in ignorance of the scope of Norris' brief and the minutiae of his findings for, although the Establishment was ratified in August 1745, the Navy Board was not told that the commission had produced its own Establishment draughts until January 1746.

Although progress was stopped on ships-of-the-line in the early stages of building, new cruisers were ordered while the commission was still in session. Two 24s were ordered in June 1745 which appear to have been an experiment or at least an interim measure for, although built to 1741 dimensions, their hull form was taken from a merchant shipbuilder's (Allen, of Deptford) model. However, the first 24 of the 1745 Establishment, the *Arundel,* was ordered on 3 October 1745 and two more followed during 1746.

Possibly the Admiralty was not very hopeful about the qualities of the compromise designs of 1745, for some of the surveys of French prizes around this time mention the 'preserving of the body' (*Subtile's* for example) as if they had been directed to look out for a swift sailing hull. This was how the Admiralty came upon the privateer *Tygre.* Her survey detailed more than the usual deficiences and recommended not purchasing her but it also stressed her 'great character for sailing'. The Admiralty decided on 31 March 1747 not to add her to the Navy but, on 29 April, ordered her lines to be taken off 'in the most exact manner' and to build to those lines two 24s 'without the least deviation' from the draught. The sense of urgency was highly unusual: one was to be built at Plymouth, at speed and 'in preference to all other new works'. Slade, the Master Shipwright at Plymouth was

1 *Phoenix,* a typical English 20 gun ship of the 1741 Establishment. With a pair of gunports, a ballast port amidships, and a row of oarports on the lower, or Gun Deck, the ship is in every respect a two decker and very high out of the water in consequence.

2 *Amazon*, ex-French *Panthère*, could not be a greater contrast to *Phoenix*, being very low indeed. She has a complete lower deck but there is no outward sign of this (even the oarports are on the upper deck), and indeed amidships the lower deck is well below the waterline. Although having advantages of stability, this form of hull would have been very wet, and the original plan shows the additional topside bulwarks the Royal Navy intended to add. Note that the ship was steered with a tiller, a feature only found on small, handy craft in the Royal Navy.

3 *Embuscade,* although much larger, has many features in common with *Amazon.* French frigates were not only low built but also had severe tumblehome (curve inwards from the waterline) in section, and therefore carried their channels (the outward projecting platform to which the lower standing rigging was set up) below the upper deck ports. This gave them more leverage but exposed them to damage from heavy seas.

4 *Renommée* was the finest of the French captures. She, like most French cruisers, carried no broadside guns forward of the foremast. This was because the fineness of the lines forward gave little buoyancy, and also because the long light hull could not stand heavy weights at the ship's extremities.

5 Following the Admiralty's dissatisfaction with the 24 gun ships of the 1745 Establishment, the two Surveyors of the Navy were instructed to produce improved designs. Sir Jacob Acworth's vessel was *Seahorse:* in many ways she was a half-way stage between two-deckers and true frigates, with only a ballast port on a Gun Deck slightly lower in the hull.

6 *Mermaid* was the other design – by Allin – with generally similar features. Neither was an entirely satisfactory ship.

7 *Lyme* and her sister *Unicorn,* however, were highly successful. Based on the lines of the privateer *Tygre,* they introduced the genuine frigate form into the Royal Navy and were the prototypes for a class of 20 vessels built between 1755 and 1766. They retained certain French features, including the rectangular window-ports above the two after-most gunports, square hances (the cut-down of forecastle and quarterdeck rails) and a tiller on the quarterdeck, although this was worked by a wheel aft of the mizzen mast.

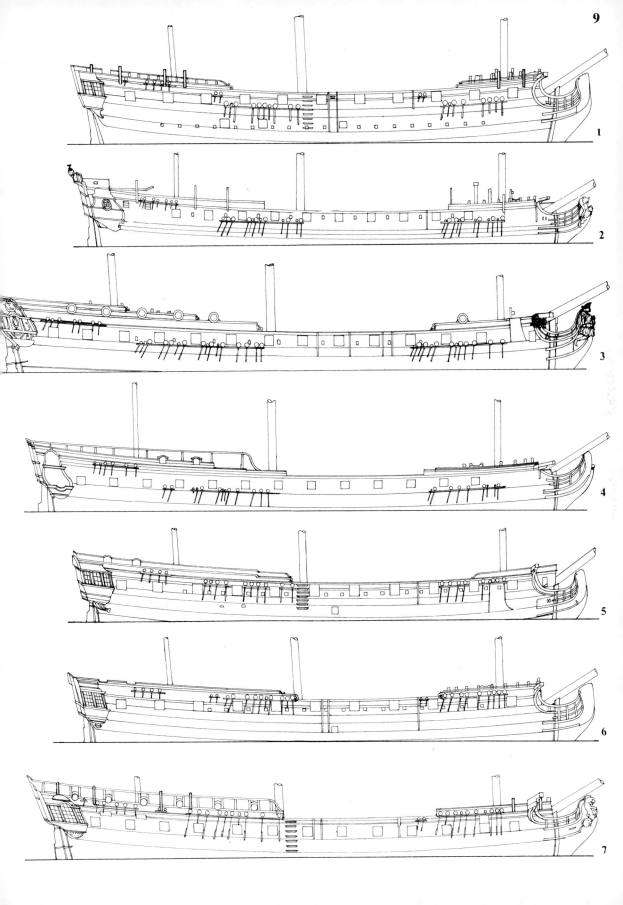

9

TABLE 2: COMPARATIVE SCANTLINGS OF FRENCH AND ENGLISH FRIGATES

In case English surveying officers' comments on French scantling be considered mere prejudice an objective comparison with English dimensions can be offered. The Adm 168/– series of Admiralty contracts contain detailed specifications and of these the earliest frigate is *Lowestoffe* of 1760, although this contract is merely a standard one for the *Niger* class (proved by the dimensions) with a few modifications for a larger ship.

The French ships were chosen because their scantlings are particularly well detailed, and except for *Hermione* and *Comête* because they particularly impressed the surveyors as well built. *Hermione, Bellone* and *Comête* were captured in the Seven Years War covered in Part 2 of this article, but are included for the sake of completeness.

*These refer to the parts numbered in Figures 1 or 2.

Name		EMBUSCADE	CASTOR	RENOMME
Tons		746	605	669
Built		1745	1744	1744
***FIGURE**	**TIMBERS**	inches	inches	inches
	Space between floor timbers	10-16	3-8	4-7
1/11b	floor, sided	9½	?	8½
	floor, moulded	9	?	9
1/11c	1st futtock, sided	?	8	8½
	1st futtock, moulded	?	8	9
1/11d	2nd futtock, sided	?	8	8½
	2nd futtock moulded	?	7¾	9
1/11e	3rd futtock, sided	?	8	8
	3rd futtock, moulded	?	6¼	7
1/11f	4th futtock, sided	7	8	7
	4th futtock, moulded	5	4½	6
1/11h	Top timber, sided	?	7½	7
	Top timber, moulded	?	4	5½
	LOWER DECK			
2/24	**Beams,** sided	13	12	9
	moulded	10	12	8
	Distance apart	36-70	44-64	42-63
	No. of beams	16	24	23
2/2 or 2/21	**Hanging** Knees, sided	NONE	9(pine)	7½
	Bolts per arm, and diameter in inches	—	4+3 of ¾	3+4
	Which beams have knees	—	All	All
	Dagger knees, sided	2	NONE	NONE
	Bolts per arm	2+2	—	—
	Which beams have knees	All except 2 4 5 7 & 10	—	—
2/11	**Lodging** knees, sided	NONE	NONE	NONE
	Bolts per arm, and diameter	—	—	—
	Which beams have knees	—	—	—
2/13	**Clamps,** thick	6½	7	4
	broad	28	12	23
2/9	**Waterways,** thick	6½	6	8
	let into beams	2	3	2
	broad	?	24	10
	UPPER DECK			
2/1	**Beams,** sided	14	8½	9
	moulded	12	8½	8
	distance apart	26-72	30-65	40-66
	No. of beams	26	26	27
2/2	**Hanging** knees, sided	10	7½(pine)	7
	Bolts per arm, and diameter	3+2	4+3 of ¾″	4+3 of ¾″
	Which beams have knees	18 midships	All except 1	All
2/11	**Lodging** knees, sided	10	NONE	NONE
	Bolts per arm, and diameter	3+2	—	—
	Which beams have knees	1st 5, last 3	—	—
2/21	Iron hanging knees, which beams	NONE	NONE	NONE
2/9	**Waterways,** thick	10½	5	4
	let into beams	3½	2	2
2/6	**Clamps,** thick	5	6	4
	broad	28	24	12

HERMIONE	BELLONE	COMÊTE	LOWESTOFFE/NIGER
812	677	647	701/679
1748	1755	1751	1761/1758-63
inches	inches	inches	inches
9	4-5	6	2½/3
?	9	9	13
?	7¾	7¾	10
9½	9	?	13
9	8	?	9½
9	9	8	11½
9	7¾	7¾	8½
?	8	?	11
8	7¾	?	7½
?	8½	8	10¾
6	5½	5	8
?	8½	8	10¼
5	3¼	3½	4

The English vessels not only have considerably heavier frames but they are also closer together.

10½	9¾	8	9
9	9¼	7	8
?	36-62	?	?/30-54
25	26	?	28
?	(iron)	6	7½
?	3+3	2+3	6+6 of 1
1st only	every other	All	All
NONE	NONE	NONE	NONE
—	—	—	—
—	—	—	—
NONE	NONE	NONE	7
—	—	—	5+4 of 1
—	—	—	All
5½	4		5
10	18¾		28
?	?	?	4
3	?		0
?	?		?

12½	10	8½	9
10½	9	8	9
?	32-60	?	26-54
27	27	?	29
9	8	7½	7
4+4	3+4	3+3	7+7 of 1″
11 beams	All	All	All
8	NONE	NONE	6½
3+3	—	—	5+6 of 1″
5 beams	—	—	All
12 beams	NONE	NONE	NONE
?	?	?	4
3	?	?	¾
5½	5¼	?	4
12	29½	?	?

The points to note are that deck beams on French vessels are slightly heavier but further apart. The English system of kneeing with every beam given one hanging and one lodging knee to each end, heavily fastened, compares very favourably with the French preference for a single knee, and slightly thicker clamps and a rebated waterway.

The same generalisations hold true for the forecastle and quarterdeck, although the English vessels are, relatively somewhat lighter - which is very wise, considering that they are loftier than their French counterparts, and unnecessary weight would affect stability.

	Gun deck	Keel for tonnage	Breadth	Depth in hold	Tonnage
Tygre	118ft 11in	95ft 7in	33ft 8in	11ft 0in	576 24/94*
Unicorn/Lyme	117ft 10in	96ft 5½	33ft 8in	10ft 2in	581 50/94*

*Because of the formula used tonnage was always given in whole tons and fractions of 94. This was known as Builders Measurement.

instructed to 'have a perfect draught drawn thereof, and to take an exact account of all the scantlings, dimensions, form and manner of the framing, scarphs, fastenings, and every particular relating to her hull, masts and yards', all of which was 'to be forwarded with all possible expedition'.

The '24s' which became the *Unicorn* and *Lyme,* were re-rated 28 gun ships and became the first English true frigates. They were highly successful but the problem is whether they were actually built as 'Chinese copies' like the Admiralty instructions indicate. The Navy Board realised that to maintain the same performance the same scantlings and weight distribution would be necessary but, given the strong antagonism to French building practices in general and the shortcomings of the prototype so thoroughly exposed in the survey, one cannot imagine the ships being built to anything but acceptable Royal Dockyard standards. No draught of *Tygre* exists for a conclusive check but, since the dimensions as taken off the *Tygre* differ considerably from the design dimensions for *Unicorn* and *Lyme,* it is safe to assume that the design was subtly altered during draughting to allow for English standards of scantling and construction.

When more vessels of this class were built after 1755, considerable internal and topside alterations further increased the tonnage. By the time *Unicorn* and *Lyme* were ready for sea, the war was over. However, the Admiralty had in the meantime ordered more 24s, although they continued to experiment. Despite the fact that the first 1745 Establishment 24 did not go to sea until March 1747, by 13 October 1747 the Admiralty informed the Navy Board that 'great complaint is made of the bad qualities of His Majesty's ships of 24 guns, especially with regard to

their sailing' and ordered them to produce two designs for 24s without confining themselves to the Establishment dimensions. The Navy's designers (confusingly called the 'Surveyors of the Navy') were put on their mettle but since one of them, the old and reactionary Sir Jacob Acworth, had been a successful opponent of the larger dimensions proposed for the 1745 ships, the Admiralty must have felt self-righteous when both designs turned out to be larger than the 1745 vessels. Neither Acworth's *Seahorse,* nor *Mermaid*, designed by the other Surveyor, Joshua Allin, was much better than the Establishment vessels.

With the war over the search for a first class cruiser design ceased but after 1749 only one other 24 gun ship was built. The superiority of the larger, faster and more seaworthy 28s was proved in sailing trials, and subsequently they took over as the Royal Navy's standard sixth rate. No other French warships such as the superb *Renommee* were considered but this is hardly surprising since a replacement was required for a 500 ton ship, not a 700-tonner. There can be no denying the debt of the *Unicorn* and the *Lyme* to the French privateer but *Tygre* was not only the right ship but also happened to find herself in the right circumstances. Because of the administrative situation the Admiralty was not able to get the improvement in ship design it knew was necessary and used the *Tygre* as an escape from the impasse it had reached with the Surveyors and the old two decked 24s.

CONCLUSIONS
Although expressed as criticisms, the consistency of the surveyors' remarks on French construction clearly demonstrates that English and French shipbuilders were following widely divergent philosophies. There is some

indication that the French use of light scantling and fastening was related to the high speeds achieved by their cruisers. This posed a problem for the English Navy Board when ordered to build exact copies of captured French vessels because they strongly disapproved of the French style of construction but realised that it was not possible simply to build a French hull shape on English principles and expect the same performance. However, the problem only arose once during the period under review, when the new frigate-form was brought into the Royal Navy as part of a wider programme of experimentation pursued by the Admiralty: even though it was ordered, it is doubtful whether *Unicorn* and *Lyme* were exact copies of *Tygre*. Perfect imitation was certainly rare in the period of the Seven Years War, to be covered in the following part of this study. It will also be possible to investigate consistent principles in French and English cruiser design, as this part has established principles of construction.

This article is based on a more detailed series by the author published in French in 'Le Petit Perroquet' (Part 1, No 21, Spring 1977).

THE KING GEORGE V
CLASS   PART 1
BY ROBERT DUMAS

By 1930 the British battlefleet consisted mainly of old vessels constructed during or before the First World War, the only exceptions being the two battleships of the *Nelson* class. The Admiralty, therefore, began an extensive programme of reconstruction and started work on the design of the battleships that were to become the *King George V* class. It was intended that these ships should be the first vessels of a battleship replacement programme and that on their completion the five *Royal Sovereign* class ships, which were the least suitable of the older vessels for reconstruction, would be sold for scrapping.

The new ships were required to be designed within the current international Treaty limitations of 35 000 tons standard displacement and 14in (506mm) maximum gun calibre. Originally the design was settled on a main armament of twelve guns in three quadruple turrets (two forward, one aft) but, in order to provide more weight for protection, the turret in B position was altered to a twin mounting. The designed speed was 27.5 knots at full load displacement.

Compared with foreign contemporaries the *King George V* class had guns of smaller calibre and, in most cases, a lower speed but their well conceived protection helped to counterbalance any possible handicap. The Royal Navy had not conceived sophisticated vessels but well built ships with good staying power.

Anson runs trials in the Pentland Firth, 21 June 1942.
NMM

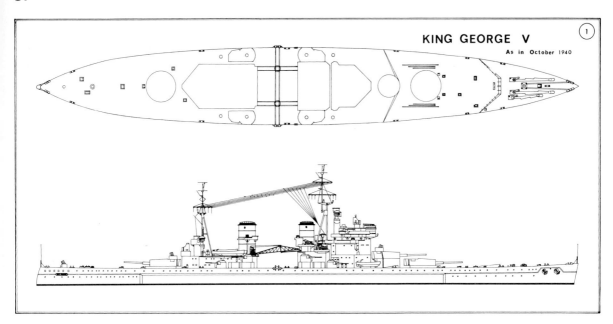

KING GEORGE V

As in October 1940

TECHNICAL CHARACTERISTICS WHEN COMPLETED

Dimensions: Length: 745ft (227.07m) overall, 700ft (213.36m) between perpendiculars; Beam: 103ft (31.39m) max; Draught: 29ft (8.84m) at standard displacement, 32ft 6in (9.9m) at full load.

Armament: Ten 14in (356mm) 2 x 4 plus 1 x 2; Sixteen 5.25in (132mm) 8 x 2; Four 8 barrelled 2pdr pom-pom AA mountings in *King George V* and *Prince of Wales*; Six 8 barrelled 2pdr pom-pom AA mountings in remainder, (the two additional 8 barrelled pom-poms were disposed on B and X turrets); Four UP (Unrotated Projectile rocket launchers) AA mountings in *King George V*, three UP mountings in *Prince of Wales*, (in *King George V* one UP was fitted on B turret, two on X and one on the quarterdeck, in *Prince of Wales* one UP was fitted on B and two on X); One Bofors AA on the quarterdeck on *Prince of Wales* only; six single 20mm Oerlikon in *Duke of York*; eighteen single 20mm Oerlikon in *Anson* and *Howe*.

Aircraft Equipment: One catapult amidship (Type DIIIH); three Walrus amphibians

Machinery: 8 Admiralty 3 drum boilers (400lb/sq in working pressure), 4 sets Parsons single reduction geared turbines, 110 000 SHP (normal), 125 000 SHP (maximum), 4 shafts and one rudder.

Note: *King George V* was engined by Vickers Armstrong (Barrow-in-Furness) *Anson* by Wallsend Slipway and the other three by their builders.

Protection: Main belt: 15in (380mm) $5\frac{1}{2}$in (140mm) lower edge – abreast magazines, 14in (356mm) $4\frac{1}{2}$in (115mm) lower edge – abreast machinery; Internal bulge, with outer air space and inner oil/water tank, torpedo bulkhead $1\frac{3}{4}$in (45mm); Main deck: 5in (127mm) over machinery, 6in (152mm) over magazines; Upper deck: 1in (25mm); Main turrets: 13in (330mm) face, 9in (228mm) sides, 7in (177mm) rear, 6in (152mm) crowns; Conning tower: $4\frac{1}{2}$-2in (114-50mm).

Radar: *King George V* and *Prince of Wales:* Type 279 air warning, with aerials on mastheads, and Type

The *King George V* in May 1942 on her return from covering the Russian Convoys PQ15 and QP11. The extensive damage to the bow, which forced her early retirement from the operation, was received when she accidentally rammed and sank the destroyer *Punjabi*.
IWM

KING GEORGE V

As in December 1941

②

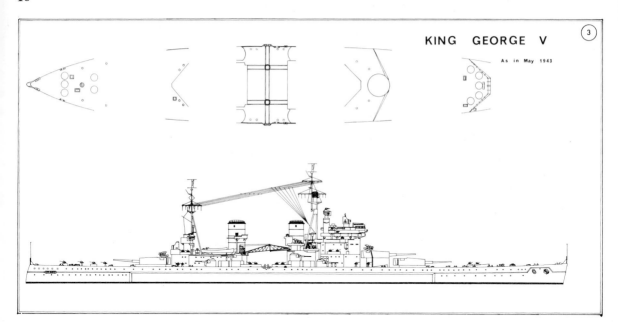

284 for main armament, with aerials on forward main director. *Prince of Wales* was also fitted with four Type 285 and four Type 282 gunnery sets, with aerials on the HACS Mk IV directors and the pom-pom directors (on the lower bridge) respectively, shortly after completion. *Duke of York:* Type 281 air warning, Type 284 for main armament, four Type 285 with aerials on HACS Mk V director and six Type 282 for pom-poms (later reduced to five). *Anson* and *Howe*: As *Duke of York* except also carried Type 273 surface warning radar on foremast starfish.

Rangefinders: Two 41ft (12.50m) in A and X turrets; One 30ft (9.10m) in B turret; Six 15ft (4.57m) in main and secondary directors.

Speed: Normal sea speed, 27.5 knots; Maximum sea speed, 29.5 knots.

Endurance: 14 000 miles at 10 knots, 7000 miles at 14 knots, 4300 miles at 20 knots, 2400 miles at 27 knots.

Bunker capacity: Oil fuel, 3700 tons, Petrol for seaplanes, 35 tons.

Complement: In peacetime, 1511; As fleet flagship, 1644; The complement of *Prince of Wales* when she was sunk was 1612.

Ships boats: *King George V, Prince of Wales* and *Duke of York*; Three 45ft (13.7m) fast motor boats, one 45ft (13.7m) motor launch, three 25ft (7.6m) fast motor boats, two 27ft (8.2m) whalers, one 16ft (4.8m) fast motor dinghy, one (*Duke of York* two) 14ft (4.2m) sailing dinghy, two 32ft (9.76m) cutters (abreast B turret); *Anson* and *Howe*: Two 45ft (13.7m) motor boats, one 45ft (13.7m) motor launch, one 36ft (10.9m) motor pinnace, four 32ft (9.75m) cutters, two 25ft (7.6m) fast motor boats, one 16ft (4.8m) fast motor dinghy, two 14ft (4.2m) sailing dinghies, one (*Howe* two) 27ft (8.2m) whaler; Note: the majority of the boats were stowed on the after superstructure between the after funnel and mainmast. There were some differences in the positioning of boats between the ships of the class and some of the smaller types (32ft and under) were stowed in various positions – abreast X turret, on the catapult deck, before the fore funnel, etc.

1 The *King George V* in a heavy cross sea off the north western tip of Scotland on 18 February 1943.
NMM

2 *King George V* in the Firth of Clyde on 10 July 1942. Note the Type 273 radar lantern and office on the foremast and the Type 284 aerial on the forward main director.
NMM

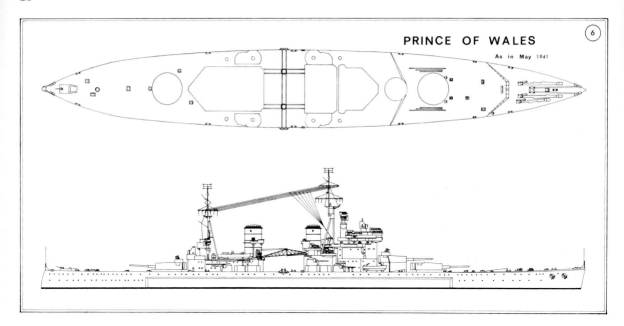

PRINCE OF WALES

As in May 1941

6

1

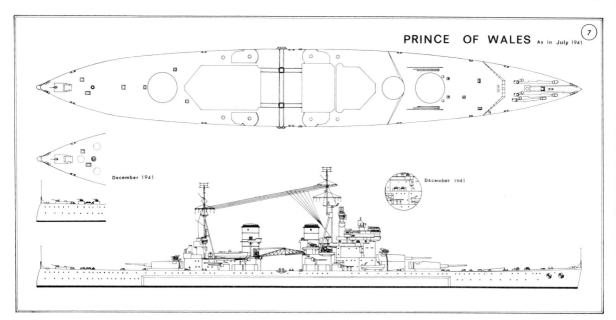

PRINCE OF WALES As in July 1941

⑦

December 1941

December 1941

1 *Prince of Wales* arrives at Singapore Naval
   Base on 2 December 1941, six days before
   she was sunk.
   IWM by courtesy of Roger Chesneau

2 One of the twin 5.25in HA/LA Mk I
   mountings of the *Prince of Wales* in May
   1941. The port side of the bridge structure
   is visible in the background; note the aerial
   for the Type 284 gunnery radar on the roof
   of the main director and the HACS MkIV
   director (behind the muzzle of the left
   5.25in gun) which had not at this time
   received the radar aerials of Type 285.
   MoD, by courtesy of Peter Hodges

2

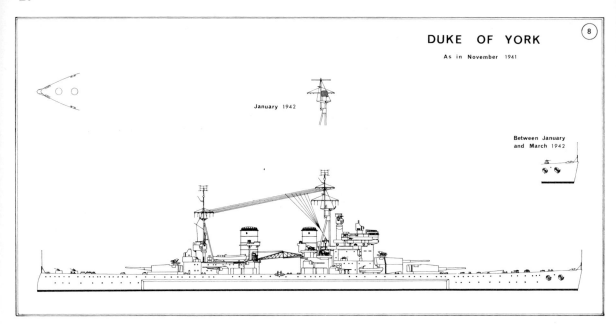

8

DUKE OF YORK

As in November 1941

January 1942

Between January
and March 1942

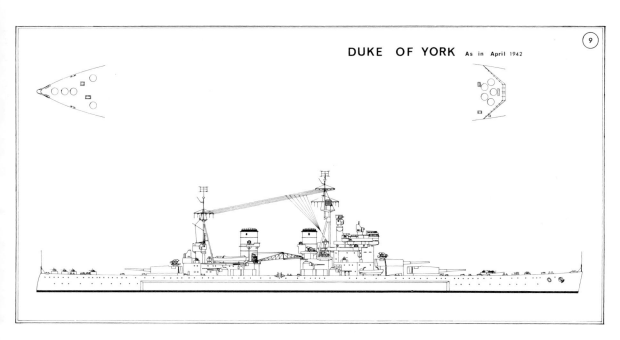

9

DUKE OF YORK As in April 1942

ALTERATIONS AND ADDITIONS BETWEEN COMPLETION AND MAJOR REFITS OF 1944/45

King George V. Early 1940: pom-pom director platform between forward HACS directors replaced by Type 271 surface warning radar. December 1940: UP mountings removed, Type 271 radar replaced by Type 273 (Lantern on foremast starfish), five Type 282 radars fitted, 18 single 20mm Oerlikons fitted (5 on forecastle, 5 on quarterdeck, 2 on each side of No 1 platform, 4 on boat deck). Early 1942: Four Type 285 radars added. May 1943: Two 32ft cutters abreast forecastle removed, 20 single 20mm Oerlikons added (2 on each side mainmast, 4 on each side catapult deck, 4 abreast B turret and 4 on quarterdeck), upper bridge extended aft and Admiral's bridge forward.

Prince of Wales: July 1941: UP mountings removed and two 8 barrel pom-pom mountings fitted (one on B and one on X turrets), Type 271 surface warning radar added between forward HACS directors as in *King George V*. December 1941: 7 single 20mm Oerlikons added (3 on quarterdeck, 4 on No 1 platform).

Duke of York: November 1941: radar Type 273 fitted on foremast starfish. January 1942: One 20mm Oerlikon fitted between hawsepipes at extreme forward end of forecastle (the position proved impractical due to the mounting's susceptibility to the weather and was removed after two or three months). April 1942: 8 single 20mm added (5 on forecastle, 3 on quarterdeck) sheet anchor on starboard side removed. March 1943: 24 single 20mm Oerlikons added (2 on after boiler room vents, 4 abreast B turret, 6 on No 1 platform, 4 on each side catapult deck, 2 on each side of deck forward of X turret) bridge

modified as in *King George V* and cutters abreast B turret removed. June 1944: Two twin 20mm Oerlikons added on No. 1 platform and 8 single 20mm removed from No 1 platform.

Anson: June 1943: 17 single 20mm Oerlikons (4 on each side of catapult deck, 8 on forecastle around B turret). Cutters abreast B turret removed.

Howe; June 1943; 22 single 20mm Oerlikons added (plus 2 transferred from abreast X turret= 24) (4 on each side catapult deck, 2 in wings of Admiral's bridge, 2 in place of 44in searchlights on after funnel, 2 on No 1 platform, 10 on forecastle deck around B turret).

TABLE 1. CONSTRUCTION

Names	Builders	Laid Down	Launched	Completed	Pennant No
KING GEORGE V	Vickers Armstrong (Walker)	01-01-37	21-02-39	01-10-40	41
PRINCE OF WALES	Cammel Laird (Birkenhead)	01-01-37	03-05-39	31-03-40	53
DUKE OF YORK (ex ANSON)	John Brown (Clydebank)	05-05-37	28-02-40	04-11-41	17
ANSON (ex JELLICOE)	Swan Hunter and Wigham Richardson (Wallsend on Tyne)	20-07-37	24-02-40	22-06-42	79
HOWE (ex BEATTY)	Fairfield (Govan)	01-06-37	09-04-40	29-08-42	32

TABLE 2. DISPLACEMENT

Design standard displacement: 35 000 tons
Estimated displacements in 1941 (tons)

Names	Standard Displacement	Full Load Displacement
KING GEORGE V	36 730	41 815
PRINCE OF WALES	36 750	41 850
DUKE OF YORK	36 820	41 930
ANSON	36 970	42 080
HOWE	36 950	42 050

TABLE 3. BREAKDOWN OF WEIGHTS OF KING GEORGE V (tons)

	AS DESIGNED		AS COMPLETED	
	Standard	Full load	Standard	Full load
Hull and fittings	13 500	13 500	13 830	13 830
Machinery	2 700	2 700	2 770	2 770
Protection	12 500	12 500	12 410	12 410
Armament	6 050	6 765	6 570	7 400
Equipment	1 150	1 465	1 150	1 620
TOTAL	35 900	36 930	36 730	38 030
Oil fuel		3 700		3 730
Lubricating oil & petrol		60		60
Reserve feed water		300		255
TOTAL		40 990		42 075

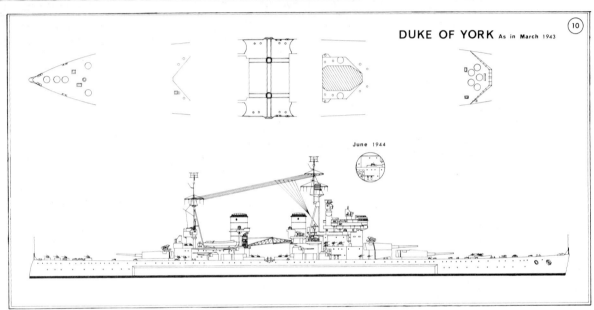

DUKE OF YORK As in March 1943

(10)

June 1944

ANSON As in June 1942

(13)

1 *Prince of Wales* in the Pentland Firth on 6
October 1941. She now has multiple
pom-poms on B and X turrets, in place of
the UP mountings originally carried, and is
equipped with a full radar outfit (Types
279, 271, 284, 285 and 282)
NMM

2 The *Anson* turning to starboard on 5
August 1942.
NMM

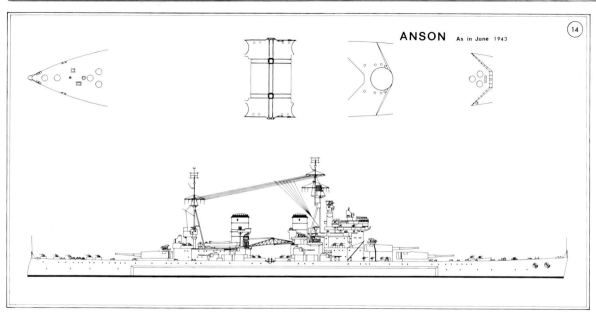

ANSON   As in June 1943

14

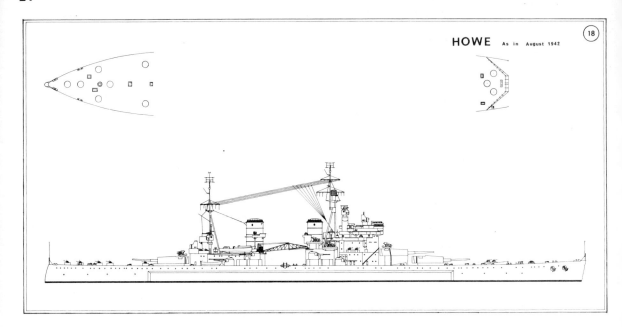

HOWE As in August 1942

⑱

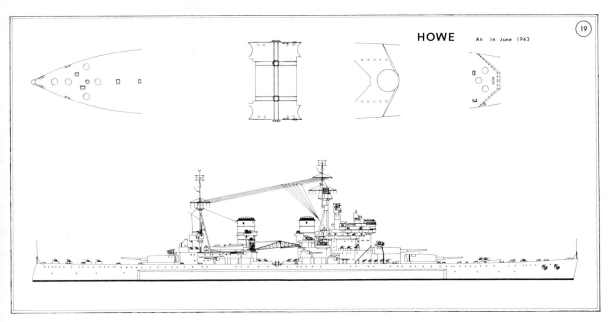

HOWE   As in June 1943

⑲

1 *Howe* leaving Fairfields yard on completion in 1942.
Authors collection

2 *Howe* turns to port at speed, March 1943.
CPL W/9/001

1 *Prince of Wales* arriving at Argentia Bay, Newfoundland, in August 1941.
IWM

3 *Duke of York* in dock at Rosyth at the end of her December 1942-March 1943 refit.
IWM

2 *Duke of York* leaving drydock at Rosyth, March 1943.
IWM

1

2

By the early 1960s the surface forces of the Netherlands Navy were based on an ageing carrier, the *Karel Doorman* (ex-HMS *Venerable)*, the cruisers *de Ruyter* and *de Zeven Provincien* and twelve large anti-submarine destroyers of the *Holland* and *Friesland* classes. One of the cruisers, the *de Zeven Provincien*, was converted between 1962 and 1964 to carry the Terrier surface-to-air missile. Consideration of cost, however, as well as doubts about the future of these large ships with their complement of about 900 men in a small navy with limited

resources of manpower, meant that this conversion was not extended to *de Ruyter*. So, in 1964 the decision was taken to build a limited number of large guided-missile frigates to replace the cruisers as flagships.

ATTEMPTS AT STANDARDISATION

In view of the increasing commitment of the Netherlands Navy to NATO following the break-up of her empire in South-East Asia, efforts were made right from the start to collaborate as closely as possible with other allied countries in the development and adoption of suitable weapons, sensors and a propulsion system. A major agreement involving the first two items was made with the Royal Navy, with which the Netherlands Navy had established particularly close connections since the War. The Dutch would adopt the British Sea Dart missile then under

development as the future area-defence weapon of the Fleet. In return the Dutch, with their highly specialised electronics industry, would be responsible for the development of a large three-dimensional radar to provide action-data and automatic tracking for the missile. Besides being installed on the new frigates the radar would be adopted by the new generation of aircraft carriers and escorts that the Royal Navy was planning to build at that time (a comparison between HMS *Bristol* as originally designed and *Tromp* as completed shows a remarkable similarity.) In the event, however, the Dutch became concerned about the amount of 'ship-space' that a high-performance system like Sea Dart would take up. As their frigate was a smaller design than the Type 82, they opted for the medium-performance (and cheaper) Tartar missile which the

The large dome above the *Tromp's* bridge provides weather protection for the aerial of the Dutch HSA three dimensional air search and tracking radar. The smaller dome forward of the bridge protects the aerial of the WM25 fire control radar (also of Dutch manufacture) which controls the Sea Sparrow system and the twin 120mm gun mounting.
C & S Taylor

TROMP

BY JOHN JORDAN

Americans had developed specifically for destroyers and which was being adopted by several other European navies. Conversely this meant that the 3-D radar was now rejected by the Royal Navy, leaving the Dutch with considerable development costs for an end product of just two installations. Whether the deal would have gone through, in view of the subsequent cancellation of the new generation of carriers and all but one of the Type 82s, is in any case open to question.

There can be little doubt that the decision to drop Sea Dart from the design, blow that it was to a common weapon system between the Royal Navy and the Dutch, resulted in other capabilities being enhanced as far as the frigates were concerned. This certainly fell into line with Staff Requirements (agreed in 1968) which included protection of a task force or convoy against aircraft, submarines and surface ships as well as shore bombardment (ie a bit of everything rather than a specialised role).

Furthermore, the Naval Staff emphasised once again that standardisation was of paramount importance by demanding that all equipment be chosen from that in use or under development – in the Netherlands or other allied NATO navies. Curiously enough this latter demand, combined with the all-important aim of economising on manpower, led the Netherlands Navy back into collaboration with the Royal Navy in the one area where this had not been considered initially – that of propulsion.

GAS TURBINES

The original Dutch frigate design was to be driven by conventional steam turbines with fixed-pitch propellers. The Royal Navy, however, was now developing a new generation of aero-derived gas-turbines to be installed in their future frigate and destroyer designs. The major attraction of gas turbines

for the Dutch was the reduction in the engine room personnel needed to operate and maintain them but a further factor was undoubtedly the lower noise-signature of gas turbines compared with steam turbines and diesels, making them better suited to anti-submarine operations. The *Tromp* class finally emerged from the drawing-board with basically the same COGOG (Combined Gas or Gas) propulsion system as the British Type 42 class destroyers: one Olympus boost turbine and one Tyne cruise turbine on each shaft driving controllable-pitch propellers. Y-ARD(Glasgow) acted as consultants for the main machinery installation and controls and the Dutch entered into a joint agreement with the Royal Navy to monitor the performance of the turbines.

The forward engine room houses the Olympus turbines, each rated at 22 000 shp, which give the ships their top speed of over 28 knots. The turbines were down-rated from the 27 000 shp version fitted in the Type 42s in order to extend the life of the gas-generators, thereby lowering maintenance costs. Outside the two Olympus modules are two 1000kW diesel generators which provide half the electrical power. Diesel rather than gas generators were selected partly because of the problems of providing additional air intakes and uptakes to those required by the propulsion machinery but also because of the high fuel-consumption of gas-turbines at low ratings.

The after engine room contains the Tynes which, at a rating of 4000shp each, propel the ships at

their cruising speed of about 18 knots. The main reduction gearing is also housed in this engine room, with one Tyne aft and one Olympus forward of each gear box. The Dutch designed their own gearing in preference to the adoption of British equipment and the gearboxes for the *Tromp* class were supplied by the shipbuilder, Royal Schelde. An auxiliary machinery room aft of this engine room houses the other pair of diesel generators.

The arrangement of propulsion and auxiliary machinery was designed to minimize action damage. Either set of turbines can continue to operate with the other engine room flooded and the gearboxes are designed as watertight units. Furthermore, the separation of the two pairs of generators by two watertight bulkheads lessens the likelihood of

1

1 *Tromp* shortly after her launch in 1973 and in the early stages of 'fitting out' at the De Schelde shipyard in Flushing.
Rolls-Royce, courtesy A Preston

2 An aerial view of *Tromp* taken at Spithead shortly after the ship's completion. Photographs 3 and 4 were also taken at this time. The vessel alongside is the British fleet tender *Lawlask*.
C & S Taylor

power failure.

All machinery is designed for the quietest possible operation:the diesel generators are fully enclosed in noise-absorbing hoods, the cruise turbines are resiliently mounted, the gearboxes are exeptionally quiet, and there are silencers housed in the intakes and uptakes.

A push-button Machinery Control Room provides remote control and surveillance of the complete machinery installation. For ease of communication it is located near the Operations Room, with command links to the latter and the bridge.

HULL AND SUPERSTRUCTURE
Seaworthiness was naturally a major consideration in a ship whose main area of operations would be the North Sea and Atlantic. It has been achieved by combining high

freeboard with a wide beam. Top-weight has been kept to a minimum by extensive use of aluminium in the superstructure, steel having been used only beneath the large 3-D radar. Full advantage has been taken of the great depth and beam of the ship to improve habitability and to provide maximum space for weapons and electronics.

ARMAMENT AND SENSORS
The armament finally fitted is both comprehensive and well-balanced, with two weapon systems provided for each of the three functions – surface-to-air, surface-to-surface and ASW – demanded by Staff Requirements.

The main surface-to-air element is the American Standard SM1 missile (of which 40 are carried). The single-arm Tartar Mk 13

launcher is mounted on a deckhouse which extends forward of the helicopter hangar, giving good all-round coverage, and the two SPG 51D tracker/illuminators overlook it from positions just aft of the mainmast. It is a system which has been adopted by a number of NATO navies and has been described in detail in a previous issue *(Warship No 6 — USS California)*. The Dutch installation differs from all others, however, in that target-tracking information for the SPG 15s is initially provided not by a radar of American manufacture, such as the SPS 52 and 48A planar radars, but by the massive HSA three-dimensional radar specifically designed for these ships. This is an advanced air-search and tracking radar capable of handling simultaneously over one hundred aircraft tracks. The

2

This view of *Tromp*, slightly off the starboard beam, shows very clearly the layout of her armament and radar aerials. The containers for the Harpoon missiles had not been fitted at the time this photograph was taken but the supporting framework for the starboard pair can be seen just forward of the funnels.
C & S Taylor

air-search functions are performed by a pair of parabolic reflectors mounted back-to-back, and the tracking functions by a similarly mounted pair of planar, phased-array antennae with integrated IFF. These antennae are mounted on a single platform with common turning gear and are housed within a large fibre-glass dome. The back-to-back arrangement gives a very high data-rate, and high and low cover is provided by the system.

Back-up for Standard is provided by the NATO Sea Sparrow short-range surface-to-air missile. Developed from the American Basic Point Defense Missile System (BPDMS), it uses a special version of the Sparrow missile which has folding wings and can therefore be launched from a new lightweight 8-cell launcher (its predecessor used a modified ASROC launcher). With an effective range of about 12km the missile can engage targets down to about 150m.

The Sea Sparrow missile has been coupled with various guidance systems. In the *Tromp* class it is the WM25, which also serves the 120mm mounting. The WM25 is the latest in the popular M20 series of radars which now equip many of the world's small ships and which, like the 3-D radar, are manufactured by Hollandse Signaal

Apparaten. It comprises a tracker/illuminator radar above a parabolic search reflector on a common mount, housed in a near-spherical radome. The tracker radar directs the Sea Sparrow missiles. The search radar provides air and surface search as well as automatic tracking for one or two surface targets. The whole system has been designed for quick reaction against medium- and close-range targets, and computer-direction ensures an all-weather capability.

In view of the modernity of the rest of *Tromp's* equipment it is perhaps surprising that the Dutch should have retained the ageing Bofors twin 120mm/50cal dual-purpose gun rather than opting for the Vickers Mk 8 or the Italian OTO 127mm. It does, however, compare well enough with more modern guns in terms of performance 85° elevation and a rate of fire of 40 rounds per minute – and the choice was no doubt influenced by the availability of two mountings from the old destroyer *Gelderland*. The turrets are fully automatic and radar-controlled and have been specially modified for use aboard the new frigates.

It took the Dutch some time to choose a surface-to-surface missile to complement the twin Bofors. The main candidates were undoubtedly

the French Exocet and the American Harpoon. Eventually a decision was made in favour of the more advanced (and more costly) Harpoon, for which ramps can be seen just forward of the twin uptakes. The missile uses inertial guidance until booster separation, after which a computer in the missile brings it on a course determined by target data inserted before launch, making the missile independent of the ship's sensors. It then cruises at low altitude under altimeter control. The active radar homing system switches on automatically at a predetermined distance from the position of the target at launch. The homing radar, which is frequency-agile to prevent jamming, then seeks out and locks onto the target. In the final phase the missile executes a climb/dive manoeuvre. At a length of 4.75m (shorter than the horizon-range Exocet) Harpoon is particularly compact for a missile with a range of over 55km. On *Tromp* and her sister four of the weather-proof canisters will be bolted to each of the two ramps for a total of eight missiles.

The principal ASW weapon carried is the Anglo-French Lynx helicopter which is only just coming into service. The Lynx is at present without a rival in the small ASW helicopter bracket and has also been

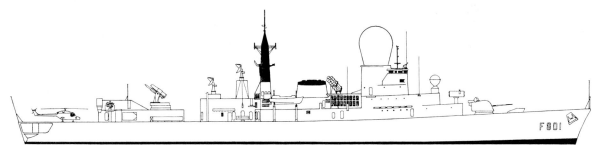

ordered by the Dutch for the new *Kortenaer* class frigates. Over twice the weight of the earlier Wasp it was designed to replace, it is still less than half the weight of the big-ship Sea King. In its ASW role the Lynx carries two American Mk 46 torpedoes. The latter weapon is also launched from the two triple Mk 32 ASW tubes mounted at upper deck level just aft of the mainmast. ASW data is provided by two hull-mounted sonars. The first is the long-range EDO(USA)CWE 610, a low-frequency sonar in production since 1969 which is also in service with the Italian Navy. The second is the even more recent Type 162M developed for the Royal Navy. This has a sideways-looking scan pattern and is designed to classify mid-water and seabed targets out to about 1100m.

For navigational purposes and for helicopter control the *Tromp* class carry the Decca dual Transar radar for which twin port and starboard antennae. above the bridge, provide 360 ° coverage. The system appears to have been chosen because of clutter problems posed by the siting of the 3-D radome. ECM sensors are carried on the mainmast, and are backed up by two British-design Corvus chaff dispensers abreast the hangar.

All weapons and sensors are linked by a command system designated SEWACO-2 (from the Dutch SEnsoren, WApens and COmmandosysteem). The electronics for this are mainly of Dutch manufacture supplemented by components from other NATO countries. The computer-based command system processes information from all sensors, evaluates threats and designates targets to the weapon systems. The operations room, in which the display sub-system is housed, is located low in the ship, with the

Displacement:	4308 tonnes
Length:	138.2 metres
Beam:	14.8 metres
Draught:	4.58 metres
Complement:	35 officers, 271 men

computer and sonar rooms.

CONCLUSION

Part of the undoubted success of the *Tromp* class can be attributed to the way in which the Dutch have selected from the best equipment available in NATO to suit their requirements and those who have called for more standardisation within the alliance now have an example to hold up to the sceptics. But the real triumph belongs to the Dutch electronics industry which, in linking up weapons and sonars from a variety of sources and matching them with high-performance above-water sensors of its own manufacture, has without question placed the Netherlands in the 'first division' of naval technology.

HMS COCHRANE
BY JOHN ROBERTS

The *Cochrane* and her three sister ships of the 1903-04 Programme, *Achilles, Natal* and *Warrior,* were among the last armoured cruisers to be constructed for the Royal Navy and enjoyed a high reputation as one of the best cruiser classes in the Fleet. This reputation stemmed from the adoption of an all turret armament which, unlike the broadside guns of earlier ships could be worked in any sort of weather. In addition the turrets substantially increased topweight which, by reducing the level of stability, made them very good seaboats and steady gun platforms. In contrast the previous *Duke of Edinburgh* class, which were virtually identical, apart from having a secondary armament of 6in guns mounted in a broadside central battery, had a very poor reputation; even the *Minotaur* class, the next and last of the armoured cruisers, were not regarded as highly as the *Warriors.* Unfortunately the appearance of the battlecruiser type with the *Invincible* class of 1906 rendered all the later armoured cruisers obsolete before they even entered service.

The *Cochrane* was laid down at Fairfields Yard in Glasgow on 24 March 1904 and launched on 20 May 1905. She was commissioned with a nucleus crew on 18 February 1907, joined the Nore Division of the Home Fleet on 6 March and shortly afterwards was brought to full commission for service in the 5th Cruiser Squadron. On 1 April, 1909 she recommissioned for service with the 2nd Cruiser Squadron with which she remained until September 1917.

She spent the majority of the war with the Grand Fleet and in May 1916 took part in the Battle of Jutland. In November 1917 she transferred to the North America and West Indies station but rejoined the 2nd Cruiser squadron early in the following year and was based at Murmansk during May –

September 1918. On 14 November 1918 she was stranded in the Mersey Estuary, while under the control of the pilot, and later broke in two becoming a total loss. The wreck had been broken up *in situ* by June 1919. Of *Cochrane's* sister ships, the *Natal* blew up and sank in the Cromarty Firth on 30 December 1915 and the *Warrior* was sunk by gunfire during the Battle of Jutland on 31 May 1916; the sole survivor, *Achilles,* was sold to T Ward for breaking up in May 1921.

PARTICULARS AS COMPLETED

Displacement: 13 550 tons (load) 14 500 tons (deep) as designed

Dimensions: 480ft 3¼in (pp) 505ft 4in (oa) x 73ft 6in x 27ft 6in (max at load displacement)

Machinery: 2 shaft, 4 cylinder triple expansion engines, 23 650 IHP = 23.3 knots (trials), 19 Yarrow large tube boilers, 6 cylindrical boilers, 2050 tons coal, 600 tons oil fuel

Armour: main belt 6in amidships, 4in forward, 3in aft; upper belt 6in amidships closed by 6in end bulkheads forming protective citadel to bases of beam turrets; turrets 7½in faces, 5½in sides, 4½in backs, 6in bases reducing to 3in on inboard side of beam turrets, 3in ammunition tubes to A and Y turrets only; conning tower 10in wall, 3in communication tube

Protective Plating: bulkheads around engine cylinders 2in; lower deck ¾in (1½in over steering gear); main deck 1in forward and aft of citadel; upper deck¾in over citadel

Armament: 6 - 9.2in BL, 45 cal, Mk X on single Mk V mountings; 4 - 7.5in BL, 50 cal, Mk II or V guns on single Mk II mountings; 26 - 3pdr Vickers QF guns on single Mk II mountings; 2 - single 3pdr Hotchkiss; 3 submerged 18in torpedo tubes, one stern, two broadside (abreast bridge)

Searchlights: 2 - 36in, on bridge wings; 7 - 24in, 1 below foretop, 2 abaft 2nd and 2 abaft 4th funnels, 2 abreast mainmast

Boats: stowed forward of mainmast, 2 - 45ft steam pinnaces, 42ft sailing launch, 36ft pinnace, 2 - 30ft gigs (stowed on quarterdeck davits when in harbour) 27ft whaler, 16ft dinghy, 13½ft balsa raft; stowed on davits amidships 4 - 32ft cutters

Anchors: bower 2 - 116cwt Wasteney-Smith; sheet 115 cwt Wasteney-Smith; kedge one 17 cwt and one 15 cwt Admiralty Pattern (stowed against starboard side of after superstructure); stream 41 cwt Inglefield (stowed against port side of after superstructure)

Complement: 712

ALTERATIONS AND ADDITIONS

1908 Topgallant masts, for wireless yards, added.

1909 Funnel bands painted up. One white on 2nd and 3rd funnels.

1910 Searchlight platforms abreast mainmast moved 8ft further aft and two 3 pdr Hotchkiss guns originally in this position removed.

1912 Funnels increased in height by approximately 6ft. Topgallant masts shortened.

1912-13 Torpedo net defence and booms removed. Control platform added on lower section of mainmast. Searchlight on platform below fore top was removed at about this time but information on this point is uncertain.

1915 6 pdr AA gun fitted on quarterdeck.

1915-16 Two searchlight platforms added on both fore and mainmasts. Compass platform extended aft. Topgallant masts and main topmast removed and fore topmast shortened. Gaff added to mainmast. Searchlight platforms abreast mainmast removed (these appear to have been replaced by 2 - 3pdr Vickers AA guns on Mk III mountings but information on this point is uncertain). 3 pdr guns on A and Y turret roofs removed. Deckhouse added below searchlight platform between 2nd and 3rd funnels.

1916 6 pdr HA gun replaced by 3in, 20 cwt, HA gun on Mk II mount.

1917 Foremast converted to tripod to provide support for director. Former searchlight platform enlarged to form director platform but director not actually fitted until August 1918. Two lower searchlight platforms on foremast removed. Aftermost pair of 3pdr guns on after superstructure and 3 pdr guns on P1 and S1 9.2inch turrets removed. This left her with a 3pdr armament of 20 guns (exclusive of 2 x 3 pdr AA). Some of these guns were landed at Murmansk in 1918 and at the time of her loss she carried a total of 17 but it is not clear if this included AA gun(s).

This and the following photograph was taken in Plymouth Sound on 29 October 1917 shortly after the *Cochrane* completed a refit in Devonport dockyard. During this refit her foremast was converted to a tripod to support the weight of a director. The empty platform below the foretop bears witness to the fact that the director was not fitted until August 1918.
(*MoD*)

Cochrane from the port quarter, the 3in HA gun on the quarterdeck is hidden by a canvas cover and most of her 3 pdr guns are barely visible among the complexity of her superstructure. The lower control position on the mainmast was added before the war but the two searchlight platforms above it were fitted in 1915 or 1916, a similar pair of searchlight platforms on her foremast were removed during her 1917 refit.
(*MoD*)

This drawing, which shows *Cochrane* as she was in 1910, is based on the official plans of the ship held by the National Maritime Museum. By this date very few modifications had been made to the ship since completion and the only visible alterations were the addition of topgallant masts and the moving of the searchlight platforms abreast the mainmast 8ft further aft, where they replaced two 3pdr Hotchkiss guns. The latter guns were of different type to the main 3pdr battery and it seems likely they were intended for saluting a function presumably transferred to the main battery. It is worth noting that this anti-torpedo boat battery of Vickers 3 pdr QF guns totals 26 weapons (10 on turret roofs and 8 on forward and after superstructure) while almost every reference book (including the Navy List) credits them with only 24 (*Brassey's* just to be different says 29). The four cutters mounted on davits amidships were stowed on the upper deck abreast the funnels in wartime and the 30ft gigs, stowed above the after wing 9.2in turrets, were carried on the quarterdeck davits when in harbour (boats shown in this position by broken line).

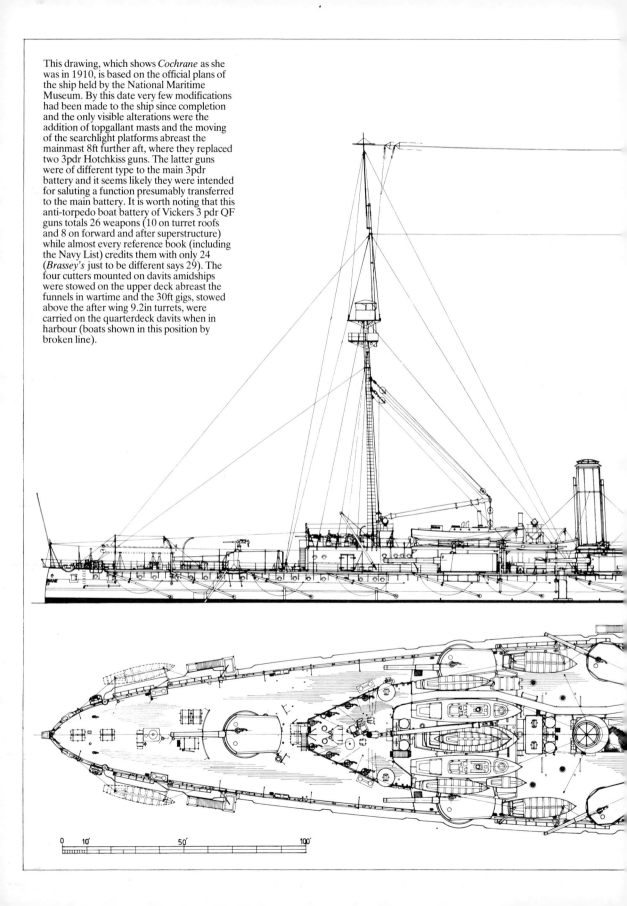

0   10'   50'   100'

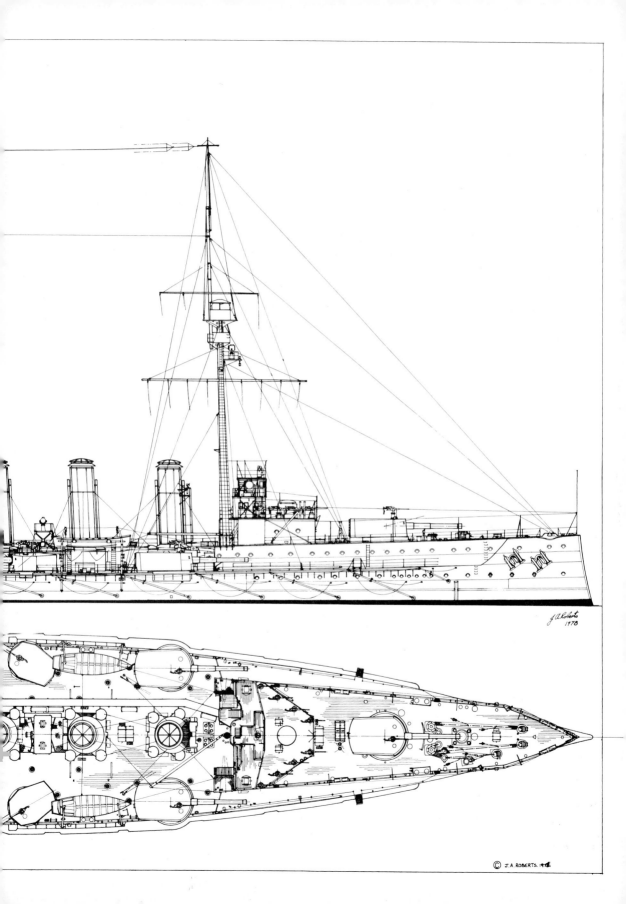

J.A.Roberts
1978

© J.A. ROBERTS. 1978.

PROJECT GUPPY

BY NORMAN FRIEDMAN

The US submarine force ended World War Two in a somewhat paradoxical state. It had just won perhaps the greatest submarine victory in history, against the Japanese Empire, but with that war over it had lost much of its mission as the next prospective enemy, the Soviet Union, had no large merchant marine susceptible to submarine attack. At the same time the large force of new 'fleet submarines' of the *Gato, Balao,* and *Tench* classes (of which 158 were in commission on 31 December 1945) had suddenly become obsolescent with the advent of the German Type XXI, examples of which the Soviets as well as the Western Allies had captured in 1945. Tests with such vessels demonstrated new standards not merely of underwater speed but also of quieting and ruggedness to resist depth-charging. These experiments were extremely discouraging for the US ASW force; in 1945 experienced Pacific submarine commanders had proven very difficult targets for equally experienced Atlantic escort goups in exercises and it was clear that the Type XXI was far more difficult to track than the fleet boat.

Meanwhile, within the submarine force, the first evaluations of the Type XXI led to the abandonment of existing plans for a new variant of the 'fleet boat' and to the beginning of the design effort which would lead to the first postwar US submarine, the *Tang.* However, it was clear that large numbers of such submarines would not be forthcoming in view of the absence of a mission for US general purpose submarines. Thus the submariners' interest in a range of special purpose types – missile firing

submarines, troop and cargo carrying types for small scale commando raids and specialized ASW submarines, which might help to counter the threat of the large Soviet submarine force. Indeed, in a sense the 'Guppy' was also a specialist type as it was intended initially to provide the ASW forces with a modern 'tame' target against which to practice. The US had been allocated two ex-German Type XXIs, *U-2513* and *U-3008,* but neither could be kept operational for very long.

PROJECT GUPPY
Hence Project GUPPY – for Greater Underwater Propulsive Power – which involved the conversion of existing fleet boats to high speed. Early in 1946 the Bureau of Ships proposed to modify fleet boats for high submerged speed by increasing storage battery power and by radical streamlining of both hull and superstructure. Sacrifices would include all of the gun armament and, it was believed, some considerable measure of surfaced sea keeping capability. On the other hand, simply because the original fleet boat had been designed largely for high speed surface operation, the conversion would lose little of its surfaced speed. Nor was there any way to provide it with the kind of deep diving capability characteristic of the 'true submersible' Type XXI

Odax (SS-484) was one of two prototype GUPPY I conversions. Her narrow sail betrays the absence of a snorkel; note the bulge to house the SV air search radar when retracted. She is shown here as built (12 March 1950); later a snorkel was fitted and she was altered to GUPPY II configuration. *USN*

and the late model fleet boats converted to 'Guppies' were limited to a test depth of 412ft.

Converted submarines would have four 126 cell Guppy batteries in place of the previous two 126 cell *Sargo* batteries (named after the submarine in which they had been introduced in 1936). Each cell was about two-thirds the weight of the earlier type but total power from the new batteries would be about twice that of the *Sargo*. In 1947 it was estimated that the Guppy would have 4520 SHP available underwater at the highest (half-hour) rate as compared to 2688 for an unconverted boat. At the lower six hour rate the Guppy installation would be about 50 per cent more powerful than the *Sargo* and at the low rate, for maximum underwater endurance, about 40 per cent more powerful. This was a reasonable allocation of priorities, given the short ranges of contemporary sonars and ASW weapons. A submarine attacking a convoy submerged might well be detected only after she had fired and a burst of speed at that point might well enable her to escape entirely.

The new batteries had disadvantages. They were more fragile than the *Sargo* type, their expected peacetime life was only eighteen months (as compared to five years for the earlier type) and they required twice as much lead. It followed that US lead resources and battery manufacturing capacity

might well limit production of Guppies. They also required considerable internal rearrangement. Of the 252 cells of the forward batteries only 184 could be placed in the former forward battery compartment which had held 126 *Sargo* cells. The others had to be placed under the control room in spaces formerly occupied by fresh water tanks, magazines (for the deck guns now dispensed with) and an ordnance storeroom. The after battery space had to be extended forward, and some bunks relocated, and four reload torpedoes sacrificed. An auxiliary engine was also removed to provide space for increased air conditioning capacity to deal with the heat generated by the new batteries.

Conspicuously absent from the Guppy project was any advance in sonar which might have made the boats particularly effective submarine killers. In 1946-7 the long range passive sonar developed by the Germans was still a matter of experimentation, under the designation GHG; it would appear in late Guppy conversions and in a series of specialized hunter-killer submarines designated SSK. Guppy itself was concentrated on high underwater speed and, to a lesser extent, underwater endurance at high speed. Readers familiar with the Type XXI design may recall that the latter was far more directed towards battery capacity and had an entire lower pressure hull devoted to batteries. So radical an approach

was impossible in a fleet boat conversion, in which the basic form and even most of the internal arrangement of the pressure hull was fixed by considerations of what had now become an obsolete form of submarine warfare in which speed and endurance on the surface was essential.

TYPE II GUPPIES
The Chief of Naval Operations approved the Guppy proposal in June 1946 assigning a high priority to the conversions of *Odax,* at the Portsmouth Naval Shipyard, and *Pomodon,* at Mare Island. It is some indication of the urgency of the conversions that snorkels were foregone, as none would be available in time. In addition the after periscope was omitted and an air-search radar (SV) installed in its place; at the time it was stated that design changes necessary to provide two periscopes would have delayed completion. In fact in October 1946, even before the first two Type I Guppies were completed, ten more were authorized for which time was now available to design an enlarged 'sail' incorporating a second periscope and a snorkel. These boats were designated Type II and a further twelve were approved during 1947. The two Type I prototypes were soon brought up to Type II standard. Four of the Type IIs were *Tench* class submarines which had been suspended incomplete at the end of World War Two.

Picuda (SS-382), a GUPPY IIA conversion in her original configuration, shown here on 23 February 1954. The dark areas are sloped parts of her superstructure painted to make them less visible from above.
USN

TYPICAL CHARACTERISTICS

	FLEET/ SNORKEL	GUPPY:	II	IA	IIA	III	
Surfaced	1827		1870	1830	1848	1975	tons
Submerged	2400		2440	2440	2440	2450	tons
Length	312		307	307	307	326.5	ft
Beam	27		27	27	27	27	ft
Draft	17		17	17	17	17	ft
Speed:							
Surfaced	18.5		18.0	17.3	17.0	17.2	kts
Surfaced (cruise)	13.5		13.5	12.5	13.5	12.2	kts
Snorkel (1 engine)	6.5		9.0	7.5	8.0	6.2	kts
Max Submerged (half hour)	10.0		16.0	15.0	14.1	14.5	kts
Submerged Cruise	3.0		3.5	3.0	3.0	3.7	kts
Engines	4		4	4	3	4	
SHP	4610		4610	4610	3430	4610	

NOTE: Complement was 8 officers, 74 (78 in Guppy III) enlisted men.
Submerged cruise rate was 36-hour rate; typically a submarine would follow a cycle of snorkel and battery operations. Of Guppy IIs, only *Tiru* had three engines.

Trials with the first two boats were extremely encouraging. Off San Francisco, the *Pomodon* made 18.2 knots submerged (batteries at the half-hour rate), as compared to 17.8 on the surface at full power. *Odax* made slightly lower speeds which were explained on the basis of hull fouling and a different propeller pitch. Even at high submerged speeds no vibration was noticed forward of the manuevering room and for the rest of the boat vibration was about the same as that in a fleet boat at full power, ie at about 9 knots. Even at maximum underwater speed water noises could not be heard within the hull. An unexpected by-product of the streamlining adopted to achieve high speed was that sonar detection range on a Guppy was 10 per cent less than sonar range on a fleet boat. This effect was probably analogous to the greater reflectivity by corners of radar pulses. On the other hand Type I was not quite Type XXI. It was far noisier and could not dive as deeply. Moreover, the maximum battery rate for a Type XXI had been *one hour* rate and that had been comparable to the half-hour rate attainable by a Guppy.

TYPE 1A GUPPIES
As the Guppy program neared completion in the Spring of 1949 the Navy began to evaluate alternatives for future production. The Center for Naval Analysis, the Navys 'think tank', compared snorkel installation, streamlining,

the Guppy battery and a variety of combinations. Significantly, the criterion chosen was exchange rate (merchant ships sunk per submarine sunk) in a classical anti-shipping campaign, not submarine vs submarine ASW, as would later become a primary preoccupation of the US submarine force. At periscope depth, over the speed range of up to 10 knots, an unmodified fleet boat would require 2.5 times the power required by a streamlined boat such as *Odax*, 2.25 times the power required by a Guppy II (streamlined with a snorkel), Type II paying a 10 percent power penalty over Type I. However, at a depth of 100 ft with speeds of 0 to 15 knots both streamlined types would match. At the half-hour battery rate Type I could make 18.5 knots underwater (Type II 16.5) but a streamlined submarine with *Sargo* batteries could make 15 (13.2 with snorkel). In view of the high cost of the Guppy battery it was a primary question whether those 3 knots were worthwhile. It was clear that the snorkel was worthwhile as aircraft contacts would decrease radically and even the best ASW radars would suffer a loss of 80 or 90 percent in range against a snorkelling as opposed to a surfaced submarine. On the other hand, the increased running speed due to a snorkel seemed less valuable. Pacific experience was held to show that only 20 percent of individual merchant ship contacts and only 15

percent of convoy contacts could not be attacked due to the low speed of the submarine.

In fact the study concluded that funds should be used to combine the snorkel with streamlining and that the Guppy battery should be foregone in future conversions. It is possible that the loss of a new Guppy II, USS *Cochino*, off Norway after a battery fire on 26 August 1949 also influenced the decision that there would be no more Guppy II conversions Instead there were two batches of conversions using modified *Sargo* batteries (*Sargo* II under the FY 51 and FY 52 programs). In addition the FY 51 program included a series of limited 'fleet snorkel' conversions intended to secure some of the essential features of the Guppy at minimum cost.

Thus the program for Fiscal Year 1951 (the year beginning 1 July 1950) included ten Guppy 1A conversions whose primary mission was 'to locate and to destroy enemy ships, surface or submarine, with torpedoes.' By this time ASW training was relegated to last place among secondary tasks, the others being offensive minelaying, reconnaissance and lifeguard duties during air strikes. The Characteristics, or staff requirements, for the conversion noted that 'this conversion is intended to increase the capabilities of the obsolescent fleet type submarine the maximum amount for a minimum expenditure of funds. To this end, it is desired that during the conversion period of this ship, no replacements or additional installation of equipments and machinery be made, other than those described below, unless prior authorization be obtained from the Chief of Naval Operations. This conversion includes the installation of snorkel and streamlining of the superstructure. The installation of snorkel is considered to be an absolute requirement to permit submarines to carry out their mission in combat areas under enemy air patrol. Streamlining the superstructure provides substantial increase in both submerged speed and submerged endurance for a reasonable cost and is therefore very desirable. Present type of storage battery will be retained.' In fact the 1A conversions received a modified battery (*Sargo* II) rather larger than that of fleet boats and intermediate in lifetime between a *Sargo* and a Guppy. One unusual feature of the conversion was that the conning tower was to be designed to permit later installation of a long range conformal array listening sonar, a relative of the type then being fitted to the bows of SSKs. Two further Guppy IA conversions were to be made for the Royal Netherlands Navy, namely *Hawkbill* and *Icefish*.

'FLEET SNORKELS'

Even Guppy IA was not the least expensive way to rehabilitate a Fleet boat. The FY 51 program also included 19 'fleet snorkel' conversions, three of which were later cancelled. It was limited to 'installation of the snorkel plus that streamlining which is an economical part of snorkel installation' although 'conversion features shall be designed to facilitate future conversion to Guppy II or IA.' In practice that meant that a 'fleet snorkel' conversion could be distinguished from a true Guppy by its retention of a ship-type bow in place of the Guppy rounded one. Thus by snorkelling on one engine the 'fleet snorkel' could maintain only 6.5 knots to the IAs 7.5 (or the Type IIs 9 knots) and at the maximum half-hour battery rate she could make only 10 knots

underwater (15 for a IA, 16 for a II).

The original 'fleet snorkel' characteristics called for a 'minimum reduction of gun armament as necessary to meet stability requirement,' and at least some of these submarines emerged from their refits retaining a 5in/25 'wet gun' abaft their conning towers. These were soon removed, presumably in the interest of greater underwater speed.

TYPE IIA GUPPIES

There remained one further series of conversions, 16 more fleet boats became Guppy IIAs under the FY 52 program. Like the IA, the IIA employed the *Sargo* II battery but was redesigned for improved sonar performance, one main engine being eliminated to allow relocation of auxiliary machinery away from the sonar transducers. There were also habitability improvements which included better air conditioning. Sonar equipment included a new passive sonar called AN/BQR-2, generally in a chin dome under the hull, there was also an active sonar, such as BQS-2, and a precision tracking passive sonar (the wartime JT or its replacement, GQR-3). By 1954 this sonar suit was standard in Guppies.

The Guppy IIA program included two boats specifically intended as ASW targets, *Thornback* and *Razorback*. Both were modified to allow for impact firings of the new generation of ASW homing torpedoes but the modifications were such that it was relatively easy to convert these boats to the standard IIA configuration.

One remaining feature of all of the Guppy and 'fleet snorkel' submarines deserves mention: all were fitted with a new underwater fire control system, Mark 106, which permitted them to fire a new generation of electrically (as opposed to mechanically) set torpedoes and all ultimately received the new generation submarine-fired ASW homing torpedoes.

Guppies were not the only 'fleet boats' modernized to extend their useful lives. Seven boats received

more extensive SSK modifications, including installation of powerful BQR-4 passive sonars (at the expense of two bow tubes); they were otherwise similar to Guppy IIA conversions. There were also two boats converted to fire Regulus guided missiles which were otherwise comparable to 'fleet snorkels,' and nine converted to radar pickets. Other conversions produced cargo carriers and even a submarine oiler. However, the specialist types died out as experience with the converted fleet boats during the 1950s apparently showed that it was possible to build an effective general purpose submarine which would also be an effective SSK. At least that became US policy with nuclear submarines.

THE FRAM PROGRAM

By the late 1950s many of the US warships built for World War II were beginning to show their age. In 1958 an extensive Fleet Rehabilitation and Modernization (FRAM) program was instituted to buy time until the mass of war construction could be replaced. It included submarine refits, and ultimately nine Guppy IIs were rebuilt, lengthened 10ft, to allow for a plotting room and a longer conning tower, their hull and machinery overhauled and their fire control systems modified to allow them to fire the new ASTOR, the Mark 45 ASW torpedo with a nuclear warhead. In a sense this paralleled the destroyer modernizations which allowed them to fire ASROC, the new surface ASW weapon contemporary with ASTOR. The main external mark of the FRAM conversion, which was designated Guppy III, was a nuclear submarine style 'sail' which replaced the stepped type characteristic of the earlier boats. However, this new superstructure was also applied to Guppies which did not undergo FRAM and even to some 'fleet snorkels.'

Another major modification was the BQG-4 fire control sonar (PUFFS – Passive Underwater Fire-control Feasibility Study), housed in three domes projecting above the hull. Together, they were intended to permit the submarine to

USS *Tiru* (SS-416) was a GUPPY III. The domes along her upper deck are part of the PUFFS (BQG-4) passive ASW targeting system, which was also fitted on some newer submarines, including *Tullibee* (SSN-597). Here she is shown on 10 June 1963. Note the speckled periscope shaft, and also the absence of an air search radar – for a modern submarine air search radar is a hindrance rather than a help, since it can be counter-detected.
USN by courtesy of Norman Polmar.

triangulate sources of noise and thus to obtain both range and bearing without itself emitting sonar 'pings'. More conventional passive sonars could not find the range without having the boats they were mounted aboard carry out specialized and precise maneuvers. PUFFS was also mounted aboard several later US diesel submarines, and on the Guppy IA submarine *Blenny*.

The original FRAM program of December 1958 called for the modernization of 35 submarines to FRAM Mark II standard, which was expected to extend their useful lives by five years – one prototype under the FY 59 program, then 4 in FY 60, 8 in FY 61, and 11 each in FY 62 and 63. This conversion was designated SCB 223 in the series of new construction and conversion projects of the Ship Characteristics Board (Guppy II had been SCB 47, IA had been SCB 47A, the 'fleet snorkel' SCB 47B, and IIA SCB 47C). In 1958 a total of 48 Guppies were active and two had been lost, *Cochino* and *Stickleback*, the latter to a 1958 collision with a destroyer escort. FRAM modernizations were to apply to those units with the longest remaining working lives and

probably would have included all 23 surviving Guppy IIs and some of the 15 surviving Guppy IIAs. However, the Guppy III program was reduced to 24 and ultimately to 9 submarines. One reason may have been a growing skepticism as to the value of such limited refits in elderly hulls with very limited sonar capabilities against modern submarines; new nuclear boats equipped with very long range sonars (and presumably able to dive deeply enough to reach optimum sonar conditions) and SUBROC must have seemed a far more economical proposition.

Even so, the Guppies were retained in service into the 1970s and many now serve in foreign navies alongside the surviving 'fleet snorkels'. During the 1960s US yards converted a number of the surviving fleet boats, as well as several which had already been transferred abroad, to the late 'fleet snorkel' configuration including the new type of sail. US 'fleet snorkels' remained in service alongside the Guppies as late as 1973 showing, perhaps, the wisdom of the austere conversion. This last is perhaps a good way to conclude this brief

account. In the late 1940s the advance of wartime technology and the magnitude of the potential Soviet threat seemed so impressive that all of the proposed solutions involved wholesale reconstruction of the existing ASW fleet, much of it well under a decade old. It was impossible for the Navy to secure that kind of funding and in retrospect one of the great surprises of the 1950s was just how well the Fleet could do with far more austere measures, such as the 'fleet snorkel'.

ACKNOWLEDGEMENTS

I am indebted to the personnel of the US Naval Historical Center, particularly Cal Cavalcante, for their assistance in obtaining material for this article.
Photographs were supplied by Robert Carlisle of the US Still Photography section.

GUPPY CONVERSIONS

No	Boat	Conversion – yard and date			Transferred/fate	
GUPPY I						
484	ODAX	P	9.46 –	8.47	8. 7.72	Brazil
486	POMODON	M	10.46 –	7.47	1. 8.70	Scrapped
GUPPY II						
339	CATFISH		8.48 –	5.49	1. 7.71	Argentina
343	CLAMAGORE*	Ph	12.47 –	7.48	27. 6.75	Turkey
344	COBBLER*	E	12.48 –	8.49	21.11.73	Turkey
345	COCHINO				?	
346	CORPORAL*	E	3.47 –	2.48	21.11.73	Turkey
347	CUBERA	Ph	7.47 –	3.48	5. 1.72	Venezuela
349	DIODON	M	8.47 –	3.48		
350	DOGFISH	Ph	8.47 –	4.48	28. 7.72	Brazil
351	GREENFISH*	E	1.48 –	8.48	19.12.73	Brazil
352	HALFBEAK	P	9.49 –	1.50	1. 7.71	Scrapped
416	TIRU*				1. 7.75	Turkey
425	TRUMPETFISH*				15.10.73	Brazil
426	TUSK				18.10.73	Taiwan
478	CUTLASS	Ph	1.48 –	2.49	12. 4.73	Taiwan
483	SEA LEOPARD	Ph	12.48 –	.49	27. 3.73	Brazil
485	SIRAGO	Ph	12.48 –	7.49	1. 6.72	Scrapped
487	REMORA*	M	2.47 –	11.47	29.10.73	Greece
490	VOLADOR*					
522	AMBERJACK	P	12.46 –	1.48	17.10.73	Brazil
523	GRAMPUS**	B	–	10.49	13. 5.72	Brazil
524	PICKEREL	P	–	4.49		
525	GRENADIER**	B	–	2.51	15. 5.73	Venezuela
GUPPY 1A						
319	BECUNA	E	11.50 –	8.51	15. 8.73	Venezuela
322	BLACKFIN	M	11.50 –	5.51	15. 9.72	Sunk (target)
323	CAIMAN	M	4.51 –		30. 6.73	Turkey
324	BLENNY	M	–	.51	15. 8.73	Sunk (target)
341	CHIVO	E	10.50 –	7.51	1. 7.71	Argentina
342	CHOPPER	E	9.50 –	5.51	1.10.71	Scrapped
366	HAWKBILL	E	6.52 –	3.53		R Neth N
367	ICEFISH	E	8.52 –	5.53		R Neth N
403	ATULE	P	.50 –	.51	15. 8.73	Peru
406	SEA POACHER	Ch	–	.51	15. 8.73	Peru
407	SEA ROBIN		–	.51	1.10.70	Scrapped
417	TENCH				15. 8.73	Sunk (target)
GUPPY IIA						
340	ENTEMEDOR	E	2.52 –	10.52	1. 8.73	Turkey
365	HARDHEAD	E	4.52 –	1.53	26. 7.72	Greece
368	JALLAO	E	–	12.53	26. 6.74	Spain
377	MENHADEN	M	8.52 –	5.53	15. 8.73	Sunk (target)
382	PICUDA	P	–	8.53	1.11.74	Spain
385	BANG	P	2.52 –	10.52	1.11.74	Spain
391	POMFRET	M	4.52 –	1.53	1. 8.73	Turkey
394	RAZORBACK	P	8.52 –	4.53	30.11.70	Turkey
396	RONQUIEL	M	5.52 –	2.53	1. 7.71	Spain
402	SEA FOX	M	10.52 –	7.53	15.12.70	Turkey
410	THREADFIN	P	11.52 –	8.53	1. 8.73	Turkey
415	STICKLEBACK	M	11.52 –	6.53	28. 5.58	Sunk (rammed)
418	THORNBACK	Ch	6.52 –	3.53	1. 8.73	Turkey
420	TIRANTE	P	3.52 –	12.52	1.10.73	Scrapped
421	TRUTTA	Ch	5.52 –	1.53	1. 7.72	Scrapped
424	QUILLBACK	P	5.52 –	1.53	23. 3.73	Scrapped

*Boats converted to Guppy III.

**Boats completed as Guppy.

Key to conversion Yards:
B, Boston Navy Yard
Ch, Charleston Navy Yard
E, Electric Boat Co
M, Mare Island
P, Portsmouth Navy Yard
Ph, Philadelphia Navy Yard

A's and A's

AIRCRAFT ON TIGER from
Adrian Vicary, Cromer

I have received today Issue 6 of
Warship and am particularly
interested in the photographs on
page 89. The photograph captions
incorrectly state the aeroplane's
serial number as S6797; this should
be N6797. However more
important than this is that it is
actually a Sopwith 2F1 Camel not a
Sopwith Pup. This is one of a batch
of 100 built by William Beardmore
& Co Ltd, of Dalmuir (Serials
N6750 - 6849). The date of the
photograph must therefore be
sometime after March 1918 as the
first Beardmore built Camel flew in
February 1918 and deliveries to
Rosyth commenced in March.
    Incidentally Culley's Camel, in
the Imperial War Museum, is also
from this batch of Beardmore
Camels (N6812). According to
*Marine Aircraft of the 1914-1918
War* the turret ramp was built on
Tiger in February 1918, and
another Camel (N6603) was
carried.

1 This aircraft, N5180, seen here shortly after
completion, was the first Pup (excluding the
six prototypes) to be manufactured by
Sopwith. Earlier production models were
however produced by Beardmore who
manufactured a large number under
sub-contract.
Courtesy H Woodman

2 An unusual view of a Beardmore built
Sopwith Camel 2F1 taking off from an
aircraft carrier (HMS *Pegasus*) in the Firth of
Forth. Note the level upper wing, which in the
Pup followed the line of the lower wing, and
the Lewis gun mounted at its centre.
R L Rimell, courtesy H Woodman

A's and A's

VIRIBUS UNITIS from Harry Woodman, London

The feature on *Viribus Unitis* was of great interest to me but I regret that Herr Prasky had to damn all previous attempts to describe these ships with his remark that . . . "Articles have been published on these ships but all of them contain errors of fact". As one of the writers of a previous article I find it a little off-putting. Apart from myself the only other accounts that spring to mind were written by an Austrian, a Czech and a Dutchman. My own feature which was published in *Battle* magazine, in three parts, in 1976 was based almost entirely on Austrian material and I had the help and advice of Ing Rene Greger of Prague and the Graf von Aichelberg of Vienna. My drawing was, as is Herr Prasky's, a tracing of the original drawing held by the Austrian State Archive. As my work was to be reduced to 1:700 scale much small detail was omitted but I did modify it to show the vessel as she appeared in 1916/17 with some of the 7cm guns removed and anti-bomb baskets fitted to the funnels. Apart from this, despite Herr Prasky's remarks, a good drawing was available some time ago in the US which was also traced from the original Austrian material. My feature was entitled *The Tegetthoffs* for the simple reason that contemporary Austro-Hungarian literature and material (which I possess) refers to these ships as *Tegetthoff Klasse*.

Finally I think that your readers may be a little puzzled by the statement at the top of page 106 that *Szent Istvan* was . . . 'completed in Poland'. It is of course a misprint for Pola.

CRUISER RADAR from Alastair H Mitchell, Sussex, UK

I was very interested in Norman Friedman's article on cruiser electronics in *Warship* 6 as, having spent seven years on radar maintenance in the RN in the 1950s, I worked on some of the later equipments mentioned. Reading the article I got the impression that Mr Friedman was more at home with US Navy radars than he was with the RN. There was a fair degree of supposition as regards some aspects of the performance and operational use of the British sets. To take a few examples **a.** Page 81 –

1. "The wide beams of the British systems (Types 79, 281 etc) presented a serious problem if their warning were to be translated into data suitable for gunnery or probably even for fighter control."
2. "The RN appeared to have had difficulty in synchronising the rotation of two aerials."

In (1) it depends on what period of the war we are talking about. Initially the sets were classified as purely early warning and were used by the few ships fitted to give the fleet warning of an impending air attack. Tracking and ranging were normally done visually by the AA directors. In 1945 the Types 79, 279 and 279M were listed as long range early warning of aircraft and ships and as AA gunnery ranging. Types 281 and 281M were listed as for long range warning and short range ranging against aircraft, and for range and bearing of surface targets. In addition, of course, facilities existed for 'putting on' the centimetric radars Type 277, 275 etc, to give accurate height and ranging guidance; eg display units Type JJ and 19.

I would therefore agree that the radar could not give accurate bearing information but then as the range lessened so would the distance of arc until visual contact was made. In any case beam-width is measured between the half power points so as you come close-in problems with main lobe width and sidelobes arise at the lower frequences. I do not know how effective the radars were in the gunnery data role as by the time I came on the scene it was all done by the 10cm radars, the Type 960 metric set having reverted to purely long range warning.

As to the rotation of the aerials (2) this was done mechanically by hand through 360° and back. The only report I have seen of this stated that one man rotated both aerials. I have no information as to how this was actually done but given that the RN could get 15in turrets weighing over 700 tons to follow a director I would not have thought the problem was beyond them!

b. Page 82 – in describing the roles of Types 277 and 293 radars there are several mistakes. The Type 293 was a 10cm radar (not 3cm) with a beam-width in the final Q version of plus and minus $1\frac{3}{4}°$ and a vertical beam-width of plus and minus 30° tilted at 15° to give air cover up to 45°. The broad elevation beam meant it did not have to be stabilised in any plane to give effective surface cover out to the horizon (12 - 25 miles depending on the height of the aerial and target size). It was primarily a surface warning and target indicating set and was only fitted to ships with a gunnery director. The very narrow beam made it a doubtful proposition as an air warning set and whether you picked up an aircraft or not depended on its size and altitude.

The same radar was used in conjunction with a dish aerial and then became Type 277. This gave a relatively narrow beam in both horizontal and vertical planes, was stabilised in one plane and was used as a combined surface/air warning set on all types of ships and as a height-finder in conjunction with Types 279M and 281BQ. The official ranges quoted for Type 277M were 25-30 miles for surface targets (including coastlines) and 50-100 miles for aircraft with maximum elevation for heightfinding of 40°. The 'P' version had an improved receiver giving 15% range increase while the elevation of the aerial was increased to 75°. In the 1950s the normal method of operation was to rotate the Type 277 with the dish vertical and when required stop it on the approximate bearing indicated by the Type 281/960 and 'nod it' up and down to obtain the elevation.

Having complained for most of this letter I would like to say that I do think Mr Friedman is correct in his general assessment of the different tactical concepts applied in the two navies with the emphasis on gunnery in the RN and that I enjoyed reading the article. Very little is ever written about the development of shipborne radar.

FAULTS IN VIRIBUS UNITIS CLASS

Friedrich Prasky the author of the article on the *Viribus Unitis* class published in *Warship* 6 has sent us the following additional information. It is taken from an official document listing the faults of the class.

1. The ships were about 2500 tons too small for their armament.
2. In battle condition the bow lay 20cm too deep in the water.
3. The freeboard at the forecastle was too low; the ships were not ocean going types. The ram bow was obsolete.
4. Because of their low stability the ships heeled over very much even in turning at low speed. Turning at full speed during a battle was impossible otherwise the side armour would have come out of the water.
5. The ships were too slow. During the raid of the Austro-Hungarian Fleet against the Italian coast at the beginning of the war *Viribus Unitis* only reached 17.5 knots as maximum speed.
6. The openings in the armoured deck were too large, especially around the smokestacks where large openings were arranged, so a projectile as small as 7cm could penetrate the wall of the boiler room. With the resultant loss of air pressure in the fire rooms the speed would have been further reduced. The funnel uptakes were unprotected and the ships carried nets on the top of their funnels against bombing – a very pointless construction.
7. The turrets also had some faults. As you can see in my drawing there was an unprotected slot between barbette and gun house. The cupola of the rangefinder on the turret roof

was too large. A hit on it would have opened the thin turret covering like a tin can. Under battle conditions the gun houses could not be ventilated and the oxygen in them only lasted for 15 minutes. Before firing the ventilation had to be turned off, otherwise the explosion gases would have been sucked in. The 15cm barbettes had no ventilation; when smoke got into them they were out of action.

In summary it can be said that the ships of the *Viribus Unitis* class were powerful looking and beautiful but they were not suited for action. The Austrian Naval Staff knew the faults of these ships as there exists a document about these drawbacks dated before the sinking of the *Szent Istvan*.

TRIBAL CLASS
FRIGATES
BY PETER HODGES

HMS *Zulu* in 1975, some eleven years after her launch. She was the last ship of the class (giving the Z of her name a hint of finality) and was the only one having Seacat systems from building. Both the 20mm junk-bashers and the 8-barrelled rocket launcher were later additions. The bluff bow at forecastle deck level is clearly seen.
HMS Osprey

The Type 81 General Purpose Frigate emerged from a 1954 design in which it was hoped to combine the attributes of the specialised Type 12 (A/S) Type 41 (A/A) and Type 61 (A/D) frigates. These three classes of six, four and four ships respectively were completed between 1956 and 1959 (together with a dozen Type 14s, the latter honestly described as '3rd rate'); but the concept proved costly. Economic strictures had already dictated that only the Type 12s would have the steam turbines necessary for them adequately to fulfil their function as AS vessels. The remaining eight diesel propelled AA and AD frigates were embarassingly slow in company

with the Type 15 conversions – and indeed with most of the existing fleet including, of course, the aircraft carriers.

The first three ships of the 'Tribal' class were ordered under the 1955-56 Estimates and soon featured in contemporary publications. The details therein proved to be so inaccurate that one is left wondering whether they were the pure conjecture of the publishers or had been collusively released from Whitehall with deliberate intent to deceive. Either way, surely only the most naive could have believed that on a displacement of 2800 tons with 20 000 shp and one shaft the class had been designed for 30 knots.

The imagined armament was equally erroneous and mysteriously suffered a multiplication factor of two. Thus, the class were to have two twin 4.5in DP, two twin 40mm Bofors and two Limbos to say nothing of eight 21in torpedo tubes. Even now they are cryptically described as having 'Optical Seacat Directors'.

ARMAMENT
The armament is in fact a strange mixture of ancient and modern. Two single 4.5in Mk 5 mountings, which are fundamentally cleaned-up 4.7in Mk XXIIs of Second World War vintage with electric power added, are set in A and Y positions. Like their valiant forebears the

present day shell and cordite loading numbers must needs take what comfort they can behind an open-backed gunshield cradling a 55lb projectile and 35lb cartridge case in their arms. No doubt the 'single four five' concept was economically attractive (since there were mountings a-plenty from scrapped 'C' class destroyers) but it seems hardly the armament for the nuclear age. The layers' and trainers' sighting ports have been plated over to improve the watertightness of the front face shield and the hand ramming arrangements removed from the spring powered loading tray to reduce maintenance effort; but the mounting as a whole cannot be

---

Nubian at anchor with the hatch-covers in position on the flight deck covering the open lift well. Note that the red 'danger' circle around the 4.5in defines the swept arc of the muzzles. The GWS 21 directors are uncovered and the aerial dish can be seen, centrally on the drum-shaped shield.
C & S TAYLOR

claimed to be other than the stop-gap it was acknowledged to be when it was first designed in the early 1940s. 'A' mounting has triple 2in Rocket Flare Launcher (RFL) rails on each side for illumination purposes which allows the gun to be supplied with HE rather than starshell. The RFLs are less flexible than conventional fused starshell since their range is less and they are at a fixed elevation. They date from the Battle of the Atlantic and were originally designed for one gun escorts to enable them to illuminate and engage surfaced U-boats without the need to change ammunition type from starshell to HE.

The 4.5in armament is controlled by the first frigate-fit of the MRS3 system which before the advent of the latest digital computers was the standard gunfire control system in the Royal Navy. MRS3, which is analog-electronic, is a 'Chinese copy' of the USN Mk 63 system and the discerning will note a similarity

FIGURE 1. TYPE 81 ('TRIBAL' CLASS) FRIGATE
1. VDS gantry operator's compartment
2. VDS gantry
3. Towed acoustic torpedo decoy winch
4. Y 4.5in main Mk5 mounting
5. Hangar roof/flight deck
6. Triple-barrelled A/S mortar Mk10
7. Secondary control for Y mounting abaft after funnel (by STD)
8. IFF
9. Type 965 long range surveillance radar
10. UHF
11. Navigation/helicopter landing control radar
12. Medium range/weapon direction radar
13. MRS3 (Gunnery) director, with radar Type 903
14. Visual gun direction positon
15. A 4.5in Mk5 mounting
16. Attack and search sonars
17. Triple 2in rocket flare launcher, left and right
18. 20mm Oerlikon, port and starboard
19. 8-barrelled 3in decoy rocket launcher, port and starboard
20. Quadruple Seacat launcher, port and starboard
21. Boat stowage space, port and starboard
22. GWS 21 director, port and starboard
23. Mortar bomb handling room
24. After capstan

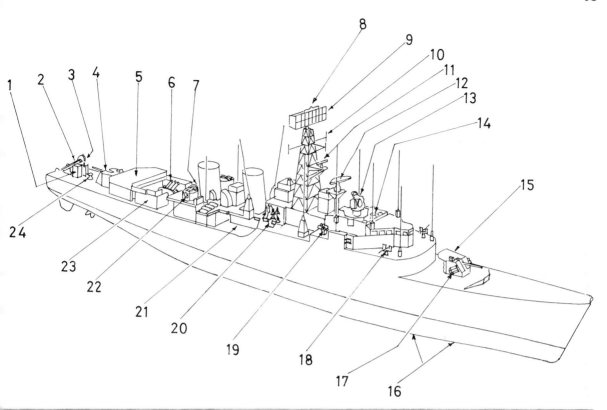

between the respective directors (fig 2). The heart of the system is the tracking gyro in the director. Designed by Sperry it has, of course, strong American associations. The Radar Type 903 aerial dish has the American style 'Cutler Feed' at the termination of the wave guide which, through a complex gearbox, nutates in a conical scan to produce a pencil-beam tracking mode. Having acquired a target in Search the system then locks-on and all target tracking and fire control computation is thereafter automatic.

The International 'Code' pennant over 'zero' warns merchant vessels that *Ashanti* has right of way as a warship. Note the sonar gantry operators 'sentry box' on the starboard quarter. *Tribals* carry a Royal Marine detachment, here drawn up on the port side amidships.
C & S TAYLOR

The class was designed to carry two Seacat systems but only *Zulu* (the seventh and last ship) received them from building while the others were given two single Mk 9 electric powered 40mm Bofors for close range AA defence and surface 'police' duty. At subsequent long refits all six earlier ships were given two sided Seacat systems and lost their single Bofors but, in keeping with the Fleet as a whole, single 20mm Oerlikons were added for the 'junk bashing' role.

The GWS21 system of the 'Tribals' employs self-contained tracking devices within the director but with the same launcher and missile guidance arrangements found in other Seacat variants. The director (fig 3) is fundamentally a modified Close Range Blind Fire (CRBF) director dating from the early 1950s and disappeared elsewhere in the Fleet when

Devonshire decommissioned after being purchased by the Egyptian Government. Its radar, Type 262, was first fitted in the STAAG twin Bofors of immediate post war years and develops a conical tracking lobe from an eccentrically spinning radar dish aerial driven by an aerial motor. The completely trunnioned aerial oscillates in both planes during the Search phase and once locked on automatically controls the movement of the director and thus, in sequence, the Seacat launcher. Tracking is tachometric (rate measuring) from a gyro and the Seacat aimer has a secondary reflector sight for visual control which perhaps accounts for the 'Optical Seacat Director' phrase mentioned earlier.

The tachometric system is commonly used in gunfire control systems and employs the characteristics of a gyroscope,

whose spin axis is maintained in gimbals along the 'present' line of sight to the target. Because such a gyro will remain fixed in space it will automatically measure ship movement between itself and its ship mounted gimbals and thus provide measurable stabilisation corrections. But a gimballed gyro can be made to precess, or shift its 'aim', by applying a force to either or both gimbals and its axis may thus be caused to constantly follow the target's present position. The rate at which it is necessary to precess it, combined with the target's present range (which is constantly measured by the Radar) allows the future position of the target constantly to be predicted (fig 4).   A Simple Tachometric Director (STD) hand worked by an aimer and fitted with a gyro gunsight is positioned abaft the second funnel for divided control of

Y mounting.

One triple barrelled Mk 10 AS mortar is positioned fractionally off the centre line to port flanked by superstructure units and appears to be in a well but is in fact at upper deck level. The mortar bomb handing room is on the starboard side and in the loading position the mortar barrels are laid horizontal to align with three bomb rammers which propel the missiles, tail first, into the barrels. The mortar mounting base is fixed and takes the form of a pair of trunnion supports in the fore and aft line. A cradle trunnioned in them is driven in the roll direction by an electric motor and the three mortar barrels are collectively trunnioned into the cradle in the athwartships plane. All are linked together and driven by a second electric motor and thus move in the pitch direction. Clearly movement in the pitch plane with

the roll plane at zero allows theoretical ahead or astern firing; while with the barrels vertical and stationary in pitch, roll will give beam firing on either side. Further, by a combination of both motions, all-round cover is again theoretically achieved but, for blast considerations, it is unlikely that firing is possible directly over the hangar. Follow is automatic by synchro transmission from the Sonar computer and is gyro stabilised to counteract ship motion (Fig 5). The combined movements of the follow-motors are used only to direct the trajectory along the computed bearing and the barrels are not elevated for range even though this is mechanically possible. Instead the barrels remain at a sensibly constant elevation and range is varied by the automatic venting of a proportion of the cordite gases.

54

FIGURE 2. MRS3 MOD1 DIRECTOR

1. Director officer's blast hood
2. Shutter
3. Screen wiper
4. Cine-camera mounting bracket
5. Director Aimer's compartment
6. Screen wipers
7. Aerial reflector
8. Aerial cover support
9. Conically/spirally scanning cutler-feed aerial
10. Forced lubrication pump
11. Electric training motor
12. Fixed director base
13. Base jacking bolt
14. Training base roller-path weathering cover
15. Electric elevation motor
16. Elevation gear box
17. Swept-arc guard rail quadrant
18. Radar electronic compartments
19. Maintenance access steps
20. Cable room

Notes.

i. Compare items 1 and 6 above with items A, B, J, of GWS 22 director on page 163 of *Warship* No 7

ii. Replace item 1 above with item A from GWS22 director for original MRS3 director officer's hood

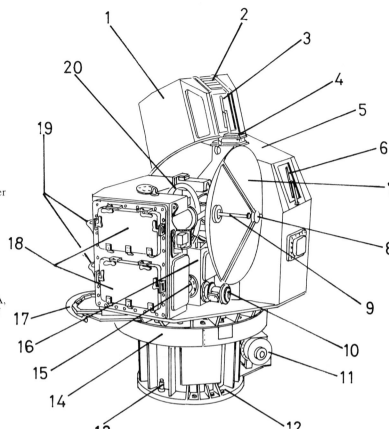

FIGURE 3. GWS21 DIRECTOR

A. Rear windscreen extension
B. Director officer's open sight bracket
C. Elevating link between open sight and gyro tachometrical unit
D. Aerial spinner-motor
E. Aerial lateral deflection axis
F Eccentric aerial dish reflector
G. Aerial elevation gearbox
H. Shaft drive to gear box
I. Aimer's reflector sight
J. Gyro safety caging lever
K. Tachometrical unit, elevating about left hand trunnion
L. Aimer's joystick
M. Aimer's footrest
N. Aimer's seat
O. Seat descending trackway
P. Power drive to aimer's seat, maintaining seat position irrespective of tacho. unit elevation
Q. Sliding access door
R. Housing locking bolt lever
S. Director officer's joystick
T. Director officer's seat
U. Director officer's control panel
V. Radar operator's screen eye-pieces

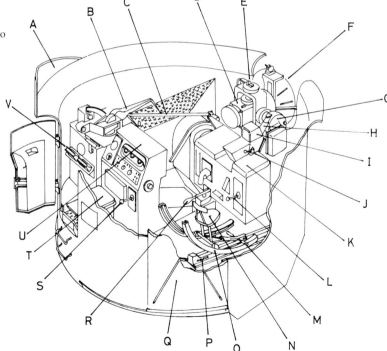

FIG 4. TACHYMETRICAL TRACKING PRINCIPLES

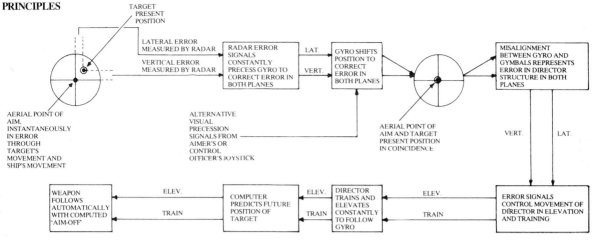

FIGURE 5. FUNDAMENTAL FEATURES OF MORTAR MK10 MOUNTING

1. Roll motion motor and gearbox on after face of mounting base
2. Mounting control selector lever
3. Mounting base
4. Automatic computer-controlled cordite gas venting valves
5. Pitch motion trunnions
6. Forward barrel impulse cartridge breech mechanism
7. Pitch motion gearbox axis
8. Control circuit conduit tube
9. Forward roll motion cradle trunnion and electrical slip-ring
10. Forward barrel, driven by pitch motion drive
11. Centre and after barrel, linked to forward barrel
12. Barrels pitch upright and roll horizontal to loading position

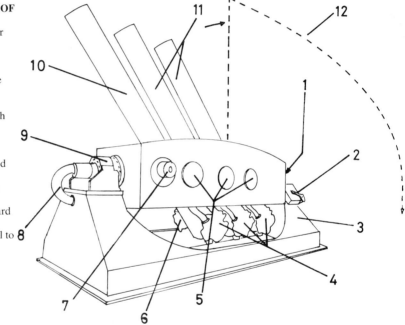

Prototype trials on this mortar were carried out in the 'Weapon' class destroyer *Scorpion* soon after the Second World War when the weapon was given the code name Limbo but, although still frequently met with in print, this name is never used in the Navy. The total system (which includes the attack sonar in a retractable Hull Outfit) was designed, and indeed first installed, as a two-mortar outfit, but has since been reduced to one except in the remaining *Blackwood* class.

The deck space taken up by the after 4.5in mounting in Y position precluded a conventional flight deck so the helicopter is launched and recovered from its lift platform which becomes the Flight Deck in its raised position. When the aircraft is stowed the, then open-topped, hangar is closed by merchant marine style sectioned hatch-covers. The retention of Y mounting is hard to understand. No other RN classes have medium range gun-coverage over the after arcs and had it been removed at major refits a *Leander* style flight deck and hangar configuration could conceivably have been built. *Tiger* and *Blake*

bear witness to the fact that stranger things have happened. As it is the second mounting doubles the workload in terms of auto follow performance and weapon alignment, compared to the one-mounting frigates, while in two ships (*Gurkha* and *Ashanti*) the after arcs are further encroached upon by the presence of the Sonar 199 gantry.

In common with the rest of the fleet, the class as a whole has multi barrel decoy rocket launchers to port and starboard.

HULL FORM, APPEARANCE AND MAIN MACHINERY

After decades of destroyer hulls stepped down one deck level abaft the bridge superstructure followed by the unusual forecastle deck of the earler New Construction frigates the flush deck of the 'Tribals' was something of a novelty. Apart from the short Seaslug deck of the 'Counties' the two classes have similar hull forms, but the 'Tribals' have none of the presence of the GMDs. The position of the two funnels is, of course, dictated by by the internal main machinery layout but the fact that their height does not follow the sheer of the continuous forecastle deck gives the ships an ungainly appearance in the view of many and the retention of a lattice mast (when most are plated) coupled with the elderly main armament presents a decidedly dated appearance.

The mast is topped by the Type 965M surveillance radar and has a projecting platform for the Type 978 Navigation set aerial. The medium range /gun direction Type 993 aerial has its own rather unsightly pylon support between the mast and the MRS3 director (with its radar Type 903). The Seacat directors have their Type 262 dishes and the usual spinney of whip aerials is clustered around the main superstructure.

The single shaft is powered by a Combined Steam and Gas (COSAG) turbine arrangement, the former plant developing 12 500shp and the latter 7500shp, control being effected from a central air conditioned machinery control room. Since there is nothing particularly unusual in the general hull form, by normal power /weight ratio standards, it would mean that on steam alone the Tribals will probably touch 20 knots and not much in excess of 25 with 'all systems go'. Thus, the gas turbine allows a comparatively rapid ability to get under way from cold but alone would give little more than manoeuvering speed under way and with steam available hardly gives the ships a sprint capability. Further, the single shaft must inevitably produce its own torque

effect and make manoeuvering astern more difficult than with a twin shaft installation.

Bearing in mind that a submerged 'nuke' will almost certainly outpace a *Tribal* it would seem unlikely that the surface vessel could ever get close enough to engage such an underwater target with her mortar except, of course, by fortuitous encounter. Hence, the need to retain the mortar looks questionable and its removal, together with Y mounting, would give even more scope for a better flight deck arrangement. One could envisage, for example, the hangar shifted forward to a position immediately abaft the second funnel and upon it a centre line Seacat director with twin Seacat launchers à la Ikara and Exocet *Leander.* But by modern standards the *Tribals,* at an average of 16 years old, are probably not destined for further major modification.

CONCLUSIONS

The oddest stories have grown up around these ships. It has been said that they were specially designed for the Persion Gulf and even that they were given two funnels because the peoples of that region set great store by the number of funnels evident in a ship. But the fact that as General Purpose Frigates they were more

expensive units than the successful *Whitbys* and additionally ran to an odd number of seven perhaps indicates that they were tacitly deemed less 'utility' than was originally anticipated. Having said that, however, the Type 81 did introduce new standards of accomodation and internal spaciousness as well as the then novel air conditioning but these are, perhaps, facets of *peace-ship* rather than *warship* design. Finally, with *Afridi* and *Cossack* notably absent from the seven ship names one is left wondering what the late Admiral of the Fleet Sir Philip Vian thought of them upon their emergence.

1 *Gurkha* showing the packed quarter
deck with the Sonar 199 gantry and
heavy towing winch. In this ship the
danger circles around the 4.5in define
only the swept arc of the gunshield. The
STD can be seen, flanked by ladders,
abaft the second funnel.
C & S TAYLOR

2 *Nubian* again, with the helicopter in the
process of being ranged. The rotor
blades are being unfolded and the flight
deck safety nets have been hinged
down. The danger circle around the
whip aerial base, forward of the
starboard Seacat launcher, defines a
dangerous radio transmission source.
C & S TAYLOR

2

Warship Pictorial
PRINZ EUGEN

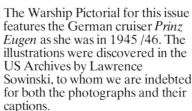

The Warship Pictorial for this issue features the German cruiser *Prinz Eugen* as she was in 1945/46. The illustrations were discovered in the US Archives by Lawrence Sowinski, to whom we are indebted for both the photographs and their captions.

The *Prinz Eugen* was commissioned in August 1940 and in May 1941 sailed into the North Atlantic with the battleship *Bismarck* to raid the British convoy routes. After the sinking of HMS *Hood* she separated from her ill-fated companion and eventually joined the *Scharnhorst* and *Gneisenau* at Brest. In February 1942 together with the two battlecruisers she returned to Germany via the English Channel (Operation Cerberus), a daring exploit which met with much greater success than expected. The British were caught off-guard by the sudden appearance of three enemy heavy ships on their doorstep and had insufficient time to do more than mount a few unco-ordinated and ill-prepared air and sea attacks,

a missed opportunity which left many with red faces.

She served most of the remainder of the war in the Baltic and during 1944-45 was employed as a bombardment vessel against the Russian army, expending for this purpose over 2500 8in shells. In April 1945 she was immobilised at Copenhagen, due to lack of fuel, and at the end of the war, in the following month, she was taken over by the British, de-ammunitioned and escorted to Wilhelmshaven.

On 13 December 1945 she was allocated to the USA and exactly one month later, on 13 January 1946, sailed for Boston where she arrived on the 22nd. After examining the ship and removing some of her guns and equipment the ship was transferred to the Pacific to take part in the two Atomic bomb tests at Bikini Atoll in June 1946. In both tests she was moored about 1200 yards from the centre of the explosion. The first bomb was detonated in the air and did only minor damage to *Prinz Eugen* but the second, detonated underwater, caused more extensive damage to her hull structure. She was later towed to Kwajalein Atoll where she ran aground, capsized and sank on 22 December 1947. The wreck was broken up during 1962-65.

The *Prinz Eugen* just prior to sailing for Bikini. The picture was probably taken at Pearl Harbor.

1

1 *Prinz Eugen* leaves the Philadelphia Navy
Yard on 3 March 1946 en route to Bikini
Atoll. She was one of three test ships with an
all-welded hull to take part in Operation
Crossroads.

2 Pictures of *Prinz Eugen*, such as this one,
taken from a crane in Philadelphia, are a ship
modeller's dream. Note the catapult abaft the
funnel.

3 This magnificent picture shows the *Prinz
Eugen* before any modifications were made at
Philadelphia (February 1946). The crane is in
the process of removing 'A' turret's armor
plate so that both 20.2cm (8in) guns can be
removed.

2

U.S.S. PRINZ EUGEN - IX 300
FEB. 1946   378-46-10

U.S.S. PRINZ EUGEN - IX3
FEB. 1946   378-46

U.S.S. PRINZ EUGEN – IX 300
VIEW FROM MAINMAST, STBD.
SIDE, LOOKING AFT.

1

1 This view, taken from the side of the mainmast, clearly shows the starboard quarter twin 10.5cm (4.1in) AA.

2 Taken at Bikini on 11 June 1946, this close-up shows one of *Prinz Eugen's* starboard side triple torpedo mounts. The US ships in the background are, left to right: the carriers *Independence* and *Saratoga*, cruiser *Salt Lake City* and a line of attacke transports with a floating drydock among them.

3 Looking down *Prinz Eugen's* starboard side from the foremast. Note the 8in gun lying at the very end of the piers.

2

U.S.S. PRINZ EUGEN - IX 300
VIEW FROM FOREMAST, STBD.
SIDE, LOOKING AFT
FEB. 1946   378-46-4

64

U.S.S. PRINZ EUGEN - IX 300
VIEW FROM FORE MAST, STBD.
SIDE, LOOKING FWD.
FEB. 1946   378 - 46 - 1

Modifications made to *Prinz Eugen's* bridge included the installation of a US Army radar van atop the comming tower. The van is still painted olive drab.

Close-up of a single 40mm mount. The picture was taken eleven days after test 'Able' on 12 June 1946.

Prinz Eugen at Bikini after the first atom blast 'Able' on 1 June 1946. Her only damage was a snapped main topmast and a bent foremast. The ship in the background, directly behind *Eugen's* stern, is the US heavy cruiser *Salt Lake City* – both of her funnels were toppled over by the blast.

BRITISH SUPER-HEAVY GUNS PART I

BY N J M CAMPBELL

The guns discussed in this article, that were actually mounted in British ships, are limited to the four RML mounted in the battleship *Inflexible* completed in 1881, the two 16.25in BL mounted in the battleships *Benbow* of 1888, and *Victoria* and *Sans Pareil* of 1890-1891, the single 18in BL mounted in the battlecruiser *Furious* of 1917 and the monitors *General Wolfe* and *Lord Clive,* as rearmed in 1918, and finally the nine 16in BL Mark I mounted in the battleships *Nelson* and *Rodney* of 1927. This is a small total when compared with the 128-15in BL mounted at one time or another in 22 ships, but the guns of 16in or over actually mounted in ships tell but a part of the story of such weapons. Also included are the 17.7in RML mounted at Gibraltar and Malta, the 16in BL built for Russia in 1914-1917, which ended its days as the first British super-velocity 8in, the 16in BL Mk II and III intended for the *Lion* class, ships cancelled because of the 1939-1945 war, and the 16in BL Mark IV project for the redesigned *Lion* class of the immediate post World War Two period. Besides these there are the four 18in/45 cal guns of 1920-1921, each of which was of different construction and three of which were actually begun. Lastly the 1885-1886 project to reinforce the Portsmouth defences by four 17in/41 cal BL may be noted, though there is more than a touch of fantasy about this as it

would have been virtually impossible to build these guns at that date and it is exceedingly improbable that they would have functioned in a satisfactory way if they had been constructed.

16IN RML MARK I

The origins of this gun go back to July 1873 when the Admiralty requested the War Office, at that date responsible for the supply of naval guns, to prepare a design for a 60 ton gun, 22ft 4in in overall length. The largest gun actually in British service at this time was the 12in/35 ton. At a meeting on 21 October 1873 a design for a 75 ton 16in of the above length, to fire a 1650lb projectile with a 300lb black powder propellant charge, was discussed and a requirement to pierce 20in of wrought iron at 1000yds was mentioned; the Italian battleship *Duilio,* laid down in April 1873, would have armour of this thickness, as also, it was erroneously believed, would the Russian battleship *Petr Veliki,* launched in August 1872. On 26 November 1873 a less ambitious design was produced for a 60 ton 15in gun, still 22ft 4in long, firing a 1350lb projectile with 230lb charge. Finally, on 11 March 1874, the manufacture of an experimental gun of about 75 tons – on a later estimate 80 tons – was approved. This was to have a 24ft bore and was to be tried successively at 14, 15 and 16in cal – when bored to 16in, it was expected to give an MV

(muzzle velocity) of 1400ft/sec with a 1650lb projectile and a 300lb propellant charge. It took 18 months to complete this gun, as enlarged plant had to be acquired at Woolwich, and meanwhile the *Inflexible,* which was to mount 4 of these guns when the design had been settled, had been laid down on 24 February 1874.

The experimental gun was eventually bored to 14.5in, not 14in, and rifled on the unsatisfactory but usual RML system with 11 grooves, studded projectiles and the twist increasing from zero to 1 in 35 at the muzzle. It was 'proved' on 17 September 1875 attaining an MV of 1550ft/sec with a 1260lb projectile and a 240lb charge. After further firings it was bored to 15in and rerifled, then chambered to 16in and finally bored to 16in and rerifled. It should be noted that in the later firings copper gas-checks were used. These were rimmed discs attached to the base of the projectile; the rim expanded into the rifling grooves on firing so that the serious erosion from powder gases escaping past the projectile was greatly reduced. After a total of 166 rounds the gun was examined on 30 December 1876 and it would found that the steel tube had cracked in a rifling groove for a length of 55 to 85ins from the bottom of the bore. This was thought to be due to holes drilled and tapped for the fitting of crusher gauges to measure the pressures in the bore on firing.

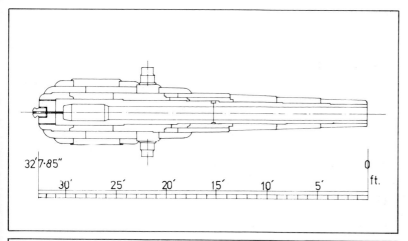

17·72 IN RML

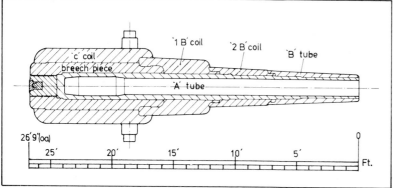

16 IN RML

However, firings continued, with some further development of the crack, and the gun was then chambered to 18in diameter and attained an MV of 1600ft/sec with a 1700lb projectile and 425lb charge. By June 1877 the total of rounds fired was 274 but, though the *Inflexible* had been launched on 27 April 1876 and construction of all 4 of her guns was under way in March 1877, important details were as yet unsettled. In particular it had not been decided whether to abandon the studded projectile in favour of an improved gas-check combined with shallower but more numerous rifling grooves, a system to be known as polygroove. Accordingly the first of the *Inflexible's* guns was bored to 15.5in and given polygroove rifling but troubles with excessive pressures and shells 'setting up' occurred so it was not until August 1878 that it was recommended that this system should be used with a bore of 16in. It had been decided a year

previously that the guns were to be chambered. The *Inflexible's* 4 guns were completed in 1880-1881 and this much delayed ship was finally ready in October of the latter year. Two more guns completed in 1881-1882 were mounted in a twin turret at Dover and one more, intended as reserve for the *Inflexible,* was completed in 1885-1886 to give, with the original experimental gun, a total of eight.

All were built at the Royal Gun Factory Woolwich which at that date had a monopoly of gun construction for the British Services. The 16in RML was built on what was known as the Fraser two layer modification. There was a steel 'A' tube which was heat-treated and quenched in oil but not tempered, and over this a wrought iron breech piece, 1B coil, 2B coil and B tube were shrunk. These were linked to one another by overlapping bayonet type joints. The C coil, incorporating the trunnion ring, was shrunk over the breech piece and

part of the 1B coil and the cascable screw, which contained the axial vent, was screwed into the breech piece and butted firmly onto the end of the 'A' tube. The cascable and trunnion ring were wrought iron forgings while the other parts were built up by hammer welding two or more coils,,themselves made by coiling wrought iron bar over a mandrel and hammer welding. No attempt was made to carry out the shrinking so as to give precise calculated stresses in the various layers. This construction was crude but cheap, and reasonably effective for relatively short guns, and gave better longitudinal strength than the more complex Armstrong construction used in the 17.72in RML. Details of the 16in RML Mark I were:

Weight 80 tons (average)
Length (oa) 26ft 9in (321in)
Length (bore) 18 cal (288in)
Diameter 72in (max) 25in (at muzzle)

68

Chamber size 59.6 x 18in, volume
14 600 cub in

Rifling length 227.4in twist 0 to 1 in
50 at muzzle, 33 grooves,
polygroove plain section 0.1 x 1in,
lands 0.523in

Projectile weight 1700lb (including
21¼lb gas check)

Charge 450lb prismatic black (4 x
112½), later 450lb prismatic brown

Muzzle Velocity 1604ft/sec with
black powder, 1540 with brown.

Brown powder charges were
approved in April 1885 as black
powder was found to expand the A
tube and, in one instance, to crack
it. The two Dover guns, Nos 6 and
7, were identical to the others
except for shorter trunnions. A
report of 23 May 1888 shows no
available reserve guns for *Inflexible*
as No 4 had had to be replaced by
No 8 and neither No 4 nor the
original No 1 were yet repaired.
Two years later it was suggested
that the two Dover guns might be
replaced by smaller BLs and
transferred to the Navy as

additional reserves but nothing
came of it, perhaps because the
trunnions would have had to be
lengthened. The life of the 16in
RML before relining was rather
dubiously estimated at 350 rounds.

The *Inflexible's* two twin turrets
allowed 10° elevation and 2° to 5°
depression depending on the
training angle with fixed loading
positions at 9°35″ depression. The
hydraulic loading gear could
accommodate a shell 60in long
which gave ample margin as the
longest common shell was a little
under 51in and the chilled iron
Palliser AP (Armour Piercing)
43.45 to 43.7in. At 10° elevation
the range at 1590ft/sec MV was
6730yds, reducing to 6430yds at
1540ft/sec. The *Inflexible* took part
in the bombardment of Alexandria
on 11 July 1882. At that date her
outfit per gun was 55 Palliser AP,
each with a 16lb black powder
burster intended to explode on
impact as there was no fuse, 15 nose
fused cast iron common shell each

with a 60lb black powder burster, 5
shrapnel, containing 860-4oz shot,
and 5 case, intended mainly for use
against torpedo boats and
containing 1920-8oz shot. Her total
expenditure in the bombardment
was 21 Palliser, 56 common and 11
shrapnel, all fired with full charges.
The Palliser AP was unlikely to
burst unless it struck a heavy gun or
mounting and the effect of the other
projectiles was much reduced by the
near uselessness of the fuses for
which the War Office authorities
were responsible. Cast steel base
fused common shell, with 112¾lb
black powder bursters, did not
become available until much later.

The next heaviest RML in the
British Navy was the 12.5in/38 ton
so the 16in was by far the largest. It
can be judged as an interesting and
fairly satisfactory gun but of
obsolescent type by 1881 when it
entered service, as two years
previously a 15.75in/21.8 cal Krupp
BL had been demonstrated with
good results at Meppen. It remains

Inflexible at Malta in her early days.
NMM

The Italian battleship *Duilio*.
Aldo Fraccaroli

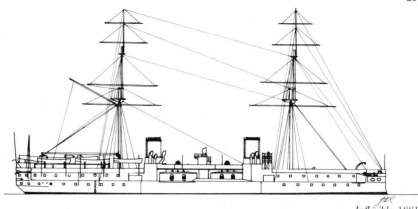

Inflexible, 1881

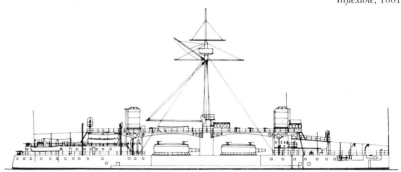

Duilio, 1895

2

to add that the two Dover 16in and turret are still extant although declared obsolete in 1902.

17.72IN RML MARK I

The origins of this gun go back to the *Duilio* and *Dandolo,* two of the remarkable but not entirely satisfactory ships designed by Benedetto Brin for the Italian Navy. When authorised in 1872 it was intended that they should have four 35 ton guns but in 1873 this was increased to four 60 ton. Both ships were laid down in the first half of that year but in 1874, as a consequence of the intention to arm the *Inflexible* with four 80 ton guns, it was decided that the two *Duilio's* should each have four 100 ton guns. A contract to build 8 of these guns was placed with Armstrong's at Elswick in July 1874, though only one was to be made initially, the others following when the first had been found satisfactory. It must be noted that the *Duilio* was about 900 tons smaller than the 11 880 ton *Inflexible* and that her beam was only 64ft 8in compared with 75ft in the latter ship. She was clearly much overgunned as is shown by her ammunition outfit of only 35 rounds per gun.

The first gun, bored to 17in and not chambered, was sent to Italy for trials in July 1876 but, on satisfactory reports of the 80 ton gun, orders to proceed with the other 7 guns of the original contract had already been given on 23 June 1876. As an unchambered 17in, 1542ft/sec MV was attained with a 2000lb projectile and a 375lb prismatic black charge. Other tests were satisfactory and the gun was returned to Elswick for boring to 17.72in and chambering. Further trials were carried out in March and April 1878 and the four guns for the *Duilio* were delivered in time for her to complete in January 1880, the *Dandolo,* which had been launched 26 months after the *Duilio,* following in April 1882. Meanwhile the British wished to increase the coast defences of Gibraltar and Malta and, as further 16in RMLs could not be delivered from Woolwich in reasonable time, it was decided to break their monopoly and order 4 of the

17.72in from Elswick which, at that time, had a far better equipped gun-making plant than Woolwich. These four guns were delivered in 1882-1883 and a further three guns were made for Italy (one for the pontoon *Forte*, which was part of the Spezia defences, and two reserve guns) giving a final total of 11 for Italy and 4 for Britain.

The construction was very different from that of the 16in RML. The steel 'A' tube was in two lengths joined by a steel ring, in halves, over the joint. Over the 'A' tube were shrunk 10 wrought iron coils, identified from the breech end as 2A, 2B, 2C, 2D, 2E, 2D¹, 2E¹, 2F, 2G and 2H. The 2D and 2D¹ coils were thinner than the rest and had the 2E and 2E¹ coils shrunk over them. The next layer, which stopped 207.85in from the muzzle, comprised the 3A and 3B coils, the trunnion piece and the 3C coil. Finally there was a layer extending to the trunnions, consisting of the 4A¹, 4A and 4B coils. The cascable, which screwed into the 2A coil, contained the axial vent and was made from a wrought iron forging as was the trunnion piece. The various parts were shrunk to more precise limits than in the Fraser construction as it was attempted to give each the designed stress. The surface of some of the coils was serrated to give a better longitudinal grip, but not all the coils had overlapping joints, and it was thought that the 'A' tube took by far the greatest part of the longitudinal stresses. Details of the 17.72in Mark I were:

Weight 102 tons (average)
Length (oa) 32ft 7.85in (391.85in)
Length (bore) 20.5cal (363in)
Diameter 76.45in (max) 29in (at muzzle)
Chamber size 59.72 x 19.7in, volume 17 049 cub in
Rifling length 302.88in, twist 1 in 105 to 1 in 50 at 2.88in from muzzle then uniform, 28 grooves, polygroove plain section 0.125 x 1.1in, lands 0.888in
Projectile weight 2000lb (including 24lb gas check)
Charge 450lb prismatic¹ or prismatic² black (4 x 112¾)
Muzzle Velocity 1548ft/sec

It will be noted that the projectile was relatively light as, if scaled up from the 16in, it would have been about 2300lb. Much heavier charges were used by the Italians and in trials 1725ft/sec MV was attained with a 2000lb projectile and a 573lb charge but on 6 March 1880 one of the *Duilio's* guns pulled apart. The fracture ran from the front end of the parallel part of the chamber to the front end of the 4B coil just behind the trunnions. The charge on this occasion was 551lb of Fossano powder, which had large irregular grains each containing a number of small high density pieces in a lower density material. Normally such a charge would have given about 17.4 tons/sq in but it was believed that the Fossano grains had broken into fine pieces which would have given a much higher pressure. The gun was repaired by building up on a new A tube and subsequently the Italians appear to have limited charges to 529 lb, which gave about 1700ft/sec MV, while in Britain a much smaller charge and lower performance was accepted.

The British projectiles were of the same type as those for the 16in, the Palliser AP being 48.6in long with a 32lb burster and the cast iron common of the same length having a 78lb burster. A later cast steel common shell had a 194lb burster and was 52.55in long.

The two Gibraltar guns were mounted at 'Victoria' and 'Napier' of Magdala's batteries and the two Malta guns at 'Rinella' and 'Cambridge' batteries. They were in the usual type of coast defence carriage with pivotted slide and not in turrets. All except the 'Victoria' guns were still operational in 1902 but were soon declared obsolete. One still survives at Gibraltar, on a reconstructed carriage and slide as an exhibit, and there is a second gun at Malta.

SPRING BOOKS '79
Conway Maritime Press

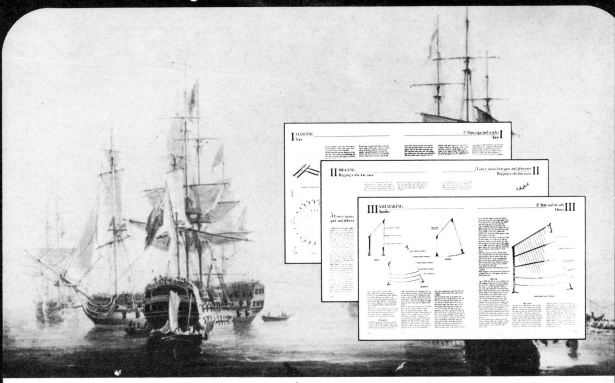

THE MASTING AND RIGGING OF ENGLISH SHIPS OF WAR 1625-1860

James Lees

The first modern study of the whole era of sail for which firm evidence is available, including the hitherto 'dark ages' of the mid-eighteenth century. As a Senior Conservation Officer at the National Maritime Museum, the author's work has allowed him to assemble — over fifteen years — minutely detailed information. Lavishly illustrated with drawings and photographs and organised for easy reference with a full index and guide to sources, appendices on mast, spar and rigging proportions for the whole period complete an indispensable book.

272 pages (11¾" x 10"). 100 photographs, 540 line drawings. February. £20.00. 0 85177 136 X.

SAILING SHIPS OF WAR

Dr Frank Howard

The wooden warship during the period 1400 to 1860, from the advent of the three-masted ship to the eclipse of sail as the principal mode of propulsion — a work of the greatest value to ship enthusiasts, model-makers and naval historians. The most accurate illustrations, and not the merely picturesque, have been chosen from a large and international selection.

256 pages (11¾" x 9½"). 150 photographs, 32 colour plates, 100 line drawings. May. £12.50 0 85177 138 6.

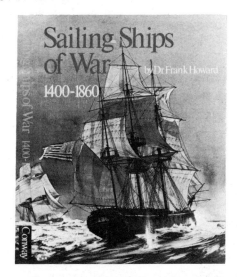

In the history of British warships there have been many occasions when technical advance has apparently been stifled by excessive conservatism, for example the reluctance to abandon sail power in the Victorian Fleet and the retention of large tube boilers in capital ships prior to the First World War when small tube boilers with a much higher power to weight ratio were available. These examples and others like them have occurred regularly throughout the period of modern warship history and have usually been characterised as a battle between the conservative and the progressive. Unfortunately, most historians have taken to describing these events in black and white terms in which the conservatives are pictured as crotchety old Admirals who prefer things the way they are for no good reason while the progressives are dynamic forward looking personalities who are seldom wrong. This, of course, is a very distorted view but this is only obvious because I have made it so by the words used. It is less obvious in studying the actual events because the arguments for and against various forms of progress are usually supported by examples to emphasise the point being made. Unfortunately, when supporting their particular case most people will pick the most extreme examples in order to give maximum force to their arguments and it is these that are often quoted by historians as being the norm rather than the exception. For example, one often reads that the officers of the Royal Navy in the late Victorian period were more interested in their ships being clean, smart and polished than efficient vessels of war and that gunnery practice was frowned upon because of the damage caused to the ships paintwork etc. I have no doubt there is truth in this statement but one of the points I have seen made in support of this is that it was not unusual for practice ammunition to be thrown over the side instead of being fired from the guns. I have read many books concerning the Victorian period and

have found only one reference to this practice – in *Reminiscences of a Naval Surgeon,* by Surgeon Rear Admiral T T Jeans CMG, published in 1927. In this book, Admiral Jeans tells that the quality of the gunnery on his ship was considered a 'screaming farce' and mentions that the practice ammunition was usually tipped over the side and the gunnery return, which had to be sent to Whale Island, faked. However, he was not serving on a battleship of the Mediterranean Fleet but the obsolete gunboat *Raven* then, 1894, serving as a fishery protection vessel in the Channel Islands. So the information is not quite as shocking as it would at first appear and, although I am sure that this was not an isolated case, and that there were many small vessels, and perhaps larger ones on distant stations, who indulged in similar practices, I doubt if the idea even crossed the minds of officers serving in the main fleets. In fact the idea of a battleship's crew hoisting 12inch shells over the side is quite ridiculous. Oddly enough Jeans appears to indicate that the main reason for dumping the ammunition was the fact that the guns (old Armstrongs BLs) were considered dangerous and that the fuss and breakages which accompanied gunnery practice were a secondary consideration. He also emphasises that the Whale Island 'bureaucrats' expected gunnery returns to be 'forwarded smartly' which at least indicates that the gunnery branch would have made a not inconsiderable fuss about such an event if they knew of it, and considering that ships' gunnery officers usually take their work seriously it seems unlikely that such events on a large scale would not have been reported to Whale Island.

Returning to my original examples, the abandonment of sail power was a gradual process which followed a logical pattern and, although with hindsight one can see that sails were retained longer than was necessary, the Admiralty were much more influenced by the

practical problems of economics and mechanical reliability than by regrets at seeing the sailing era pass away. My second example raises another interesting problem which like the change over to sails relates to the Admiralty's preference for reliability. Small tube boilers as I have said gave higher power for less space and weight – a point often made – but it is seldom mentioned that they also demanded a higher level of maintenance and it was this that made the Admiralty reluctant to adopt them in capital ships. However this form of conservatism does have a secondary danger not often considered. When new technology is not adopted because it is not as reliable as that already in use, the chances of improving its reliability are limited by lack of practical experience. Thus the French, Italian and United States Navies made great strides in machinery design between the wars by adopting new technology and ironing out the problems as they progressed while the Royal Navy, wishing to ensure absolute reliability, were much slower in adopting such things as higher boiler pressures, lighter turbines and so on. In the short term this gave the British an advantage, as new technology is seldom fully successful, but in the long term left the Navy in a position where it had to make these advances in a much shorter time and with much less experience. In general these things tend to balance themselves but, of course, there is always the danger that an enemy has fully developed an item just at the point when you decide it worth adopting.

The moral to all this, if one can call it that, is that it does not necessarily follow that all the arguments against a successfully adopted advance in warship design are without foundation and that in many cases the pros and cons are very finely balanced. The point to remember is that nobody who is trying to sell you something is going to tell you what is wrong with it.

John Roberts

SHELLS AT SEVASTOPOL

BY D K BROWN

The resistance of wooden battleships to shell fire had been tested on many occasions before the Crimean War but the results were little known and virtually no consideration had been given to the problem. It seems likely that the first operational use of shells at sea was in 1788 when a flotilla of Russian long boats used shell fire to destroy a Turkish squadron in the Liman river mouth in the Sea of Azov.

In a more recent example the Danish *Christian VIII* was destroyed by Prussian batteries at Eckenfjorde in 1849. It seems likely from an eye witness account by Lt Col Stevens RMA that the *Christian VIII* was set on fire by shells but that the fire was extinguished. She was then becalmed and could not be towed out by her accompanying steamers because one ship had had a paddle smashed by shot, a very rare, perhaps unique, example of such disablement. The Danish battleship was then destroyed by red hot shot from the four 18pdrs of the South battery.

Both the British and French Navies had carried out a number of test firings with shells. In the former series, 80 time fuse shells were fired against the old two-decker *Prince George*, of which 38 failed to explode while the remainder caused very considerable damage. Similar results were obtained by the French. These results were known to very

few and it was only with the destruction of a Turkish squadron by a Russian force using shell fire that the menace of the shell became apparent. At Sinope, on 30 November 1853, a Turkish force of seven frigates, three corvettes and two small steamers was lying at anchor when it was attacked by six Russian sail of the line (three 120s, three 84s), two frigates and three steamers. The most formidable Russian ships were the *Knias Konstantin* and the *Paris,* both of which mounted fourteen 60pdrs firing shells. It seems that each of these two ships destroyed a frigate within minutes while the remaining Turkish force, except for the steamer *Tarf*, had been sunk by nightfall. The Russian force was overwhelming and even without the use of shells the result was certain. Shells may well have hastened the inevitable end but this too could have been expected by anyone who had studied the results of pre-war tests. The general public and much naval opinion were not well informed and Sinope came as a great shock.

Early actions in the Crimean War did not add much to the fleets experience of shell fire though a few ships were hit by coastal batteries. By mid October 1854, the British and French armies had been successfully landed on the Crimea and the siege of Sevastopol had begun. The allied generals intended

to launch an assault on the town on 17 October and requested the assistance of the fleet. Dundas and Hamelin met in the *Mogador* on the 15th to discuss the 'urgent request' of the army. Dundas was understandably reluctant to commit his ships to close action against such formidable granite forts since there was still a Russian Black Sea fleet and if any substantial part of the Allied fleet was destroyed or disabled command of the sea, on which the whole enterprise depended, could be lost.

Dundas proposed to limit the naval action to a bombardment of the harbour entrance and it is believed that Hamelin shared this view. It is also probable that both fleets, aware of the suffering and sacrifice of their armies, wished for more active participation. The Admirals decided that there would be a bombardment of the forts from ships in motion, firing successively, while those not in action formed a floating reserve. The British captains were called to the *Britannia* early on the 16th to receive their instructions. At midnight on this day Dundas was visited by Hamelin, who said that he had been directed by Canrobert to anchore across the mouth of the harbour. Dundas still opposed this proposal but eventually agreed when it was explained that Hamelin was under orders from Canrobert and that the French fleet would carry out these

orders with or without the support of the Royal Navy. A contributory factor seems to have been the acute shortage of men in the French fleet. Some 1300 had been landed to help the army and the toll of cholera had been high. Guard boats had to be manned and detached to take care of the topgallant masts and other spare yards which had been put over the side in preparation for battle. In consequence the ships were too short handed to handle under sail or to fight both broadsides simultaneously. Dundas had to call another, hurried, conference with his captains, further delaying the start. During the night preceding the battle the Masters of three ships had taken boats with muffled oars close under the forts to take soundings. They found a channel suitable for big ships some 800yds from Fort Constantine. The disposition of ships and batteries is shown on the map. The French ships were to engage the southern forts – Fort Alexander, the Quarantine battery and adjoining works. The Royal Navy was to engage the northern forts – Fort Constantine, the Telegraph

batteries and their earthworks. Midway between the two fleets were the two Turkish ships, out of harm's way. The battle zone was fairly small and virtually all the ships were within the range of all the forts, both north and south.

The bombardment opened from the land guns at 0630 but it was much later before the navies were ready. The French had four screw battleships and, as these were based at Kamiesh with a shorter distance to travel, were first into action. Dundas gave the order to weigh anchor at 1050 but most of his ships were off Kotcha and the sailing battleships had to be towed by steamers. On shore the start of the battle was signalled by three maroons at 0630 and a heavy bombardment continued until 0900 when a large French magazine blew up. As a result, firing ceased at 1030 and the attack was abandoned though the fleets were not informed. Dundas gave the order to weigh anchor at 1050 but most of his ships were off Kotcha and since the sailing ships had to be towed it would be a long while before they could get into action.

Typical of the last generation of wooden ships of the line, HMS *London* was launched in 1840 although not converted to screw propulsion until 1860.
CPL W/10/002

The French ships opened fire at about 1230 on Fort Alexander, initially at a range of 2000yds and then gradually closing to about 1500yds. The British followed slowly. All ships had sent down topgallant masts and stunsail booms and these together with spare spars had been sent on board the *Vulcan* for safe keeping. The sailing ships had a steamer lashed to the port side. The British ships came in behind the French who were keeping up a heavy fire which was being vigorously returned. The steamer *Circassian* led the way followed by *Agamemnon*. Coles says 'We proceeded in at very slow speed, passing by the forts in the vicinity of Wasp Fort at very low speed, merely firing one or two guns from the bow, and we did not open our broadside until we had been twenty minutes under the fire of the Russians; we then opened our broadside on Fort Constantine'. Dundas' report says that

Agamemnon anchored head and stern at 1400, in 4¾ fathoms, 750yds from Fort Constantine. Five minutes later *Sans Pareil* (the other steam liner) anchored and engaged the Star Fort and nearby earthworks. At 1420 *Albion* (towed by *Firebrand)* anchored and engaged the Wasp battery and later fired on Fort Constantine. She was followed by *London* (*Niger* as tug) and *Arethusa (Triton).* The advantage of the steam ship in tactical mobility was already clear.

The sea was absolutely calm and with only a very light offshore wind firing had to be interrupted from time to time to allow the dense, black clouds of powder smoke to disperse. 'The firing was terrific. At a distance the sound was like a locomotive at full speed but infinitely grander.' *(The Times).* 'Britannia led the outer line and opened fire at about 1420. The steam ships *Sampson, Tribune, Sphinx, Lynx* and *Terrible* came close inshore and engaged the forts most gallantly. A large explosion in Fort Constantine is believed to have been due to a shell from *Terrible* and, after this, the Fort's barbette guns did not fire again.'

After an hour and a half *Albion* was heavily hit. She had received four shell hits and had been on fire twice. Though the fires were put out by her own crew she was seriously damaged, had lost 11 killed and 71 wounded and had to be towed out

stern first by the *Firebrand.*

At about the same time *Arethusa,* which had been engaging the Wasp battery, also had to withdraw. The Wasp and Telegraph batteries, being high up, could keep up an accurate fire since the Russian officers could measure the exact range to the ship with a quadrant. The *Agamemnon* found that the Wasp and nearby earthworks caused most damage and she had to use her after guns against them, reserving only the forward batteries for her designated target, Fort Constantine. She was also engaged from across the harbour by Fort Alexander at a range of 1800yds. The French ships firing on Alexander were dropping their shot short, close ahead of *Agamemnon.*

After some time *Sans Pareil* withdrew, since, according to Dundas' report, she had expended her ammunition allowance. The *Bellerophon* was called in and succeeded in silencing the Wasp. She was followed in by the *Queen* which was quickly set on fire by red hot shot and forced to withdraw. *Rodney,* following *Queen,* grounded aft and was quite heavily hit aloft before being towed off by the *Spiteful.*

At about 1830 the general withdrawal commenced; *Bellerophon,* the last ship still firing, ceased at 1900. 'The change was magical from hot sun, mist, smoke, explosions, shot, shell, rockets and

the roar of ten thousand guns, to a still, cool, brilliant starlit sky looki[ng] down on to a glassy sea, reflecting long tremulous lines the lights at t[he] mast heads of the ships returning amid profound silence.' *(The Time[s])*

Since the land attack had been abandoned before the naval bombardment began it was a pointless operation from the start. Had the land attack continued it seems likely that the navies would have provided a valuable diversio[n] preventing reinforcement of the land defences by men and guns from the forts. Actual damage to the forts was negligible. Only the barbette guns of Fort Constantine were silenced, by a shell in their ammunition supply. A *Morning Herald* reporter writing some time after the attack says 'We passed close by the forts of Sevastopol. W[e] were quite within range and therefore with glasses we could se[e] every chink and cranny in the fortresses. Every Fort towards the sea, those of Alexander Paul, on t[he] South, and Nicholas and Constantine on the North was perfectly covered from base to summit with shot marks. In this there was no difference between those attacked by the British or French except that Fort Constantine, to the North, had tw[o] of the casemented ports knocked into one. It was at the spot where *Agamemnon* had been moored an[d] where her whole broadside had

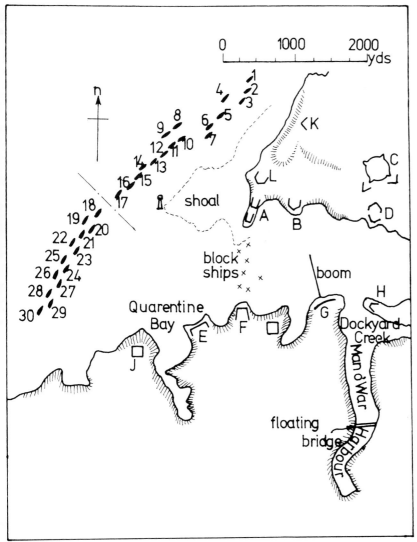

BOMBARDMENT OF SEVASTOPOL
17 OCTOBER 1854

SHIPS

British

1 Terrible
2 Albion
3 Arethusa
4 Sampson
5 London
6 Sans Pareil
7 Agamemnon
8 Sphinx
9 Tribune
10 Spitfire
11 Lynx
12 Queen
13 Bellerophon
14 Rodney
15 Vengeance
16 Trafalgar
17 Britannia

French & Turkish

18 Napoleon
19 Henri Quatre
20 Mamudieh
21 Valmy
22 Ville de Paris
23 Jupiter
24 Friedland
25 'Turkish'
26 Marengo
27 Montebello
28 Suffren
29 Jean Bart
30 Charlemagne

FORTS & BATTERIES

A Constantine
B Casement
C Star
D Michael
E Quarantine
F Alexander
G St Nicholas
H St Paul
J Old Fort
K Wasp
L Telegraph

The 17 October 1854 off Sevastopol, a general view of the bombardment fleet
NMM

been concentrated with something like effect the amount of damage is literally nothing. Where several shot have struck in the same place the granite is splintered and broken away to the depth of a foot or even less. Where only one or two balls have struck there are mere whitish marks as if the spot had been dabbed with flour.'

'To restore these forts to their original look would, of course, be expensive, because unnecessary. As forts they are as strong as if a shot had never been fired against them – a few inches of stone make little difference where walls are 14-18ft thick.'

Russian casualties are said to have totalled 11 killed and 39 wounded including Admiral Komilov who was killed.

It is not surprising that damage to the forts was so slight since shallow water prevented any ship getting closer than 750yds and most were much farther away. After the capture of Bomarsund, some two months earlier, the *Edinburgh* had carried out firing trials against some stone casemates and these trials showed that 500yds was the maximum effective range. Sir Howard Douglas has some interesting points to make about the gunnery of the flagship *Britannia*. She fired at 2000yds and the only shot capable of causing any damage were the 710 fired from the 32pdr/56cwt guns. The 700 shot fired with 8lb charges and 85 with 6lb together with 320 hollow, 8in shot and an unknown number of Moorsom fused shell had no chance of success. Damage to the ship was not excessive for an action against heavily armed forts lasting five hours. Fort Constantine mounted 97 guns, of which 43 could bear on the ships. Half were in casemates and 27 en barbette. These were mostly 32pdrs. The Wasp had 5 guns and the Telegraph 5 to 12, probably 68pdrs. Fort Alexander had 51 guns pointing seaward together with 48 more in the earthworks nearby and the Quarantine Fort had 48 guns mounted in the open. Total losses in the British fleet were 44 killed and 266 wounded while the French had

a total of 212 casualties and the Turks one or two.

With the exception of *Albion* and *Arethusa* all the British ships were fully ready for action within 24 hours. *Albion* was hit by several shells close to the waterline of which three entered the cockpit. She was on fire twice and had to cease fire when the magazines were closed to minimise the fire risk.

Arethusa too was heavily hit. One shell burst on the gun deck and knocked over the crew of the two guns, another knocked 3 cabins into one and set fire to a bed (close to a shell room containing 300 shells). A third blew in seven planks just above the waterline and a fourth in the thickness of the waterline timbers. If there had been a sea running she would have been in some danger. These were the only two ships seriously damaged and they were able to make their own way to Constantinople for temporary repairs before going to Malta for full repairs. It must be remembered, too, that *Arethusa* was only a frigate, not intended for prolonged close action against heavy guns such as those mounted by the forts of Sevastopol.

Agamemnon (and *SansPareil*) suffered heavily aloft. *Agamemnon* was hit in all 214 times including 3 shells and a rocket. Two of the shells burst in the masts (one setting fire to the main yard, briefly) and the other on deck. Coles says that there was hardly a rope left uncut and the upper deck was covered in splinters. Luckily, the upper deck guns were those usually manned by the Marines, who were ashore with the Naval Brigade. In consequence, these guns were unmanned and there were few casualties (4 killed, 25 wounded). The rocket hit 6ft below the waterline and caused a violent concussion but little damage. The case of the rocket was found still sticking out of the hull by a diver. *London* was hit in the hull by shot and shell from the Telegraph and was on fire three times in two hours. *Queen* was forced to withdraw after a fire caused by red hot shot. *Rodney's* damage while aground was mostly aloft and not serious.

Of the French ships, *Ville de Pari* was hit under the poop by a shell, probably from a mortar, which caused extensive damage and killed and wounded many of her crew. In all she was hit by 41 shot or shell in the hull and almost as many again in the masts. Despite this damage her crew was able to carry out repairs overnight and she was ready for action the following day.

Moving on a few years, the most remarkable proof of the resistance of wooden ships comes from the experience of the Austrian ship *Kaiser* at Lissa. Early in the battle she was hit by a 300lb shell from *Affondatore* which merely disabled 6 men and dismounted a single gun. Seventeen minutes after the battle started, *Kaiser* rammed the Italian ironclad *Re di Portogallo*. The Italian ship lost anchors, boats, portlights and 60ft of her side armour was displaced, but she was able to fire a broadside of one 10in and thirteen 6.3in into *Kaiser*. The Austrian lost her bowsprit and the foremast fell across the funnel causing a small fire. The *Re di Portogallo* continued to fire until *Kaiser* withdrew to put out the fire. The missing funnel had reduced her speed and she had many casualties.

This did not prevent her from re-engaging the *Affondatore* which made three unsuccessful attempts to ram before being set on fire by the Austrian liner. Eventually *Kaiser* made for the port of San Giorgio and anchored there at 1330, with springs on her cable, ready and able to defend herself.

Kaiser had fired 850 rounds, three times as many as any other ship, and was hit 80 times, twice as many as any other ship. She had suffered 24 killed, 37 severely wounded and 38 slightly wounded.

Altogether the effect of shellfire on wooden ships with well disciplined crews was far less than had been anticipated. In fact the old-fashioned red hot shot remained a bigger menace.

1 A quarter view of *London*. With the funnel lowered, there was little to distinguish these vessels from their sailing predecessors. *CPL W/10/003*

2 The paddle frigate *Terrible,* which is believed to have heavily damaged Fort Constantine during the bombardment. *CPL W/10/004*

1

2

FRIGATE DESIGN IN THE 18th CENTURY PART 2

BY ROBERT GARDINER

Models of the *Southampton* class are very rare, despite the fact that many museums catalogue their 32s as such. Both the National Maritime Museum's 32s of this period are labelled as *Southamptons,* for example – but they are both *Richmonds,* the extra (bridle) port right forward being the most obvious difference. This view of the Science Museum's model is also a *Richmond,* thought from iconographical evidence in the decorative work to represent the *Juno* of 1757.

Photo by courtesy of the Science Museum, London

In the years following the Peace of Aix-la-Chapelle (1748) the Royal Navy underwent a period of administrative reform usually associated with the appointment of George Anson to the Admiralty Board. Anson and his Board showed as much concern with the quality of the Navy's ships as with its management and it seems likely that he was responsible for the decision to build the *Unicorn* and *Lyme,* described in the previous part of this article. However, it is certain that his Board drew up the requirement for the first English 32-gun frigates.

In peacetime it was unusual to construct small cruisers, since they could be built inside a year whenever war threatened (much the same argument resulted in the rush to build escorts in 1914 and 1939). However, the Admiralty was dissatisfied with the 1745 Establishment and the period after 1748 saw the construction of many experimental vessels, one thread of development leading to the classic line-of-battleship, the '74', and the other to the classic frigate, the '32'. The old-style two-decked 24- and 44-gun ships rapidly fell from favour and in sailing trials the *Unicorn,* of the new frigate-form, established a reputation as the best all-round sailer in the fleet. The initiative in design matters, which had been held by the Navy Board,

was wrested by the Admiralty as the disappointment with the 1745 ships became widespread. The 1745 Establishment had been conservative not only because the size of ships had been contained, but also because it sought to lay down in traditional fashion the precise dimensions and scantlings, allowing a designer only very limited scope for ingenuity and originality. However, after 1748 the Admiralty introduced a radical innovation: they specified only a general 'staff requirement' and invited competitive designs.

THE ADMIRALTY AND SHIP DESIGN

This may seem obvious in retrospect but at the time it was a major breakthrough in the process of formulating requirements and producing designs to meet them. It was first applied in 1749 to two fast-sailing sloops for the suppression of smuggling for which each of the Royal Dockyards produced a design, but it is possible to see a prefiguring of this concept in the Admiralty order to the two Surveyors which produced the *Mermaid* and *Seahorse (* as outlined in the previous part of this article). By 1751 the principle had been extended to embrace the actual construction of two different designs of the same approximate specification and, as far as frigates

are concerned, this remained essentially unaltered for 60 years. During the whole of this period there were usually two Surveyors and it was common for both to produce ships of very similar dimensions but different hull forms. This has had an interesting result since when listed alphabetically (as in most eighteenth-century publications) ships of any one rate appear to spread over a wide range of dimensions, leading modern historians to claim that wooden warships could not be said to belong to proper classes. In fact, once they are sorted out, the variation from design dimensions within a class is small and the system is comparable with that for modern vessels.

THE SYSTEM OF PARALLEL EVALUATION

However, in the 1750s the Admiralty had less faith in the Surveyors so the usual system was to evaluate a French-derived design alongside a native English one. For the 4 sloops ordered in 1751, 2 were to be built from the reduced lines of the *Monarch,* a captured French 74, and the others to the lines of the yacht *Royal Caroline,* which was itself the product of a design competition among the Dockyards and the representative of a type of English fast-sailing hull that went back to at least 1700.

A new type of frigate-built 20-gun ship was introduced in 1753 and the *Royal Caroline* was again chosen as the model for the indigenous design (which became the *Seaford* class). However, for the parallel design the Admiralty turned to the highly successful *Unicorn* (for the *Gibraltar* class). *Unicorn* herself had been considered a replacement for 24-gun ships but in 1755 she was re-rated as a 28; a sign that the Admiralty was throughly satisfied with this type was that there was no parallel design, and a large number of ships (called the *Tartar* class) were subsequently built to the *Unicorn* design, with only internal modifications to improve habitability.

However, when the specification for the 12pdr-armed 32-gun frigates was drawn up in 1756 it was clear that a very different type of ship was required and therefore two designs were called for. One Surveyor, Bately, produced a vessel based on the *Royal Caroline* but the other, Slade, produced a completely original design (the *Richmond* and *Southampton* classes respectively). Slade also designed the 36-gun *Pallas* class which had a very similar hull form to the *Southampton*. It is sometimes said that these first English 12pdr frigates were inspired by the *Renommée*, captured in the previous war, but there is no

evidence for this. France had produced a 12pdr frigate in 1748 (the *Hermione* at Rochefort) and, as war was looming in 1756, it must have been clear that an armament of twenty-six 12pdrs would be the minimum requirement for a big frigate in the impending conflict. Having determined the approximate tonnage and weight of armament, the other primary factor in the English staff requirement was the height of the gunports above water, an important element in the kind of all-weather cruising ship always favoured by the Royal Navy. Given these criteria the rest of the design followed naturally, without any 'inspiration' from captured French examples.

Although the *Richmonds* proved satisfactory sailers, the *Southamptons* were considered very slow. Therefore towards the end of 1757 a new class to the same overall specification was called for and Slade submitted three designs. The Admiralty chose one based on the *Unicorn*, perhaps feeling that he should have used this model in the first place instead of bothering with the *Southampton* design, but because of the difference in size and the relative weight of ordnance the *Unicorn* design had to be significantly modified. Nevertheless the result was possibly the most outstanding and successful frigate class ever to serve in the Royal Navy.

To prove that this was not simply the result of a straight imitation of a French hull form, Slade took the midship section of the *Unicorn*, lengthened the design to the usual French proportions and constructed the hull in the lightweight French manner. The result was the *Tweed* and the report on her sailing qualities is salutary (see Table 1).

Thus by the beginning of the Seven Years War the Royal Navy had a range of good frigate designs, utilising the best English and French design features, combined with the traditionally robust English construction.

THE SEVEN YEARS WAR 1756-1763

During the course of the war several fine French frigates were captured (Table 2) but because of the general satisfaction felt with the latest *Niger* class, the Navy Board was not instructed to look out for a possible model among captured frigates. However, in 1759 the senior of the two Surveyors, Thomas Slade, happened to see the large Canadian-built *L'Abenakise* in drydock and he was impressed by her very sharp lines and obvious potential for speed. Although she was very large for her armament by British standards, Slade managed to communicate his enthusiasm for this design to the Admiralty and two frigates were ordered to her lines in

TABLE 1: PARTICULARS OF ENGLISH FRIGATE CLASSES 1755-57

TARTAR class, 28-gun sixth rates, 20 vessels

Armament:	24 x 9pdrs (a 7ft, 23½cwt weapon) on upper deck, 4 x 3pdrs (a 4ft 6in, 7cwt gun), 12 x ½pdr swivel-guns. Upper deck ports 6ft 3in apart, and sills 7ft above water (minimum)				
	Gundeck length	**Keel length for tonnage**	**Extreme breadth**	**Depth in hold**	**Tonnage**
Design dimensions:	119ft 10in	96ft 10½in	33ft 8in	10ft 2in	583 (first two) 586 (others)
Sailing qualities:	Very fast and weatherly. 9-10kts close-hauled to 12-13kts broad-reaching or running. Very stiff, but easy in a sea, rolling deeply but easily and shipping very little water. *Hussar* (one of this class) was not quite as fast as *Unicorn* herself, but faster than anything else except *L'Abenakise* which was better directly before the wind.				

SOUTHAMPTON class, 32-gun fifth rates, 4 vessels

Armament:	26 x 12pdrs (a 7ft 6in, 28½cwt gun designed specially for the new '32's and '36's) on upper deck, 6 x 6pdrs (a 6ft, 16½cwt gun, also designed specially) all on quarterdeck at first but 2 moved to forecastle, 12 x ½pdr swivel-guns. Upper deck ports a minimum of 6ft 6in apart, and 7ft 6in from the water (ship loaded with 4 months provisions).				
	Gundeck length	**Keel length for tonnage**	**Extreme breadth**	**Depth in hold**	**Tonnage**
Design dimensions:	124ft 4in	102ft 3½in	34ft 8in	12ft	652
Sailing qualities:	Not as fast as other English frigate classes but reasonably weatherly. 12kts before the wind. Very quick in tacking and wearing, going about in a short distance relative to length. Performed well in a seaway and pitched easily, and being stiff ships would sail faster in these conditions as more canvas was pressed upon them.				

RICHMOND class, 32-gun fifth rates, 6 vessels

Armament:	As *Southamptons*. Upper deck ports a minimum of 6ft 3in apart, and 8ft from water at average draught.				
	Gundeck length	**Keel length for tonnage**	**Extreme breadth**	**Depth in hold**	**Tonnage**
Design dimensions:	127ft	105ft 1in	34ft	11ft 9in	646
Sailing qualities:	Faster than *Southamptons* but not as good as *Nigers*. Not a great variety of speeds on different points of sailing but tended to be best on a beam wind when over 13kts was achieved when ships were new. Very weatherly, but this advantage over other frigate classes increased as the seas became heavier – of the *Thames* it was said, 'the harder it blows she is more weatherly'. Remarkably dry ships in high seas.				

NIGER class, 32-gun fifth rates, 11 vessels

Armament:	*As Southamptons*. Upper deck ports a minimum of 6ft 6in apart, and 7ft 6in from water at average displacement.				
	Gundeck length	**Keel length for tonnage**	**Extreme breadth**	**Depth in hold**	**Tonnage**
Design dimensions:	125ft	103ft 4in	35ft 2in	12ft	679
Sailing qualities:	Very fast (13½kts broad reaching) and very weatherly. Fast and dependable in staying and wearing. Worst point of sailing before the wind. Tendency to pitch in a head sea but preferred a stiff gale, were very stiff, rolled easily and shipped little water. Would carry sail in heavy weather, without detriment to sailing qualities, as long as the masts would bear it, and gained greater advantage over other classes as weather conditions worsened.				

April 1760. These became the *Lowestoffe,* 32 guns, and *Mermaid*, 28, and although they were larger than other vessels of their rate, they were similarly armed and equipped.

DESIGN CHARACTERISTICS OF FRENCH FRIGATES

From the proportions in Table 3 it is obvious that French frigates tended to be longer in relation to beam than their English counterparts. Except for the *Richmond* class, which via the *Royal Caroline* represented an older design tradition, the major English classes – *Southampton*, *Pallas* and *Niger* – adopted a length-to-breadth ratio which was close to the 3.5 favoured for all English ships from 1733. *Tweed*, which utilised a 'stretched' '28's' hull, is nearer to French proportions and not unnaturally both *Lowestoffe* and *Mermaid* have the ratio of *L'Abenakise*.

The breadth-to-depth ratio is particularly significant because it plays a large part in the determination of the stability of the vessel, the capacity of the hull and how far the guns are carried from the water. In this respect – apart from the French-inspired *Tartar* and *Tweed* – the English vessels display remarkable consistency. The ratio of around 2.90 applies equally to the longer *Richmonds* and significantly to the *L'Abenakise*-derived vessels, which retained the French length but adopted a depth much more in keeping with English practice.

Combined with longer, shallower hulls the French favoured relatively fine lines at the bow and stern and a sharp midship section with a characteristic 'two-turn' bilge, all of which meant that French frigates had a lower displacement (or put another way, a lower carrying capacity) for a given set of overall dimensions compared to English designs. Furthermore, the topsides of French vessels had an enormous tumblehome, which tended to be lower and more snug than in English ships.

TWEED, 32-gun fifth rate

Armament:	As *Southamptons*. Upper deck ports 6ft 3in apart, height above water unknown.				
	Gundeck length	**Keel length for tonnage**	**Extreme breadth**	**Depth in hold**	**Tonnage**
Design dimensions: (as built)	128ft 4½in	107ft 9in	33ft 11½in	10ft 4in	660
Sailing qualities:	Very fast – 10kts under topgallants alone and once did 13kts when 6 months foul – but also weatherly. Better than *Nigers* in smooth water with a quartering wind but shipped much water when close-hauled. Not a good foul-weather ship, was tender, and strained her upperworks, being so lightly built. Directly before the wind was her worst point of sailing although she was still fast.				

PALLAS class, 36-gun fifth rates, 3 vessels

Armament:	As *Southamptons*, except 4 extra 6pdrs on quarterdeck. Upper deck ports 7ft apart, 8ft from water.				
	Gundeck length	**Keel length for tonnage**	**Extreme breadth**	**Depth in hole**	**Tonnage**
Design dimensions:	128ft 4in	106ft 2⅝in	35ft 8in	12ft 4in	718
Sailing qualities:	Faster (12½-13kts in a stiff gale on a broad reach) but otherwise similar to *Southamptons*. Very good heavy weather performance.				

LOWESTOFFE, 32-gun fifth rate

Armament:	As *Southamptons*.				
	Gundeck length	**Keel length for tonnage**	**Extreme breadth**	**Depth in hold**	**Tonnage**
Design dimensions:	130ft	107ft	35ft	12ft 6in	701
Sailing qualities:	Very fast – up to 14kts in a stiff gale on a broad reach – and very weatherly, particularly in strong winds. Quick in stays but slow in wearing.				

MERMAID class, 28-gun sixth rates, 3 vessels

Armament:	As *Tartars*.				
	Gundeck length	**Keel length for tonnage**	**Extreme breadth**	**Depth in hold**	**Tonnage**
Design dimensions:	124ft	102ft 8⅛in	33ft 6in	11ft	619
Sailing qualities:	Not particularly fast – 11kts is highest quoted, although it was claimed that these vessels forereached on many other frigates, but very weatherly. Good in heavy weather.				

SAILING QUALITIES

In general French frigates were lighter, longer, shallower and finer-lined than their English equivalents and the different design emphases are apparent in their respective sailing qualities. From the 1740s the Royal Navy kept detailed records of the performance under sail of most of its vessels including those captured or bought in. From a study of these reports it is obvious that vessels of the same class had a roughly similar performance under sail and that there was a striking difference between the conditions in which English and French frigates were at their best. The English reports all stress their performance in heavier weather, whereas the French vessels exhibit a strong preference for smooth water and, to a lesser extent, lighter winds. In fact the sailing qualities of English vessels often improved as weather conditions became more boisterous – even the sluggardly *Southamptons* became relatively faster as wind and sea rose, and the *Richmonds* became more weatherly.

In contrast, French vessels were said to dislike heavy weather, and frigates like *Bellone* and *Brune* suffered a dramatic loss of speed in such conditions. Furthermore, most French vessels rolled and/or pitched greatly and shipped water, whereas the motion of English ships was easier and consequently they tended to be far drier. While French vessels were noted for their speed, they were not particularly weatherly (*Blonde, Danae*) and some were stated explicitly to be very leewardly (*Bellone, Vestale, Boulogne*), and this deficiency was put down to their relatively shallow draught. This may also explain why the rather leewardly French vessels were not good performers when close-hauled, as is implied in the report on *Bellone,* and even the all-round excellence of *L'Abenakise* did not extend to this point of sailing.

The performance of the *Tweed* is particularly noteworthy, for in many ways she was an English attempt to build a typical French frigate – long, low, and light. It is significant that she was faster than even the *Nigers* on her chosen point of sailing, but that her superiority did not apply when close-hauled or in heavy weather. She proved to be a wet, lively – and uncomfortable – cruiser which lacked stability and her motion quickly strained the lightly-built hull.

Summing up, it seems that French cruiser design emphasised speed, especially in light conditions, at the expense of a 'sea-kindly' hull; English frigates, though not as fast in some sea-states, were more weatherly, and better all-round performers, particularly in heavy weather.

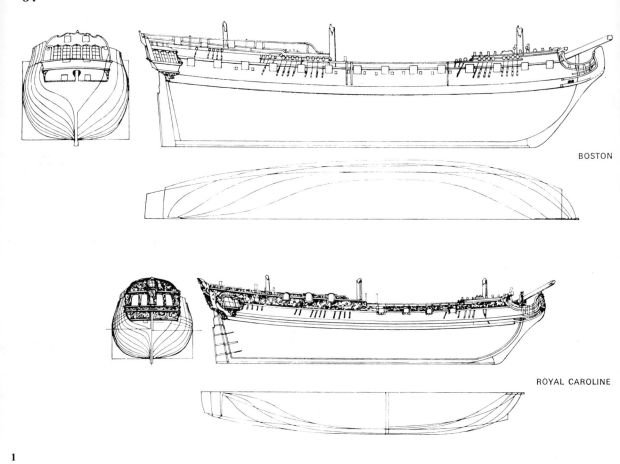

BOSTON

ROYAL CAROLINE

1

1 A comparison between the yacht *Royal Caroline* of 1749 (taken from Chapman's *Architectura Navalis Mercatoria*) and the Bately design for the *Richmonds*. Just as the *L'Abenakise* hull form was developed for a series of designs, so was this native English hull shape – the 20s of the *Seaford* class and the 74 gun *Fame* being among them.

2 Slade's first attempt at a frigate hull has no obvious models, but neither the 32 gun *Southampton* nor the 36 gun *Brilliant* class were outstanding sailers.

FRENCH DESIGN CHARACTERISTICS AND BUILDING STYLE

Speed, then, was the principal requirement of French frigate design and the long, fine-lined hulls certainly achieved this. Furthermore, the lightweight French system of construction was simply another aspect of the desire for superiority on a chosen point of sailing. However, in naval architecture it is rare to attain outstanding characteristics without sacrificing others and there is strong evidence that the French Navy bought its fair-weather speed at a high cost.

Among English shipwrights surveying French prizes, the most common cause for concern was the effect of the light construction and fastening on a very long, shallow hull. The transverse framing of wooden ships always lacked longitudinal strength and rigidity but the French style of building emphasised this deficiency. A deeper hull form would have increased the longitudinal girder strength but French designs were shallow both in draught and topsides, which further reduced the possible rigidity of the hull. In the *Maréchal de Belle Isle,* for example, the slightness of frame in relation to her great length had resulted in hogging and racking, and although only 3 years old her hull had 'worked', opening seams and exposing the frame to wet rot. In the case of the *Melampe,* the Surveyors found that her fine lines fore and aft did not give adequate support to the ends of the hull and actually augmented the hogging stresses.

It was the rapidity with which French hulls distorted that decided the Navy Board against many French prizes. *Hermione* and *Comète,* both large national frigates, were not bought in because of the state of their hulls. In fact, so certain

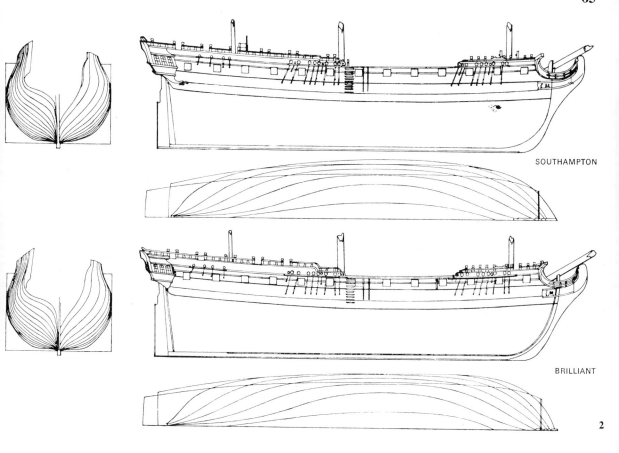

SOUTHAMPTON

BRILLIANT

2

were English shipwrights that French hulls would distort that they always recommended stiffening with extra knees and riders even if the ship was not hogged at the time of survey. The two-year-old *Danae,* for example, was recommended for a radical strengthening as a pre-emptive measure. Some French frigates, like *Renommée* and *Brune,* became favourite cruisers and so were often repaired or totally reconstructed, making their apparent longevity very misleading – but no amount of mere strengthening could extend the short active lives of most French frigates.

Oddly enough the popularity of French frigates with English naval officers and the Admiralty was based on the same factors that made them so strongly disliked by dockyard officials and the Navy Board. Because they were fast they could make a fortune in prize money for a lucky captain and the

Admiralty considered this good for the service; because they were driven hard, under conditions for which they were not designed, their fragile hulls suffered and they required frequent and costly maintenance. French frigates were about 10-15% more expensive in terms of running costs and required major attention earlier in their lives, all of which was deprecated by the frugal administrators of the dockyards. Furthermore, by a singular irony, the speed which was the principal object of these long, light hulls declined dramatically as hogging and racking set in. In many cases, it is not going too far to say that the optimum performance of a French frigate could last as little as 3 years.

The light scantling also affected armament. As early as 1745 the Admiralty and the Navy Board had disagreed over rearmament policy for French prizes, the Navy Board preferring lighter weight of metal so

as not to strain the hull. However, in the case of the *Ambuscade* the Admiralty could not conceive of a 740-ton vessel carrying the proposed 9pdrs and insisted on 12pdrs instead. This policy was usually followed in the Seven Years War. English vessels were often criticised for being over-gunned, but their fabric was built to carry the weight, and on an armament-to-tonnage basis English frigates were more powerful and, for a large navy, more cost-effective. The lightweight structure of French frigates (of the size of English 12pdr '32's) restricted their main armament to 8pdrs, while their fine lines meant that they could not bear the weight of guns forward of the foremast. Thus, although they had longer gun decks, French frigates had no more room between the ports to fight their guns, and the deck space was further restricted by the exaggerated tumblehome. The low,

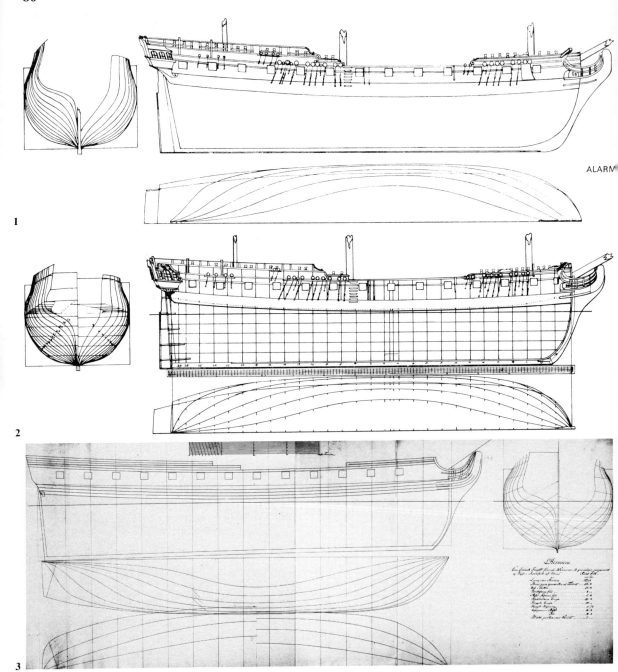

ALARM

1

2

3

L'Hermione

1 The really successful frigates of 1757-58 were the *Alarms,* derived in a general way from the 28s of the *Unicorn* (and the following *Tartar*) class. The satisfaction felt with these ships standardised the English 32 at around 670 tons and 126ft gun deck length until the late 1780s.

2 This design draught of the *Lowestoffe* shows the contribution of the *L'Abenakise* hull form to English practice – the 'two-turn' midship section, upright stempost, and slight rake of sternpost. This hull shape was also used in the less successful 28s of the *Mermaid* class of 1761, but when the design was revived in 1771 for three more 28s, the hull was modified somewhat, although two further 32s were also completed unaltered in underwater body.

3 A Danish copy of the sheer draught of the *Hermione,* the first 12pdr armed 32. Note the unusually deep hull.

Plan by courtesy of the Rigsarkivet, Copenhagen

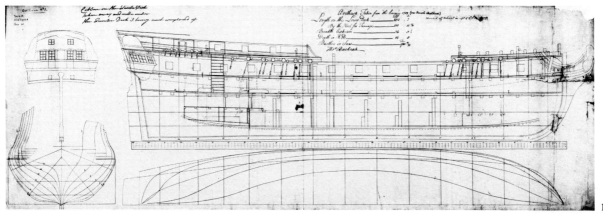

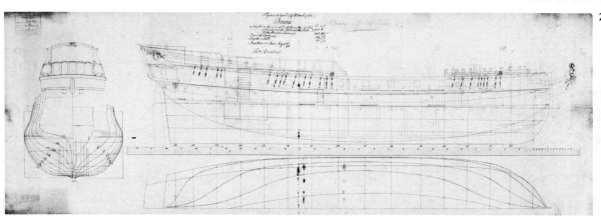

1 *Arethuse,* as captured: the poop cabin, or 'roundhouse', was removed to cut down windage in RN service.

Plan by courtesy of the NMM, Greenwich

2 *Brune* as captured.

Plan by courtesy of the NMM, Greenwich

shallow hull also meant that French frigates carried their guns closer to the water, which must have put them at a disadvantage in a seaway or when close-hauled – interestingly, both conditions in which French frigates did not excel.

The Admiralty policy of rearming prizes based on a conventional armament-tonnage ratio should not have had much effect on ships with an adequate reserve of stability (except to increase the strains on the hull) but at least three French frigates, *Vestale, Danae* and *Arethuse* had to have their masts and spars reduced. In *Danae's* case it was thought that the great spread of sail on the fore- and mainmasts caused her to labour and at sea to strain a long and weak hull. Thus her topmasts were reduced, but it is important to notice that this was not a question of stability but of damage to the hull.

It was normal policy at this time to retain the mast and spar plan 'as captured' when French frigates

were commissioned into the Royal Navy. However, *Vestale's* captain complained of her crankness (instability) under her original rig but, since there had been no complaints from her sister ship *Brune* nor from the very similar *Blonde,* this seems to have been a question of handling. French frigates usually had a substantial metacentric height which gave them reasonable initial stability, but the excessive tumblehome would have reduced the righting moment at moderate or large degrees of heel. Furthermore, the top hamper of French frigates constituted a high proportion of the displacement and all this weight aloft would cause them to roll. English frigates with their deeper and broader hulls were stiffer and could be driven by larger areas of canvas even in high winds, whereas an equivalent amount of sail would make a French ship heel at an alarming angle. In this case it seems that the English captain was unfamiliar with the characteristics of

88

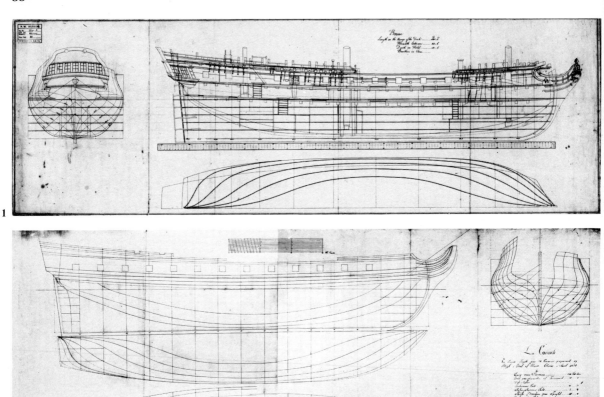

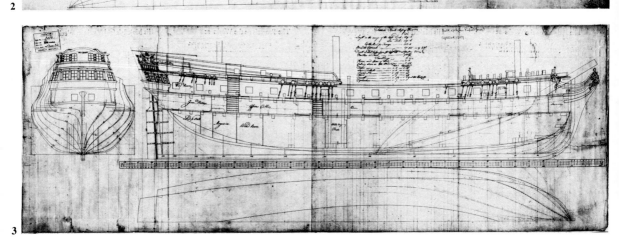

1

2

3

Brune as she appeared after her 'Great Repair' of 1770-72. As compared with her plan 'as captured', the radical alterations to give her English style stern galleries and topside detail partly account for the vast amount of money spent on her refit.

Plan from the Hilhouse Collection, Bristol

A Danish Navy copy of the French official draught of *La Comête.*

Plan by courtesy of the Rigsarkivet, Copenhagen

The 'sheer and profile' of *Danae,* as captured.

Plan by courtesy of the NMM, Greenwich

TABLE 2: PARTICULARS OF PRINCIPAL FRENCH FRIGATES CAPTURED 1756-1763
A. THOSE EQUIVALENT TO 28-GUN SHIPS IN THE RN

VICTORIE, also referred to as MARIE VICTOIRE and supposed by the English to be a privateer, taken 17 February 1757 by *Tartar,* 28. Bought in by Order 30 March 1757 as *Tartar's Prize,* 24.

Armament:	24 x 6pdrs, 4 x 9pdrs, disposition uncertain, 160 men in RN.					
	Gundeck length	**Keel length for tonnage**	**Extreme breadth**	**Depth in hold**	**Tonnage**	**Built**
Design dimensions:	117ft 3in	99ft 5½in	28ft 4in	13ft 3in	425	1757?
Sailing qualities:	No report.					

EMERAUDE, taken 21 September 1757 by *Southampton,* 32. Bought in by Admiralty Order 25 October 1757 and became *Emerald,* 28.

Armament:	24 x 9pdr on upper deck, 4 x 4pdrs on quarterdeck and forecastle, 180 men in RN. 24 x 8pdrs and 2 x 6s in French Navy.					
	Gundeck length	**Keel length for tonnage**	**Extreme breadth**	**Depth in hold**	**Tonnage**	**Built**
Design dimensions:	115ft 4in	93ft 1⅝in	33ft 11½in	9ft 3¾in	571	1741
Sailing qualities:	No report.					

VENGEANCE, privateer, taken February 1758 by *Hussar,* 28. Bought in by Order 11 March 1758 under her own name, rated 28.

Armament:	As *Emeraude.* 200 men in RN.					
	Gundeck length	**Keel length for tonnage**	**Extreme breadth**	**Depth in hold**	**Tonnage**	**Built**
Design dimensions:	116ft 11in	95ft 10¾in	32ft 4in	11ft 3½in	533	1757
Sailing qualities:	No report.					

VALEUR, taken 18 October 1759 by *Lively,* 20, and/or *Favourite,* 20. Bought in by Order 13 December 1759, registered *Valeur,* 28.

Armament:	18 x 9pdrs and 6 x 6pdrs on upper deck, 4 x 3pdrs on quarterdeck, 200 men in RN.					
	Gundeck length	**Keel length for tonnage**	**Extreme breadth**	**Depth in hold**	**Tonnage**	**Built**
Design dimensions:	115ft 6in	93ft 4in	32ft 6in	10ft 10in	524	1753
Sailing qualities:	No report.					

LA CHERZINE (?), taken early in 1760 by the *Rippon,* 60. Probably a privateer, although the survey suggests she is a naval vessel. Not bought in.

Armament:	6 ports on lower deck but impossible to fight guns because of lack of headroom, 24 ports on upper deck – guns of mixèd calibres but mainly 6pdrs. No ports on quarterdeck or forecastle.					
	Gundeck length	**Keel length for tonnage**	**Extreme breadth**	**Depth in hold**	**Tonnage**	**Built**
Design dimensions:	119ft 6in	99ft 9in	30ft 2½in	12ft 8½ft	484	estimated 1758
Sailing qualities:	No report.					

B. THOSE EQUIVALENT TO 32-GUN SHIPS IN THE RN

HERMIONE, taken 23 November 1757 by *Unicorn,* 28. Not bought in.

Armament:	26 x 12pdrs on upper deck, 2 x 12pdrs on forecastle as captured.					
	Gundeck length	**Keel length for tonnage**	**Extreme breadth**	**Depth in hold**	**Tonnage**	**Built**
Design dimensions:	130ft 10in	108ft 3¾in	37ft 6½in	13ft 5in	812	1748
Sailing qualities:	No report.					

ROSTAN, privateer, taken in February 1758 by *Torbay,* 90, and *Chichester,* 74. Bought in by Admiralty Order 13 March 1758 as *Crescent,* 32.

Armament:	24 x 12pdrs on upper deck, 6 x 6pdrs on quarterdeck, 2 x 6pdrs on forecastle, 220 men in RN. Upper deck ports 6ft 9in apart, height above water unknown.					
	Gundeck length	**Keel length for tonnage**	**Extreme breadth**	**Depth in hold**	**Tonnage**	**Built**
Design dimensions:	130ft 5in	107ft 6½in	35ft 9in	11ft 2in	731	?
Sailing qualities:	No report.					

BELLONE, taken 21 February 1759 by *Vestale,* 32. Bought in by Order 14 June 1759 as *Repulse,* 32.

Armament:	28 x 8pdrs on upper deck, 4 x 4pdrs on quarterdeck when captured. 26 x 12pdrs on upper deck, 4 x 6pdrs on quarterdeck, 2 x 6pdr on forecastle, 220 men in RN. Upper deck ports 6ft 3ins apart, 7ft above water.					
	Gundeck length	**Keel length for tonnage**	**Extreme breadth**	**Depth in hold**	**Tonnage**	**Built**
Design dimensions:	128ft 7in	104ft 1in	34ft 11½in	10ft 10½in	677	1755
Sailing qualities:	Fast (13kts with wind abaft beam) in smooth water but did not like a seaway. Best points of sailing were running and reaching but was not very good close-hauled. 'Very leewardly because of flat floors and small draught of water, but forereaches'. Did not like winds above a fresh gale when she was very uneasy and plunged greatly.					

ARETHUSE, taken 18 May 1759 by *Venus,* 36, *Thames,* 32 and *Chatham,* 50. Bought in by Order 10 July 1759 as *Arethusa,* 32.

Armament:	As *Repulse* in RN. Upper deck ports 6ft 3in apart, 6ft 10in above the water.					
	Gundeck length	**Keel length for tonnage**	**Extreme breadth**	**Depth in hold**	**Tonnage**	**Built**
Design dimensions:	132ft 1in	110ft 10³/₈in	34ft 5½in	10ft 8in	700	Purchased 1758
Sailing qualities:	No report.					

BLONDE, taken 28 February 1760 with *Maréchal de Belle Isle,* 46, and *Terpsichore,* 28, by *Aeolus,* 32, *Pallas,* 36 and *Brilliant,* 36. Bought in by Order 6 May 1760 as *Blonde,* 32.

Armament:	26 x 8pdrs on upper deck, 4 x 4pdrs on quarterdeck and 2 x 6pdrs on forecastle when captured. 26 x 12pdrs on upper deck, 4 x 6pdrs on quarterdeck and 2 x 6pdr on forecastle, 220 men in RN.					
	Gundeck length	**Keel length for tonnage**	**Extreme breadth**	**Depth in hold**	**Tonnage**	**Built**
Design dimensions:	133ft	109ft 0¼in	34ft 10in	10ft 7in	704	1755
Sailing qualities:	Fast – 11-12kts reaching and 12-13 before the wind. Not a particularly weatherly ship, but forereached on most vessels. Rolled 'deep but easy' and behaved well even in a head sea.					

VESTALE, taken 8 January 1761 by *Unicorn*, 28. Bought in by Order 16 February 1761 as *Flora*, 32.

Armament:	As *Blonde* in RN.					
	Gundeck length	**Keel length for tonnage**	**Extreme breadth**	**Depth in hold**	**Tonnage**	**Built**
Design dimensions:	131ft 7in	110ft 1¼in	34ft 6½in	10ft 9in	699	1756
Sailing qualities:	Best with the wind aft of the beam, when she would do 12kts, and forereach on many English frigates. Close-hauled in a topgallant or topsail gale she was undistinguished and in heavy weather – under reefed topsails or courses – she was very leewardly and slow.					

BRUNE, taken 30 January 1761 by *Venus*, 32 and *Juno*, 32. Bought in by Order 16 February 1761 as *Brune*, 32.

Armament:	As *Blonde* in RN. Upper deck ports 6ft 3in apart, 6ft 3in from water.					
	Gundeck length	**Keel length for tonnage**	**Extreme breadth**	**Depth in hold**	**Tonnage**	**Built**
Design dimensions:	131ft 2in	108ft 11¾in	34ft 7½in	10ft 8in	695	1755
Sailing qualities:	Fastest (12kts) before the wind; was not very fast close-hauled or in heavy weather. Suffered from pitching, and laboured and shipped water even when lying to. (However, this is based on reports from late in the ship's career which almost certainly do not represent her best performance.)					

COMÈTE, taken 16 March 1761 by *Bedford*, 64. Not bought.

Armament:	26 x 8pdrs on upper deck, 4 x 4pdrs on quarterdeck, 2 x 4pdrs on forecastle as captured.					
	Gundeck length	**Keel length for tonnage**	**Extreme breadth**	**Depth in hold**	**Tonnage**	**Built**
Design dimensions:	126ft 3¾in	103ft 9in	34ft 3in	10ft	647	1751
Sailing qualities:	No report.					

BOULLONGNE, East Indiaman, taken by *Venus*, 36, in March 1761. Bought in by Order 20 February 1762 as *Boulogne*, 32.

Armament:	As *Blonde* in RN.					
	Gundeck length	**Keel length for tonnage**	**Extreme breadth**	**Depth in hold**	**Tonnage**	**Built**
Design dimensions:	133ft 8in	111ft 10⁵⁄₈in	33ft 3in	13ft 4in	658	1758
Sailing qualities:	Best speed 11½kts broad reaching in a fresh gale with a smooth sea. Very leewardly, which was put down to her shallow draught. Rather crank when close-hauled in a stiff blow, and was very slow (4kts).					

C. THOSE LARGER THAN 32 GUN FRIGATES IN THE RN

L'ABENAKISE, taken 23 November 1757 by *Unicorn*, 28. Bought in on 13 June 1758, and registered as the *Aurora*, 38.

Armament:	8 x 18pdrs on lower deck, 28 x 12pdrs on upper deck, 2 x 6pdrs on forecastle, 250 men in RN. (Apparently the same armament when captured).					
	Gundeck length	**Keel length for tonnage**	**Extreme breadth**	**Depth in hold**	**Tonnage**	**Built**
Design dimensions:	144ft	118ft 9in	38ft 8½in	15ft 2in	946	1756
Sailing qualities:	Very fast on most points of sailing in moderate conditions. 14kts on a beam wind, 13kts quartering, and 9½kts close-hauled in 'smooth water'. Also fast under reefed topsail conditions with a beam or quartering wind (11-10kts) and was also very weatherly. However, close-hauled in a stiff gale her sailing was described as 'but indifferent'.					

French frigates and assumed that *Vestale* was over-sparred, since in his own words she would 'not carry sail unless buried in ballast, and then not move through the water'.

French frigates were not built to be 'driven' but, like British clippers of the 1860s, excelled in light conditions, a fact brought home to the captain of the *Arethuse* while on the American station in 1772; she lost her main- and mizzenmasts in a gale as a result of her shallow depth in the hold and great tumblehome, neither of which gave adequate support to the masts. However, like *Danae*, *Arethuse* 'laboured exceedingly in bad weather' but, to the surprise of her captain, sailed faster under a reduced jury rig.

These instances serve to reinforce the totally different emphases in British and French frigate design. French vessels in many ways were refined thoroughbreds, which required delicate handling to get the best from them. However, their light construction and fine-lined hulls were seen at a disadvantage in the lengthy heavy-weather cruising conditions common in the Royal Navy, and they were by no means suited to all of the tasks required of their more robust English counterparts.

ENGLISH 'IMITATIONS' OF FRENCH DESIGNS

During the 1750s considerable interest was shown in French designs but the drawbacks of the lightweight construction and the long shallow hull prohibited direct copies. *Tweed* was a particularly valuable experiment because, although not an imitation of any specific design, she was the most 'French' frigate in the Navy, and taught her designer, Thomas Slade, that these characteristics did not fulfil English requirements for seaworthiness nor heavy weather performance. However, Slade continued to study French hull forms and in 1760 he produced a design based on *L'Abenakise* 'to see if there could be any improvement by using this model', but the Admiralty ordered a whole range of designs from a 74-gun ship to a

MELAMPE, taken 2 November 1757 by *Tartar*, 28. Bought in by Order 3 January 1758 as the *Melampe*, 36. Regarded by the English as having been a privateer.

	Gundeck length	Keel length for tonnage	Extreme breadth	Depth in hold	Tonnage	Built
Armament:	26 x 12pdrs on upper deck, 8 x 6pdrs on quarterdeck, 2 x 6pdrs on forecastle, 240 men in RN.					
Design dimensions:	134ft 6in	111ft 6½in	35ft 6in	11ft 3½in	748	1757
Sailing qualities:	No report.					

DANAE, taken 28 March 1759 by *Melampe*, 36 and *Southampton*, 32. Bought in on 6 July 1759 as *Danae*, 38.

	Gundeck length	Keel length for tonnage	Extreme breadth	Depth in hold	Tonnage	Built
Armament:	30 x 12pdrs on upper deck, 6 x 6pdrs on quarterdeck, 2 x 6pdrs on forecastle, 250 men in RN. Upper deck ports 6ft 3in apart, and 6ft 3in from waterline.					
Design dimensions:	147ft 6in	123ft 11in	37ft 9½in	11ft 4½in	941	1756
Sailing qualities:	Fast but leewardly – 'tends to forereach rather than weather'. Preferred smooth water but could do 11kts in a stiff gale. Tendency to roll but pitched easily.					

MARÉCHAL DE BELLE ISLE, taken with *Blonde* and *Terpsichore* by *Aeolus*, 32, *Pallas*, 36, and *Brilliant*, 36, 28 February 1760. Not bought in.

	Gundeck length	Keel length for tonnage	Extreme breadth	Depth in hold	Tonnage	Built
Armament:	4 x 18pdrs on lower deck, 30 x 12pdrs on upper deck, 8 x 6pdrs on quarterdeck, 4 x 6pdrs on forecastle as captured.					
Design dimensions:	?	?	?	?	951	1757
Sailing qualities:	No report.					

TABLE 3: PROPORTIONS OF ENGLISH AND FRENCH FRIGATES

		RATIOS		
Name	Tonnage	Length-to-breadth	Breadth-to-depth	Length-to-depth
Tartar class, 28 guns	583	3.56	3.31	11.79
Southampton class, 32 guns	652	3.59	2.89	10.36
Richmond class, 32 guns	646	3.74	2.89	10.81
Niger class, 32 guns	679	3.56	2.93	10.42
Tweed, 32 guns	660	3.78	3.29	12.42
Pallas class, 36 guns	718	3.60	2.89	10.41
Lowestoffe, 32 guns	701	3.71	2.80	10.40
Mermaid class, 28 guns	614	3.70	3.05	11.27
Victoire, 28 guns[1]	425	4.14	2.14	8.85
Emeraude, 28 guns	571	3.40	3.65	12.38
Vengeance, 28 guns[1]	533	3.62	2.86	10.35
Valeur, 28 guns	524	3.56	3.00	10.66
Cherzine, 28 guns[1]	484	3.96	2.38	9.40
Hermione, 32 guns	812	3.49	2.80	9.75
Rostan, 32 guns[1]	731	3.65	3.20	11.68
Bellone, 32 guns	677	3.69	3.21	11.82
Arethuse, 32 guns	700	3.83	3.23	12.38
Blonde, 32 guns	704	3.82	3.29	12.57
Vestale, 32 guns	699	3.81	3.21	12.24
Brune, 32 guns	695	3.79	3.25	12.30
Comète, 32 guns	647	3.69	3.43	12.63
Boullongne, 32 guns[2]	658	4.02	2.49	10.02
L'Abenakise, 38 guns	946	3.72	3.45	12.90
Melampe, 36 guns	748	3.79	3.14	11.91
Danae, 38 guns	941	3.90	3.32	12.92

sloop based on the lines of the prize. In a very interesting reply the Navy Board explained why they could not do this, in the course of which they expounded their concept of 'imitation'. This involved adopting some of the *principles* of the design but altering proportions according to the widely different needs of a '74' and a sloop.

In essence, they were saying that the 'model' was little more than a starting point, as for any design study, and that the process was far removed from the simple 'scaling up or down' conceived of by the Admiralty.

Following this policy, the resulting *Lowestoffe* and *Mermaid* class were given the usual deeper English hull, although the midship section was generally similar to *L'Abenakise*. Despite being more heavily constructed *Lowestoffe* almost matched *L'Abenakise's* performance under sail, although the *Mermaids* were rather disappointing.

CONCLUSIONS

Like the constructional features, the design emphases of English and French frigates were consistent and strikingly different. Therefore, from this point it will be possible to reconstruct the 'staff requirements' – the duties, general parameters and the tactical rationale – of the two navies' cruising ships, which will be the aim of the third and final part of this article.

[1] privateer
[2] East India ship

Warship Pictorial

THE ITALIAN FRIGATE
LUPO

The warship pictorial for this issue comes from Doctor Stefano Cioglia who took the accompanying photographs of *Lupo* at Cagliari during April and May 1978. *Lupo* is the name ship of a class of fast frigates designed by CNR (Cantieri Navali Riuniti), in co-operation with the Italian Navy, and constructed at Rivo Trigosa near Genoa. She is heavily armed for her size (2200 tons) and combines the abilities of surface, submarine and air defence with seaworthiness and handiness and this together with moderate cost has aroused much interest in the design. Besides the *Lupo* three other ships of the class have been constructed for the Italian Navy, while Peru has four and Venezuela six completed or under construction. The *Lupo* herself was laid down in October 1974, launched in March 1976 and entered service on 12 September 1977.

The frigate manoeuvring in Cagliari harbour on the day of her arrival

1 The *Lupo* at the pier in Cagliari harbour on 1 May 1978. The gun mounting at upper deck level is one of a pair of twin Breda-Bofors 40mm/70cal gun mountings which, combined with the Dardo fire control system, provide defence against missile attack

2 The *Lupo* entering Cagliari harbour on 29 April 1978 after carrying out missile launch practice off the Sardinian coast

3 The port side looking forward. Note the telescopic hangar structure designed to accommodate one ASW helicopter (initially an AB204 which will later be replaced by the AB212)

1

2

1 A close-up from abaft the bridge
structure. The pendant number, F564,
has been changed since she was launched
when the prefix was D

2 A general view of the midships and
forward structure. Note that she carries
only two Otomat Mk 2 missile launchers
on each side, at the rear of the bridge and
abaft the funnel, the supporting structure
for the remaining four being, at this time,
unoccupied. Radars carried include air
warning Selenia RAN 10S (on E/F band),
surface navigation SMA SPQ-703 and
surface warning Selenia RAN 11L/X

3 The unique structure of the bridge
showing the dish radar aerial for control
of the 127mm gun via the NA-10 Mod 2
fire control system

4 *Lupo's* bridge structure

1

2

1 The *Lupo's* main anti aircraft weapon, the Oto-Melara 8 cell launcher for the Nato Sea-Sparrow missile (RIM-7H). The second Italian Navy ship of the class, *Sagittario,* is also to be equipped with this system but the remaining pair, *Perseo* and *Orsa,* are to carry the Oto-Melara launcher for the Italian Aspide missile. The missile director, also visible in this photograph, is a Raytheon Ex 77, Mod 0, with radar EX 91, Mod 0

2 The bows and forward section of the bridge showing the single 127mm/54cal Oto-Melara dual purpose gun mounting

3 A close-up of the midships structure showing the port 40/70 gun mounting and forward of it, on the raised platform, one of the Otomat Mk 2 surface to surface missile launchers. Above the latter just abaft the funnel is the port RTN 20X Orion director for the twin 40mm, which has a telescope attached for optical guide

4 A close up of the funnel and midships structure. Note the triple Mk 32 torpedo tube mounting, for Mk 46 A/S homing torpedoes, on the upper deck below the seaboat.

1

2

F 564

THE US FLEET CARRIER DESIGN OF 1945

BY NORMAN FRIEDMAN

The current series of large US attack carriers is descended from the abortive *United States* (CVA58), which was designed in 1946-49 as a special purpose carrier. At that time there was a second design in existence and, had it been chosen instead of CVA58, the course of US carrier development might well have been very different. That design was for a medium sized vessel of about 40 000 tons, intended as a successor to the standard wartime carriers of the *Essex* class which, in 1945, were already perceived as cramped and probably unsuitable for the coming generation of naval aircraft. Far too much had happened since their design in 1939-40 for them to have remained entirely satisfactory.

In the spring of 1945 the navy faced a dilemma. Its war construction programme had been extremely successful but it had consisted largely of ships designed as early as 1940. None could fully reflect the lessons of the war, nor could they comfortably

accommodate the fruits of rapid wartime technological advance. However, it was clear from the experience of the First World War that, however obsolescent these advances might make the existing fleet, Congress was unlikely to appropriate large funds in peacetime to replace ships only two or three years old. Moreover, it appeared that the prospective postwar slump might well destroy the design teams which had made the war programme so successful. On the 10 May 1945 James Forrestal, the Secretary of the Navy, ordered a programme of four designs to reflect war experience: a fleet carrier, an AA cruiser, a destroyer and a new fleet submarine – the latter has been described in *Warship 4*. Only the destroyer, which emerged some years later as the *Mitscher*, ever saw the light of day. The carrier, whose design had actually begun somewhat earlier, died in favour of the special-mission nuclear attack carrier.

The first to propose a new carrier

appears to have been Vice Admiral Marc Mitscher, commander of the Fast Carrier Task Force. When the carriers began to shift from island-hopping to prolonged assault on land targets it became evident that longer range and much heavier bomb loads for their attack aircraft were very desirable. After his experience off the Philippines in the autumn of 1944, Mitscher proposed the establishment of an Advisory Board for DCNO (Air) and also began to press for carrier bombers to take loads as great as 12 000lbs. The Board, which was formed on 27 April 1945, envisaged a ship with aircraft facilities comparable to those of the new *Midway* but on a smaller hull so as to achieve a new mass-production design. Thus an internal memorandum of the Bureau of Ships indicated a desire to limit displacement to 35 000 tons. In fact, of course, both *Essex* and *Midway* incorporated concepts of flight deck operations no longer accepted and in the end the new carrier (and of course its larger brother, the *United States*) had radically different flight deck configurations.

WAR EXPERIENCE

Probably the greatest single factor in the minds of carrier commanders late in the war was the need to achieve smooth, quick flight deck operations. The standard US tatic was the deck-load strike which involved up to half the air group being bombed-up, readied and fired off. The quicker the tempo of launch, the less fuel some members of the strike might waste orbiting the carrier to form up, hence the greater their effective range. Similarly, quick landings would reduce the need for aircraft to burn fuel while awaiting their turn to land. In 1945 it was estimated that landings could occur once every 30 seconds while catapults had reduced the take-off interval to as little as 20. Catapults also allowed parking on the midships portion of the flight deck, as catapulted aircraft required no take-off run. It followed that half a 96-plane *Essex* air group could be launched and the other half recovered in about 40 minutes as the carrier steamed into the wind. At this time standard schedules called for a maximum of 6 deck load strikes per day, which involved 4 hours steaming into the wind. Since the wind might not be favourable, the carrier would have to turn away from her course, then steam back to recover her position. Then the maximum time available in unfavourable winds might be about one-third of daylight time; flying at night was possible but not large scale night strikes. One interesting consequence of these considerations was that the larger air group of the *Midway* was largely wasted, since a *Midway* would require 6 hours for six half-group strikes. The larger air group could only be used effectively if provision were made for *simultaneous* launch and recovery but on the carrier decks of 1945, it was common practice to move recovered aircraft forward to the bow (to leave room for returning ones to land on) where they occupied space formerly taken up by the deckload strike just off and by the catapults. Moreover, elevators set in the flight deck could only be used when aircraft were not flying off or landing and it therefore followed that deck-edge elevators were far more useful. Indeed in the spring of 1945 it was proposed that the last few *Essex's* be completed with their forward centreline elevators replaced by a second deck-edge type; however, the *Essex* hull form forward made such a proposal impractical. The deck-edge elevator was also favoured because it was smaller and lighter, far less susceptible to the blast of hangar deck explosions, would not reduce armour protection over the hangar deck, did not require an elevator well (with its drainage system and its cut in the ship girder) and was less susceptible to misalignment. Note that most of the predictions were predicated on Kamikaze experience of 1944/5, which was fresh in everyone's mind. Moreover, the US carrier force was operating in the Pacific, where sea damage to the relatively exposed deck-edge elevators was comparatively rare. Although the deck-edge type was a standard

feature of postwar US carriers, the fleet did operate in much rougher seas in the post-war period and it is interesting that carrier commanders occasionally called for a restoration of the old centreline type.

PROTECTION AND ARMAMENT

The other major lesson of war operations was that the usual belt of side armour, applied to all existing carriers, was inefficient use of protective weight. If the future threat was likely to come from bombs, rather than from shells, then the side protection would have to defeat bomb fragments which might strike any part of the ship's side. Thus, in a 28 July 1945 synopsis of protection policy, the CNO (Chief of Naval Operations) noted that

'...the best distribution of armour would be to provide a reasonable degree of protection and at least force the enemy to carry more than a simple aircraft and engine combination in inflicting serious damage to the ship...
'...within the weight and stability limitations of a design, horizontal armour should be provided in the flight deck, hangar deck and at a lower level over the ship's vitals. On the flight deck it is recommended that armour, minimum thickness of 2in, should be provided to extend over all hangar spaces, 40lb(1in)STS should be provided at the ends of the flight deck. Hangar deck level should be armoured with a minimum thickness of 2.5in...throughout the length of the hangar covering magazine spaces, engine rooms and aviation fuel storage; steering gear, although outside these spaces, should also be protected. A lower deck of at least 60lb(1½in)STS should be provided over machinery spaces, magazines, steering engines and similar vital machinery.
'Fore and aft vertical armour should not be concentrated in an armour belt but should be distributed uniformly over the ship's side adjacent to the hangar and in the way of machinery spaces and ship's vitals from a point at least 8ft below the waterline to the hangar deck level...The minimum thickness of

the material should be 1.5in...division of the hangar into protective subdivisions open at the sides but protected one from the other by athwartships vertical armoured bulkheads as in *Midway* is sound and should be continued. Provision of at least four armoured bulkheads is recommended, one at each end of the hangar space and two which serve to divide the hangar into three subdivisions.
'...all elevators should be of the deck-type in order to preserve the maximum integrity of the protective features of the flight deck and hangar deck...in the fore and aft locations they would also eliminate the necessity of piercing forward and aft transverse armoured bulkheads. It is recommended that the current methods of providing adequate underwater protection be retained...'

For the future, it was expected that aircraft would grow in size, speed and thirst for fuel. The latter was a very sore point as aviation fuel was extremely explosive and had to be carried in carefully protected tanks. As such it consumed space in the internal armoured box where it competed with bomb stowage (which would also grow as aircraft bomb and other weapon capacity grew) and with propelling machinery (which would have to grow with the ship size). In 1945 the Bureau of Aeronautics was already beginning work on a new hydraulic catapult, the H8, which would be installed, beginning in 1950, aboard rebuilt *Essexes*. It was working, too, on a new generation of arrestor gear to take the new aircraft it was designing, one of which would materialise as the first US ship-borne atomic bomber, the North American AJ Savage. Neither was as yet so fully designed that its characteristics could be specified for the carrier designers, yet the new carrier would have to have provision for both. To some extent carrier flight deck could be specified in terms of the two largest carrier aircraft whose characteristics had been fixed, the Grumman F7F Tigercat twin-engine fighter and the

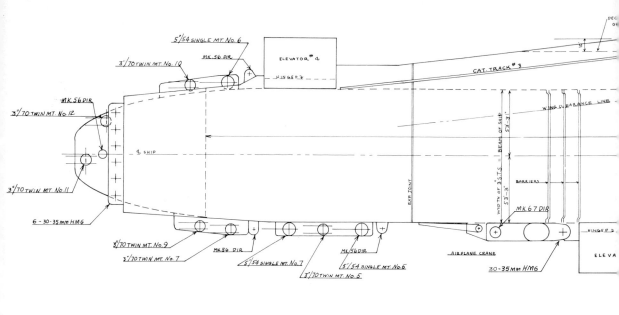

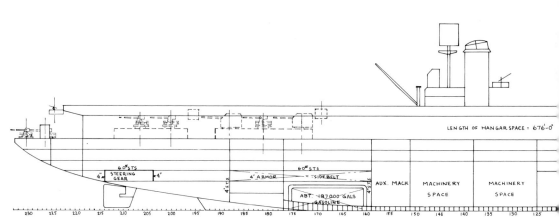

Profile and plan of aircraft carrier 'C2' dated 8 May 1946
(Drawn by A D Baker III)

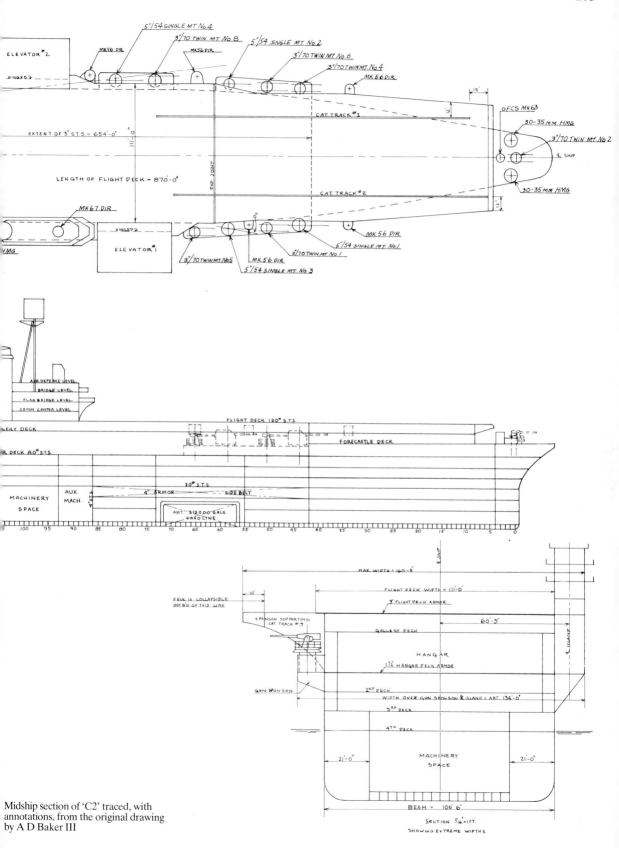

Midship section of 'C2' traced, with
annotations, from the original drawing
by A D Baker III

Douglas BT3D twin-turboprop attack plane; the latter would later materialise as the A2D Skyshark. An air group of 54 of the former and 36 of the latter was accepted by the Advisory Board on 9 July and fuel capacity was set at 500 000 gallons (compared to 250 000 for an *Essex* and 365 000 for a *Midway*)

Note that, although at this time no *Midway* class carrier had been commissioned, there was wide agreement within the Office of the CNO that the *Midways* would be inadequate and represented a wrong turning in carrier evolution: it was considered better to accept fewer aircraft and better facilities.

Kamikaze warfare also made heavy gun batteries attractive. The Bureau of Ordnance proposed four twin 5in/54, a design it had prepared for the abortive *Montana* class battleships and for a new AA cruiser study, mounted around the island as in an *Essex*. They would be backed by three twin 3in/70 in each port side and two in each starboard side quadrant, in place of the earlier single open 5in/38. There would also be 'as many 40mm quad mounts as may be practicable, but not less than twelve,' and 'as many free-swinging automatic weapons of the 37mm or twin 20mm type as may be practicable after the above installations are considered. It is recommended that the minimum of 30 such mounts be provided. The arrangement of armament should provide for the maximum number of guns practicable which will bear ahead and astern and will be capable of tracking and firing across bow or stern, respectively...A sufficient number of free-swinging mounts is considered necessary to augment fire power and for use in the event of a power failure...'

SKETCH DESIGNS
The Bureau of Ships began its series of design estimates with modified versions of its latest carrier, the *Midway*. Thus a 12 April 1945 calculation showed that without her side belt and third deck armour (4232 tons) *Midway* would displace 38 220 tons light and 52 610 on trial; 450 tons of side armour would however have to be retained to

balance her bridge. Reductions in flight deck armour were also considered but she was still too large. In a scheme I of 2 May the 5in/54 battery was cut to 16 guns and the number of quadruple Bofors from 21 to 20, while deck armour was cut to a 3.5in flight deck and 1in (as against 2in) hangar deck. Standard displacement now fell from 46 050 tons in the *Midway* to 37 560 and only 180 000shp was required. It was also possible to shrink the hull to a waterline length of 860ft, which began to approach *Essex* class dimensions.

In another sketch design, Scheme III, in which 4 more 5in/54 were sacrificed, length and displacement fell to 36 080 tons. This was so close to an *Essex* that a new design, Scheme IV, was based on the smaller carrier. However, even with a reduced air group (73 fighters and 30 attack aircraft, in place of the *Midway's* 96 and 48) it was too small and a compromise, Scheme V, 840ft long, 34 980 tons, with the armour of Scheme I and twelve 5in/54, was then evolved. It would have a flight deck wider but no longer than that of an *Essex* while an increase of 10 000shp over the earlier carrier would give a speed of 32.7 knots (vs 33.1 for an *Essex*). This design was presented to the Advisory Board on 31 May. It was followed by another stripped-down *Midway* (2.75in armour on the flight deck and hangar deck bulkheads but nothing else) of 38 210 tons and 34.2 knots. The higher than required speed implied that something smaller might be possible, with less power. Thus the ultimate Scheme VIII, the smallest ship which could carry a *Midway* flight deck, with no protection, a speed of 33.5 knots (on 165 000shp, a CVB air group and a battery of twelve single 5in/54, twenty quadruple 40mm and 28 twin 20mm. The length of 875ft on the waterline was determined not by the usual speed considerations but by the length of the *Midway* flight deck – 930ft. It turned out that such a ship could be built on a standard displacement of 35 200 tons (45 620 on trial). In effect its design was a demonstration of how far the *Midway* design had been

driven by protective considerations

This sketch design was not much more than an exploration of the consequences of various combinations of flight deck dimensions and protection and it did not yet take into account the war experience of carrier air group operations already cited. The Advisory Board heard testimony on that question from Captain W T Raisseur of the air component of the Office of the Chief of Naval Operations on 31 May. He proposed a radically new flight deck with one port and two starboard (amidships and forward) deck edge elevators. In addition to the two usual bow catapults, one would be angled out to port, served by the port elevator (the two forward catapults would be served by the starboard forward elevator). Finally, a fourth catapult would be mounted atop the forward superstructure, clearing the starboard catapult *from above*. It would be served by the after (two-level) starboard elevator. Catapult clearance would be sufficient for the launch of aircraft with 50ft wingspans to give maximum launch rate while other catapults were occupied. Note that the fourth catapult, brought out on a starboard sponson, was employed in the abortive *United States* design in which the flight deck was to have been flush (in this case, however, it was too radical and was rejected) while the third catapult, sponsoned out to port, was not. The 1945 carrier would have had an angled deck although, of course, it would not have corresponded to the angled decks of carriers of the 1950s and later.

THE FINAL DESIGNS
Scheme VIII convinced the Advisory Board that a useful carrier could indeed be built on 35 000 tons. It asked for two more studies to test the effects of particular characteristics. The first, Scheme A was extrapolated from *Midway* with equal aviation facilities (hangar and flight deck dimensions), moderate armour, equal or higher speed and Raisseur's flight deck arrangement. An air group of 54 F7Fs and 28 to 36 (the former had to be accepted)

BT3Ds and a fuel capacity of 500 000 gallons were specified. Oddly enough, armour did not follow the latest ideas. It was to comprise a 2.5 or 3in flight deck, a heavy hangar deck (this thickness was needed for strength in any case), 2in armour over the main magazines, aviation fuel stowage and isolated 3 and 5in magazines, and a 4in belt abreast aviation fuel stowage and magazines. The hangar deck bulkheads were not even mentioned. The second, *Scheme B,* was held to 35 000 tons but was otherwise to match Scheme A; BuShips worked up from *Essex* class flight and hangar deck dimensions, with a 2in flight deck and a 1.5in third deck over the vitals. Vertical armour was to be reduced or even eliminated but underwater protection was to match *Midway*, which implied a greatly increased beam. The gun battery was to follow that of Scheme A (although 5in/38 guns might have had to be substituted for 5in/54) and machinery was to consist of two of the new lightweight 80 000shp units contemplated for what would become the *Mitschers* – according to an internal BuShips memo 'take whatever speed we get'. The Bureau of Aeronautics estimated that the air group would fall to 36 F7Fs and 18 BT3Ds, and petrol stowage was reduced proportionally to 330 000 gallons.

The outcome of the A-series cannot have been heartening. Its originators made a common mistake in that they thought that omission of some armour weights would lead to major economies in size and displacement. However, other additions more than balanced this saving and both A-1 (900ft on the waterline) and A-2 (950ft) were heavier than *Midway* at 46 550 and 47 850 tons respectively, as well as less stable. They did have three catapults, three deck-edge elevators, the Buord battery already described and the *Midway* power plant.

The B-series was more encouraging; the use of lightweight destroyer machinery may have been partly responsible (3430 tons dry as against 3212 for *Essex* and 5165 for *Midway*). By September 1945 an

860ft hull of 35 030 tons and 31.8 knots had been adopted and the flight deck enlarged to 880 x 103ft. The battery now met the BuOrd standards except that there would be only 8 quadruple Bofors and 20 twin 20mm. BuShips presented these studies to the General Board of senior Admirals in October. It observed that the low speed of Scheme B might well be improved at a relatively low cost by adoption of yet another new powerplant. The design now incorporated both internal protection around magazines, aviation fuel and steering gear (primarily against rockets and other medium calibre missiles) and the side splinter plating already described as well as deck protection. In fact BuOrd noted that studies of bomb explosions and war experience suggested that increasing the flight deck from 2 to 3ins would give more than a 50 per cent improvement in protection. It suggested a third study, with heavier deck armour and speed increased to 33 knots, on about 37 000 tons.

This became Scheme C, the ultimate series. It used the 212 000shp *Midway* powerplant which, together with the 1in increase in deck armour, caused a rise to 38 000 tons, but speed also rose to an acceptable 33.2 knots. However, now, in November, the Advisory Board asked for stowage for 500 000 gallons of aviation fuel – the jets were proving even thirstier than had been supposed. Although the fuel itself would weigh only about 465 tons, BuShips estimated that piping, armour and the consequent growth in the ship itself would cost 1600 tons more. Aviation fuel alone added 20ft to the 860ft length of the ship while, at the same time, a more refined estimate of machinery dimensions showed the need for a further 8ft, so the ship was rounded off at 890ft. Power was soon boosted to 220 000shp for 33.2 knots (39 610 tons standard, 50 210 full load) and by now the medium carrier was not far short of *Midway* dimensions, but it was vastly different and far better suited to the new generation of aircraft.

The Advisory Board took up this Scheme C1 at its 3 January 1946

meeting. At this time the flight deck was 111ft wide, as in an *Essex*, except at the island where it reduced to 96.5ft. The aviators wanted to offset the island so as to avoid this reduction but costs would have included more structure to support the overhang, some problems of stability and the increased weight of 3in armour over the now clear flight deck area. In April, BuShips estimated only 200 tons to move the island but a net weight growth of 775 tons (and 1ft of beam), for the added protection.

In April a new C2 study was prepared in which the combination of island and sponson for the third catapult increased overall beam to about 150ft, which exceeded by 10ft 'the assumed maximum width of future aircraft carriers on which were based the recommendations for a clear breadth of 154ft for the projected third set of locks for the Panama Canal' – a project on which the *Montana* and *Midway* class designs had been predicated. The United States did not however, really give up its requirement for free passage through the Canal until the *Forrestals* and the chief remedy to this problem was a collapsible outboard end to the catapult sponson.

The island was reduced in overall bulk and split into two units, each with its own funnel, to reduce both airflow disturbance and the risk of losing both uptakes to one hit. The starboard elevators were moved closer to amidships, the after one forward to 'where it can be more advantageously used for striking planes below immediately after landing or for bringing planes up to flight deck during launching operations'. The forward starboard elevator was moved aft to where the flare of the ship's side was less, reducing structural complexity and also the potential for sea damage. A fourth elevator was added on the starboard side between the two islands.

All of these improvements in aviation facilities had to be paid for from the armament as ship survivability (armour) could not be sacrificed. The 5in/54 flight deck guns were given up, which allowed the island to be cut down by two levels and blast effect problems on the flight deck to be avoided. What is remarkable in retrospect is how late in the design evolution (April 1946) this step, which in the *Essex* reconstructions is considered a natural consequence of war experience, was taken. As compensation, 3 twin 3in/70 were added but only 4, rather than the original 8, quadruple 40mm could be accommodated. As the design progressed these too were eliminated and the battery rationalised to 16 twin 3in/70 with no lesser weapons. This C2 design, which was the basis for characteristics presented to the new Ship Characteristics Board on 12 June 1946, would have displaced 40 400 tons, still short of a *Midway*.

C2 would have been a new general-purpose carrier capable of accommodating jet fighters and light bombers but not the new generation of strategic attack aircraft which formed the basis of the much larger *United States* and *Forrestal* designs. It was doomed by the shift in American thinking away from conventional warfare and towards nuclear attack. In 1946 the latter meant a 10-12 000lb bomb and, if that weapon were to be delivered at any substantial

distance, its carrier would have to be a very large aircraft. The irony of the story is that by the time new carriers could appear, in the mid-1950s, nuclear weapons had shrunk so far that A-1 Skyraiders, quite capable of flying off unmodified *Essexes*, could carry them over great distances. In fact the most enduring rôle of the US carriers has been limited warfare. It is certainly true that very large carriers are much more efficient than small ones per ton but one wonders wistfully whether the small ones, in the greater numbers practicable under budgetary constraints, would not pose a greater problem to a Soviet commander bent on annihilating them. Perhaps, too, in a world of more numerous carriers, it would not be quite so necessary to claim that they are invulnerable, since the loss of one, although unfortunate, would not be quite the calamity that the loss of a super-carrier would be.

In any case by mid-1946 the Bureau of Aeronautics was emphasising a new class of very heavy carrier-based bomber and the rest of the Navy was working on a new heavy carrier to launch it so interest in the mass-production ship waned and then vanished entirely as

the new heavy carrier was modified to embody a secondary general-purpose rôle. The legacy of the 1945 carrier design study was a series of flight deck arrangement and protection ideas which were carried over to the larger ship and then, in very modified form, to its predecessors – a rather more constructive fate than that suffered by its contemporary, the 1945 submarine design.

ACKNOWLEDGEMENTS
This article is based on two sets of papers: General Board files held by the Operational Archives at the Washington Navy Yard (including reports of the Advisory Board) and design files of the former Bureau of Ships, held at the Federal Record Center at Suitland, Maryland. For access to the former I am grateful to Dr Dean Allard and his staff, notably Jathy Lloyd (now retired) and Gerri Judkins. For the latter, I am grateful to Charles Wiseman (now retired) formerly of the Naval Ship Engineering Center. Other material was taken from the CNO/Secretary of the Navy classified files at the Operational Archives and I am grateful to Nina Statem for assistance in using them.

CHARACTERISTICS

	Midway	Scheme B	Scheme C2
Standard displacement (tons)	46 050	35 030	40 590
Trial displacement (tons)	57 160	43 340	54 790
Flight deck (ft)	932 x 113	880 x 103	870 x 111
Length on wl (ft)	900	860	890
Beam (hull) (ft)	113	103	107
Draft (trial) (ft)	33.2	28.9	31.75
Power (shp)	212 000	160 000	212 000
Trial speed (knots)	33.0	31.8	33.0
Endurance (miles)	15 000	16 000	11 600
Air Groups:			
Fighters	97	35	35
Attack aircraft	48	18	18
Aviation fuel (gallons)	365 000	330 000	500 000
Armament:			
5in/54	18	4 twin	–
Twin 3in/70	–	10	13
Quad 40mm	21	8	4
Twin 20mm	28	20	20

NOTE: *Midway* and Scheme B figures are from a Bureau of Ships comparison sheet of November 1945. Scheme C2 is taken from several Bureau of Ships memoranda. Some caveats are required. Trial condition was essentially full load in all cases. Criteria for endurance varied from ship to ship: for *Midway* and Scheme B it is at 15 knots, assuming split plant operation, which was not the most economical. For Scheme C2 it is split plant operation at the new post-war standard cruising speed of 20 knots. Air groups are not directly comparable. The *Midway* air group assumes wartime types: Hellcat or Corsair fighters, and Helldiver and Avenger attack aircraft. However, Schemes B and C2 were based on the *largest* types in prospect in 1945: the F7F Tigercat twin-engine fighter and the BT3D twin-turboprop attack plane.

SMS VON DER TANN

BY JOHN ROBERTS

Von der Tann as built; note the forward gunports for the 8.8cm guns.
Drüppel

Von der Tann steaming at speed, possibly
on trials.
Drüppel

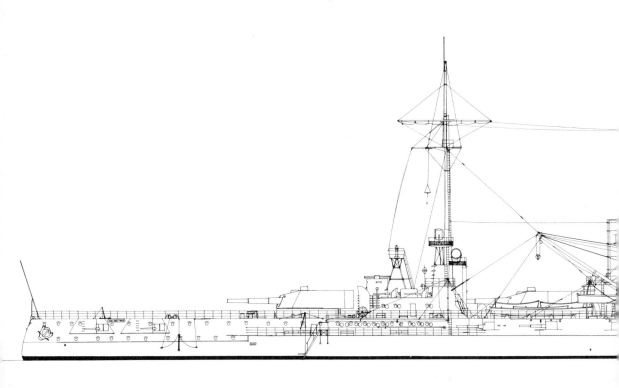

The *Von der Tann* was Germany's first battlecruiser and the first large German warship to be propelled by turbines. Built in answer to the *Invincible* class she was in most respects superior to her British rivals, being virtually a fast second class battleship rather than an over-sized armoured cruiser. Compared with the *Invincible* she had a lighter main armament but was superior in protection (both in respect of armour and internal subdivision) and secondary armament. She was also nominally of about equal speed but as the Germans, unlike the British, found high boiler forcing rates acceptable she was theoretically capable of a higher speed and on trials achieved over 27 knots with 79 000 SHP.

During 1914-18 she served with the Scouting Group of the High Seas Fleet and saw action during the raids on Yarmouth and Scarborough in 1914 and at Jutland in 1916. During the latter she sank the British battlecruiser *Indefatigable* and was herself damaged by four heavy shells (two 15in and two 13.5in). She was surrendered with the rest of the German Fleet in November 1918 and interned at Scapa Flow where she was scuttled on 21 June 1919. She was raised in 1930 and scrapped at Rosyth during 1931-34.

Builders:	Blohm and Voss
Laid down:	25 March 1908
Launched:	20 March 1909
Completed:	1 September 1910
Cost:	£1 833 000
Displacement:	19 064 tons (load), 21 082 tons (deep)
Length:	562ft 8in (wl), 563ft (oa)
Beam:	87ft 2½in
Mean load draught:	26ft 6¾in
Armament:	8 – 11in (28cm) 4 x 2
	10 – 5.9in (15cm) 10 x 1
	16 – 3.45in (8.8cm) 16 x 1
	4 – 18in submerged torpedo tubes (1 bow, 1 stern, 2 broadside)
Armour:	Belt 10inch amidships tapering to 6inch at upper edge, 4¾in/4in forward and aft; secondary battery 6in; bulkheads 7in and 4in; turrets 9in faces and backs, 7in sides, 3½/2½in roofs; barbettes 9in to 6¾in; forward CT 10in walls, 3.2in roof; after CT 8in walls, 2in roof; middle deck 1in flat, 2in slope amidships; lower deck 2in forward, 3in – 1in aft; main deck 1in fore and aft of secondary battery; upper deck 1in over secondary battery; torpedo bulkhead 1in – 1.2in
Machinery:	4 shaft Parsons turbines, 43 600 SHP = 24.75 knots, 18 Schulz-Thornycroft boilers, coal capacity 2760 tons
Complement:	998

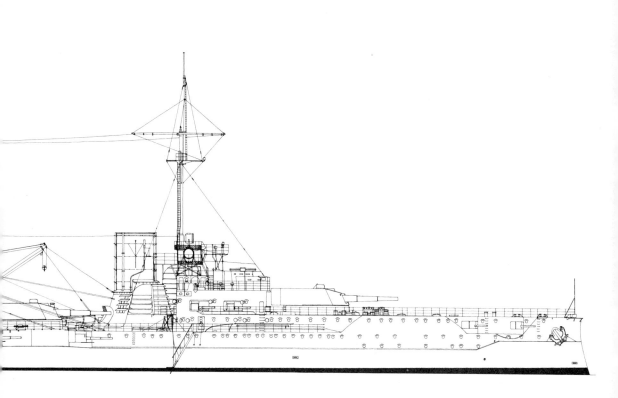

Von der Tann as built – *drawn by John Roberts*

THE KING GEORGE V CLASS PART 2
BY ROBERT DUMAS

The *Duke of York* leaving Portland in September 1948 for Home Fleet exercises. By this time her close range armament had been reduced to 64 2pdr pom poms (8 x 8) and 6 40mm Bofors (6 x 1)

CPL W/10/005

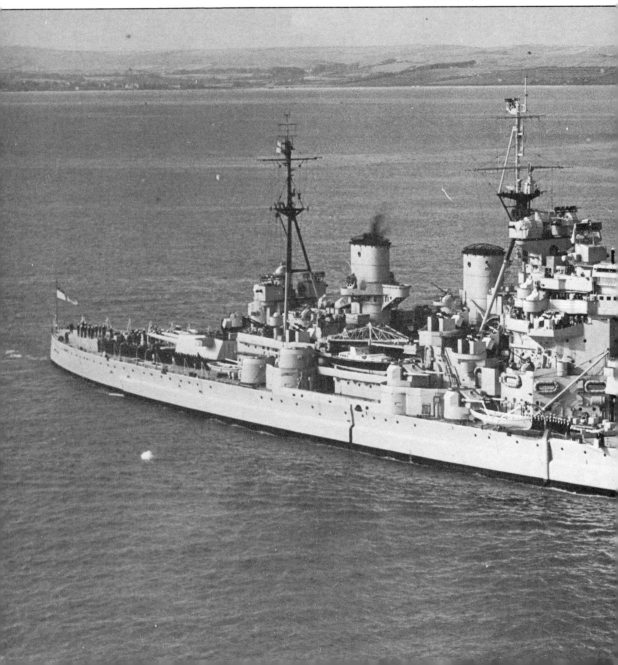

With the virtual elimination of German capital ship strength in European waters the emphasis of the naval war, with the exception of the anti-submarine campaign, shifted to the Pacific and Far East. During 1944-45 therefore, the four ships of the *King George V* class were extensively refitted in preparation for their transfer to the British Pacific Fleet. With air attack representing a much greater danger in this new area these refits were mainly concerned with providing additional AA guns and radar equipment but other alterations, resulting from war experience, were also carried out.

ALTERATIONS CARRIED OUT DURING LARGE REFITS OF 1944-45

Howe. Refit at Devonport January-May 1944.

REMOVED: 6 single 20mm Oerlikons, radars Type 281, 284 and 273 and the aircraft, their equipment and catapult. A large number of scuttles were plated over.

ADDED: (a) armament: 2-8 barrel pompoms, 2 US quad Bofors and 4 twin 20mm Oerlikon mountings on the former boat deck, 2 pompom directors and 2 US-pattern 40mm directors on the after superstructure; (b) gunnery radar: Type 274, with aerial on forward main director, Type 285, with aerial on after main director, 2 Type 282 with aerials on new pompom directors each side of after funnel; (c) boats: main boat stowage shifted

112

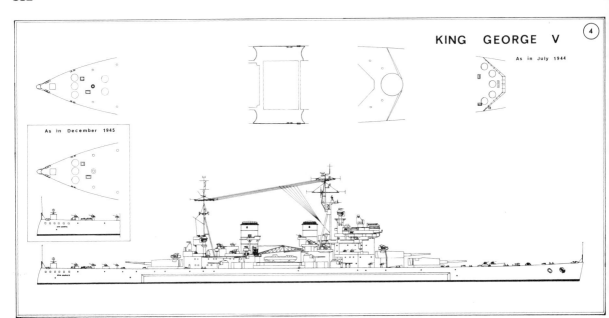

KING GEORGE V

4

As in July 1944

As in December 1945

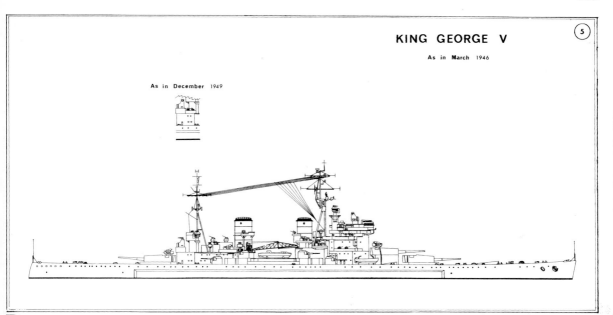

KING GEORGE V

As in March 1946

(5)

As in December 1949

A close up of the superstructure of *King George V* in December 1948. After the loss of *Prince of Wales* she was the only ship of the class fitted with Mk IV HA/LA directors. Her quadruple 40mm Bofors on the after superstructure have been removed and the remaining AA mountings together with their directors and the searchlights are covered with canvas except for the single 20mm mounting (with barrel unshipped) fitted abaft the fore funnel. The aerial on the fore topmast head is for Type 293 air and surface warning radar, the 'H' aerials below it are for the 242 IFF and Interrogator and the dish aerial on the starfish platform is for the Type 277 height finding radar. The aerial at the main topmast head is for Type 279 air warning radar, the small aerial above it being for the associate Type 243 IFF

Wright & Logan

from after superstructure to new structure built over former catapult deck amidships; (d) detection and communication equipment: combined air/surface warning radar Type 277 with aerial at top of foremast, combined air/surface target indication radar Type 293 with aerial on foremast, air warning Type 281B with aerial on the mainmast, two IFF Type 242, for use in conjunction with Type 281B, with aerials on the mainmast, 'Headache' with aerial on foremast, TBS types 86 and 87 with aerials on yard arms, D/F hut and aerial on quarterdeck; (e) other modifications: platform on after funnel fitted with roof, after HACS director platform modified, hangars converted for use as cinemas and new crew space provided on catapult deck. Note: the main yard on the foremast of *Howe* was lower than in the other ships of the class which is particularly useful in differentiating her from *King George V* in bow views. On completion of her refit the displacement of *Howe* had risen to 39 520 tons (standard), 44 510 tons (full load).

King George V. Refit at Liverpool February-July 1944.
Alterations and additions as for *Howe* except as follows:
REMOVED: 8 single 20mm Oerlikons, quad pompom on 'Y' turret, 2 searchlights on forward funnel and 2 on signal deck, external degaussing coil, radar Type 279.
ADDED: 6 twin 20mm Oerlikon mountings, air warning radar Type 279B with aerial on mainmast, 8 barrel pompom on 'Y' turret, former searchlight platform on forefunnel modified to accommodate single Oerlikons, internal degaussing coil. On completion of her refit the displacement of *King George V* had risen to 39 460 tons (standard), 44 460 tons (full load)

1

2

3

115

The forward superstructure of *King George V*

CPL W/10/006

The *King George V* arriving at Devonport Dockyard for refit on 21 November 1946

CPL W/10/007

The after quad 14inch turret of *King George V* taken during Home Fleet exercises on 4 November 1946. Note the aerials for Type 285 gunnery radar on both the Mk IV HA/LA directors and the after main armament director and the 3pdr saluting guns and US pattern quadruple 40mm Bofors mountings on the after shelter deck

CPL W/10/008

The *King George V* in September 1949 arriving at Portsmouth to pay off prior to being placed in reserve

Wright & Logan

4

DUKE OF YORK As in March 1945

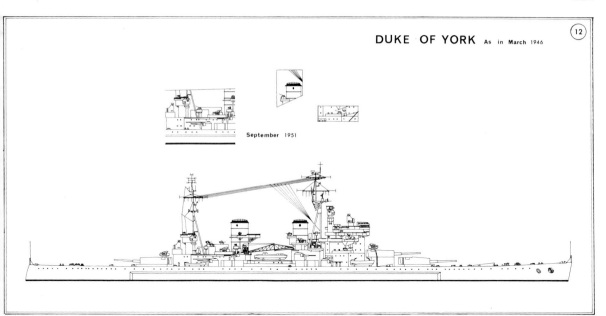

DUKE OF YORK As in March 1946

(12)

September 1951

Duke of York. Refit at Liverpool September 1944 – March 1945. *Duke of York* received more substantial additions to her AA armament as a result of the appearance of the Kamikaze in the Pacific. Alterations and additions were generally as for *Howe* except as follows:

REMOVED: 18 single 20mm Oerlikons.

ADDED: 6 quad pompom mountings (2 on quarterdeck, 2 on sponsons abreast bridge, 2 on upper deck abreast 'B' turret), 6 twin 20mm Oerlikon mountings, gunnery radar Type 274 (fitted on the after director as well as the forward director), platform on after funnel extended forward (this served to distinguish her from the other ships of the class). On completion of her refit the displacement of *Duke of York* had risen to 39 780 tons (standard) 44 790 tons (full load).

The *Duke of York* dressed overall during a royal review of the fleet on 24 July 1947. At this time *Duke of York* and *King George V* were part of the Home Fleet, the latter vessel being flagship of the C in C. The remaining pair were serving in the training squadron

CPL W/10/009

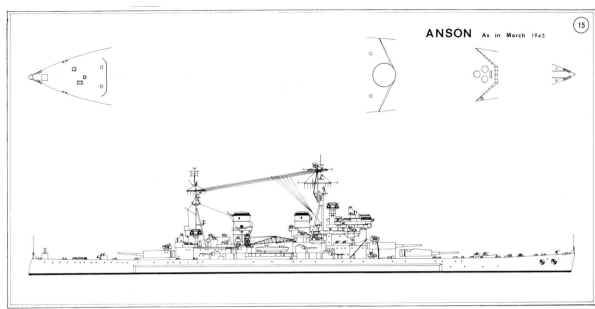

ANSON   As in March 1945

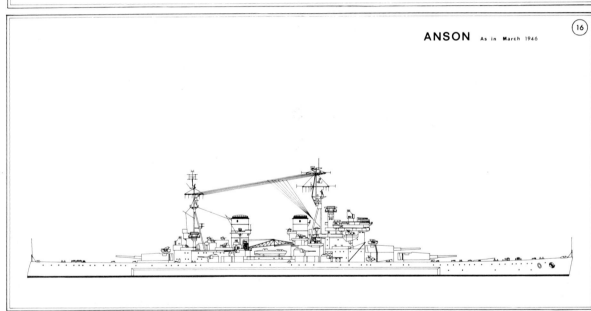

ANSON   As in March 1946

Anson. Refitted at Devonport Dockyard June 1944 – March 1945. Modifications were generally as for *Duke of York* except as follows:
REMOVED: 20 single 20mm Oerlikons, four secondary directors Mk V and associate radars Type 285
ADDED: Four secondary directors Mk VI and four sets associate radar

Type 275, missile jamming equipment Type 651, two aerial stays at top of after funnel, short mast on after funnel platform. On completion of her refit the displacement of *Anson* had risen to 40 150 tons (standard), 45 360 tons (full load).

Right: The *Anson* entering dry dock at Devonport on 11 September 1947. Note the Mk VI HA/LA directors above the bridge which were added during her major refit of 1944-45 – she was the only member of the class so equipped

CPL W/10/010

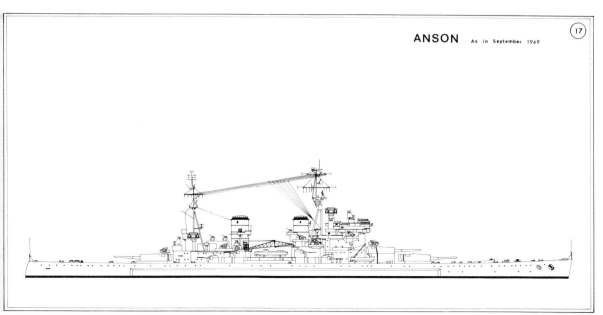

ANSON As in September 1949 17

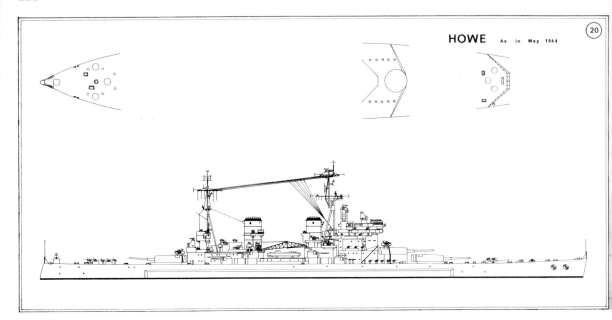

HOWE As in May 1944 20

POST-WAR ALTERATIONS

Howe. September 1945:
REMOVED: all single 20mm guns, searchlights on after funnel, DF hut on quarterdeck and sheet anchor.
ADDED: 6 quad pompom mountings (2 abreast 'B' turret, 2 on No 1 platform and 2 on quarterdeck) 18 single 40mm Bofors (2 abaft breakwater, 2 on 'A' turret, 2 on signal platform, 2 on after funnel platform, 2 abreast after main director and 6 on quarterdeck).
Late 1945: 6 single Bofors removed and side scuttles re-opened.
March 1946: All quad pompons and 6 single Bofors on quarterdeck removed.
Final condition: Two US quad 40mm removed.

King George V. December 1945: 2 single 20mm on quarterdeck removed and some of side scuttles re-opened.
March 1946: All 20mm mountings on forecastle and quarterdeck, including those abreast 'B' turret, removed; US quad 40mm removed and their directors replaced by British pattern with radar Type 282; 2 twin 20mm on after superstructure replaced by 2 single 40mm Bofors; DF hut on quarterdeck removed and 32ft cutters and davits abreast 'B' turret replaced.

Final condition: 4 single 20mm added abreast mainmast.

Duke of York. March 1946: All single 20mm and DF hut on quarterdeck removed, 4-3pdr saluting guns added, 2-27ft whalers added on upper deck and 32ft cutters and davits abreast 'B' turret replaced.
Final condition: All twin 20mm and 2 quad 40mm mountings removed and 6 single 40mm Bofors fitted (2 on after superstructure, 2 on platform abaft forefunnel and 2 on No 1 platform abreast bridge), two 27ft whalers on upper deck removed.

Anson. March 1946: All single 20mm (except 2 abreast mainmast) and the quad pompom mountings on quarterdeck removed. DF hut, sheet anchor and two small platforms on after boiler room vent removed; 4-3pdr saluting guns added on No 1 platform abreast bridge.
September 1949: All remaining 20mm mountings and 2 quad pompoms abreast 'B' turret removed and 4 single 40mm Bofors (2 abreast mainmast and 2 on platform abaft forefunnel) and a 20mm Oerlikon (abaft breakwater) added, 32ft cutters and davits abreast 'B' turret replaced.

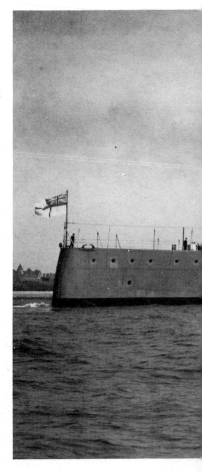

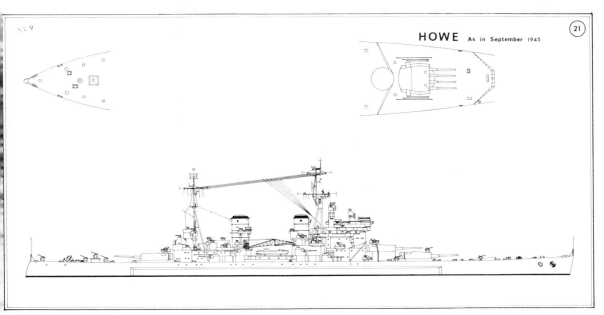

HOWE As in September 1945

21

Howe leaving Portsmouth Harbour on 19 March 1946 after the removal of the quadruple pom poms and single Bofors from her upper deck
Wright & Logan

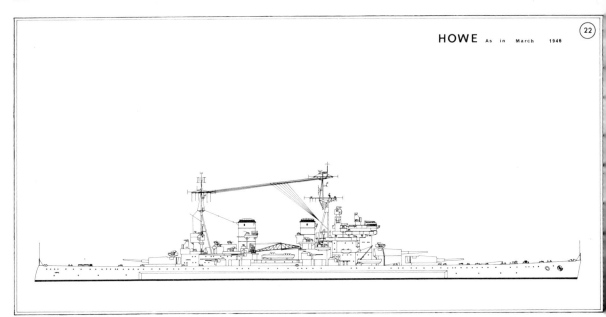

HOWE As in March 1946 (22)

The bridge and forward turrets of the
Howe early in 1945. The Mk V directors
above the bridge are facing astern

NZ Herald and Weekly News

The subject for the two parts of this article are the well known patrol submarines of the *Triton* or *T* class. Part one will cover the class during the Second World War period and part two the post war conversions. The subject matter will focus upon my detailed drawing of HMS /M *Tabard*, a late war built unit of the final or third group. The drawing has been redrawn from plans supplied by the draught room at the National Maritime Museum, Greenwich, with additional information and photographs from the Royal Navy Submarine Museum at HMS *Dolphin*, Gosport.

The effects of the submarine and mine during the First World War were to emphasize the lack of development in those fields prior to the outbreak of hostilities, but during the war substantial efforts were made to correct this situation. Pre-war submarine development had been cautious but, by utilising the potential of British industry, almost 150 new units were constructed by the specialised shipyards under the war emergency programmes. The Germans by contrast had developed diesel machinery on modern lines and their early engine designs of 1908 were ready for new construction during 1911/12. Their first diesel powered unit, *U19*, was placed in service in 1913 and served throughout the war. The British also had diesels in service from 1910, in the *D* class, but the later German engines were more efficient.

The British did not, however, lack ideas and extended the development of conventional boats' by building the *K* class, steam powered units with a surface speed of almost 25 knots (see *Warship* 8), the *J* class, which utilised three diesel engines in an attempt to achieve the same result, and the *M* class, which mounted a 12in gun. When the war ended in 1918 the 890/1070 ton *L* class were under construction capable of a speed of 17.5 knots on the surface (10.5 submerged), they were armed with six 18in torpedo tubes (4 bow, 2 beam) and carried a crew of 36.

At the close of the war the Royal

T CLASS SUBMARINES
PART 1
BY JOHN LAMBERT

Navy, as with other armed services, was pruned back and a number of building contracts were cancelled while many other ships were placed in reserve or sold abroad. As the years passed additional financial restrictions were imposed and the submarine service was further cut but new developments were continued at a slow pace and efforts concentrated upon improving existing designs and machinery.

POST WAR SUBMARINES
Although the submarines in service between the wars could do little more than the boats of 1918 they were able to submerge more quickly and to greater depths and carried a heavier offensive armament, the 21in torpedo having been introduced at the closing stages of the Great War. The diesel engine was now lighter in weight and had better performance, hulls were stronger and the internal high pressure and low pressure air systems, and other vent and blow systems, were improved by the use of more reliable auxiliary machinery and components. Crew training too had improved and, although limited in numbers, the submariners of the Royal Navy were probably the most highly trained in the world.

Although funding was restricted new designs were introduced and progressive development was continued. The 1923 Estimates provided for a new overseas patrol

design which became the *O* class and this basic design was later developed through to the *P* and *R* classes. Minelaying designs were also introduced, although subsequently discontinued with the development of mines which could be laid through torpedo tubes.

In 1930 the London Naval Treaty resulted in additional restrictions. The life of the submarine was fixed at 13 years and the United Kingdom was bound by the treaty to a total submarine tonnage of 52 700 (standard surfaced displacement) and individual units had to be below 2000 tons. With 53 boats in service, totalling 43 331 tons, and a further 19 units of 26 110 tons under construction, the limit was exceeded by some 16 741 tons. Seventeen submarines, displacing 17 040 tons, had therefore to be withdrawn from service and disposed of which left 7 over age units still in service. This resulted in a slowing down of the submarine construction programme to between 4 and 5 new 'boats' laid down each year, during the time of the depression when shipyards had little or no work. During this period design requirements for a new patrol submarine with a high surface speed were put forward and this resulted in the construction of the three units of the *River* class. These were followed by the large minelaying submarines of the *Porpoise* class.

THE T CLASS DESIGN

The *River* class, with a displacement of over 2000 tons proved costly and by 1935 a smaller and cheaper design was being requested. The requirements for these boats called for a lighter displacement, shorter range and a good 5 knot reduction in speed but an increase in torpedo tubes (10 instead of 6) and the same gun armament. This new project was intended to replace the larger *O, P* and *R* classes, and the few remaining post war *L*s. The result was the *Triton* or *T* class general service patrol submarines capable of undertaking a 42 day patrol and suitable for any ocean. (The medium sized *S* class had been designed earlier for the European theatre of operations, the first *S* boat being authorised under the 1929 estimates.)

The *T* class introduced a heavy torpedo armament – six internal bow tubes and four external tubes, the latter mounted under the upperdeck casing and all positioned to fire forward, two being amidships angled out from the centreline. Ten torpedoes were carried in the tubes and six reloads for the internal tubes. The bow casing, where it concealed the two external forward tubes, was bulbous – the foredeck then sloping down towards the bridge where it climbed to cover the midships tubes before it again sloped downwards to the slim stern. The bridge casing extended forward to give protection to the 4in gun crew during surface action. The hull was divided into eight watertight sections and had two escape hatches.

A variety of diesel engines were built into the new *T*s in order to gain data on operational performance for new engine developments. The new Vickers diesel was employed in units constructed by Vickers-Armstrongs, the Sulzer diesel in boats built by Cammell Laird, MAN diesels in those built by Scotts and the new Admiralty design in the units completed by Chatham Dockyard. Thus the new *T*s underwent a very useful period of settling down just prior to the outbreak of war.

T CLASS CONSTRUCTION

The boats were constructed under the following programmes:

1935 Estimates: 1 *Porpoise*, 1 *S*, 1 *T (Triton)*
1936 Estimates: 1 *Porpoise*, 4 *T*, 3 *U*
1937 Estimates: 7 *T*
1938 Estimates: 3 *T*
1939 Estimates and additions: 5 *S*, 7 *T*, 12 *U*
1940 Emergency War Programme: 13 *S*, 9 *T*, 29 *U*
1941 Emergency War Programme: 15 *S*, 17 *T*, 12 *U*, 8 *V*
1942 Emergency War Programme: 12 *S*, 14 *T*, 19 *V*
1943 Emergency War Programme: 9 *S*, 15 *V*, 46 *A*

It must be remembered that eac

The Group I *T* class submarine, *Triton* in June 1939.
Wright & Logan

PARTICULARS OF T CLASS SUBMARINES

	FIRST GROUP	SECOND & THIRD GROUP
Displacement tons	1090 (1325 full load)/1573 tons submerged (*Triton* 1095 (1330 full ld.)/1585 subd	1090 (1321 full load, later increased to 1422)/1571 tons submerged
Dimensions	245'6"(pp) 275'(oa) x 26'6" x 14' 3" (*Triton* 277'3" (oa)	245' 6"(pp) 273'6" (oa) x 26'6" 14'3" (full load) later increased to 15'3"
Machinery	Two shafts, 6 cylinder Admiralty, Vickers, Sulzer or M.A.N. diesels 2500 BHP ——— Laurence Scott electric motors 1450 SHP	Two shafts, 6 cylinder Admiralty or Vickers diesels 2500 BHP ——— Laurence Scott electric motors 1450 SHP
Performance	15.25 knots surface/8.75 knots submerged	15.25 knots surface/8.75 knots submerged
Fuel	132 tons diesel = 8000 miles at 10 knots	132 tons, later increased to 230 tons = 1100 miles
Armament	1-4in gun, 3-.303 LMGs. 10-21in T/tubes 16-21in torpedoes	1-4in gun, 1-20mm Oerlikon (not in group 2) 11-21in T/tubes 17-21in torpedoes
Complement	56	61
Diving Depth	300ft	300ft (All-welded boats 350ft.)

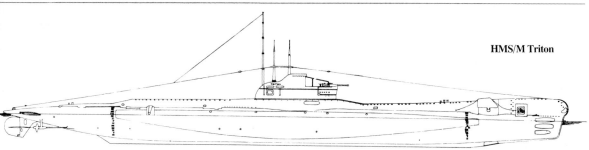

HMS/M Triton

1

2

3

boat took between 24 and 30 months to complete after the keel had been laid and the required materials had been ordered.

I have drawn HMS *Triton*, from the information received, to show the general appearance of the first group as built or ordered pre-war. She was laid down in August 1936, launched in October 1937 and completed in December 1938. She was followed by 21 similar sisters. The first major alteration made to the class was to modify the bow shape, by fining, which exposed the forward end of the external bow tubes but reduced the wave problems encountered whilst proceeding at periscope depth. The bridge shape was also altered.

The units ordered early in the war were to undergo other alterations as the war progressed. They were re-designed with their midships tubes sighted to fire aft and were thus able to fire astern at targets as they departed. An additional external tube was also added on the centreline of the casing right aft, to provide a total of 5 external tubes. The new orders gradually had new equipment built in. Radar was

added, construction was altered to part welded and part riveted and the third group had a 20mm Oerlikon mounting added aft of the bridge. The surviving units of the earlier groups were similarly modified as they underwent refit.

The vessels of the class constructed during 1943 had hulls of all welded construction (from *P332* onwards) and this resulted in the ability to utilise the external ballast tanks as additional bunkerage space. This increased the diesel fuel stowage by 74 per cent, from 131 tons to 230 tons, with a corresponding increase in range from 8000 miles to 11 000 at a surface speed of 10 knots.

Referring to the drawing of HMS/M *Tabard*, the first ship of the RN to carry the name, she was built by Scotts, at Greenock, who had constructed submarines during the Great War including the steam powered *Swordfish* and the *K15*. The *Tabard* was laid down on 6 September 1944, launched on 21 November 1945 and completed for trials and service on 25 June 1946. There were few differences between her and her earlier sisters. Her 4in

QFSA (quick firing semi-automatic) Mark XII gun on the S1 mounting is protected by a full shield. Further aft on the bandstand is the 20mm Oerlikon on a Mark VIIA submarine mounting. This was a mounting modified for 'boats' by having drainage holes cut in the lower part of the pedestal.

Of the 62 *T* class units authorised, a total of 16 were lost during the war. HMS *Thetis* of the first group was lost whilst undergoing acceptance trials in Liverpool bay in June 1939 which resulted in heavy loss of life, both among the civilians on board and the crew. She was subsequently raised and refitted, having her bow fined in the process, and joined the service as HMS/M *Thunderbolt*. Eight *T*s were subsequently cancelled and the design was subsequently replaced by the all-welded *A* class (these vessels will be another of my subjects at later date). Part 2 will examine the *T* class during the post war years and will include a number of new photographs and data.

1 The *Tantivy*, a Group III vessel, in June 1945.
IWM

2 A Group III *T* class in floating drydock.
Author's collection

3 HMS /M *Tabard* in September 1946, showing her appearance as completed.
Wright & Logan

130

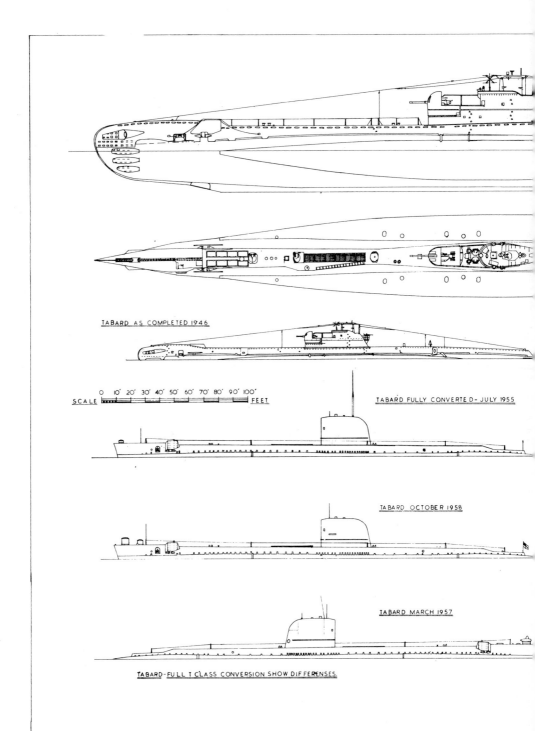

TABARD AS COMPLETED 1946

SCALE ┣━━━━━━━━┫ FEET
0 10' 20' 30' 40' 50' 60' 70' 80' 90' 100'

TABARD FULLY CONVERTED - JULY 1955

TABARD OCTOBER 1958

TABARD MARCH 1957

TABARD - FULL T CLASS CONVERSION SHOW DIFFERENSES.

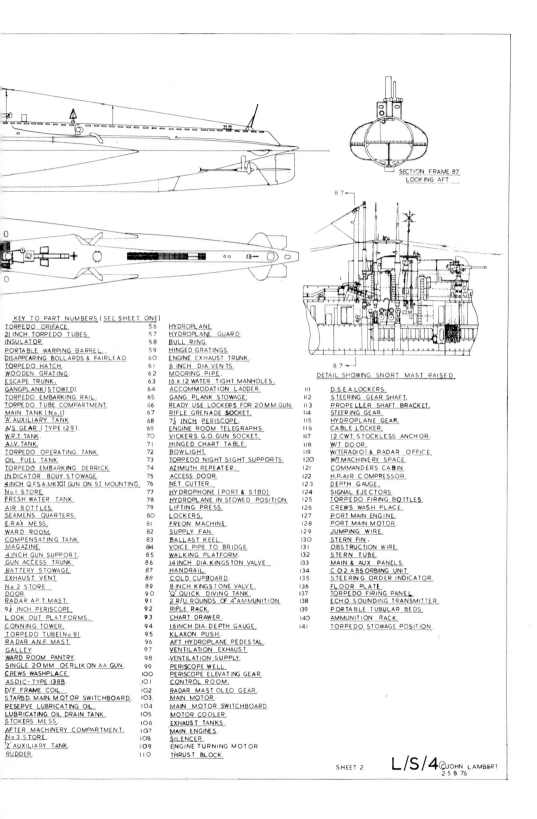

SECTION FRAME 87
LOOKING AFT

B 7→

DETAIL SHOWING SNORT MAST RAISED

KEY TO PART NUMBERS (SEE SHEET ONE)

TORPEDO ORIFACE.		HYDROPLANE.	56
21 INCH TORPEDO TUBES.		HYDROPLANE GUARD.	57
INSULATOR.		BULL RING.	58
PORTABLE WARPING BARREL.		HINGED GRATINGS.	59
DISAPPEARING BOLLARDS & FAIRLEAD.		ENGINE EXHAUST TRUNK.	60
TORPEDO HATCH.		8 INCH DIA. VENTS.	61
WOODEN GRATING.		MOORING PIPE.	62
ESCAPE TRUNK.		16 x 12 WATER TIGHT MANHOLES.	63
GANGPLANK (STOWED).		ACCOMMODATION LADDER.	64
TORPEDO EMBARKING RAIL.		GANG PLANK STOWAGE.	65
TORPEDO TUBE COMPARTMENT.		READY USE LOCKERS FOR 20MM GUN.	66
MAIN TANK (No.1).		RIFLE GRENADE SOCKET.	67
'A' AUXILIARY TANK.		7½ INCH PERISCOPE.	68
A/S GEAR (TYPE 129).		ENGINE ROOM TELEGRAPHS.	69
W.R.T. TANK.		VICKERS G.O. GUN SOCKET.	70
A.I.V. TANK.		HINGED CHART TABLE.	71
TORPEDO OPERATING TANK.		BOWLIGHT.	72
OIL FUEL TANK.		TORPEDO NIGHT SIGHT SUPPORTS.	73
TORPEDO EMBARKING DERRICK.		AZIMUTH REPEATER.	74
INDICATOR BOUY STOWAGE.		ACCESS DOOR.	75
4 INCH Q.F.S.A.MKXII GUN ON SI MOUNTING.		NET CUTTER.	76
No.1 STORE.		HYDROPHONE (PORT & STBD).	77
FRESH WATER TANK.		HYDROPLANE IN STOWED POSITION.	78
AIR BOTTLES.		LIFTING PRESS.	79
SEAMENS QUARTERS.		LOCKERS.	80
E.R.A's MESS.		FREON MACHINE.	81
WARD ROOM.		SUPPLY FAN.	82
COMPENSATING TANK.		BALLAST KEEL.	83
MAGAZINE.		VOICE PIPE TO BRIDGE.	84
4 INCH GUN SUPPORT.		WALKING PLATFORM.	85
GUN ACCESS TRUNK.		14 INCH DIA. KINGSTON VALVE.	86
BATTERY STOWAGE.		HANDRAIL.	87
EXHAUST VENT.		COLD CUPBOARD.	88
No.2 STORE.		8 INCH KINGSTONE VALVE.	89
DOOR.		'Q' QUICK DIVING TANK.	90
RADAR A.P.T. MAST.		2 R/U ROUNDS OF 4" AMMUNITION.	91
9½ INCH PERISCOPE.		RIFLE RACK.	92
LOOK OUT PLATFORMS.		CHART DRAWER.	93
CONNING TOWER.		16 INCH DIA. DEPTH GAUGE.	94
TORPEDO TUBE (No 9).		KLAXON PUSH.	95
RADAR A.N.F. MAST.		AFT HYDROPLANE PEDESTAL.	96
GALLEY.		VENTILATION EXHAUST.	97
WARD ROOM PANTRY.		VENTILATION SUPPLY.	98
SINGLE 20MM OERLIKON AA GUN.		PERISCOPE WELL.	99
CREWS WASHPLACE.		PERISCOPE ELEVATING GEAR.	100
ASDIC - TYPE 138B.		CONTROL ROOM.	101
D/F FRAME COIL.		RADAR MAST OLEO GEAR.	102
STARBD. MAIN MOTOR SWITCHBOARD.		MAIN MOTOR.	103
RESERVE LUBRICATING OIL.		MAIN MOTOR SWITCHBOARD.	104
LUBRICATING OIL DRAIN TANK.		MOTOR COOLER.	105
STOKERS MESS.		EXHAUST TANKS.	106
AFTER MACHINERY COMPARTMENT.		MAIN ENGINES.	107
No.3 STORE.		SILENCER.	108
'Z' AUXILIARY TANK.		ENGINE TURNING MOTOR.	109
RUDDER.		THRUST BLOCK.	110

D.S.E.A. LOCKERS.	111
STEERING GEAR SHAFT.	112
PROPELLER SHAFT BRACKET.	113
STEERING GEAR.	114
HYDROPLANE GEAR.	115
CABLE LOCKER.	116
12 CWT. STOCKLESS ANCHOR.	117
W/T DOOR.	118
W/T (RADIO) & RADAR OFFICE.	119
W/T MACHINERY SPACE.	120
COMMANDERS CABIN.	121
H.P. AIR COMPRESSOR.	122
DEPTH GAUGE.	123
SIGNAL EJECTORS.	124
TORPEDO FIRING BOTTLES.	125
CREWS WASH PLACE.	126
PORT MAIN ENGINE.	127
PORT MAIN MOTOR.	128
JUMPING WIRE.	129
STERN FIN.	130
OBSTRUCTION WIRE.	131
STERN TUBE.	132
MAIN & AUX PANELS.	133
C.O.2 ABSORBING UNIT.	134
STEERING ORDER INDICATOR.	135
FLOOR PLATE.	136
TORPEDO FIRING PANEL.	137
ECHO SOUNDING TRANSMITTER.	138
PORTABLE TUBULAR BEDS.	139
AMMUNITION RACK.	140
TORPEDO STOWAGE POSITION.	141

SHEET 2 L/S/4 ©JOHN LAMBERT
25 8 76

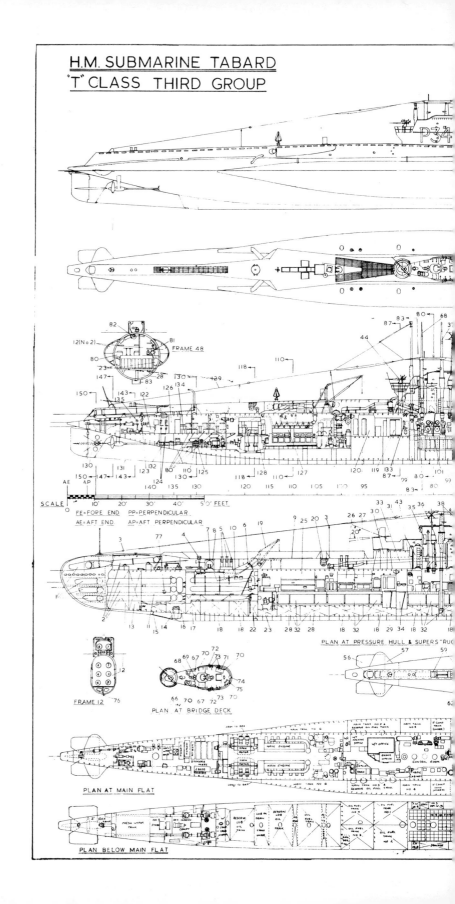

H.M. SUBMARINE TABARD
"T" CLASS THIRD GROUP

P34

FRAME 48

SCALE

0   10'   20'   30'   40'   5'0' FEET

FE=FORE END   PP=PERPENDICULAR
AE=AFT END   AP=AFT PERPENDICULAR

PLAN AT PRESSURE HULL & SUPERSTRUC

FRAME 12

PLAN AT BRIDGE DECK

PLAN AT MAIN FLAT

PLAN BELOW MAIN FLAT

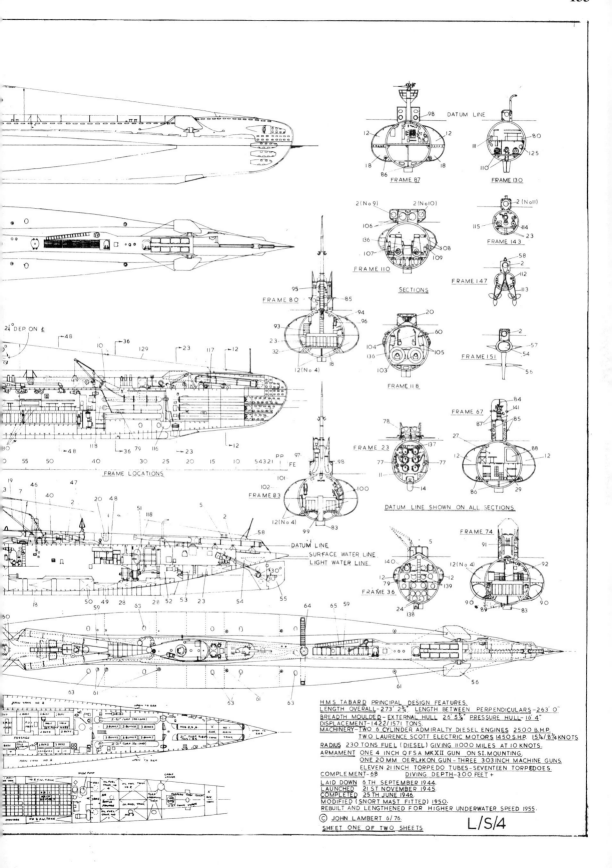

H.M.S. TABARD PRINCIPAL DESIGN FEATURES.
LENGTH OVERALL – 273' 2¾". LENGTH BETWEEN PERPENDICULARS – 263' 0".
BREADTH MOULDED – EXTERNAL HULL 26' 5¼". PRESSURE HULL – 16' 4".
DISPLACEMENT – 1422/1571 TONS.
MACHINERY – TWO 6 CYLINDER ADMIRALTY DIESEL ENGINES 2500 B.H.P.
       TWO LAURENCE SCOTT ELECTRIC MOTORS 1450 S.H.P. 15¼/8¾ KNOTS.
RADIUS 230 TONS FUEL (DIESEL) GIVING 11000 MILES AT 10 KNOTS.
ARMAMENT ONE 4 INCH QFSA MK XII GUN ON SI. MOUNTING.
       ONE 20 MM OERLIKON GUN – THREE 303 INCH MACHINE GUNS.
       ELEVEN 21 INCH TORPEDO TUBES – SEVENTEEN TORPEDOES.
COMPLEMENT – 68   DIVING DEPTH – 300 FEET +
LAID DOWN 6 TH SEPTEMBER 1944.
LAUNCHED 21 ST NOVEMBER 1945.
COMPLETED 25 TH JUNE 1946.
MODIFIED (SNORT MAST FITTED) 1950.
REBUILT AND LENGTHENED FOR HIGHER UNDERWATER SPEED 1955.
© JOHN LAMBERT 6/76.
SHEET ONE OF TWO SHEETS.   L/S/4

LIST OF T CLASS SUBMARINES. BUILT 1938-1946.

Pennant No.	Name	Launched	Fate
First group			
15T	TRITON	5/10/37	Lost Mediterranean 18/12/40
11T	THETIS	29/6/38	Renamed *Thunderbolt* Lost Mediterranean 13/3/43
76T	TRIBUNE	8/12/38	Scrapped 1947.
52T	TRIDENT	7/12/38	Scrapped 1946
18T	TRIUMPH	16/2/38	Lost Aegean 14/1/42
38T	TAKU	29/5/39	Scrapped 1946
17T	TARPON	17/10/39	Lost North Sea 14/4/40
24T	THISTLE	25/10/38	Lost North Sea 10/4/40
63T	TIGRIS	31/10/39	Lost Mediterranean 10/3/43
53T	TRIAD	5/5/39	Lost Mediterranean 20/10/40
68T	TRUANT	5/5/39	Scrapped 1946
94T	TUNA	10/5/40	Scrapped 1946
78T	TALISMAN	29/1/40	Lost Mediterranean -/9/42
77T	TETRACH	14/11/39	Lost Mediterranean 2/11/41
79T	TORBAY	9/4/40	Scrapped 1946
Second group			
N86	TEMPEST	10/6/41	Lost Mediterranean 13/2/42
N11	THORN	18/3/41	Lost Mediterranean 6/8/42
N37	THRASHER	28/11/40	Scrapped 1947
N48	TRAVELLER	27/8/41	Lost Mediterranean -/12/42
N91	TROOPER	5/3/42	Lost Aegean Sea 17/10/43
N45	TRUSTY	14/3/41	Scrapped 1947
N98	TURBULENT	12/5/41	Lost Mediterranean 23/3/43
Third group			
P311	EX P91	5/3/42	Lost Mediterranean 8/1/43
P312	TRESPASSER	29/5/42	Scrapped 1961
P313	TAURUS	27/6/42	Scrapped 1960
P314	TACTICIAN	20/7/42	Scrapped 1964
P315	TRUCULENT	12/9/42	Lost 1950, salved and scrapped
P316	TEMPLAR	26/10/42	Scrapped 1959
P317	TALLY-HO	23/12/42	Scrapped 1967
P318	TANTALUS	24/2/43	Scrapped 1950
P319	TANTIVY	6/4/43	Expended as a target, 1951
P321	TELEMACHUS	19/6/43	Scrapped 1961
P322	TALENT	17/7/43	Scrapped 1963
P323	TERRAPIN	31/8/43	Scrapped 1945, as constructive total loss
P324	THOROUGH	30/10/43	Scrapped 1961
P325	THULE	22/10/42	Scrapped 1962
P326	TUDOR	23/9/42	Scrapped 1963
P327	TIRELESS	19/3/43	Scrapped 1968
P328	TOKEN	19/3/43	Scrapped 1970
P329	TRADEWIND	11/12/42	Scrapped 1955
P331	TRECHANT	24/3/43	Scrapped 1963
P332	TIPTOE	25/2/44	Scrapped 1975
P333	TRUMP	25/3/44	Scrapped 1971
P334	TACITURN	7/6/44	Scrapped 1971
P335	TAPIR	21/8/44	Scrapped 1966
P336	TARN	29/11/44	Scrapped 1967
P337	TASMAN	13/2/45	Scrapped 1970
P338	TEREDO	27/4/45	Scrapped 1945
P341	THEBAN	–	Cancelled 1945
P342	TABARD	21/11/45	Scrapped 1968
P343	TALENT (II)	–	Cancelled 1945
P344	THREAT	–	Cancelled 1945
P345/8	Unnamed	–	Cancelled 1945
P349	THOR	18/4/44	Cancelled 1945
P351	TIARA	18/4/44	Cancelled 1945
P352	TOTEM	28/9/43	Sold to Israel 1964. Lost 1968
P353	TRUNCHEON	22/2/44	Sold to Israel 1968
P354	TURPIN	5/8/44	Sold to Israel 1965
P355	THERMOPYLAE	27/6/45	Scrapped 1970

BRITISH SUPER-HEAVY GUNS PART 2
BY N J M CAMPBELL

16.25IN BL MARK I

The twelve guns of this type were all built at Elswick but the differences between them were such that the designation of Mk I was abolished in July 1892 and they were known individually by their serial numbers. The origins of this gun go back to March 1883 when the Admiralty decided to arm the battleship *Benbow*, laid down on 1 November 1882, with two 100 ton guns to be supplied by Armstrong instead of the four 13.5in guns of the original design. It must be noted that the four ships of the French *Terrible* class, of which the first had been launched in 1881, were to have two 16.5in, though of a short and not very powerful type, and that Armstrong had already built 17in 100-ton guns for the Italian navy, while Woolwich were having great trouble in designing and building much smaller BL (Breech Loading) guns. In April 1883 Armstrong sent the design, No 12746, of the 17in gun they were then making for the *Lepanto*, the second of the Italian 17in gun ships, to the Ordnance Committee. After discussion two more 17in designs were submitted, Nos 12866 and 12867. These had chambers only 84.5in long instead of 102in and No 12866 was 31 calibres instead of 27, while the weights were 113-116 tons, which

the Admiralty objected to, in May 1883, as they did not wish the weight to exceed 100 tons. The Ordnance Committee therefore confined themselves to the *Lepanto* design, which they objected to on the grounds of too long a chamber, too short a gun and a jointed A tube.

The Admiralty then agreed to accept a weight of over 100 tons if this were essential and on 27 July 1883 Armstrong submitted design No 13375. This was for a 16.25in/30 cal gun with an 84.5in chamber, an improved method of jointing the A tube and a weight of 110½ tons. With a 900lb charge and a 1800lb projectile, the MV (muzzle velocity) was variously estimated at 2020 to 2127fs with a maximum pressure of 17 tons/sq in. After further discussion this design was altered to include a single piece A tube, at a price of 4 to 6 months delay, and on 16 September 1884 design No 15215, which incorporated this feature, was finally approved, orders for *Benbow's* two guns and one reserve having been placed on 16 February 1884. Slow burning cocoa powder – SBC – was approved for the guns on 24 August 1886 and the charge weight was later fixed at 960lb.

The history of the twelve guns is now given under their serial numbers.

NOS 1 AND 2

The construction was: A tube/breech piece (taking breech block), 17 hoops extending to muzzle/1 long hoop and 10 short hoops/8 hoops/7 hoops. All parts were made from steel forgings. The breech piece was secured to the A tube longitudinally by a serrated metal ring and the hoops of the 3 outer layers were secured by shoulders, apparently with yellow metal run in. The foremost hoop of the outer layer was held by a serrated metal ring. As the *Benbow* had been launched on 15 June 1885 the two guns were required in 1886 but No 1 was not proved until 1887 when it was found that the projectiles were not being properly rotated due to the rifling grooves being only 0.04in deep, as in the Italian guns. Nos 1 and 2 were, however, too urgently needed for the grooves to be deepened and in *Benbow's* gunnery trials in April 1888 the projectiles were reported as steady in flight. *Benbow* was completed in June 1888 but in December it was directed that her guns should be limited to half charges and Nos 1 and 2 were eventually replaced by Nos 11 and 12 in about May 1894.

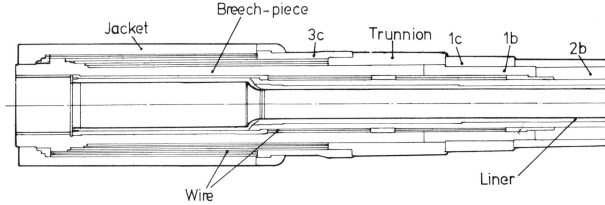

Jacket | Breech-piece | 3c | Trunnion | 1c | 1b | 2b | Wire | Liner

NO 3

Intended as a reserve gun for *Benbow* this was returned to Elswick for the rifling to be deepened to 0.06in and for the shot seating to be altered to take a 16.5in diameter driving band. The gun was delivered in December 1888 and used for range table firings, but it developed flaws in the bore and was also found to droop 0.75in. Further firings extended the flaws and slight openings appeared between the exterior hoops. It was accordingly sent to Elswick to be fitted with a short bore liner and for some alterations to the hoops. This comprised replacing the 14 forward hoops of the first layer by 3 long hoops or tubes and the 5 forward hoops of the second layer by a single long hoop. The third layer, of 9 hoops, and the fourth layer, of 7 hoops, were not altered. Further experimental firings caused flaws to develop forward of the liner and it was decided to fit a full length liner, the design of which was approved in October 1896.

NO 4

Completed with 0.06in rifling grooves and with a coned section at the start of the shot seating which gave a reduced MV of 2066fs at 14.5 tons/sq in pressure. After firing trials in the new battleship *Victoria* on 17 October 1889 it was found to have drooped by 0.7in with slight opening between hoops. As soon as the gun could be spared it was sent for strengthening which in this case comprised a long final hoop in the second layer replacing 5 short hoops and an additional short hoop beyond it. On re-proof in 1890 the droop increased from 0.3in to 0.75in with slight opening between hoops but further firing caused little change and it was accepted in September 1890 and sent to the *Victoria's* sister ship *Sans Pareil*. It was found to be oversize and a small amount had to be cut from the *Sans Pareil's* turret port to allow full depression.

NO 5

Completed with 0.06in rifling grooves as were all the later numbers. This gun was built up on a softer A tube than usual and during proof in April 1889, and subsequent rounds fired with the gun turned over, developed a droop of 1.4in with a bend of 0.7in to one side. Openings of up to 0.135in also occurred between the hoops. The Elswick authorities blamed this on the use of the usual proof carriage with the recoil not in the direction of the gun's axis. It was then mounted in *Victoria* but as after 12 rounds the droop increased to 2.5in there was nothing for it but to rebuild the gun on a new A tube, which was eventually decided upon 14 months later in December 1890. As rebuilt the hoops were as given for the short lined No 3 above except that there was one less short hoop in the second layer and the third layer comprised 2 fairly long and 4 short hoops. After reproof the gun was accepted in August 1892 and was sent to Malta as reserve gun.

NO 6

After two proof rounds in May 1889 openings appeared between the hoops and the gun seemed to be bending. There was a delay until October 1889 when it was decided to return the gun to Elswick for the second layer to have a long final hoop in place of the 5 short ones. The altered gun was proved and sent to Chatham for the *Victoria*, as a replacement for No 4 gun, by March 1890.

NO 7

This gun was altered before delivery in the same way as No 6, passed proof in January 1890 and was sent to the *Victoria* as a replacement for No 5 gun. In August 1891 a crack appeared in the A tube face at the muzzle which extended 5¼in into the bore. This was removed at Malta later in the year by cutting back the gun by about half a calibre.

NO 8

This gun was completed, like the strengthened No 4, with a long final hoop in the second layer in place of 5 short hoops and a short hoop beyond it. It was slightly larger than No 4 and was sent for proof in September 1890 when openings were found to be developing between the chase hoops, but the gun still went to the *Sans Pareil* for gunnery trials in December 1890. Two ¾-charge rounds were fired and it was then discovered that the foremost short hoop of the second layer had cracked through. The hoop was renewed at Woolwich and further rounds fired at the proof butts and at Shoeburyness, making a total of 18, but, as the separation of the hoops had increased and the gun now had a droop of 1.25in and was bent 0.95in to the right, it was rejected in March 1891. It was sent

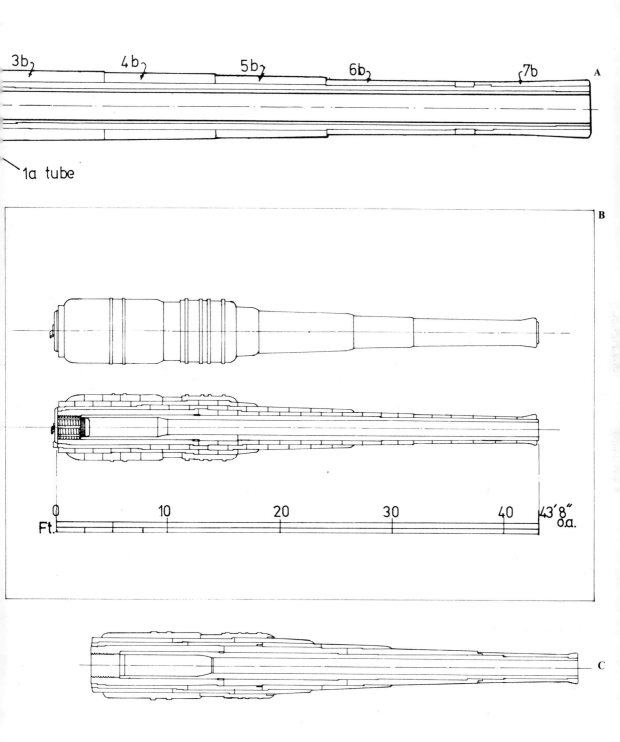

3b 4b 5b 6b 7b A

1a tube

B

10 20 30 40 43′8″ o.a.

Ft.

C

A 17in BL

B 16.25in BL Mk I

C 16.25in BL Nos 11 and 12

back to Elswick at the end of the year for the hoop to be cut off, from the muzzle to the thrust bands, the A tube straightened cold and the gun rebuilt with two long hoops in the forward part of the first layer and one in that of the second layer. It was however found necessary to use a new A tube. The gun was sent for re-proof in January 1894 when some movement of the outer hoops occurred and also some expansion of the bore and chamber. Two further rounds were fired in June which caused a little further expansion but it was decided to accept the gun in July 1894 and it was stored in England as a reserve gun.

NO 9

This was built to a different construction with A tube/breech piece (taking the breech block), 1 medium hoop, 2 short hoops, 2 long hoops or tubes, 1 short hoop, 1 long hoop or tube to the muzzle/1 long hoop, 4 short hoops, 1 long hoop/2 medium hoops, 1 short hoop, 1 medium hoop/7 short hoops. It passed proof in 1891 and was mounted in the *Sans Pareil*. A report of March 1898, when a total of 5 proof, 16 full, 40 practice and 18 reduced charges had been fired, shows that the first layer of hoops had then moved forward by a total of 0.26in.

NOS 10, 11 and 12

On 24 January 1890 the Admiralty approved that three more guns should be obtained from Elswick to an improved design provided that they were interchangeable with the other guns. Two Elswick designs, Nos 31305 without wire and 31306 with wire, dated 10 April 1890, were considered by the Ordnance Committee who recommended the wire design with some modifications. The Admiralty were concerned at the extra cost of £1000 for one wire wound gun or £2100 for three, and also at the presence o wire in that part of the gun outside the *Victoria* class turrets, and asked

for the DGOF (Director General of the Ordnance Factories) to be consulted as the design differed considerably from that of the experimental 9.2in/40 and 13.5in/30 which had successfully been made at Woolwich. The DGOF produced design No 8514C3, in which the wire was kept within the *Victoria's* turret, and eventually the Ordnance Committee recommended that the three guns should be made to a modified Elswick design, No 31306C of 27 November 1890, unless any were made at Woolwich when 8514C3 was to be used. The Admiralty, who had postponed

ordering the guns on 20 November 1890, agreed on 4 February 1891 on the understanding that the guns would be interchangeable with earlier ones and that the War Office were responsible. It should be noted that the Admiralty became responsible for naval guns in 1888-89 but the 16.25in remained a War Office responsibility. For reasons of cost the Admiralty wanted at least one built at Woolwich but this was vetoed, without doubt correctly as Woolwich had enough troubles with smaller guns.

The Elswick works would give no delivery date for a wire wound

16.25in as they had no experience of winding guns of that size and eventually, on 25 September 1891, it was recommended that No 18 be built to a modification of the 10 April 1890 design No 31305C as some forgings were already partly machined, and that Nos 11 and 12 be built to 31305D which had a thinner A tube at the muzzle end to bring it within the then safety conditions for a burst A tube. In explanation it should be said that Elswick usually worked on the 16.25in well in advance of formal sanction. The drawings were sealed on 17 December 1891.

The construction was as follows: A tube/breech piece (taking breech block), 1B hoop, 2B hoop, B tube to muzzle/1C, 2C, 3C hoops/1D, 2D, 3D hoops/jacket, E hoop machined for thrust rings. All hoops were long. There were screwed collars at the forward ends of the breech piece, 2C and E hoops where they were over the A tube, 1B and 3D hoops respectively.

No 10 was proved in 1893 and sent out to Malta as a reserve gun, while Nos 11 and 12, proved in the same year, both showed some expansion in the bore which was attributed by Elswick to a rather soft A tube and to the driving band which was considered to be excessively large. The expansion was worst in No 12 but was not very serious and the two guns replaced Nos 1 and 2 in *Benbow* in about May 1894.

It is clear that the 16.25in was an over-ambitious venture at a time when smaller guns such as the 12in/25 and 13.5in/30 had many troubles. Details were:
Weight (including breeech fittings) 112 tons 15cwt 90lb
Weight (less breech fittings) 110 tons 12cwt 51lb
These figures apply to Nos 1 and 2. The individual weights for the later guns are not known. They are usually listed as 111 tons nominal.

The battleship *Benbow,* the first vessel to be fitted with the 16.25in gun. The weight involved meant only one gun could be mounted in each barbette instead of two as in the earlier ships of the *Admiral* class which carried 13.5in guns

NMM

Length (oa) 43ft 8in – 524in
Length (bore) 30 cal – 487.5in
Diameter 65.5in max, 28in min
Chamber size 84.5 x 21.125in,
volume 28 660 cu in
Rifling 397.2-397.4in, Nos 1, 2 and
3 twist of 1 in 130 to 1 in 30 at
77.2in from muzzle then uniform,
Nos 4-12 1 in 60 to 1 in 30 at
muzzle, 78 grooves, polygroove
EOC section, 0.04 x 0.45in (in Nos
1 and 2) 0.06 x 0.45in (in Nos 3 to
12) lands 0.2045in. As relined No 3
had Mk III rifling with 396.9in
straight to 299.4in from muzzle
then increasing to 1 in 30 at muzzle,
78 grooves, polygroove modified
plain section, 0.06 x 0.42in, lands
0.2345in.
Projectile weight 1800lb
Charge 960lb slow burning cocoa
SBC (8 x 120lb)
Muzzle velocity 2087fs
Design pressure 17tons/sq in

A charge of Mk I Cordite was
considered but not adopted; 317$\frac{1}{2}$lb
size 50 + 8lb 6oz size 3$\frac{3}{4}$ gave an
MV of 2278fs at a pressure of 15.01
tons/sq in. The breech block was a
cylindrical screw with 6 plain
segments and a de Bange obturator.
There was no carrier and the block,
which was operated by hydraulic
power, was normally kept at the
fixed loading position as in the
contemporary 13.5 and 12in guns.
The mountings in all three ships
allowed 13° elevation and 5°
depression, with loading at
maximum elevation, and the range
at 13° was 12 400yds at the new gun
MV of 2087fs. The probable life
was 104 full charges. The rate of fire
was slow with 3 to 3$\frac{1}{2}$ minutes
between rounds but the 12in and
13.5in 'Admirals' were no faster,
and it was not until the introduction
of the improved 13.5in mountings
in the battleships *Nile* and *Trafalgar*
that the interval was reduced to
about 2 minutes 10 seconds.

The ammunition outfit was 100,
later 92, rounds per gun in *Benbow*
and 80 in the *Victoria* and *Sans
Pareil*. The proportions for 1892
were, in *Benbow*, 37 AP (armour
piercing), 44 Common and 11
Shrapnel and in the other two 32
AP, 38 Common and 10 Shrapnel.
If available 20 of the AP were to be
hollow steel shot. This had a

maximum length of 59.31in and
was required to be 'substantially
whole' after piercing a 20in
compound plate backed by 6in
wrought iron at normal impact and
at a velocity of 2100fs. The chilled
iron Palliser AP short was 43.57in
long and the nose fuzed common
and shrapnel 55in long. The forged
steel common shell had a burster of
187$\frac{1}{2}$lb of black powder and the
later, and cheaper, cast steel
common shell one of 179$\frac{1}{4}$lb. The
shrapnel shell contained 2330 4oz
iron shot. Later a base fuzed
pointed common was introduced;
this was 57.35in long with a 182lb
black powder burster. Figures dated
1890 give 58$\frac{1}{2}$in as the extreme
length of shell for power loading but
presumably it was found possible to
accommodate the steel AP shot at
its maximum length.

**PROJECTED 17IN COAST
DEFENCE GUN.**
The dreams of gun designers are
excluded from this article but an
exception has been made for the
17in/41 calibre of 1885-86. The
intention was to construct two
turrets each containing two of these
156 ton guns, as a reinforcement for
the Portsmouth defences. One
turret was to be located 400yds east
of Horse Sand Fort and the other
400yds south of No Man's Land.
No drawings of these turrets have
been found but it seems probable
that they would have resembled the
Torre Umberto which was erected
at Spezia by Armstrong. This
hydraulically powered work
completed in 1892 contained two
15.75in 119 ton Krupp guns firing a
2028lb projectile at an MV of
1804fs and had a revolving weight
of about 2000 tons of which 1400
tons was contributed by the cupola
roof of Gruson chilled iron. In any
event the cost of the Portsmouth
turrets was considered prohibitive
and the plan was altered to two forts
each containing two guns on the
usual single carriage and slide
mounting. The whole project seems
to have been abandoned in 1886.

Drawings of the gun show a liner
extending from the forward end of
the chamber to the muzzle inside
the 1A tube and joined to it and the

chamber liner by a curved threaded
ring. There was a 2A tube over the
chamber liner and this was joined to
the 1A tube by a shoulder. The line
of the 2A tube was continued for
about 14ft by wire and stop rings.
Over this was shrunk a complete
layer comprising the breech piece,
into which the breech block
screwed, and the 1B to 7B hoops
extending to the muzzle. A thick
layer of wire was wound over that
part of the breech piece which
covered the chamber, shot location
and part of the breech screw. This
was continued by the 3C hoop
which was partly over the forward
end of the wire, the trunnion piece,
1C and 2C hoops to a distance of
29ft 3in from the muzzle. Finally
the jacket, and what appears to be a
ring brazed to the 3C hoop,
extended for 159.8in from a point
2in from the breech face. Details
would have been:
Weight 156 tons
Length (oa) 61ft 11in – 743in
Length (bore) 41.12 cal – 700in
Diameter 69in max, 30in min
Chamber size 100 x 27in
Projectile weight 2240lb
Charge weight 1700lb
Muzzle velocity 2500fs
Design pressure 18 tons

It is as well that no attempt was
made to build this design.

**16IN GUN FOR RUSSIA,
VICKERS PATTERN A**
This gun was begun in 1914 before
the outbreak of the First World War
and was proved at Eskmeals on 22
August 1917. It was originally
intended as the prototype gun for a
class of three projected 32 000 ton
battleships to be built in Russia for
the Black Sea Fleet and which were
to be armed with three triple 16in
turrets. Although wire wound guns
were standard in Britain at that
time, they had never been accepted
by most foreign countries and
Vickers had already built
satisfactory wire free 10in guns for
the Russian cruiser *Rurik* and had
an order for twenty-four 14in guns
for the *Borodino* class
battlecruisers. The construction of
this gun, Vickers No 1712A –
known during the War as the '15
inch A', was thus very far from

1 The battleship *Victoria* fitting out during
  1889/90. The left 16.25in gun has been
  fitted in her single turret but the right gun is
  still to be installed

  NMM

2 The *Victoria* at Malta shortly after
  completion in 1890

  NMM

contemporary British practice. There were the usual tapered inner A and A tubes but with the favourite Vickers cannelured rings between the locating shoulders. Over the A tube were the B1, B2 and B3 tubes reaching to the muzzle and over these the C1 and C2 tubes for about two thirds of the gun's length. The next layer comprised the jacket and a screwed collar and finally the breech ring. The breech screw, held by the carrier, worked in a breech bush which was screwed into the C1 tube. Details were as follows:–

Weight (including breech mechanism) 107 tons 14cwt
Length (oa) 60ft – 720in
Length (bore) 43.65 cal – 698.45in
Diameter 56.6in max, 27in min
Chamber size 127 x 18.24in, volume 33 000 cu in
Rifling 565.5in long, grooves 0.12in deep – believed to have had the start of the rifling slightly coned so that the full depth was not attained for about 8in, a refinement present in the Vickers 10in and 14in guns for Russia.
Centre of gravity 248.2in from breech face (loaded) 249.45in (unloaded)
Projectile weight 2461lb
Charge weight 732lb NCT (Nitrocellulose tubular)
Muzzle velocity 2485fs
Working pressure 16.3 tons/sq in

At proof an MV of 2513fs was recorded at a temperature of 69°F and a pressure of 16.6tons/sq in. This was with a 734lb NCT charge of grain size 15.2in long, 0.79in outside diameter and 0.283in inside diameter. It was anticipated that 2600fs would be reached with a 765lb charge and a pressure of 18.7 tons/sq in. The nearest comparable standard British gun of that time, the 15in Mark I of 42 calibres, weighed 100 tons including the breech mechanism, had a larger diameter chamber of 107.505 x 20.0in and 30 590 cu in volume, was 68.5in diameter over the breech ring and had an unloaded centre of gravity 209.7in from the breech face. It fired a 1920lb shell at an MV of 2472fs, with a 428lb MD45 cordite charge at 80°F and 20 tons/sq in working pressure. The

performance of the Vickers 16in was very high relative to the gun's weight but the centre of gravity was far forward which would have meant large turrets, so that there was good reason for the 15in guns large breech ring. Unfortunately it is not know what the regularity of the 16in would have been with NCT but with MD45 its performance would have been drastically reduced, as is shown by the 14in for the *Borodino* class. This gun, the Vickers 14in Pattern 'B', was 50.4 cals in bore length, weighed 82 tons 28lb with breech mechanism, had a 21 940 cu in chamber and, with a 1648lb shell, was designed to attain an MV of 2700fs using a 540lb NCT charge of 18.5 tons/sq in pressure. A few entered British service in 1918-19 as the 14in Mk VI and at this pressure with a 1586lb shell the best that could be achieved with MD45 was a 313lb charge giving 2470fs MV.

In August 1917 the question of what to do with this gun arose, and there were discussions about its employment on land but its weight was considered too great. However, on 23 March 1918 the German long 21cm guns began to shell Paris at about 70 miles range and the production of a similar weapon became an urgent matter. It was thus decided to convert the 16in into a 205mm – 8.07in 'super velocity' gun to be known as the 8in sub-calibre Mk I. The A tube was cut back 42in at the muzzle and it, and the inner A tube were extended for 267.45in past the original muzzle by a new 2A tube. The B3 tube was cut back by 182.05in and was continued to the new muzzle by a B4 tube, with a screwed external guide ring joining B3 and B4. A new full length rifled liner was inserted in the 2A and inner A tubes. The details of the rifling and projectile were based on what could be learnt from fragments of the German shells which had been picked up. Details of the gun were as follows:
Weight (including breech mechanism) 138 tons 16cwt
Weight (less breech mechanism) 136 tons 19cwt
Length (oa) 82ft 3.35in – 987.35in

Length (bore) 119.9 cal – 968in
Chamber size 128.35 x 11.0in, volume 11 500cu in
Rifling uniform twist 1 in 45, 64 grooves 0.1005 x 0.198in, lands 0.198in (The shell body and forward driving band were pre-rifled)
Centre of gravity 333.5in from breech face (loaded) 333.85in (unloaded)
Projectile weight 249lb
Charge 313lb MD oval, 0.60 x 1.20in
Muzzle velocity 4901fs
Pressure 29.47tons/sq in

The conversion was completed in February 1919 and the above figures are those for the highest velocity reached in the trials. The wear at 1in from the commencement of rifling was about 0.02in per round. Unfortunately the heat treatment of the very long liner had to be carried out with improvised equipment at Vickers and it developed a crack so that only six rounds were fired and the forging for the replacement liner, which was to be heat treated at Woowich who had equipment that would take it, had to be scrapped. Thus no more was done with the gun and it was scrapped in late 1928. All rounds had been fired from the proof mounting with muzzle support and the service mounting, which allowed elevation from 40 to 58°, was never completed.

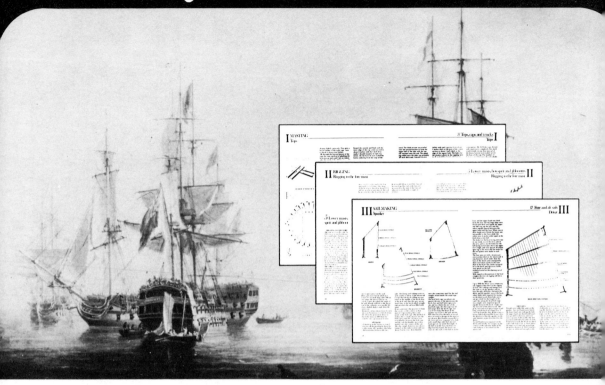
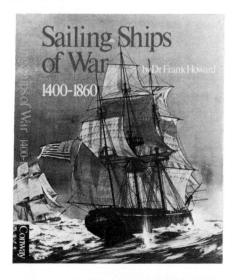

Editorial

I have never been a great believer in the often repeated opinion that in war the quality of the man has a greater influence on the outcome of the battle than the quality of the machine, mainly because it is far too great a generalisation and is little more than an extension of the mythical superiority of one race over another. I would however say that the quality of personnel training, morale and equipment efficiency are of almost equal importance and while limitations in the latter can often be made up for in the former the reverse seldom applies.

The high quality of the British seaman has often been used to explain why the Royal Navy with, supposedly, inferior ships were so successful against the French during the Napoleonic Wars. Robert Gardiner's recent articles on 18th Century Frigate design (Parts 1 and 2 in Warships 9 and 10, Part 3 to appear in Warship 12) reveals that British warships were not in fact inferior in design and moreover showed operational superiority over their French counterparts in many ways. Added to this the British spent far more time at sea (personnel training) and were extremely confident (morale) and thus possessed an all round superiority. Hardly surprising then that the British were so successful against an enemy with specialised ships of limited capability, whose personnel training was limited by lack of sea experience and whose crews, being subjected to a long series of defeats and extended periods in harbour, could hardly have had a high morale.

The old argument could more sensibly be applied to more recent events. During the many naval actions off the Solomons in 1942/43 the Japanese often demonstrated a very marked superiority in night fighting despite the American advantage of radar. Their greatest success was the Battle of Savo Island, of 9 August 1942, in which the Japanese sunk four cruisers, HMAS *Australia* and the three *New Orleans* class ships (whose design history is described in this issue by Norman Friedman) *Astoria, Vincennes* and *Quincy,* with only minor damage to themselves. Theoretically this should not have happened as the Americans had superior ships, and certainly had personnel of high quality and morale. The Japanese, however, had developed their night fighting technique to a high degree, both with equipment and training, to a point where it was quite usual for a Japanese lookout to make a sighting before American radar picked up his own ship. Added to this they had the great advantages of the long-lance torpedo, with a range well in excess of anything else in the world, and flashless cordite. In most other technical respects the Japanese were inferior but the advantages they did have more than made up for this, much to the cost of the US Fleet. On the American side one can see lack of training and lack of knowledge of the performance of the long-lance as prime causes of their early defeats. (It should also be said that the performance of early radar sets was not particularly good). Americans are, however, quick learners and by the end of the Solomons campaign they had corrected many of their deficiencies while the Japanese had begun the downward spiral which was marked by a general lack of further technical advance and a much reduced emphasis on training.

Had the superiority of men over machines really been valid then the Japanese would have had a substantial advantage for much longer, not because they were superior to Americans but because their approach to war was so fanatical. In the event Japan was defeated by superior technology, training and weight of numbers; in the end they had only their fanaticism as a substitute for morale while the allies had all three legs of their tripod – training, moral and equipment – fully developed.

John Roberts

THE NEW ORLEANS CLASS

BY NORMAN FRIEDMAN

In common with the other major navies, the US Navy approached the problem of the 10 000 ton 'Washington Treaty cruiser' by emphasizing speed and firepower. Indeed, early sketch designs of the *Pensacola* class included no armour at all, although ultimately protection against 5in destroyer fire was provided. At the time it appeared that no more could be achieved under the Washington Treaty weight of 10 000 tons, as long as a relatively high speed (32.5kts) and nine or ten 8in guns were required. Thus, although the General Board, responsible for the outline Characteristics of US warships, was concerned with the vulnerability of cruiser guns and of their fire controls as early as 1925, the second class of US heavy cruisers, the *Chester* class (CA 26-31), showed no great improvement in armour over the first. These ships did show a concern with underwater damage; in particular they sacrificed one gun in order to buy a rearrangement of their machinery. With alternate engine and boiler rooms no single torpedo hit could leave them dead in the water. In the course of their design a plotting room was added below decks to permit them to employ effective director control of their 8in guns at very long ranges.

The original concept of the 8in gun cruiser had been that it would engage lighter forces at relatively short ranges, overwhelming them by weight of fire rather than by outranging them. It was assumed that there was little hope of protecting such ships against 8in fire, particularly as that fire would be delivered at short range. However, with the advent of effective director control for 8in guns, battle range between two heavy cruisers might well open to a point at which armour protection might be practicable, a point realized in the US Navy in the *New Orleans* class. These ships are representative of a shift in the other navies building heavy cruisers as well, as typified by the French *Algerie* and the Italian *Zara*.

An important factor in the designs of the *New Orleans* class was that it was not until the end of the 1920s that the US Bureau of Construction and Repair (C&R), responsible for warship design, learnt to build ships up to the treaty limit. The problem was that the standard displacement specified by the Washington Treaty was not a realistic operational displacement and so could not be the basis of a design. Rather, some estimate of operational (normal) displacement, which included fuel and reserve (boiler) feed water, had to be made, from which machinery power (hence weight) could be estimated, but the type of machinery selected determined just how much fuel and feed water was needed to achieve a

The New Orleans class cruiser *Minneapolis* on 15 September 1941. She, together with the *New Orleans, Tuscaloosa* and *San Francisco* survived the coming war but her remaining three sisters, *Astoria, Quincy* and *Vincennes* were all lost on 9 August 1942 during the Battle of Savo Island
USN

required steaming endurance. Moreover, the US treaty cruisers were designed to employ machinery and weapons not previously used in any other US ships. The constructors knew that it was absolutely essential to come in under the 10 000 ton limit and consequently left themselves generous margins for error, in addition to the usual margin of several per cent provided in any design. The building yards were encouraged to save weight and received bonuses for tons below design.

The results might be described either as better than expected or as embarrassing. While representatives of C&R were explaining at General Board Hearings that extra protection was impossible on the weights, the new cruisers were coming out very light indeed: *Pensacola,* designed for 10 000 tons with a 252-ton margin, actually displaced 9138 and

Northampton, with a 318-ton margin, displaced only 8997 tons. Although these ships were not completed until 1929 or later, C&R was aware of this situation rather earlier. It received quarterly reports of weights placed aboard ships under construction with estimates of totals. Thus by 1928 the C&R cruiser designers were ready to consider better protected ships, just as the General Board was ready to request them.

At that time the US Navy expected to receive authorization for a long-term cruiser programme of fifteen ships in three groups: CL (later CA, heavy cruisers) 32-36, 37-41, and 42-46. C&R expected to prepare a design for each group, and hoped that changes from group to group would be relatively small. On 5 April 1928 the General Board approved the Characteristics for CA32-36: they were to duplicate the *Chesters*, except that 'any weight which might be found available be used in the increase of protection, primarily of the magazines.' By this time it was evident that enough weight was available to increase magazine sides from 3.75 to 5in and magazine crowns from 2 to 2.5ins. The length of CA32 was increased 10ft to compensate for the elimination of the bulbous bow of the previous class: 'it is considered that vessels of the size and type of the Light Cruisers will have a greater tendency to pound when driven at speed in a seaway if fitted with a bulbous forefoot'. Finally, it would be possible for the plotting room to be accommodated within the protected magazine area forward.

The result was still less than well protected. Its guns were mounted in light gunhouses, essentially no more than splinter-proof, with very thin barbettes. Machinery protection against shellfire was still good only against destroyer fire. However, it appeared that the C&R design was the best the General Board could hope for and on 28 February 1929 it recommended that the design be approved, and indeed that CA37-41 be built to the same design, except for two to be built as flagships.

MAGAZINE PROTECTION
There was one controversial point in all the cruiser designs. Magazines were above the waterline, in order to keep them as far as possible from the outer skin of the ship, a practice that reflected the concerns of the First World War in which underwater damage was far more frequent than damage by shell fire. However, magazines projecting above the waterline depended entirely upon their side and crown armour for protection against shellfire, whereas those below water were largely shielded by the water through which shells would have to pass. By late 1929 there was considerable criticism of the basic

1

magazine design, especially since the potential of director-controlled 8in cruiser fire was beginning to be appreciated. For example, the Director of Fleet Training argued that

'The seriousness of this situation becomes apparent when the tactical uses of these vessels are considered. They are badly needed in the fleet to support our destroyers. This means going in with them, beating off light craft opposition which would consist of light cruisers, probably of equal power. Another tactical use of our light cruisers is to repulse enemy destroyer attacks. When so employed these vessels might have destroyers as their targets but they would themselves be the targets of the enemy light cruisers supporting the attack . . .

'The new cruisers as designed are so very vulnerable to 8in gunfire that to employ them tactically as described would be to court disaster, yet unless we do so employ them we cannot hope to make our destroyers really effective against 'Red' or 'Orange'. It would seem that we are in danger of forgetting the lesson of the battlecruisers at Jutland, where the German vessels justified their existence because of their defensive strength and those of the British proved such failures because of the vulnerability of their magazines.'

C&R noted that it would indeed be possible to lower the magazines of CA32-36, provided a loss of 576 tons of fuel oil were accepted; 50 tons more armour would be required to protect the forward bulkhead of the engine room spaces

where it would be uncovered by the lowered forward magazines. By way of compensation the magazine armour would have to be reduced by 1.2in on the sides; alternatively the ship might be lengthened about 8ft to increase oil stowage but then magazine side armour would have to be reduced by 2.9ins. The situation aft was far less favourable because of the hull form there. For example, the shafts could not be lowered without bringing the tips of the propellers below the line of the keel, and C&R noted that 'the possible amount of lowering shafts is very small in any event. Since some working space is required in shaft alleys over the shafts, these alleys will project into the magazines, reducing their floor areas and the cubic capacity available for stowage of ammunition.' At best the magazines could be lowered about 30in and then at great cost in redesign and crowding.

There was one other problem. The contracts for CA33 and 35, which would become *Portland* and *Indianapolis,* had been awarded to private yards and any change from the original C&R design, then, would be extremely expensive. On the other hand, Navy Yards had been assigned the construction of the other three ships, CA32, 34 and 36, and in that case there would be no contractual problems, although any massive change would involve considerable delays. Meanwhile, in the late summer of 1929, the General Board was beginning to reconsider its action on the next group, CA37-41.

'IMMUNE ZONES'

The Bureau of Ordnance in particular was urging that in future Characteristics be written, not in terms of particular armour thicknesses, but rather in terms of *immune zones* in the face of particular guns – zones defined by the *least* range at which belt armour would keep out shells and the *greatest* range at which deck armour would keep out plunging shells. The great advantage of specifying an immune zone was that it made clear the balance of protection represented by the design, where otherwise deck protection might correspond to a range *inside* that corresponding to side armour.

In December 1929 the General Board called for a new design for CA37-41 to reflect immune zones, measured against 8in fire at a target angle of 60° (90° would be dead abeam, so that this was a less stringent requirement), of 12 000 to 24 000 yards for magazines, and 15 000 to 24 000 for engines, boilers and plotting rooms. This improvement had to be achieved without any reduction in speed below 32.5kts and without any reduction in battery below nine 8in indeed, a requirement for eight rather than the previous four 5in/25AA weapons was stated. In contrast to the *Chesters,* all aircraft were to be carried abaft the after funnel – this was at the request of the Bureau of Aeronautics, which really wanted a catapult on the fantail. One improvement the new Characteristics did not show was any increase in gun mount protection. The new design, like the

USS *Astoria* (CA34) shows only a few modifications in this November 1941 post refit photograph. Splinter protection has been applied to her eight 5in/25 guns and four quadruple 1.1in machine gun mountings have been added, two on top of the pilot house and two on the fantail (where the tubs for their directors are also visible). The foremast carries a platform intended for later installation of an SC air search radar. The big liferafts on the sides on the searchlight tower amidships were probably also new
USN

USS *San Francisco* (CA38) in October 1944 after refit at Mare Island showing an appearance typical of the *New Orleans* class late in the Second World War. Her modifications were dictated by considerations of air attack; a large open bridge, a searchlight platform cut away to clear the arcs of fire of AA weapons and a substantial increase in AA firepower
USN

old ones, would show little more than blast and fragment cover over the 8in guns.

C&R was not entirely happy with the new Characteristics. In December it offered five sketch designs, two of them armed with twelve 6in guns and two with speed reduced to 31kts. The alternative, the one the General Board accepted, was a radical redesign. Magazines and shell rooms were lowered beneath the waterline: 'in case of damage to the shell, water still spread athwartships, reducing stability by introducing free water surface to the full width of the ship, and putting the vessel down by the head due to the weight of entering water. This danger did not exist in the same degree in the earlier vessels where the magazine protection extended above the waterline. In the new design the magazine floor forward is about 9ft above the keel line and a greater amount aft, so that there is some protection against explosion of torpedoes or mines, although not as much protection as if the magazines were on the same level as in preceding cruisers. Also there are but two skins instead of three in the previous designs'.

As a means of weight saving the machinery spaces were lowered and the draughts increased to reduce the vertical extent of the belt armour over them. In addition, each boiler room was shortened by 4ft, on the assumption that a new boiler would become available. A more detailed study by the Bureau of Engineering showed that the reduction in headroom in the machinery and

boiler spaces could be achieved only if both engine rooms and both boiler spaces were together, ie if the immunity to a single torpedo or shell hit was given up. The justification cited at the time was the vastly improved armour protection achieved, but this did not answer the torpedo problem.

DESIGN MODIFICATIONS
All this came at some considerable expense. In order to increase draught from 19ft 6in as on previous ships to 22ft 6in in the new one, without paying a high price in hull weight, it was necessary to decrease freeboard by about 3ft (28ft forward and 15ft aft, as compared to 31ft forward and 19ft 6in aft on the *Chesters*); moreover, beam decreased 5ft. 'This is of great importance in reducing the weight of deck protection, but it may be accompanied by a small decrease in range of stability'. Yet another weight-saver was a reduction in length, originally to 570ft; the bulbous bow was reintroduced to make up for the shorter waterline length. It turned out that the hoped-for savings in machinery space length were not forthcoming, as the Bureau of Engineering could save 4ft on each engine room but not on each boiler room; ultimately length (waterline) was set at 578ft.

Rear Admiral Rock, Chief of C&R, was not too enthusiastic: 'it will be noted that the net result will be a moderate sacrifice in comfort and convenience; less comfortable quarters for the crew since they either have all to be quartered in the upper decks in a smaller total space

1 An excellent view of the midship structure of *San Francisco* showing some of the alterations made to the ship in 1944. The starboard aircraft crane was landed to reduce topweight and allow the addition of a quadruple 40mm Bofors mounting in its place. Note also the new, very heavy mainmast which seems far too strong for the SG and other light aerials it carries. Its platform, however, was reserved for an SP fighter-control radar
USN

2 Another view of *San Francisco* at Mare Island; the vessel in the background is a *Cleveland* class cruiser
USN

than on present designs of 10 000 ton Light Cruisers or else a portion of them be assigned to spaces without natural light or ventilation; less convenient because of reduced head room in machinery spaces and possibly more congested machinery rooms than at present . . . It should be noted, as pointed out in some of the hearings before the General Board, that neither the No 37 to 41 class as contemplated nor the preceding classes will have waterline protection forward and aft of the machinery spaces, although this deficiency will not be so serious on the No 24 to 36 ships as in No 37 to 41, because the box protection of magazines on the earlier vessels extended above the waterline and so would tend to prevent a complete spread of water athwartships in case of damage to the shell plating . . .

'. . . the Bureau believes that a degree of protection never before realized in any navy on a vessel of such seaworthiness, high speed and heavy gun power has been realized but the various studies that have been made so far, including this latest one, all point to the conclusion that 10 000 tons standard displacement is too small displacement on which to ensure a well balanced design, if the ship be armed with an efficient battery . . . and if high speed be an essential requirement . . .'

Even more was squeezed into the design in the course of preliminary studies. Thus when it presented its final sketch design at the end of March 1930, C&R proudly noted that it had provided full turrets with 6in face plates, 2.25in crowns, and 1.5in sides, compared to a previous

standard of 2.5, 2, and 0.75in respectively; they sat on 5in barbettes (1.5in) and there was an 8ft diameter, 2.5in (1.25in) conning tower. Further weight saving details included the provision of combination boat and aircraft cranes, made possible by the location of the catapults abaft the second funnel; now that the aircraft crane was no longer stepped from the mainmast, that could be reduced to a simple pole carrying radio antennas. The tripod foremast could also be reduced for a further saving in weight.

On the other hand, the design was now so tight that it could not be adapted as a flagship. The original CA37-41 Characteristics had called for one cruiser of the group to be fitted as a cruiser division flagship and another as a Fleet flagship. The first remained practical but the second would add about 75 tons; C&R 'brought out the point that, in order to obtain the greatly increased protection desired by the Department in these vessels, it had been necessary to reduce the margin to a point not previously accepted as satisfactory, and that this point, and the necessity of making no changes during construction which would add weight, must be recognized by the Department'.

Indeed, the only major changes still to be made in the design were the elimination of torpedo tubes and of the tripod foremast, the latter in favour of a tower bridge of the type also fitted in the *New Mexico* class battleships as reconstructed at the same time. Rock was able to overcome some of the problems he had raised by providing a short waterline belt forward, sufficient to keep out destroyer fire at 'moderate ranges'.

The General Board was sufficiently impressed with the new C&R design to suggest, on 25 April 1930, that it be applied to the Navy Yard built CA32 *(New Orleans)*, 34 *(Astoria)* and 36 *(Minneapolis)*. The cost, $700 000 per ship and a delay of twelve months, was considered acceptable. However, the other two ships of the five-ship programme, privately built, could not be redesigned, although they did receive some additional protection. As for the series to which the design had originally been addressed it fell victim to a combination of the Great Depression and the London Naval Conference of 1930. Only four more ships were built to the

New Orleans design, and all were modified to some extent. In CA37 *(Tuscaloosa)* and 38 *(San Francisco)* small weight savings, including a lighter 8in gun, bought more barbette armour 6.5 rather than 5in, but the very small design margin was more than wiped out. Thus when quadruple 1.1in machine guns were requested for CA39 *(Quincy)*, a general redesign was already in progress to bring the ship below the Treaty limit. The barbettes were reduced to 5.5in, turret No 1 was moved aft 8ft and the forward end of the magazine moved aft 16ft (to make up for the reduction in length of magazine spaces forward, the armour side of the magazine was moved out to the side of the ship), turret No 2 was raised 6in and the steering gear enclosure was reduced in size. For the first time in a US cruiser, emergency electrical power was to be provided by diesel generators rather than by storage batteries. The final ship in the series, CA44 *(Vincennes)*, repeated the *Quincy* design.

The quarterdeck of *San Francisco* at Mare Island in 1944
USN

CONCLUSIONS

The *New Orleans* class was the direct design ancestor of all later US large cruisers; it developed into the *Brooklyn* and *Wichita* which were the direct ancestors of the World War II *Clevelands* and *Baltimores*. For example, it introduced the turret to US practice and the submerged magazines fore and aft of a waterline machinery space. Perhaps more importantly, the *New Orleans* design introduced into US design practice the explicit use of an immune zone, against which design

trade-offs could be evaluated.

Clearly their designer, Admiral Rock, considered them unbalanced. The General Board saw them as the first case in which all of those 10 000 tons had actually been used – in fact the *New Orleans* class was somewhat overweight as completed. In battle, they were unfortunate: the Japanese had developed surface torpedo warfare to a high art, and in the Solomons US cruisers were subjected to it, as well as to intense 8in shellfire. Both contributed to the loss of three ships of this class, but here it is impossible to go further and say just how much better or worse the earlier *Portlands* would have have fared. The one simple conclusion is that no 10 000 ton cruiser could be entirely adequate, which is no great surprise, given the evolution of cruisers as soon as the Treaty restrictions were allowed to lapse.

A NOTE ON SOURCES

Material for this article was taken from files of the General Board held by the US Navy Operational Archives (Washington Navy Yard), from files of the former Bureau of Construction and Repair (National Archives) and from the former classified correspondence files of the Secretary of the Navy (National Archives). I am particularly grateful to Dr Dean Allard and to Kathy Lloyd, formerly of the Operational Archives, for their assistance in connection with General Board files. The specification is from a notebook kept by the Preliminary Design Division of the Bureau of Construction and Repair.

	Portland	*New Orleans*
Std Displacement (tons)	10 283	10 047
Normal Displacement (tons)	11 833	11 515
GM (Normal) (ft)	3.40	3.75
Length (OA) (ft)	610	588
Length (WL) (ft)	592	578
Beam (ft)	66-0½in	61-9in
Draft (ft)	19-5¹/₈in	21-7in
At (tons)	11 574	11 515
Armour (lb)		
Belt abreast Machinery	90 over 30	200 tapering to 130 over 30
Magazines (side)	230	160 tapered to 120
Protective Deck:		
Machinery	60 over 40	90
Magazines	85	90
Designed SHP	107 000	
Designed speed (knots)	32.5	32.7
Radius (miles/knots)	10 000/15	10 000/15

Each ship is armed with nine 8in/55 and eight 5in/25 AA guns and carries four aircraft which use two catapults.

Note Displacement data above are taken from inclining experiments of the ships as built (*Indianapolis* for *Portland* class); note that both ships came out heavy. Armour data is given in lb per square foot, with (roughly) 40lb per inch thickness. In *New Orleans*, deck armour is reinforced by some armour applied to other decks. Note too, that a single thickness of 90lb plate is more than equivalent to a combined thickness of 60 and 40lb, in resistive strength.

The *Varyag* as completed
CPL W/11/014

Sunk at Chemulpho 1904
re floated 8th Aug 1905
now "Soya"

IMPERIAL RUSSIAN NAVY CRUISER VARYAG

BY ADAM SMIGIELSKI

The protected cruiser *Varyag* was built in America according to Russian specifications prepared and published in 1897. These called for four classes of warship (battleships of 13 000 tons, protected scout cruisers of 6000 tons, small scout cruisers of 3000 tons and torpedo boat destroyers of 350 tons) which were to be built as a reinforcement to the Russian Far Eastern Fleet. The 6000 ton cruisers, considered as possible commerce raiders and officially known as first class cruisers, were to be fast (23-24kts) and well armed with quick firing 152mm (6in) guns. A detailed specification for these ships is given in Table 1.

Varyag was ordered together with the cruiser *Askold*, the battleships *Retvisan* and *Cesarevic* and the small cruisers *Bojarin* and *Novik*. As the Russian shipyards were at the time overloaded with naval construction, ships were ordered in France, Germany, the USA and Denmark. *Varyag* and *Retvisan* were ordered from William Cramp & Sons of Philadelphia, the contract for *Varyag* being signed on 11 (23) April 1898 by Admiral V R Vierhovskij for the Russians and by Mr C Cramp for the builders. The contract for the cruiser specified

that the price should not exceed 2 138 000 dollars (4 233 240 roubles). The details of the ship were as follows:

DIMENSIONS
Length: 129.56m, 425ft (oa) 121.90m, 400ft (pp) Beam: 15.85m, 52ft (moulded) Draught: 5.94m, 19.5ft (mean at normal displacement). Length/beam ratio was therefore 7.69 and beam/draught ratio 2.67. Block coefficient was 0.57 and actual metacentric height 0.7m (2.3ft) at normal load and 0.6m (1.97ft) at full load.

DISPLACEMENT
Normal displacement was calculated at 6500 tons and the full load displacement was about 7020 tons; it was later to be increased to over 8000 tons.

MACHINERY
The machinery of *Varyag* was typical for cruisers of her time. She carried thirty Niclausse boilers arranged in three boiler rooms, with ten in the forward boiler room, eight in the midship boiler room and twelve in the after boiler room. They were divided into four groups with one funnel for each group.

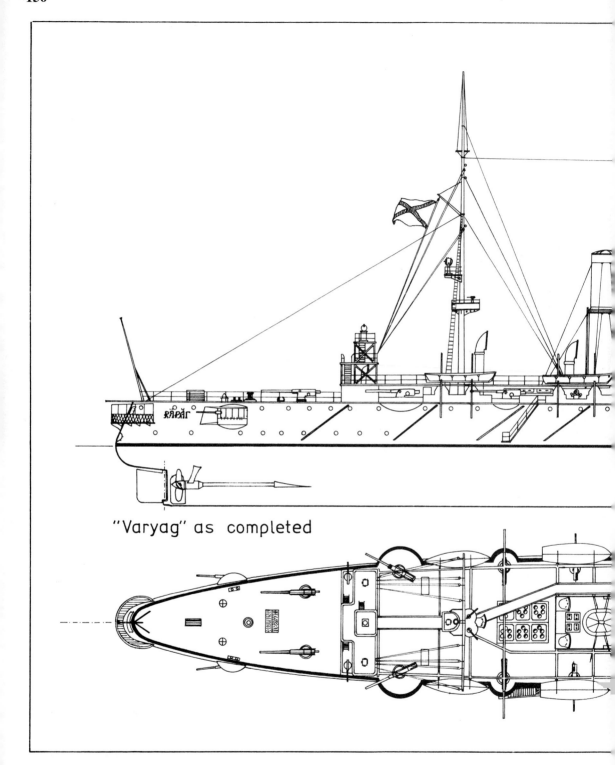

"Varyag" as completed

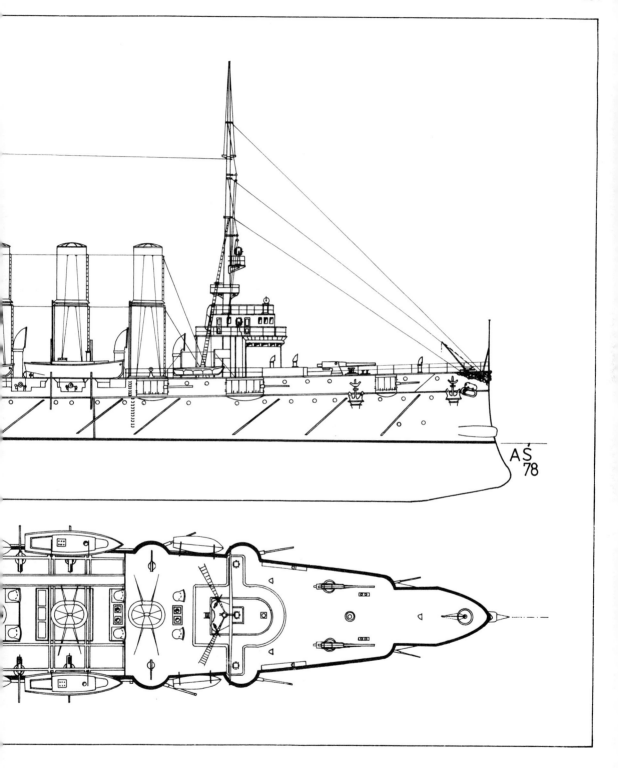

AŚ
78

FIGURE 1

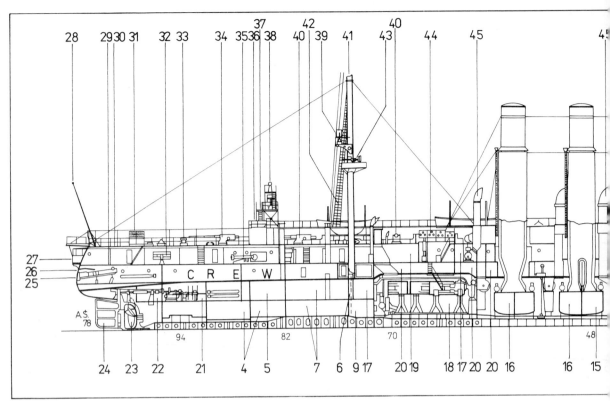

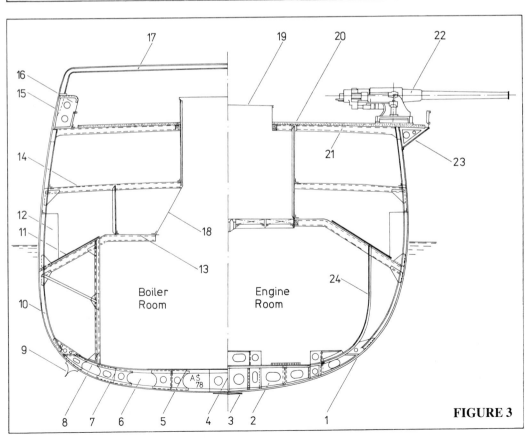

FIGURE 3

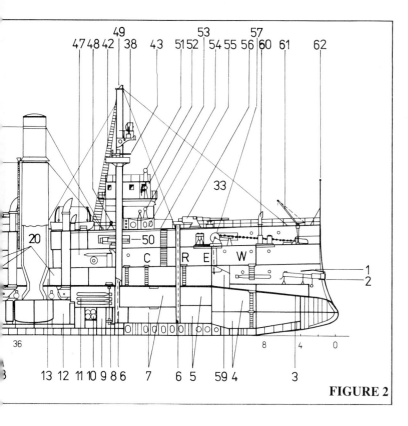

FIGURE 2

Total heating surface was 5786sq m (62 250sq ft) the working pressure 18kg cm (256psi) and the strength test pressure 28kg/sq cm (398psi). The boilers were 3m (10ft) high and contained 9240 tubes in all. Normally the ship carried 120 tons of feed water in the double bottom and in the boilers themselves and the evaporators could provide 180 tons of water every 24 hours.

The two main steam engines were of the vertical triple expansion type and were designed for 20 000ihp. They were 14m (46ft) long, 4.5m (14.76ft) high (including base) and were installed in two parallel compartments separated by a longitudinal bulkhead. This was a dangerous arrangement in view of preserving stability after damage as flooding would be restricted to one side of the ship. Each engine had four cylinders; one high pressure, one intermediate pressure and two low pressure with respective diameters of 1.02 (3.35), 1.58 (5.18) and 1.73m (5.68ft) and working pressures of 14 (199), 8.4 (119) and 3.5kg/sq cm (50psi). Piston stroke was 0.91m (3ft) and maximum shaft speed 160rpm. The shafts drove two 3-bladed bronze screws, of about 4.4m (14.4ft) diameter, the pitch of which could be altered for docking. The rudder was of a standard streamlined type with a surface area of 12sq m (170sq ft).

Western sources incorrectly state that *Varyag* was fitted with thirty Miyabara boilers when in service with the Japanese Navy, in fact she retained her original installation until the end of her career.

ELECTRIC PLANT

The electric plant, providing power at 105 volts DC, consisted of three main dynamos driven by fast rotating steam engines; two, of 132kW output each, were located below the armoured deck, one forward and one aft, and one, of 66kW, was installed in the living quarters. In addition the ship's two steam boats each had a dynamo of 2.6kW supplying power at 65 volts. The total output was very small by today's standards but it was sufficient for the time. The boiler

Figure 2
Longitudinal section of *Varyag*:
1 Armoured cover on bow torpedo tube **2** Bow torpedo tube **3** Armoured deck **4** Storage **5** 75mm magazine **6** Ammunition hoist **7** 152mm magazine **8** Bilge pump **9** 47mm magazine **10** Magazine for mines **11** Magazine for torpedoes **12** Forward boiler room **13** Armoured cover to funnel uptakes **14** Electric motor for bilge pump **15** Middle boiler room **16** After boiler room **17** Dynamo room **18** Engine room **19** Mechanical workshop **20** Coal bunker **21** Steering compartment **22** Helm **23** Port screw **24** Rudder **25** Stern torpedo tube **26** Armoured cover on after torpedo tube **27** Stern gallery **28** Ensign staff **29** Living quarters **30** Upper deck **31** Commander's companionway **32** 75mm gun **33** Capstan **34** Stern 152mm gun **35** Side torpedo tube in the officers' messroom **36** Skylight of officers' messroom **37** After command post **38** Main after compass **39** Searchlight **40** 152mm gun **41** Mainmast **42** Shrouds **43** 47mm guns in fighting top **44**

Engine room skylight **45** Boiler room ventilators **46** Steam launch **47** Port torpedo tube **48** 64mm gun **49** Foremast **50** 152mm gun below forecastle deck **51** Main forward compass **52** Pilot house **53** Conning tower **54** Base of conning tower **55** Forecastle deck **56** Forward 152mm gun **57** Anchor capstan **58** 75mm gun **59** Chain locker **60** Bollard **61** Anchor davit **62** Jackstaff

Figure 3
Cross-section of *Varyag* looking forward:
1 Hull plating **2** Floor **3** Keel plate **4** Vertical keel **5** Double bottom plating **6** Double bottom tanks **7** Stringer **8** Longitudinal boiler room bulkhead **9** Bilge keel **10** Frame **11** Armoured deck slope **12** Compartments filled with cellulose **13** Armoured deck flat **14** Deck beam **15** Bulwark **16** Hammocks **17** Boat skids **18** Armour cover of funnel uptakes **19** Skylight **20** Upper deck **21** Upper deck beams **22** 152mm gun **23** Sponson **24** Longitudinal bulkhead in engine room

TABLE NO 1

Some of the proposals for 6000 ton protected cruisers sent in by various shipyards and worked out according to Russian Admiralty specifications

Firm (name of ship)	Place won by project (Date of contract)	Displacement tons	Dimensions m(ft)				Metacentric height m (ft)
			Length	Beam	Height	Draught	
1 Russian Admiralty Specification		no more than 6000	not given				not less than 0.76 (2.5)
2 Germania, Germany (Askold)	–1– (August 1898)	5900	130 (426)	15 (49.2)	10.2 (33.5)	6.2 (20.3)	
3 Vulkan, Germany (Bogatyr)	–1bis– (August 1898)	6250	124 (406)	16.2 (53.1)	10.5 (34.4)	6.3 (20.7)	0.76 (2.5)
4 W Cramp & Sons, USA (Varyag)	–5– (April 1898)	6000	121.9 (400)	15.8 (51.8)		5.9 (19.4)	0.76 (2.5)

ARMOUR mm (in)

	Armoured deck		Side armour			
Flat	Slope	over engine spaces	elevators	bases of funnels	conning tower	
1 not given	not given	not given	38 (1½)	38 (1½)	152 (6)	
2 40 (¾)	76 (3)	100 (4)			150 (5.9)	
3 37-51 (1½-2)	73 (2.9)	84 (3.3)				

TABLE NO 2

Particulars of guns and machine guns

Type	naval	naval	Baranovski	Revolver 5 barrels	naval
Calibre (mm)	152	75	63.5	47	130
Calibre (in)	6	2.95	2.49	1.85	5.1
Weight of barrel (tons)	5.8	0.9	0.1	0.57 mount.	5.3
Length of bore (calibres)	45	50	19	–	55
Powder charge					
AP shot (kg/lbs)	–	2.36/52	–	–	–
Common shot (kg/lbs)	–	–	0.41/0.9	–	10.8/23.8
Weight of shell					
AP (kg/lbs)	40.5/89	4.8/10.6	–	–	–
Common (kg/lbs)	50/110	5.98/13	2.95/6.5	0.99/2.2	36.9/81.4
Muzzle velocity (m/sec/fs)	793/2600	819/2700	372/1200	425/1400	823/2700
Muzzle energy (mt/ft)	1330/4363	186/610	–	–	850/2788
Perforation at muzzle (cm/in) Krupp steel	19.3/7.6	12/4.7	–	–	–
Range (m/yds)	9800/10 700 at 15°	7000/7650 at 15°			16 500/18 000 at 20°
Weight of mounting (tons)	11			0.57	13.7
Remarks		rate of fire 10 rpm	fitted with wheels for land use	rate of fire 40rpm	rate of fire 8rpm designed by Vickers

Coal tons		Max range		Engines & Boilers			
ormal	full	nautical miles	No of screws	Boiler type	IHP		Speed on 12hr full power trial
		5000	2	Belleville			23
'10	1100	6500	3	Schultz	19 000		23
'20	1070	5000	2	Normand	19 500		23
'20		5000	2	Niclausse			23

Varyag in 1916 after her return to Russia
Courtesy A Preston

43°C in the other. Trial displacement was calculated as 6500 tons with a mean draught of 5.94m (19.5ft).

After some serious difficulties with the engines, the next series of trials was begun on 15 July 1900. This time the high pressure cylinder of the port engine was destroyed but this defect was repaired by 15 September 1900 when the *Varyag* went to sea once more. This time she reached 23kts and maintained this speed for 12 hours with 14 157ihp, 149rpm and boiler pressure at 17.5kg/sq cm (250psi); without forced draught. It was calculated that endurance would be 5270nm at 10kts, with 62rpm and 1200ihp. The normal coal capacity was 770 tons with the maximum coal stowage of 1350 tons.

HULL AND ARMOUR
The extreme length of the *Varyag's* hull caused some difficulties at the design stage, the length to beam ratio being much higher than in other cruisers of the time, but these were successfully overcome. The armour protection was arranged on the same lines as most of the protected cruisers of the period. The armoured deck was placed 6.48m (21.3ft) above the base line generally and at 7.1m (23ft) over the engine rooms, while the lower edge of the slope of the armour deck terminated 1.1m (3.6ft) below the waterline. The horizontal part of the armour was made up of a double layer of 19mm (¾in) plates and the slope of a double layer of 38.1mm (1½in) plates. These gave the total thickness of 38 (1½in) and 76.2mm (3in) respectively. The plates were made of nickel steel by Carnegie. Being a protected cruiser *Varyag* had no vertical armour but the coal bunkers were placed to give protection to the ships sides. This can be seen in the transverse sections of the ship shown in Figure 3.

ARMAMENT
The main armament consisted of twelve Obukhoff 152mm (6in) L/45 cal QF guns without splinter shields, 18 of which were placed on the upper deck and 2 on the

room ventilator fans needed only 96kW and those in the engine room only 23kW, while the searchlights and boat davits took the most power at 54kW and 90kW respectively. There was also a storage battery of 60 accumulators for emergency use to run the lighting and signalling equipment.

SEA TRIALS
Progressive trials were carried out for speeds of 16, 18, 21 and 23kts on the measured mile near Boston with the sea state 4-5 and the wind up to Force 6. The highest speed recorded on trials was 24.59kts, with 16 198ihp and a steam pressure of 15.5kg/sq cm (220psi), on 9 July 1900. After the trials the chief of the Russian commission said that in his opinion it was possible for *Varyag* to reach 25kts, if properly steered. During the trials the temperatures in the boiler rooms varied from 36°C to 71°C while in the engine rooms it was fairly constant at 31°C in one and

TABLE 1A

Weights

Weight sheet (extract) for IRN cruiser *Varyag* as designed:

Hull and fittings	2647.8 tons
Armour plating	632.3 tons
Main engines	349.8 tons
Auxiliary engines	44.4 tons
Armament (gunnery)	186.0 tons
Armament (torpedoes)	20.0 tons
Rig	52.5 tons
Ammunition	229.8 tons
Crew	77.0 tons
Drinking water and food	85.5 tons
Feed water	180.4 tons
Boilers	113.6 tons
Electric plant and equipment	156.0 tons
Ship's boats	29.3 tons
Spare parts for engines and armament	265.7 tons
Ballast (concrete)	200.0 tons
Coal (normal)	770.0 tons
Anchors, their equipment and chains	114.0 tons
Torpedoes and mines	23.7 tons
Normal displacement	about 6500.0 tons
Full load displacement	7022.0 tons

The *Varyag* shortly after arrival in home
waters
Author's collection

forecastle. The four foremost guns on the upper deck were carried in unprotected casemates, the remainder being in open positions, and all except the quarterdeck and forecastle pair were mounted in sponsons very similar to those of the museum cruiser *Aurora* currently moored in Leningrad. The guns were of a new type to the Russian Navy and were provided with separate projectiles and charges. The latter were contained in brass cartridge cases which were much safer than the silk cloth bags used in earlier Russian guns. The 152mm gun had a muzzle velocity of 793m/sec (2600fs) which gave a range of 9800m (10 700yds) at 15° elevation. The mounting weighed about 11 tons and the rate of fire was 6rpm; more detailed data on the *Varyag's* armament is given in Table 2.

The anti-torpedo boat armament consisted of twelve 75mm (3in) L/50 QF pieces, each of which weighed less than two tons, had a rate of fire of 10rpm and a range of 7000m (7650yds) at 15° elevation. The Russian Navy considered it very important to have on board light QF guns for engagements at close quarters. Four 47mm guns were therefore placed on the fighting tops and another four, together with two 37mm QF and two 7.62mm machine guns, were mounted on the upper deck. Two of each of these weapons could also be mounted in the ship's steam launches if required, as could two Baranowski 64mm which were carried for use by the ship's marines. Fighting tops were omitted in the next classes of Russian cruisers (*Askold, Bogatyr*) as useless.

The ship had nine magazines, grouped forward and aft, with ammunition stowage as follows: 2388-152mm, 3000-75mm, 1490-64mm, 5000-47mm and 2584-37mm. Shells and powder were transported to the hoists in the magazines by means of overhead rails. Similar rails were fitted under the boat skids above the upper deck to transport the ammunition from the hoists to each gun. There was a separate rail system for the guns of each calibre. Hoists for the guns mounted in the fighting tops were placed inside the steel masts.

The torpedo armament consisted of six 381mm (15in) above water tubes of which two were mounted on each beam, adjacent to the living spaces fore and aft, and one each in the bow and stern. The broadside tubes were retractable and the bow and stern tubes were fitted with light armour shields. The ship carried two reloads for each tube. Four short 381mm (15in) torpedoes (4.57m (15ft) long compared to 5.18m (17ft) for the main torpedoes), 6 thrower mines and 35 anchor mines were also carried for use by the ships boats.

When taken over by the Imperial Japanese Navy, as *Soya*, *Varyag* retained her old 152mm Obukhoff guns but her other guns were replaced by 12-76mm (3in) guns and 2-42mm guns. The beam torpedo tubes were also removed while, according to Western books, 457mm (18in) tubes replaced the 381mm bow and stern tubes. When *Soya* was re-purchased by Russians in 1916, with this well worn armament, the eight upper deck 152mm amidships were fitted with shields while the forecastle and quarterdeck pairs were moved to centreline positions to give them better arcs of fire. The Imperial Russian Navy planned to rearm *Varyag* with ten modern 130 (5.1in) L/55 guns but this was never done.

CAREER
Varyag was laid down early in October 1898 as the shipyard's job No 301. Her name was entered on the Navy List on 11 January 1899 and the official ceremony of laying down, according to Russian custom, took place on 10 (22) May when 1102 tons had already been worked into the ship. Launching took place on 31 October 1899 and she was commissioned on 2 January 1901 under Captain, First Class, W I Ber. She left the USA for Russia on 10 March 1901 and on passage encountered heavy weather (Force 11 on the Beaufort scale) and suffered a few mechanical defects. At the time the crew consisted of 565 men which included 24 officers,

1 *Varyag* on the building slip prior to launching. Note the prominent streamlined shield of the bow torpedo tube
Author's collection

2 The forebridge of *Varyag* shortly after completion showing the two foremost 152/L45 QF guns on the forecastle and the two 47mm guns mounted in the fighting top
Author's collection

1

55 petty officers and three passengers – representatives of Cramp, General Electric and Niclausse. During the voyage she called at Cherbourg (14 April), Revel (30 April) and Kronstadt (3 May). She was inspected by the Tsar on 18 May and was then detailed to escort the Tsar's yacht *Schtandart,* together with other ships to Danzig (Gdansk), Kiel and Cherbourg. In September she was released from this service and on 16 September left Cherbourg for the Salerno Gulf to join the Russian Mediterranean Squadron. At the time the Squadron consisted of the battleship *Imperator Nikolaj I,* cruiser *Abrek,* gunboats *Terec* and *Chrabry* and the two torpedo boats Nr *119* and Nr *120.* Later she was ordered to proceed to the Far East and on passage visited several ports including Suez (8 November), Karachi (25 December), Singapore (15 January), Nagasaki (13 February) and finally Port Arthur (25 February). In May 1902 she paid a visit to German-held island of Taku.

On speed trials in July she attained 20kts for short spurts and 16kts for long periods. The beginning of 1903 was spent under repair after which the *Varyag* was repainted grey, like the other ships of the Far East Fleet, the work being completed on 18 September. During this time, on 1 March, a new commander was appointed, Captain, First Class, W F Rudniev. She left Port Arthur for Tschemulpo (in Korea) on 27 December and arrived there on 29 December, where on 18 February 1904, together with the gunboat *Korejez* (under Captain, Second Class, G P Bielajev), she was surprised by a powerful Japanese cruiser squadron commanded by Admiral Urigu. At the time *Varyag* was capable of only 14-16kts because of the bad state of her boilers (according to the Sudovoj Spisok of 1904) while the gunboat was even slower. There was little chance for the Russians and under overwhelming Japanese fire the heavily damaged Russian ships were scuttled at 1800. *Korejez* was

1 *Varyag* coaling on her way to the Far East
Author's collection

2 A rare photograph of *Varyag* at Chemulpo shortly after her battle with Japanese cruiser
Author's collection

blown up beyond repair but *Varyag* was found by the Japanese to be worth raising and work on her resulted in the ship being floated by the Japanese salvage steamers *Santo Maru* and *Kyoto Maru* on 8 August 1905. On 23 October she was towed to Sasebo (according to other sources she proceeded under her own steam) where she was repaired and fitted with a new superstructure and funnels. Renamed *Soya*, she was placed in service with the Japanese Navy as a training ship for midshipmen. In 1916 she was considered obsolete and was offered to Russia which was now an ally of Japan and seriously short of warships.

The ship was repurchased in March 1916 for 4 million yen, together with two other former Russian ships, *Tango* (ex-*Poltava*) for 4.5 million yen and *Sagami* (ex-*Peresvet*) for 7 million yen. They arrived at Vladivostok for refit and repair on 21 March 1916 as part of Admiral Yamanaka's Squadron. Reverting to her old name of *Varyag*, she was

commissioned on 27 March under Captain K I Den. At the time her crew consisted of 22 officers and 570 men. According to the Russian archives *Varyag* still had her old Niclausse boilers at this time, the Japanese having limited themselves merely to a renovation of the old boilers before putting the ship into service. The cruiser had these boilers to the very end of her career despite the fact that, on 20 May 1916, the ship was capable of only 16kts because only 22 out of her 30 boilers were in serviceable condition. At this time some minor changes were made to the armament, including re-positioning the quarterdeck and forecastle 152mm guns on the centreline. After numerous trials *Varyag* left for Murmansk on 18 June. On passage she called at Colombo (27 July) and Tulon (19 September) and arrived at the Ekaterina Gulf port of Alexandrovska (now Polyarnyj) on 17 November 1916.

During the winter of 1917 talks were held with the British shipbuilders Cammell Laird

concerning the much needed refit and repair of the ship. In the meantime the Russian Admiralty Technical Department ordered *Varyag* to be re-armed with ten Vickers 130mm guns, in place of the worn out 152mm pieces, and the after torpedo tube to be removed. The ten bases for the 130mm guns were sent from the Obukhoff works on 1 February 1917 and before going to England she had all but four of the 152mm guns removed and the bases for the new guns fitted. The cruiser left Murmansk for England on 25 February and arrived at Liverpool on 4 (17) March where, as the shipyards were overworked, *Varyag* had to wait for some time before being taken in hand. In April and May all but fifty of the crew left the ship to man new vessels purchased in America. The last four 152mm guns were eventually removed, together with their ammunition supply and sent to Russia aboard the steamer *Altaj* and not long after this the twelve 130mm guns ordered from Vickers were sent first

1

to Archangielsk and then by rail to the Obukhoff works. Later these guns, together with the old 152mm from *Varyag*, were fitted as a part of the coast defences in the Baltic area.

After the outbreak of revolution in Russia the red flag was hoisted on *Varyag* but it was hauled down on 8 December 1917 by armed British sailors and the ship was taken over by the Royal Navy. On 15 February 1918 she was beached off the Irish Coast while under tow but was later refloated and served the Royal Navy as a hulk until 1919. In 1920 she was sold for scrap but was accidentally beached once again, this time off the coast of Scotland, approximately in position 55°N 5°W. She was scrapped *in situ* between 1923 and 1925.

CONCLUSIONS

As can be seen from this short article the cruiser *Varyag* had rather an unhappy career. During her life she encountered one mishap after another and the only bright spot in her career was the battle with Japanese squadron on the roadstead of Tachemulpo.

The use of Niclausse boilers in the ship was a fateful choice. The Russians had carried out successful trials with these in the gunboat *Chrabri* in 1896 but they generally preferred another French boiler, the Belleville. However W Cramp and Sons wished to fit Niclausse boilers in the *Varyag* and the Russians

unfortunately acceded to the builder's wishes. They proved a complete disappointment in service and were never again fitted in a Russian ship. Even the French Navy, the greatest user of this type of boiler, had phased most of them out of service by the time of the First World War. It is possible that *Varyag's* engagement with the Japanese in 1904 might well have ended differently if she could have achieved her designed speed of 23kts. The *Varyag* also exceeded her designed displacement, causing a further loss in speed, which resulted from inaccurate calculation of weights by Cramp during the design stage. Furthermore it was found, during her action with the Japanese, that the crew casualty rate was very high due to half their number having battle stations in open unprotected positions – in particular at the unshielded guns.

However, despite these deficiencies, the *Varyag* proved to be a reasonably good design which set the pattern for subsequent classes of fast Russian cruisers.

SOURCES

R M Mielnikov, *Krejser Varyag*, Leningrad 1975
R Greger, *Die Russische Flotte im Ersten Weltkrieg 1914-1917*, München 1970
W L Clowes, *Naval Pocket Book 1905*, London

Morskoj Sbornik 1897-1906, St Petersburg
Jane's Fighting Ships 1906, 1919, London
Taschenbuch der Kriegsflotten 1901-1918, München
Sudostroyenie 1974, 1975, Leningrad
Warship International 2/1975, 1/1978, Toledo
Les Flottes de Combat 1909, 1915, Paris
Modelarz 4, 5/1964, Warszawa
Modelist Konstruktor 3/1968, Moscow
H Jentschura, *Die japanischen Kriegsschiffe 1869-1945*, München 1970 (plus Errata)
Various other publications such as the German *Schiffbau* or *Zeitschrift Vereine des Deutschen Ingenieure* (popularly known as 'VDI')

1 *Varyag* in 1916
Courtesy A Preston

2 *Varyag* in 1916. Note the new funnels installed by the Japanese
Courtesy A Preston

3 The cruiser *Bogatyr*, built to the same specification as *Varyag* by Vulcan of Stettin but of substantially different design
Courtesy A Preston

THE HELICOPTER GOES TO WAR

BY ROBERT L SCHEINA

On 16 January 1944 a Sikorsky YR-4B rose from the pitching deck of the British motor vessel *Daghestan* in mid-Atlantic, and the helicopter had gone to war! A more demanding trial could not have been devised: *Daghestan*, deeply loaded, rolled and yawed during the entire 16-day voyage due to rough weather. Ten degree rolls were routine and, as the weather worsened, 45 degree rolls were experienced. The flight deck, fitted on the stern, rose and fell by 30ft as the bow slammed into the heavy seas and 40kt winds whipped across the landing area. A few days out, a winter gale had struck and the wind blew at 80kts for a short period. This was reality – a merchantman battling the North Atlantic during the winter.

The helicopter, and for that matter all the ingenuity of the Allies, was needed to fight the U-boat. The merchant ship *Daghestan* had been selected for the third and final test 'to determine . . . [the helicopter's] practical value for operating from merchant ships in ocean convoys'. What were the limiting conditions for conducting helicopter flight operations from a merchant ship? On 2 January 1944 the British Helicopter Service Trial Unit embarked at Bridgeport, Connecticut, and two fragile

Sikorsky YR-4B helicopters were carefully lifted on board. *Daghestan* proceeded to New York, where US Coast Guard and Navy observers boarded. The motor vessel then joined a convoy and sailed for England on 6 January.

Daghestan's design was a forerunner of the now famous mass produced 'Liberty Ship'. She was 7213 gross register tons, 10 325 dead weight tons, 442ft 11in long, 56ft 6in wide and diesel driven – she was a typical Second World War merchantman and had been completed in 1941. In 1943 a wooden platform 50ft by 96ft had been fitted over the stern, 22ft above the waterline. The port and starboard edges of the platform were pierced by small rectangular openings permitting the erection of wind screens consisting of individual 2 x 4s. When in place, these stood 17ft above the flight deck. Twenty 30ft and 40ft squares were marked off on the landing deck as a guide for the pilots. Personnel safety nets, extending 10ft outboard, surrounded the three exposed edges of the platform. A 500gal tank for aviation fuel was located beneath the flight deck.

The YR-4B was a fledgling but one generation removed from the first successful US helicopter design, the Vought-Sikorsky VS-300. This craft had flown under controlled conditions on 14 September 1939. Daring pilots and demanding tests led to a US Army Air Corps

Waiting – the YR-4Bs lashed to the deck. *USN*

Manufacturer:	Sikorsky Aircraft Corp, Bridgeport, Conn
Cost:	$43,940 each
Engine:	Warner R-55-3
Dimensions:	Length 48ft 3⅜in, height 12ft 5in, empty weight 2020lb, gross weight 2600lb, total rotor diameter 8ft 2in, main rotor diameter 38ft
Payload:	Crew 2, fuel 30gal, oil 3gal
Performance:	Top speed 75mph, cruising speed 60mph, radius 65miles, sea level climb 780fpm, hover ceiling none, service ceiling 8200ft, take-off power 200hp

contract for the XR-4, which flew on 14 January 1942. Soon the limited production models, the YR-4A (3 built) and YR-4B (27 built), were commissioned by the American and British military. The characteristics of the YR-4B reflect the primitive state of the helicopter.

The YR-4Bs which were hoisted on board *Daghestan* were equipped with float-type landing gear. This provided good traction on the wooden deck, but when the helicopters were positioned on the beam, the rubber floats had insufficient rigidity to withstand the side force induced by the ship's roll. Therefore, the Sikorsky craft had to be lashed to the deck during most of the crossing. Lacking wheels, the helicopters were moved about on tricycle dollies but could not be secured to them and, as *Daghestan* rolled and yawed, the helicopters were found to be difficult to manoeuvre. Sixteen men had to wrestle with the wingless aircraft in order to jockey them into the launching position. For 10 days *Daghestan* ploughed through the Atlantic experiencing heavy seas and the helicopters remained lashed to the deck but finally, on 16 January, the weather abated.

The Sikorsky YR-4B helicopter was stripped to spartan necessities. Only a crew of one and 20 gallons of aviation fuel were permitted, bringing the flight weight to 2360lb, well below the helicopter's operational gross weight. No electronics were fitted, not even a radio. The Sikorsky YR-4B soared out beyond the large convoy, passing over an escort carrier, and remained airborne for 30 minutes. The landing was made athwartships into the relative wind. *Daghestan*, abiding by convoy regulations, was

not permitted to manoeuvre to reduce rolling or alter wind direction across the landing area, and in order to land on the pitching deck, the helicopter had to set down on its leeward edge, allowing the tail rotor to hang over the side of the ship. This prevented the rotor from striking the deck as the ship rolled but left the helicopter precariously balanced near the edge. On the following day a second 30-minute flight took place and the deck-edge landing had to be repeated again, but on 18 January the weather worsened and no further flight operations could be conducted during the voyage.

The helicopter was not yet mature enough to be an open-ocean anti-submarine weapon. The evaluating board concluded:

1 'Ten degrees is considered the maximum roll . . . for safe landing . . .'
2 'The YR-4 lacks sufficient power . . .'
3 'The wind screen provided was . . . too cumbersome . . .'
4 'Some orientable gear for securing the helicopter to the deck immediately upon making contact during landing is a necessity . . .'
5 'The flight deck should not be less than 40ft by 60ft . . .'
6 '. . . anti-corrosion measures taken were inadequate . . .'
7 '. . . the YR-4B helicopter is not suitable as an anti-submarine weapon.'

The board recommended that additional testing and development take place.

Crucial firsts for the helicopter, like those for a child learning to walk, are more numerous and bear greater significance for the proud

parents than for the family friend. Being but curious observers, let us focus only on the helicopter's milestones which led to that flight on 16 January 1944.

The first shipboard helicopter tes took place on board the US tanker *Bunker Hill* on 7 May 1943, a few miles east of Stratford Point Light, Connecticut. Fifty observers watched as Colonel Frank Gregory, USAAF, lifted-off and landed an XR-4 helicopter almost two dozen times on a small strip of deck, whic had originally been provided for carrying deck cargo. Conditions varied from flat calm at anchor to *Bunker Hill* making 15kts with 12k winds breezing across the landing area. This Army test proved the versatility of the helicopter but had no goal for shipboard deployment.

Governmental reaction to this success was predictable – a committee was needed in order to guide the helicopter's maritime deployment. A 'Combined Board for Evaluation of the Helicopter in Anti-Submarine Warfare' was formed, ultimately representing the US Army, Coast Guard, Navy, National Advisory Commission for Aeronautics and the War Shipping Board, as well as the Royal Air Force and Navy. The board concluded that a three-phase shipboard testing programme woul determine whether the helicopter was ready to go to war in a convoy:
Phase 1 'Calm water, as in Chesapeake Bay, to familiarize the pilots with shipboard take-off and recovery technique'
Phase 2 'Open sea tests to establish the effect of ship's motion in a seaway on the problem of taking of and alighting'
Phase 3 'Operations from a ship in a regular convoy to Europe and return'

In Phase 1 the merchantman *T James Parken* embarked on a two-day cruise between New York and the Virginia Capes on 6 July 1943 to determine the practicality of operating a helicopter for short-range anti-submarine patrol. Two Sikorsky helicopters were employed, the XR-4 and the first of three YR-4As. The landing platform, mounted 40ft above the

1 The British motor vessel *Daghestan,* owned by the Hindustan Steam Shipping Co and managed by Common Brothers. This photograph, possibly taken at Liverpool, shows her with the helicopter platform over the stern and an aircraft catapult over the forecastle
NMM

2 Preparation – the wind screen being put in place. *USN*

waterline, was trapezoidal, 50ft athwartships forward tapering to 40ft aft, with a 60ft length. During three days 98 flights were conducted with winds ranging from 5 to 25kts and varying visibility. The test was a complete success.

On 26 November 1943 shipboard helicopter trials were conducted on board *Daghestan* in Long Island Sound (Phase 2). Two YR-4B helicopters were embarked, one each from the British and American navies. *Daghestan* raised anchor and proceeded into the Sound. The wind was variable, the sea smooth and visibility six miles in hazy weather. *Daghestan* built up to 10kts. Lt Commander F A Erickson, USCG, led more than 300 lift-offs and landings. All 26 evaluators and observers took turns as pilots and as observers. The only difficulty encountered was with the main rotor blades. In high winds, the vessel had to be turned down wind in order to permit starting and stopping motors. The helicopter was ready for Phase 3 – the convoy test.

The helicopter had not adequately matured by January 1944 to allow employment against submarines. Had the German submarine offensive continued to grow rather than peaking in the summer of 1942, perhaps a reorientation of national priorities would have resulted in a greater commitment of finance to helicopter development. This did not happen, and besides, technology is most often evolutionary and seldom revolutionary. Additional resources would probably have had but slight catalytic effect. The helicopter was not yet ready to go to war.

1

2

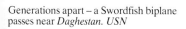

Generations apart – a Swordfish biplane passes near *Daghestan*. *USN*

Lift-off – 16 January 1944, the helicopter goes to war! *USN*

Challenge – a YR-4B soars past a Mac ship (escort carrier). *USN*

Landing – precariously balanced near the edge. *USN*

Warship Pictorial

THE GERMAN NAVY IN THE 1870s

The entire staff of *Warship* has been involved for over 18 months in the production of *Conway's All the World's Fighting Ships 1860-1905*, and in one sense this pictorial feature celebrates the completion of a monumental task. It is also an ideal opportunity to print some of the excellent photographs collected but not used, and the following set on the German Navy of the 1870s is particularly attractive in having a unifying theme. Not only are a number of early German ships portrayed, but also the ports and dockyards of Wilhelmshaven and Kiel in their formative years.

1

Wilhelmshaven Dockyard in the early 1870s, with three of the principal ironclads of the German Navy at that time. Nearest the camera is the unrigged *König Wilhelm* of 10,590 tons built at the Thames Ironworks and launched on 25 Apr 1868. Ahead of her is the French-built *Friedrich Carl* of 6820 tons launched on 16 Jan 1867 and the *Kronprinz* of 6197 tons built by Samuda Bros on the Thames and launched on 6 May 1867
CPL W/11/001

The first armoured ship designed in Germany was the centre battery corvette *Hansa* of 4334 tons built at Danzig Dockyard and launched on 26 Oct 1872. The building period was protracted, stretching from 1868 to May 1875, and she was probably photographed during fitting out
CPL W/11/002-3

2

3

The first large German-designed capital ships
were the three rigged turret ships of the
Grosser Kurfürst class, the other two being
the *Friedrich der Grosse* and the *Preussen*.
They were laid down in 1868, 1869 and 1870
respectively at the new Imperial Dockyards at
Wilhelmshaven and Kiel, with the *Preussen*
being constructed by the established firm of
Vulcan at Stettin. Not surprisingly, the
Preussen was completed first in July 1876,
with the *Friedrich der Grosse* following in
Nov 1877, but the Wilhelmshaven-built
Grosser Kurfürst was not ready until May
1878

1 The bow of the *Friedrich der Grosse* showing
the spur ram
CPL W/11/006

2 The *Preussen* at an early stage of framing
about 1872
CPL W/11/004

3 The *Preussen* being prepared for launching in
1873
CPL W/11/005

Before the formation of the Imperial German
Navy in 1871 the Prussian Navy had built a
number of conventional wooden screw
frigates at Danzig, including five very similar
ships of the *Arcona* type of about 2500 tons.
One of these was the *Vineta* shown here

4 *Vineta* in a floating dock at Kiel. Note the
sheathing below the waterline
CPL W/11/008

3

4

1 The German Navy only built two monitor-type ships, the *Rhein* (seen here) and *Mosel* (A G Weser, 1872-4). They were only 279 tons, were armed with two 120mm RMLs, and were designed specifically for use on the Rhine
CPL W/11/012

2 The roadstead at Kiel in the late-1870s. The principal ships (left to right) are the ironclads *König Wilhelm, Kronprinz, Kaiser* or *Deutschland* and the *Hansa.* The brig under sail is probably the *Musquito* or *Rover,* both ex-British sloops used for training
CPL W/11/013

3 The *Nymphe* class at 1180 tons were smaller than the *Arcona* class and were rated as 'flush-decked corvettes'. Like the frigates they were copper-sheathed and used extensively for overseas service; the second ship of the class, *Medusa,* is seen here at anchor in Valetta Harbour, Malta
CPL W/11/011

1

2

MILNE

The sixteen destroyers of the *L* and *M* Flotillas, although constructed during the early years of the war, were the last and largest of Britain's pre-war Fleet destroyer designs. They had a distinctive profile with a very large single funnel and three fully enclosed 4.7inch gun mountings. These latter, were the main improvement over previous destroyer classes. 50° was provided, compared with 40°, to improve their AA capability but, as the war was to prove, this was still insufficient to deal adequately with air attack.

The *Milne* was leader of the *M* flotilla and differed from her sisters in having the after deckhouse extended further forward to provide additional accommodation. On completion she joined the 3rd Destroyer Flotilla which operated with the Home Fleet unitl November 1944 and then transferred to the Mediterranean. In 1942 she covered the landings in North Africa but was mainly employed escorting arctic convoys. On 30

May 1944 she sank the German submarine *U289* in the arctic. In 1946 she was placed in reserve and thereafter saw little active service in the Royal Navy. In 1957 she was sold to Turkey and after undergoing refit was officially handed over in April 1959 and renamed Alp Arslam. The *Milne* survived until the early 1970s when she was deleted from the active list and sold for breaking-up.

The drawing shows *Milne* as completed and is based on the official as fitted drawing held by the National Maritime Museum. Note that she carried a 4inch AA gun in place of the after bank of torpedo tubes and five 20mm Oerlikons – two abreast the bridge, two abreast the searchlight platform and one on the quarterdeck.

Dyeline copies of this drawing (scale 1/16in = 1ft) are available from Sambrook Marine (Plans), 84-86 Broad Street, Teddington, Middlesex, TW11 8QT, price £1.25 plus 30p post and packing.

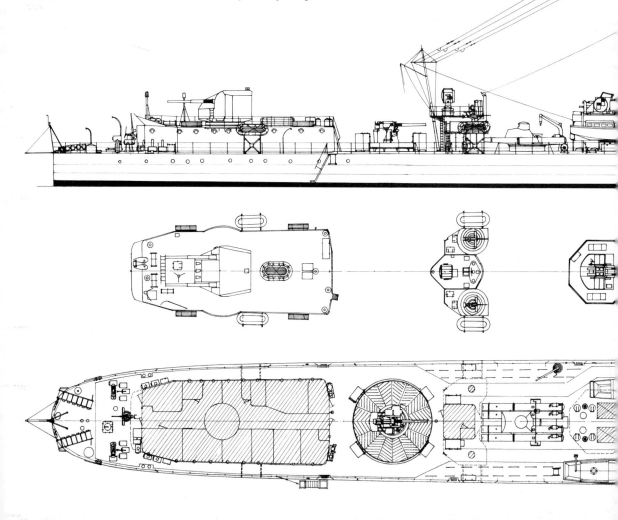

Builders:	Scotts (completed by J Brown due to bomb damage at Scotts yard)
Laid down:	24 January 1940
Launched:	31 December 1941
Completed:	6 August 1942
Displacement:	1935 tons (standard) 2750 tons (full load)
Length:	345ft 6in (pp), 362ft 3in (oa)
Beam:	37ft
Draught:	10ft
Armament:	6 – 4.7 inch Mk XI guns, twin Mk XX mountings (150 SAP, 100 HE, 25 LA practice and 16 HA practice rounds per gun plus 50 starshell for B mounting); 1 – 4inch Mk V gun, single Mk III AA mounting (207 rpg); 4 – 2pdr Mk VIII pompoms, quadruple Mk VII mounting (1800 rpg); 5 – 20mm Oerlikons, single mountings; 1 – quadruple Mk X 21inch torpedo tube mounting; 2 – DC throwers; 2 – DC rails, 36 depth charges
Machinery:	Parsons geared turbines, 2 shafts, 48 000 SHP = 36 knots at 480 rpm, 2 Admiralty 3 drum boilers, fuel capacity (100%) 565 tons fuel oil, 31.3 tons diesel fuel
Complement:	224

THE
KING GEORGE V
CLASS   PART 3
BY ROBERT DUMAS

The *King George V* in dry dock at Rosyth showing the unusual camouflage pattern she carried at the time of her completion *IWM*

The bridge and forward turrets of *King George V* in late 1940 *IWM*

Providing details of the camouflage of the *King George V* class has been one of the more difficult parts of this monograph as it is complicated, and in some cases almost impossible to determine accurately the exact shade of a colour. The shades used were mixed from several basic colours and I, unfortunately, have no information on the proportions employed so can only give the approximate colour and its official number.

Two main types of camouflage were used by the Royal Navy. The disruptive or dazzle type was intended to break up the outline of the ship in order to make it difficult to determine its speed, course, range and, to a lesser extent, its identity. The second type was true camouflage intended to make the ship blend into its background. These patterns and colours were chosen to suit the most likely conditions of the area in which the ship was intended to operate. The

actual patterns worn by the *King George V* class during the Second World War are listed below.

KING GEORGE V

Trials period 1940. Intermediate type consisting of 507A and 507B arranged in a geometric pattern. Similar patterns were worn by the battleships *Warspite* and *Valiant* around 1942. It is believed that the port side pattern was the same as the starboard.

December 1940-February 1941. Modified dazzle type with different patterns to port and starboard, as shown in the drawings. It appears that the paint or the preparation were of poor quality as the pattern flaked off comparatively quickly. Colours employed were 507A, 507B and 507C.

February 1941-June 1942. Overall medium grey.

June 1942-February 1944. Intermediate disruptive type, colours 507A, B5, B6 and 507C.

July 1944-end 1945. Admiralty standard type B with a B20 panel placed approximately over the ships vitals and the rest of the ship painted G45.
1946 onwards. Overall light grey.

PRINCE OF WALES
As completed. Overall medium grey.
August-December 1941. Admiralty first disruptive type, colours 507C, MS4, PB10, B20 (actually B5 as B20 was not introduced until 1943 – editor) MS3 and MS2. This type of camouflage was not very successful as the pattern was too complex and insufficiently bold to effectively break up the outline of the ship.

DUKE OF YORK
September-November 1941. Experimental Admiralty disruptive type, colours 507C, MS3, 507A. Port and starboard patterns were identical.
November 1941-March 1943. Overall medium grey.
March 1943-September 1944. Hull G10, superstructure G45.
March 1945-late 1945/early 1946. Admiralty standard Type B as for *King George V*.
Early 1946 onwards. Overall light grey.

KEY TO CAMOUFLAGE COLOURS
A. 507A/G10 (dark grey)
B. 507B/MS3 (medium grey/medium grey green)
C. 507C/G45 (light grey)
D. B5 (medium blue)
E. B6 (light blue)
F. MS4 (light grey/green)
G. PB10 (dark ultramarine blue)
H. MS2 (dark grey green)
I. B20 (medium blue)

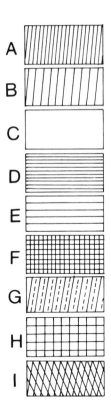

1 2

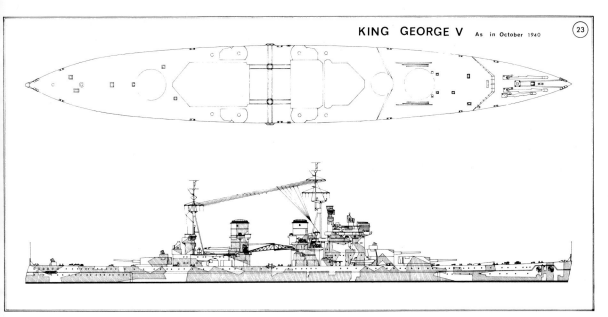

KING GEORGE V   As in October 1940   (23)

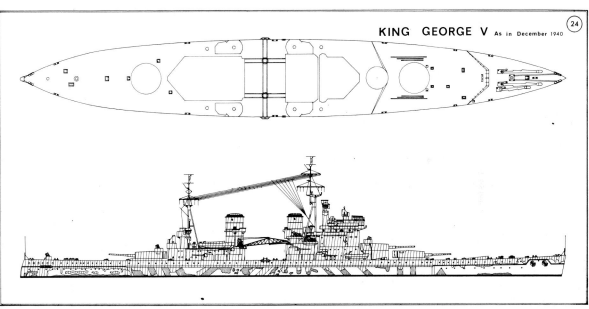

KING GEORGE V   As in December 1940   (24)

Viewed from the quarterdeck, 'Y' turret and
the superstructure of *King George V* shortly
after completion
IWM

An unusual view of *King George V's*
starboard quarter at Rosyth in 1940. Her
name plate, framed by the de-gaussing coil,
has been covered with a steel plate, probably
for reasons of security
IWM

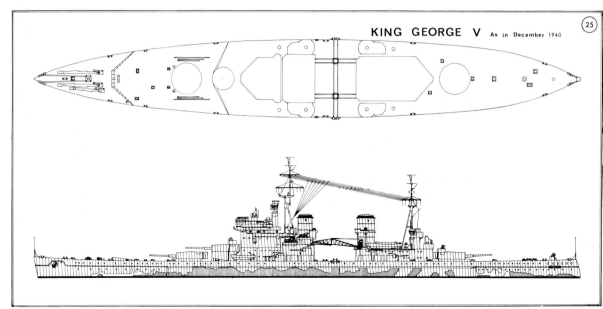

KING GEORGE V *As in December 1940*

㉕

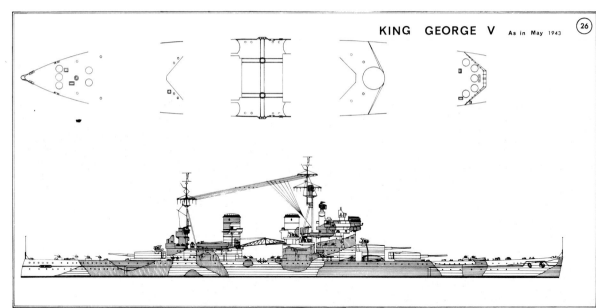

KING GEORGE V *As in May 1943*

㉖

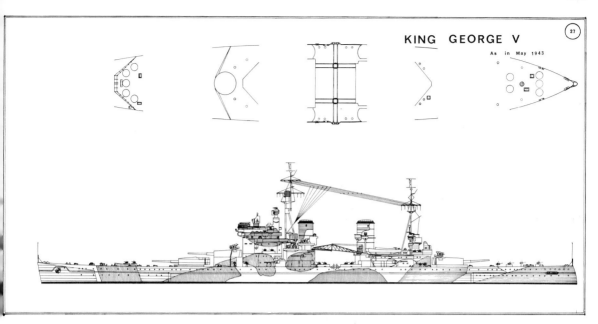

KING GEORGE V

As in May 1943

27

1 The *Prince of Wales* off Northern Scotland on 6 October 1941
NMM

2 The *King George V* on 15 April 1943
NMM

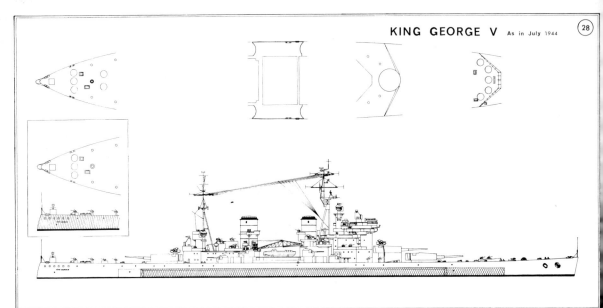

KING GEORGE V As in July 1944

28

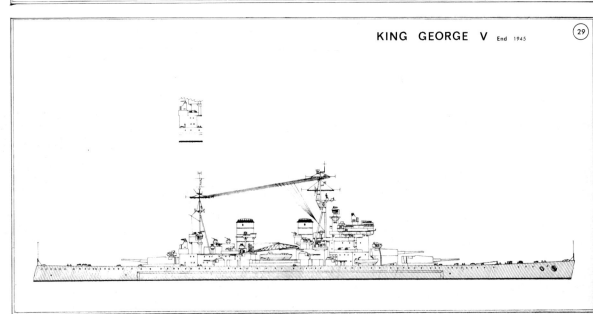

KING GEORGE V End 1945

29

1

The *King George V* in late 1940 or early 1941 with her dazzle camouflage pattern heavily eroded
CPL

The King George V on 10 July 1942 wearing her newly acquired intermediate disruptive type camouflage
NMM

2

1 The four guns of *King George V's* 'Y' turret, their ends plugged with crude wooden tompions
IWM

2 *Duke of York* in heavy weather
IWM

3 *King George V*
Author's collection

4 *The Prince of Wales* sporting the elaborate Admiralty disruptive camouflage which she wore from August to December 1941
MoD

3

4

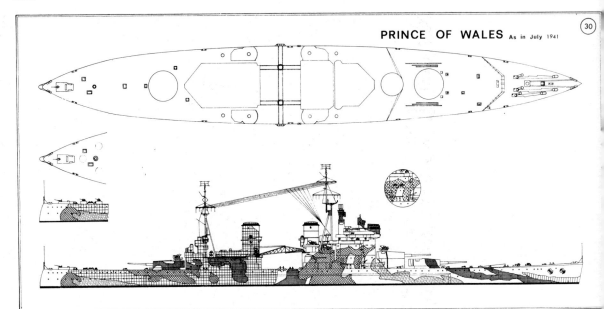

PRINCE OF WALES As in July 1941

30

PRINCE OF WALES As in July 1941

31

The *Prince of Wales* sailing south through the
Little Minch, between the outer Hebrides and
the Isle of Skye, on 23 October 1941. Two
days later she sailed from the Clyde as
flagship of Admiral Sir Tom Phillips, C in C
Eastern Fleet
NMM

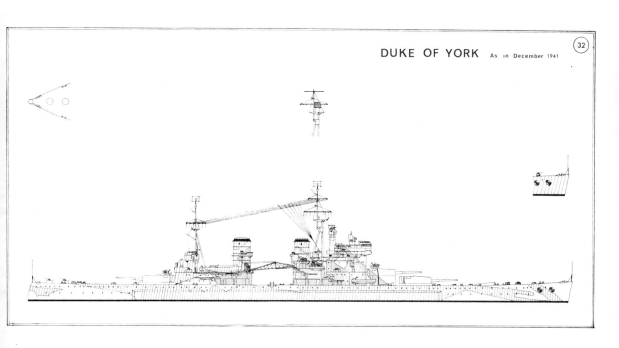

DUKE OF YORK As in December 1941

32

1 The *Duke of York* post war in overall light grey
Ralston

2 Damage to the port strut of *Duke of York's* tripod foremast caused by an 11in shell from the *Scharnhorst* during the Battle of North Cape in December 1943
NMM

1

BRITISH SUPER-HEAVY GUNS PART 3
BY N J M CAMPBELL

1 The 18in gun, *Furious* 1917
NMM

2 *Furious* with aircraft and flying-off platform, 1917
NMM

2

18IN MARK I

This gun was the heaviest ever completed in Britain and, except for the 18.1 guns of the Japanese battleships *Yamato* and *Musashi,* the largest mounted in any ship. It was originally intended for the light battlecruiser *Furious,* laid down on 8 June 1915, which was to carry two 18in gun in single turrets fore and aft. Only the Armstrong works at Elswick could build a gun of this size without considerable difficulties and the two guns plus one spare were ordered in the Spring of 1915 to Elswick drawing 14237, RGF11349/1 being the official Woolwich drawing.

The first gun was proved at Ridsdale, the Elswick proving ground, in September 1916, the second followed in late 1916 and the third in early 1917. Since the days of the 16.25in the construction of British heavy guns had been much simplified by the use of wire winding. The 12in Mark VIII mounted in the *Majestic* class battleships, laid down from December 1893, had been the first standard British wire wound heavy gun and this had been followed by the 12in Marks IX to XII, the 13.5in Mark V and the 15in Mark I, the two latter being highly satisfactory in most respects. Serious difficulties had arisen in the 12in Mark VIII, and also in the Mark IX, as a result of the inner A tube closing in near the muzzle –

'steel choke' – and also cracking. This was due to a great part of the longitudinal stresses in the inner A tube being concentrated at the foremost locating shoulder. Various expedients improved this by better stress distribution and the trouble was virtually eliminated by the introduction of a slow taper fit between the inner A and A tubes in the 13.5in Mark V of later manufacture. The earlier guns of this mark retained forward shoulders until relined. With tapered inner A tubes the locating shoulders were kept well to the rear of the gun.

In most respects the 18in, which was known as the 15in B during the war for reasons of secrecy, actually resembled an enlarged version of the 15in with a relatively small breech ring but there was an important difference in the breech mechanism. The standard Welin stepped screw block was used with 15 segments of which 3 were plain, but the Vickers 'pure couple' mechanism was replaced for reasons of excessive slam by the Elswick short arm mechanism. In this the breech screw withdrew through the carrier, which complicated the actuation of the lock but was fast acting, the time to open or close the 18in breech being 3 seconds with hydraulic power, and slam was much reduced. It may be noted that this mechanism would in all probability have been standard

in the 15in if trials in E597, the experimental gun fitted with it, had not been delayed for too long by a failed A tube. A further unusual feature of the 18in was the 'slow cone' obturator. The construction of the gun was normal comprising: tapered inner A tube with 5 locating shoulders a little forward of the Chamber/A tube in which the breech bush (taking the breech block) was located/wire layers with necessary stop rings and fastenings/B tube and Jacket overlapping the rear end of B tube/breech ring. There was the usual shrunk collar on the rear of the A tube. Nickel steel was used for the various forgings except for the jacket and breech ring which were in unalloyed carbon steel.

To return to the history of the three guns, the *Furious* had her two guns and mountings shipped in early 1917 but on 2 March 1917 it was decided to remove the fore turret and replace it by a flight deck. She commissioned on 26 June 1917 and on 17 October 1917 it was decided to replace the after turret by a second flight deck. Meanwhile Vice Admiral Bacon, in Command at Dover, had been told of the existence of these guns and that two would be available. In August 1917 he proposed mounting them inside the shell of the Palace hotel at Westende, when that place should fall to the Army, and use them to bombard the German docks at

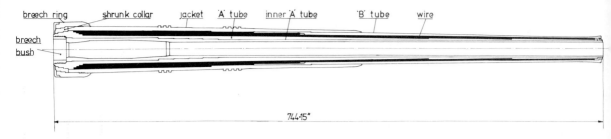

breech ring   shrunk collar   jacket   'A' tube   inner 'A' tube   'B' tube   wire

breech
bush

744·15"

The 18in BL Mk I

Bruges and the Zeebrugge locks at about 36 000yds.

It soon became clear that the Army would not reach Westende quickly, if at all, and Bacon conceived the idea of mounting them in 12in gun monitors, whose guns were by then badly outranged by the German coastal batteries. Approval for this was given on 23 September 1917 but the mountings for *Furious* had been designed to suit the roller path of the twin 15in turret and were actually heavier and of greater overall diameter. Thus new mountings for all three guns were ordered to be designed and built at Elswick. Although always called the 15in B Coast Defence or CD mounting, they were actually land bombardment mountings with a forward pivot and only 20° total training. There were various troubles but eventually the first was installed in *General Wolfe* training over the starboard beam aft and the second was similarly fitted in *Lord Clive*. The third mounting was to have been in *Prince Eugene* but this was cancelled. No 2 gun, originally in *Furious* A turret, was shipped in *General Wolfe* on 9 July 1918 and removed to the Portsmouth gun ground on 14 December 1920 where it remained until scrapped and sold in July 1933. No 3 gun, the original spare, was shipped in *Lord Clive* on 7 September 1918 and removed to the Portsmouth gun ground on 11 October 1920. In January 1921 it was sent to Woolwich to be relined for experiments in connection with the proposed 18in/45 cal and when the relining was cancelled, in November 1921, remained at Woolwich until scrapped and sold in July 1933. No

1, the gun in *Furious* Y turret, arrived at Portsmouth for the *Prince Eugene* on 13 September 1918 and was sent to the Silloth range for various trials in March 1920. It had been intended that Elswick should reline the gun for experiments for the proposed 18in/45 but this was cancelled and in November 1921 it went to Elswick for relining to a 16in/45 cal Mark I. This was done

by January 1924 and the gun was used for various trials until January 1942 when it was sent to Woolwich and eventually scrapped in July 1947.

The myth that the three guns were mounted at Singapore dies hard in the nature of myths and it was thought worthwhile to give their true history. Details were as follows:

Weight (including breech mechanism): 149 tons
Weight (less breech mechanism): 146 tons 4 cwt
Length (oa): 62ft 0.15in – 744.15in
Length (bore): 40cal – 720.2in
Diameter: 72.5in max, 30.5in min, 32in over muzzle
Chamber size: 127.05 x 23.85in, volume 51310cu in (The intended chamber dimensions were 125.8 x 24in but they were altered owing to a machining error)
Rifling: 585.42in long, uniform twist 1 in 30, 88 grooves, polygroove plain section, dimensions not certain but believed 0.124 x 0.459in with lands 0.1835in
Centre of gravity: 250.5in from breech face (loaded)
Projectile weight: 3320lb
Charge: 630lb MD45 (6 x 105) Supercharge 690lb MD45 (5 x 105 + 1 x 165)
Muzzle velocity: 2270ft/sec (with supercharge 2420ft/sec)
Design pressure: 18.0tons/sq inch

The main fault was the low muzzle velocity for which the impracticability of making MD Cordite in a size greater than 45, due to the time taken to evaporate solvent and wartime conditions which prevented experiments with other grain forms or propellants, were responsible. Trials at Silloth in 1920 with the charge at a temperature of 49/50°F instead of the standard 80°F gave an MV of 2277ft/sec with 660lb of MD45 cordite and 2438ft/sec with 820lb of the new oval Ardeer Solventless (SC) cordite with an 0.32 x 0.64in section, the respective pressures and mean differences in muzzle velocity being 16.92 tons/sq in and 2.0ft/sec

with MD45 and 16.90 and 4.6 with SC.

In point of fact the supercharge could have been used as the standard full charge as wear was remarkably small and the gun could well have withstood the likely new gun, 80°F, pressure of 21 tons/sq in. The only gun that did much firing, No 2 in *General Wolfe*, expended 60 proof and supercharges, 41 full and 2 reduced charges calculated as equivalent to 161⁵⁄₁₆ full charges. The mean wear at 1in from the commencement of the rifling was 0.379in compared with at least 0.45in for the same number of equivalent full charges in the 15in Mark I.

The mountings for *Furious* allowed 30° elevation and 5° depression giving a range, with 4crh (calibre radius head) shells and full charges, of 28 800yds. The monitor mountings allowed firing at 22° to 45° elevation and 8crh shells were used giving a range of 36 000yds with full charges and 40 100yds with supercharges. All these ranges are for new gun muzzle velocities as given above. *Furious* had a war outfit of 120 rounds per gun, 60 being APC (Armour Piercing Capped) and 60 CPC (Common Pointed Capped). Length was limited to 77in but it would seem that this was not attained by the 4crh shells, the APC not exceeding

67¼in and the CPC 75.7in. The CPC burster was 243lb black powder and that of the APC 119lb lyddite. The monitors carried 60 rounds intended to be 8crh nose fuzed HE (High Explosive) with a maximum length of 84¾in. These were however not delivered in time and they fired APC shells fitted with ballistic caps to give an 8crh head.

In conclusion it must be regretted that this good but very heavy gun was never mounted in a suitable ship, although alternative designs for the *Hood* with this gun was considered.

Stern view of *General Wolfe* in 1918, showing her fixed 18in Mk I
CPL

18IN/45 CALIBRE

Although none of these were completed, their history is important to the development of British heavy guns. In 1919 the Admiralty decided that the standard main armament of future battleships and if possible battlecruisers was to be the 18in/45. At the same time it was desired to reduce the weight and also the muzzle droop of future gun designs and it was hoped that this might be achieved by improved wire wound construction or by using a partly wire wound or wire free design. The possibility of obtaining a 30tons/sq in yield point from heavy forgings made in nickel chrome molybdenum steel would make it easier to solve these problems. Designs for all three types of construction were called for from Elswick, Vickers and Woolwich and their designers produced 11, 13 and 13 designs respectively which were carefully considered by the Ordnance Committee. As a result 5 final designs were produced by the Royal Gun Factory (RGF), Woolwich. It was realised that the test programme on the partly wire wound and wire free guns would take a long time and that the first production guns would probably have to be made to the improved wire wound design. Orders for 18in No 5, the partly wire wound gun, and No 6, the wire free gun, were placed with Vickers and Elswick respectively on 22 December 1920, while No 4, the wire wound gun, was ordered from Woolwich on 20 January 1921. It was intended to order a second wire free gun in the following year, to be made on Krupp principles as far as they could be adapted to the use of bag charges, but this was never done. Krupp guns were built at that time by the precision shrinking of relatively short tubes and not as in No 6 above, where long tubes should be used.

It should be noted that only Elswich were suited for making 18in/45 guns in production as is shown in the following table of manufacturing limits, though Vickers and Woolwich could have made a few.

Works	Maximum Diameter (breech end)	Length (oa)	Weight
ELSWICK	84in	73ft	200 tons
VICKERS	72in	70ft	100 tons (150 possible)
WOOLWICH	72in	76ft	120 tons (can be increased in emergency)

In the event the 18in/45, generally known as the 16in/50 for reasons of secrecy, was too large for the first new British ships which were to be battlecruisers and, as negotiations at the Washington Conference which had begun on 12 November 1921, made it clear that 18in guns would be ruled out, the three prototype guns were cancelled on 30 January 1922.

No 4 would have been built on similar lines to the 18in Mark I but with the wire wound in one continuous length, a process known as taper winding. No 5 would have had an unwired chase with inner A, A and B tubes and the wire over the rest of the gun was not to have been taper wound, while No 6 would have had a chase, comprising inner A, A and B tubes, with the B tube continued by a C tube towards the rear where there was also the usual jacket. All would have had the Elswick short arm breech mechanism. The A tube forging weighed 57 tons.

There was never any intention of building 20 or 21in guns and Sir Robert Hadfield of the famous steel company of that name was asked to stop talking about APC shells of this size.

Details of the three 18in/45 guns were:

Design	Wire RGF 11459	Part Wire RGF 11460A	No Wire RGF 11462
Weight (including breech mechanism)	134 tons 10cwt	134 tons 15cwt	130 tons
Diameter (max)	66in	66in	65.2in
Diameter (min)	29.6in	29.5in	29.0in
Centre of gravity from breech face (loaded)	276.8in	277.3in	271in
Droop	0.55in	0.51in	0.48in

The following details were common to all:

Length (oa): 69ft 5in – 833in
Length (bore): 45cal – 810in
Chamber size: 147.3 x 22.14in, volume 55,000cu in
Rifling: Not decided
Projectile weight: 2916lb
Charge: About 810lb MD oval (0.37 x 0.74in)
Muzzle velocity: Probably about 2650ft/sec
Design pressure: 20 tons/sq in

The triple mounting designed by Elswick would have given 40° elevation and 3° depression with an estimated rate of fire of one round per gun every 29 seconds. It will be noted that the projectile was very light. In August 1920 the intended new 18in APC with an 8crh, would have weighed 3320lb with a length of 79.72in and a burster of 2.37% of the projectile weight. A maximum length of 92in would have been allowed to cover any HE design and also the possibility of increasing the weight to 4000lb. Inadequate trials at oblique impact appeared to show that a 1688lb 15in shell behaved better than the 1920lb one. This result was not substantiated by later trials but it was decided prior to these to fix the 18in/45 calibre shell at 2916lb with a $2\frac{1}{2}$% burster and a conical head – $6/\infty$ crh – the max length being taken at 82.66in to allow for HE.

Rifling details were to await 15in trials between a gun with the standard rifling of uniform twist 1 in 30 with 76 grooves, each 2.5 x land width, another gun similar but with a uniform twist of 1 in 40, as used in Italian 15in guns, and a third gun with a uniform twist of 1 in 30 and 100 grooves of equal width to lands, which was based on modified German practice.

General Wolfe taken at the same time as the previous photograph
CPL

T CLASS SUBMARINES
PART 2
BY JOHN LAMBERT

HMS/M *Thermopylae* in July 1950. Note that her 4in gun has been removed and that her 'snort' mast is laid flat abaft the conning tower, its normal stowed position
Wright and Logan

At the end of the Second World War the early *T* class units, of all riveted construction, were reduced to reserve or sold abroad while the later war construction units, of part- or all-welded construction, remained in service, particularly on the Far East station. However, despite the fact that they were of comparatively recent construction it soon became clear that the *T* class design would become obsolete within a few years as a result of advanced German developments.

Access to German records and the opportunity for allied scientists to examine ex-enemy units under construction at the end of the war revealed, as had been feared, that the latest German U-boats were very highly developed, with greatly advanced submerged performance and a much improved offensive armament. There were two basic lines of development, the first involving the adoption of a new type of propulsion system, the 'Walther' turbine, and the second the improvement of existing types.

THE WALTHER SYSTEM

The 'Walther' turbine gave the promise of providing a 'true' submarine which could operate submerged continuously, while having a high speed and a radius of action comparable to a normal diesel engined boat. The arrangement consisted of a very complex closed-circuit turbine system, activated by the thermal energy produced by the decomposition of a high concentration of hydrogen peroxide (perhydrol). This latter generated a high temperature, pressurised gas which, in itself, was able to drive a turbine, but the fuel was also very hazardous due to its instability when any impurity was present. Any impurity served as a catylist causing rapid decomposition and a rise of temperature resulting, ultimately, in spontaneous combustion. It was found that absolute clinical cleanliness was essential in preparing and storing this new fuel and, after a series of experiments, flexible synthetic rubber was found

to be the most suitable coating for its storage containers.

The perhydrol was forced up by water pressure, from its stowage tank in the bottom of the hull, into a porcelain lined chamber where it was joined by the catalyst to bring about its decomposition. This break down and change produced steam and oxygen at a high temperature ($1765°F$) which was then passed to a combustion chamber. Here they ignited the oil fuel while, at the same time, water was sprayed on to the gas to reduce its temperature (to $986°F$) and increase its volume. The combination of gas and steam was used to drive the turbine and then, after giving up its energy in this way, passed through a condenser, where the water was extracted and the residual carbon dioxide, generated in the combustion chamber, was drawn off. Whilst this new system was capable of producing high power for a low weight ($11\frac{1}{4}$lb/SHP) and was quite independent of the use of the atmosphere, it had the disadvantages of a high rate of

consumption at full speed, giving a limited range, and high cost, about eight times as expensive as oil fuel.

Development of the 'Walther' turbine had started with the experimental submarine *V80* in 1940 and trials had continued throughout the war. The first naval unit to receive the new machinery was the *U791*, which had a two shaft arrangement developing 4360 SHP for a speed of about 19kts. One 'Walther' powered coastal U-boat, *U1407,* which was scuttled at Cuxhaven on 2 May 1945, was salvaged by the British and brought to the United Kingdom to serve as a test bed in the Royal Navy as HMS *Meteorite.*

HIGH SPEED U-BOATS

The second line of development – the improvement of existing types – involved a different solution to high underwater speeds and silent approach. New high capacity batteries were developed and the number of cells almost trebled which, combined with a fully

streamlined 'figure of eight' hull section, resulted in the maximum submerged speed being increased from 9 to about 15.5kts. In addition the 'Schnorchel' mast, introduced in 1943, was improved and employed principally to run the diesel engines while submerged in order to re-charge the batteries. The new U-boat designs were also fitted with silent running auxiliary motors, to give a creep speed of 5kts, and the torpedo armament was increased to six bow tubes, with 17 internal reloads, and automatic re-loading gear was provided. Finally AA defence was improved by fitting remotely controlled gun mountings in the fin. A few of these new all-electric boats became operational in the last months of the war while large numbers were either working-up or on trials.

These new developments caused much radical re-thinking by the Allies particularly as a large part of the German submarine war construction had fallen into the hands of the Russians who, it was

soon realised, would make the most of their new found knowledge. Designs were modified and improved to the new standard as opportunity offered; the first change being the fitting of the 'Snort' mast, the British version of the 'Schnorchel', as standard in all new construction and in the war built *S, T* and early *A* class boats when refitted.

T CLASS CONVERSIONS

HMS/M *Tabard,* as mentioned in Part 1, was one of the final units of the *T* class to complete. Her hull was of ¾in welded steel and her ballast tanks could therefore be utilised for the stowage of oil fuel without the risk of oil leaking to the surface to betray the presence of a submarine. She was fitted with a 'Snort' at Chatham Dockyard in 1950 and the differences from her original configuration can be seen in my drawing. The 20mm Oerlikon mounting was also removed and the bandstand replaced by a faired tail fin.

The *T* class proved capable of undergoing both limited streamlining and major 'super' conversion. The former was carried out in five part-welded *Ts (Talent, Tapir, Teredo, Tireless* and *Token)* in the early 1950s. It involved the removal of all the upper deck tubes, except the single stern tube, and rebuilding and streamlining the casing. The bridge was also rebuilt and raised to enclose all the masts, radar aerials and periscope standards. The first to complete was *Tireless* and, in view of the many improvements undergone by the class since the trials of *Triton* in 1938, it was decided to carry out comparative trial between her and an ordinary 'Snort' fitted *T*. The chosen vessel, *Tudor*, was docked, cleaned and fitted with standard *T* class bronze propellers of 5ft 4in diameter and 4ft 6½in pitch. Six trials were carried out to compare: (i) submerged speed; (ii) surface turning; (iii) submerged turning; (iv) acceleration and deceleration; (v) diving trials; and (vi) depth changing.

The trials, carried out by *Tireless* in October 1952 showed that the effect of streamlining was to increase the 'quiet' speed, maximum submerged speed and submerged endurance (high capacity batteries – 6560 as against 5350 – were also fitted). Minor changes were also obtained in submerged turning, control and depth changing and in diving times. The surface performance was the same since no changes had been made to the form below the surface waterline but the increased height of the bridge gave a considerable improvement to surface watchkeeping in moderate and rough weather.

Due to improved form underwater the effect of streamlining is two-fold. The speed for a given rpm is greater and the rpm at which cavitation occurs is greater because of the improved slip. The trials showed an increased of about 1kt or 40% between the two ships (*Tireless* gave 125rpm = 3.25kts and *Tudor* 110rpm = 2.3kts). The maximum speed at periscope depth was 9.5kts at 380rpm in *Tireless* and 8.1kts at 380rpm in *Tudor,* an increase of 1.4kts. The increased submerged endurance was the result of a 23% increase in battery capacity and a reduction in resistance for a given speed. These gave an increase in endurance of between 30-40 miles throughout the speed range. Thus it was shown that by modification, and removal of the gun and upper deck bulk, the performance of war-built submarines could be improved.

Between 1951 and 1956 eight all-welded boats underwent a 'super' conversion. (*Tabard, Taciturn, Thermopylae, Tiptoe, Toten, Trump, Truncheon* and *Turpin*). The pressure hull was cut at the engine-room and the hull increased in length by about 20ft (*Taciturn* by 14ft and *Thermopylae* by 12ft). The extra space was utilised for the addition of a second pair of electric motors, clutches between which and the original motors made diesel-electric drive possible. A fourth section of improved capacity battery cells was also added, giving a maximum underwater speed of about 15kts, and new asdic and radar equipment were fitted. *Tabard* and *Trump* also had the bridge reconstructed as a large fin, housing two periscopes, two radar masts, two Snort masts and an aerial. The remaining six super conversions had the bridge reduced to a small area in the fore part of the fin. Other work on the vessels followed the previous description, with recontoured casing, removal of the external tubes and gun, etc. The post war units of the *A* class were similarly modified. The life of the *T* class was considerably lengthened by these reconstructions and a few remained in service until the early 1970s before being replaced by new construction.

1 HMS/M *Tabard* as completed in 1946. Note the 20mm Oerlikon mounting at the rear of the conning tower
MoD

2 HMS/M *Tabard* after 'super' conversion with lengthened hull and streamlined upper works. Compare this view with her original appearance in the 1946 photograph and also the larger fin with that of the other converted 'boats'
Author's collection

3 The *Truncheon* on 18 May 1958. The extension at the base of the fin, forward, is the bridge, a common feature to all the streamlined and reconstructed boats except *Tabard* and *Trump* which had a larger fin
MoD

1

2

3

DETAILS OF POST WAR T AND A CLASS SUBMARINES

	T CLASS	T CONVERSIONS	A CLASS
Number of units	**11/4**	**4/4**	**15**
Surface displacement (tons)	1424 (deep)	1588 (deep)	1443 (deep)
	1327 (light)	1554 (light)	1370 (light)
Submerged displacement (tons)	1571	1696/1734	1620
Standard displacement (tons)	1090	1269/1460	1120
Length overall	273ft	285ft/290ft 6in	282ft
Maximum beam	26ft 7in	26ft 7in	22ft 3in
Maximum surface draught	15ft 10in	16ft	18ft 1½in
Pressure hull diameter	16ft 4in/16ft 4in	16ft 4in	16ft
and thickness	.625in/.75in	.75in/.75in	.875in
Pressure hull material	HST riveted/	'S' welded	'S' welded
	'S' welded		
Main tank capacity (tons)	263	207	265
Diving depth (feet)	300/350	350	500
Surface BHP (Diesel)	2500	2400/2500	4300
Surface speed (kts)	15.25	14.15	18.6
Surface endurance (miles/kts)	7500/15.25	–/–	5000/18.6
Snorting BHP	200	1900/–	3500
Snorting speed (kts)	7.4	9.4/–	8.5
Snorting endurance/kts	4920/7.4	–/–	4050/8.5
Submerged SHP	1450	6000	1250
Submerged speed (kts)	8.6	15.4/–	7.5
Submerged endurance (miles, kts)	80, 4	100, 4/-	80, 4
Maximum Oil Fuel carried (tons)	209	200 approx	213
Internal Torpedo Tubes	6-Fwd	6-Fwd	4-Fwd, 2 Aft
(Torpedoes)	(12)	(12)	(16)
External Torpedo Tubes	2Fwd, 2Mid, 1Aft	–	2 Aft
(Torpedoes)	(5)	–	(2)
Gun armament	1-4in	Nil	1-4in
Complement	63	68	63

COMPARISON BETWEEN TIRELESS AND TUDOR – SUBMERGED TURNING

RPM	Rudder Angle	Tactical diameter (yards)		Advance (yards)		Time to turn (min-sec)		90°	180°	360°
		TUDOR	TIRELESS	TUDOR	TIRELESS					
370	20°P	640	750	410	430		TUDOR	2-23		8-54
							TIRELESS	2-12		8-22
370	20°S	680	730	415	440		TUDOR	2-26		9-22
							TIRELESS	2-31		8-49
370	35°P	455	410	290	240		TUDOR	1-52		7-10
							TIRELESS	1-36		6-02
370	35°S	440	415	270	305		TUDOR	1-49		6-59
							TIRELESS	1-43		6-08
250	35°P	460	390	310	275		TUDOR	2-39		10-32
							TIRELESS	2-06		8-09
250	35°S	430	370	275	280		TUDOR	2-26		9-48
							TIRELESS	2-08		8-18
130	35°P	450	395	250	300		TUDOR	4-53	9-50	
							TIRELESS	3-48	7-18	
130	35°S	560	400	315	310		TUDOR	5-18	11-14	
							TIRELESS	4-07	7-46	

It is evident from these results that *Tireless* turns about 10% smaller at most speeds with 35° rudder but with 20° rudder the conditions appear to be reversed. It would be expected that the large fin-like bridge in *Tireless* would reduce her turning circle.

Depth changing:

Generally, *Tireless* reached the required depth and returned to periscope depth faster than her sister. This can be attributed almost wholly to the increased speed of *Tireless*. The hydroplane response appears similar in both cases. At full speed 15° bow down was reached about 50 seconds after the order in both submarines.

COMPARISON BETWEEN TIRELESS AND TUDOR
ACCELERATION AND DECELERATION

Condition	TIRELESS	TUDOR
Stopped submerged to full ahead 'Group Up'	1min 50 sec 380yds	1min 15sec 230yds
Full ahead both engines on surface to full astern, both motors 'Group Up'	1min 45sec 460yds	1min 38sec 454yds
Maximum RPM 'Snorting', to full astern, both motors 'Group Up'	1min 45sec 340yds	1min 15sec 175yds
Full ahead 'Group Up' both motors to full astern 'Group Up' both motors	1min 30sec 236yds	0min 55sec 135yds

Note: The above results are not considered representative of the submarines capabilities. The differences can almost all be attributed to the reactions of crew members carrying out orders.

Two views of the *Talent,* which was streamlined during 1954-56, moored at Fort Blockhouse, Gosport, in 1960. The vessel in the background is the un-modernised *Tally Ho* (S87) whose single 4in gun and raised 'snort' mast are clearly visible
MoD

1

1 The *Thermopylae* whose 'super' conversion involved a 12ft increase in length. Note the large 'sonar' dome at the extreme forward end of her casing
MoD

2 The 'super' conversion boat *Taciturn* leaving Portsmouth harbour, October 1960
Wright and Logan

3 HMS/M *Tabard* in March 1957
Wright and Logan

1 The *Token* off Portsmouth in May 1948; she was streamlined at Devonport Dockyard in 1955
Wright and Logan

2 Modernised at Devonport Dockyard during 1951-52, the *Tireless* was the first *T* class boat to be streamlined
MoD

THE PADDLE FRIGATE GUADALOUPE

BY D K BROWN

For several years before they built the *Nemesis* (see *Warship 8*), Laird's had been trying to persuade the Admiralty to order an iron frigate from them. It was an unrealistic proposal, as their Lordships fully appreciated, since there could be no ocean-going iron ships until the completion of Airey's work on the correction of compasses. However, Laird's design of 1836 for an iron paddle frigate ultimately developed into their Ship No 42, which was finally launched in April 1842 as the Mexican frigate *Guadaloupe*. At this time she was the world's largest iron ship. Her principal particulars were:

Dimensions:	Length 187ft (on deck), 169ft 6in (keel), beam 30ft 1in, draught 9ft
Displacement:	878 tons (with 10 days coal), depth 16ft
Tonnage:	788bm
Machinery:	2 cylinder, 5ft stroke, 4ft 4in dia, 180nhp
Paddle wheels:	21ft dia, 22rpm giving 9kts at 9ft 2in draught

She originally carried a 68pdr pivot gun at each end but two long 24pdrs were added on arrival in Mexico and two more some time later.

While she was building, Dupuy de Lôme, the brilliant young French naval constructor, was working at Lairds studying the building of iron ships for his Admiralty. In his report he says that Lairds had aimed for exceptional strength in the design of *Guadaloupe*. The hull weight was 410 tons, 46.7% of her displacement compared with 25.6% in Brunel's *Great Britain*. The keel was fabricated from best Low Moor iron at £20 per ton whilst the remainder of the hull was constructed of the cheaper Coalbrookdale iron at £10 per ton. Altogether, the cost of the hull came out at £40 per ton with an average of £12 for material and £28 for labour, wastage, overheads and profit. *Guadaloupe's* keel was $\frac{3}{4}$in thick, reducing to $\frac{5}{8}$in at stem and stern. There were 121 frames, each with a reverse bar to give a 'Z' shape, spaced at 16in intervals in the engine room, 20in intervals at the ends and 18in intervals between. Her bottom plates were $\frac{5}{8}$in thick reducing to $\frac{1}{2}$in at the waterline and $\frac{3}{8}$in above.

Dupuy de Lôme regarded *Guadaloupe* as the finest and strongest iron warship at sea and he advised the French Navy to copy her. However, the French were not interested in a proposal by Laird for a frigate of 180ft length, 32ft beam, 20ft depth and 12ft draught, propelled by Forrester engines (62in dia, 6ft stroke). The cost of the hull for this vessel was quoted as £18 000 and that of the machinery as £13 500. Equipment at £4500 made up a total of £36 000.

Dupuy de Lôme's enthusiasm for *Guadaloupe* was shared by her first Captain, Edward Phillip Charlwood, a Commander RN on leave (!) Charlwood joined the *Guadaloupe* in 1841 and stood by her till completion, remaining in command for nearly two years, which included the Mexican expedition against Yucatan when she was under fire from both ships and forts. He told a Parliamentary commission in 1847 'For general purposes I am decidedly of the opinion that in several points iron is much preferable to wood for steam vessels. I allude now to vessels for general purposes. There are various points of superiority'. He listed:
Buoyancy;
Roominess due to the thin sides and small deck beams;
Watertight bulkheads which make an iron ship far safer from the risk of grounding; and
Economy in timber, a material then becoming very scarce.
Charlwood said that the only drawback was fouling (see *Warship 12*). On the effect of shot he said 'the damage was considerably less than is usually suffered by a wood vessel; and I should also consider that there were nothing like the number of splinters which are generally forced out by a shot sent through a wooden vessel's side'. Under questioning he said that he had, at Acre, been under fire in *Benbow*, which had been repeatedly hit by shot when the wood gave off enormous splinters. Iron ships were much safer.

During the Mexican campaign against Texas in 1843, *Guadaloupe* was under fire daily for 4-5 weeks and was hulled a number of times by 18 or 24pdr shot:

1 A 24pdr shot struck the bow, where the woodwork of the head was joined on, at a range of 1000yds. The hole was smooth and the same size as the shot
2 A shot struck the counter
3 A spent shot struck the bulwark on the disengaged side and started the plate, tearing the rivets for about 9in
4 A 24pdr struck under water abreast the mainmast and lodged in a bunker. The range was about 1000yds and the hole was clean and circular
5 Another shot also struck about 2ft below the waterline and lodged in a provision cask. The hole was plugged by the engineers who put a plate outside and screwed it into the hole
6 A smooth hole was produced by an 18pdr above the waterline
There was no sign of the jagged edges or the showers of splinters which were seen in the Woolwich trials.

Guadaloupe not only received damage but inflicted it. During the action of 16th May 1843 she hit the Texan corvette *Austin* (20 guns) about a dozen times with her 68pdrs and caused the *Austin* to withdraw.

Charlwood finished his evidence by saying that *Guadaloupe* was a better gun platform than *Salamander,* a smaller Symonds' wooden sloop, and that iron ships were safer in a gale because they were more buoyant. He would prefer to command an iron ship provided that it was properly built

and of the best iron. There had never been any difficulty with the compass; it was a simple but length job to adjust it and well within the capacity of a Naval Officer once he had been taught how to do it.

Charlwood had an interview with Sydney Herbert when he returned to England but this was of little consequence as the Board had already decided on a big expansion of the iron fleet. *Guadaloupe* was followed by the even bigger *Montezuma,* built on the Thames, which was 210ft long and of 34ft beam.

There is a simple builder's mode of *Guadaloupe* in the reserve collection of the Science Museum and a plan in the National Maritime Museum.

Janes Fighting Ships 1978-79
Macdonald & Janes, 1978 (Price: £31.00)

Jane's Fighting Ships has come a long way from its inception in 1898. As the prime source of information on the world's warships it has always been of as much interest to the ship-lover as the naval officer. Today this is still true, despite an enormous increase in price.

As a reference it resembles Rolls-Royce cars in the sense that it has created its own mythology. For example, the Russians believe that it is published on behalf of Western Naval Intelligence. Many laymen think that *Jane's* contains all that there is to know; some people question the need for any new books or magazines on warships on the grounds that 'It's all in *Jane's*'.

The truth is somewhat different. *Fighting Ships* has varied greatly in quality over the years and, in any given year, is better at some things than others. The very early issues, for example, are largely of curiosity value and do not match *Brassey's* for detail and accuracy. This was inevitable because *Jane's* was intended for popular consumption and the information was so abbreviated and simplified as to be almost pointless. The 1914 edition is valuable but not outstanding, whereas the 1919 edition is very good, and much better than either the 1918 or 1920 editions. This is because it contains so much about wartime construction and alterations to older ships.

In the 1920s the quality remained good but, in my opinion it declined in the 1930s to some extent. To cite one example of this decline, it was not the Italian Navy but *Jane's* which perpetuated the myth that Italian cruisers achieved their extraordinary speeds with full armament and fuel aboard. *Jane's* always pandered to the ship-lover's infatuation with statistics and had a tendency to quote speeds out of context, ie without making clear whether it was a designed speed, at light displacement, in smooth water or at full load (see *Warship* No 3 – 'Speed on Trial' by D K Brown).

It must have been almost impossible to keep up to date during the Second World War but the 1944-45 edition cleared up many of the doubts about war-construction, although adding its own contribution to mythology and misinterpretation. In the 1950s there was a marked improvement in quality, largely in the observations made on each class of ship and in the captions under the photographs. The quality of printing and reproduction then slumped dramatically and by the late 1960s became very bad. A pernicious practice crept in of using undated and extremely elderly photographs coyly credited 'Added 1969'; in one case a Chinese Nationalist destroyer was shown in a pre-Pearl Harbor configuration, before the Nationalists even existed as such!

The appointment of a new editor, Captain John Moore, coincided with a long overdue improvement. Now it is possible to change text and update photographs more often. Today it certainly contains more information about more navies than ever before. There is even an entry for Switzerland.

Whether a professional reader or merely a layman dedicated to keeping abreast of naval developments, everyone ultimately turns to the illustrations for they are the link with the ships themselves. *Jane's* uses photographs lavishly but also uses line-drawings to illustrate important ships, scale waterline profiles and silhouettes. Of these the line-drawings are the most important, for an accurately drawn plan and profile are an invaluable aid to understanding photographs and even descriptions of a weapon-fit. In this respect the US Navy comes off a clear winner, with fine drawings by Arthur D Baker III and John Humphrey. The Royal Navy, surprisingly, merits only some poor profiles with no scale shown, which is a poor reflection on a reference work published in the United Kingdom. To be fair I suspect that this can be blamed on the obstructive attitude of the Ministry of Defence, whose Technical Security people labour under the delusion that the Russians will build a copy of HMS *Invincible* from an accurate 1:1800 plan and profile (don't laugh – I have heard a senior official of Procurement Executive say this!). What else can one believe of an organisation that recently refused to allow a shipbuilder to quote the length and beam of a new minehunter?

Photographs are also important, but they must be current and they need interpretation. The reader of the 1978-79 edition cannot help wondering about the rest of the information when he finds a Turkish missile patrol boat credited with 76mm OTO-Melara guns while a photograph of the same vessel showing a twin Oerlikon-Bührle 35mm mounting is printed alongside. He will also be puzzled by oddities like the Admiralty Mk 6M fire control director in a South African frigate when it is labelled as a GDS 5 system – a designation not known to this reviewer. When two ships of the same class of Indian-built *Leander* class frigates sport very different radar aerials it is not enough to say that the ships have Dutch HSA radars in place of British types, especially when one of the photographs shows a GEC-Marconi Type 965 long-range air warning array.

Inevitably the Soviet section is the hardest to assess, for no matter how hard one tries to find out there are the twin perils of Russian silence on the subject and Western navies' willingness to puff the Russians in order to get more money out of their governments. In this respect *Jane's* leans towards the latter fault, and tends to accept some of the wider estimates of performance without question. For example the Kara class are credited with 120 000 shp for 34 knots on 8200 tons (standard) or 10 000 tons (full load) whereas the nuclear-powered USS *California* makes a similar speed on half the power and a slightly larger hull. Where do the Russians put the machinery? With gas turbines there must be a proportionate increase in volume, even without the provision of access trunks and removal routes. The implications are that the Russians are either ahead of both General Electric and Rolls-Royce in gas turbine technology by a very big margin or they have accepted crippling limitations on the use of gas turbines. If the latter is true, why worsen the problem by cramming so much power into a hull, especially when it has been recognised for many years that ultra-high speed has no tactical value? The Russians are neither fiendishly clever nor totally stupid and the laws of hydrodynamics apply to them as much as the Western constructors.

The most dubious feature of the Soviet section is the last part dealing with auxiliaries. This is padded out with civilian survey ships, hydrographic and meteorology vessels, satellite trackers, etc, etc, which have nothing to do with the Soviet Navy or the Defence Ministry. If it is claimed that they are para-military this is no truer than it is of hundreds of similar Western ships. If it is to make the Soviet Navy look bigger, all I can say is that it seems quite big enough to me.

To sum up, *Jane's* is an immensely valuable guide to the warships of today but it can never be taken literally. For one thing it is so big that it cannot be uniformly accurate. For another it takes so long to produce that the information in this edition can only have been correct up to, say, the end of 1977 or at best the first two months of 1978. However, these are not faults of the editor and the compilers, and until the day that *Jane's* changes to a different format such as a quarterly loose-leaf publication on the lines of the Tax Law amendments, they are inherent. *Jane's* is still the premier naval reference book and we would be incomparably worse off without it.

Antony Preston

Big Gun Monitors
by Ian Buxton, World Ship Society and Trident Books, 1978.
(Price: £9.95 + postage and packing)

The monitor has always had a strange appeal. Certainly the most ungainly of ships, they were also the quintessential fighting ship, a pair of big guns sent to sea.

Ian Buxton is well qualified to write this book, being both a naval architect and a distinguished warship enthusiast, who has used official records and personal reminiscences to write a first-rate technical and operational history.

The British never showed much interest in the classic monitor but the peculiar circumstances of the First World War led them to develop their own special variant of the type. Under the dynamic duo – Churchill and Fisher – ships were rapidly built to bombard the vulnerable right flank of the German Army on the Belgian coast. Using American 14in gun turrets illicitly bought from Bethlehem Steel and 12in guns

A line of monitors laid up awaiting disposal after the First World War.
CPL/W/11/015

from old battleships, a scratch force of a dozen monitors was created in a short space of time. Subsequently they saw action from East Africa to the White Sea.

The monitors took long-range gunnery several stages further than it could be taken by the battlefleet. What I find fascinating in this book is the involved story of how techniques evolved to meet the need to fire (and hit) at ever-greater ranges. As an example the 9.2in in the *Gorgon* and *Glatton* ranged to 39 000 yds in 1918, a figure only surpassed by the 18in with modified ammunition, which ranged to 40 100 yds.

The book takes each class in chronological order, with full description, drawings and service careers. Many of the drawings are by the author but some of the best official drawings have been reproduced, giving an idea of what a monitor looked like on the drawing board. All 42 monitors are there, with a separate chapter on the guns and gunnery, illustrated with drawings of the guns and their mountings.

The chapters on the monitors which served in the Second World War throw many interesting sidelights on the art of shore bombardment, and these will be valuable to historians of combined operations and amphibious warfare. In his final chapter the

author concludes that monitors were extremely cost-effective ships, costing about £8 million to build and a further £9 million to run, a large sum but only 1.6 per cent of the cost of the naval war to the RN. They served in nearly all theatres of the war and were a constant source of annoyance to the enemy; one of the German Navy's worst problems was the shortage of heavy guns, many of which were appropriated by the Army for the defence of the Belgian coast. In the Second World War there were only four monitors but they also caused maximum disturbance for minimum cost. The decision to use heavy naval bombardment at Normandy was a direct result of the failure of destroyers' gunfire at Dieppe in 1942.

There was nothing a monitor could do which a battleship could not do better, except go in close to the shore. In the Second World War the new *Roberts* and *Abercrombie* had an added value because of their powerful AA batteries and radar coverage; they were the equivalent of cruisers, but unlike a cruiser, the monitor was there to be risked close inshore. In the First World War the monitors also had a deterrent effect against the German surface fleet, particularly off the Belgian coast.

Disciples of Lord Fisher will not

be pleased by the evidence of his stupidity when meddling in ship-design and refusing to listen to professional advice. As early as December 1914 AEW at Haslar warned that a designed speed of 10kts could not be achieved unless the lines were altered or the installed power was increased. It was typically Fisher to refuse to hold up the building of the hulls but he could easily have prevented the error from being repeated in the two following classes. Egged on by the gadget-minded Churchill he went on to insist on using untried diesel engines in the *Marshall Ney* and *Marshal Soult*, with the result that two of the most powerful, expensive and scarce gun-mountings were installed in ships which behaved like the notorious Russian *Popoffkas*. A side-effect of this obstinacy was to damn the diesel in the eyes of the Navy for another 20 years.

All this and more makes *Big Gun Monitors* a fascinating book. Its presentation is particularly good, with a clear layout, good reproduction and hardly any literals. A point of interest is that it is published jointly by the World Ship Society and Trident Books, a bold and praiseworthy venture. The address is: Trident Books, 12 Grand Parade, Tynemouth, North Shields, Tyne & Wear NE30 4JS, UK.

Antony Preston

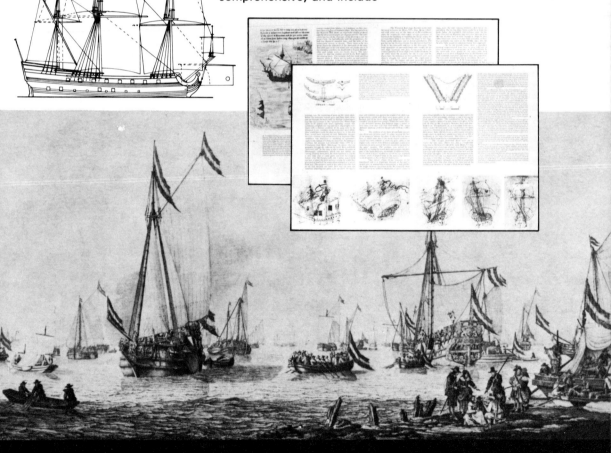

Editorial

In this issue of Warship Norman Friedman describes another warship (the USS *United States*) that was never built and which, without doubt, will raise considerable interest among our readers. This interest in projected ships is, in part, indicative of the enthusiasts' delight in discovering details of ships of which, hitherto, only a few intriguing generalities were known or, in some cases, details of a completely unknown project. For those with a detailed knowledge of vessels actually built the opportunity to study the particulars of such a vessel give a refreshing new edge to their interest and the scope for additional conjecture on what might or might not have happened had naval history taken a slightly different course. The importance of these designs does however vary considerably and some consideration of their place in the history of warship development is always worth considering.

Broadly speaking designs fall into two categories, namely proposed designs and projected designs. The former come in many forms and are usually prepared for discussion either (a) to assist in the formulation of design requirements (b) to show what variations are possibly within the requirements or (c) to demonstrate what possibilities there are in major variations from standard practice. In effect (a) and (b) represent the two initial stages of the design process and their importance is limited to their effect on the design which is finally decided upon. Individually they have little value except where the various proposals have been reduced to two or three possibilities from which one is chosen. In these cases those designs rejected have come very close to being a reality – a classic example of this is the 5.25inch gun *Fiji* class cruiser design (see drawing by A Raven in *Warship* 5) which in slightly different circumstances might well have been chosen in preference to the 6inch gun design actually accepted.

The third category (c) often produced the most extreme and unlikely designs and normally have no more than curiosity value. Among these are several British and US battleship/aircraft carrier and cruiser/aircraft carrier projects and the US giant battleship designs of 1916-17 (70-80 000 tons, 18inch guns) and 1944 (106 500 tons, 16inch guns).

Projected designs are of course of much greater importance as they represent a definite intention to build and therefore have a very definite place in the design history of the group to which they belong. As examples one could mention the British *G3* battlecruisers, the *Gibraltar* class aircraft carriers and the *Northumberland* class cruisers, the US battleships of the *Montana* class and many more. Some of these vessels went well beyond the projected stage with construction well advanced (in some cases to early fitting out) and again there are many examples – the German aircraft carrier *Graf Zeppelin*, the US battleships of the first *South Dakota* class, the Russian battleships of the *Sovietsky Soyuz* class and so on.

One asset of a projected ship not usually found in ships constructed to a normal programme is the major modification of the original design usually as a result of extensive delays in their laying down. Such vessels were the British *Lion* class of the 1938 Programme. But for the outbreak of war they would certainly have been constructed to the original design which provided for an armament of nine 16inch guns on a displacement of 40 550 tons with dimensions of 785ft (oa) x 104ft x 30ft. There would, of course have been some detail changes while the vessels were under construction but these would have been limited by the existing dimensions of the hull. In fact as the ships' construction did not progress, a considerable amount of re-design was possible and by 1945 the *Lions* were projected as 59 100 tons (standard) with dimensions of 960ft (oa) x 120ft x 35ft with the same armament. Although never built, the story of how the *Lion* class design gained 50% in displacement would be of great value in illustrating the effect of war experience on the design of battleships in a single line of development between 1938 and 1945.

While on the subject of projected designs; I recently came across some basic particulars of the Soviet *Sovietsky Soyuz* class which were given, by the Russians, to the British in 1937 and included in the intelligence files on foreign ships. The details given were as follows: Standard displacement: 44 190 tons, dimensions: 794ft x 119ft x 29ft 10in, machinery: turbo-generators 150 000 SHP = 29 knots, armament: nine 16inch, twelve 5.9inch, twelve 3.9inch, twenty smaller, two aircraft. In dimensions these particulars vary substantially from those I have found in published sources, so did the Russians deliberately provide false information, was the design later modified like the *Lion* class or is it simply a case of the particulars of several proposed designs becoming confused?

John Roberts

THE FIRST OF THE SUPER CARRIERS
USS UNITED STATES

By NORMAN FRIEDMAN

Since the *Forrestal* class was laid out during 1950-52 US aircraft carriers have been fixed in their basic design despite the major transition from conventional to nuclear power and many detail changes. Indeed, the attack carrier design goes back a step further to a much larger ship, the *United States* (CVA 58), designed just after the Second World War, laid down and then cancelled as a result of Air Force-Navy animosity. The *United States* herself was developed as an alternative, and then as a successor, to the new fleet carrier designed in 1945-46 and described in *Warship 10.* She was intended from the first for naval strategic attack with long range bombers capable of carrying

An artist's rendering of the large carrier *United States* (CVA 58), 1949. The final plans show a different arrangement of uptakes, but the flight deck configuration had been fixed by this time. Along and around the flight deck, the single gun mounts are rapid-fire 5inch/54s, the twins, 3inch/70s. Note the arrangement of catapults to avoid mutual interference, with one elevator serving each. The aircraft shown are not in scale nor are they representative, but they were the types in service at the time: F2H fighters and P2V Neptune bombers (aft).
USN

the very heavy nuclear weapons of the early postwar period and as such was perceived by the Air Force as a direct challenge to their own basic mission. This mission, incidentally, made the Air Force by far the most dominant service in a postwar Military Establishment based upon nuclear attack.

The precise origins of the heavy attack carrier are difficult to establish but it is clear that by the end of 1945 interest within the naval aviation community had begun to shift away from the wartime general-purpose carrier and towards a more specialized type optimized for the operation of a small group of heavy bombers. More than anything else, the size of

such aircraft would dominate hull design; for example, it seemed that truly efficient operation of aircraft with long wings demanded a flush deck, a dream of naval aviators in the 1920s and 1930s and which had actually been designed into the old *Ranger*, the first purpose-built US carrier.

For example, on 28 December 1945 Rear Admiral Sallada of the Bureau of Aeronautics recommended a new type to the CNO: 'It is believed that the 39 600 ton carrier will be well adapted to general all-around naval warfare . . . However, in order for the Navy to maintain an equitable position in air-sea warfare of the future, it is believed that serious consideration

should immediately be given to the development of an additional type . . . that will accommodate aircraft of about 100 000lbs with a 2000 mile radius. The ship may be rather radical in design with, for example, no island and no hangar. A flight deck equivalent to the CVB 41 class would accommodate about 14 planes . . . 500 000 gallons of gasoline would permit each plane about eight full-range flights. Such a carrier would be capable of long-range bombing as opportunity afforded; at other times it would be available for more conventional operations.'

At this time Admiral Mitscher, who had commanded the Fast Carrier Task Force during the war

and who had begun the development of the 39 600 ton carrier, became DCNO (Air) and on 8 January 1946 recommended to the CNO the development of both the 100 000lb bomber and a carrier, to accommodate 16 to 24 such aircraft, capable of supporting a total of about 100 sorties without replenishment. There would be no hangar because the aircraft would be so large that they could not fit any conceivable hangar space. The small number of sorties per aircraft may well reflect the assumption that nuclear weapons would be used, as Mitscher had met Captain William Parsons and Cdr John T Hayward, both of whom had worked on the Manhattan Project. The VCNO approved these studies on 7 February and work within BuShips began on 4 April. In fact some preliminary studies had been conducted even earlier, as CVB-X. It is interesting that the Bureau of Ships did contemplate provision of a hangar to permit operation of smaller aircraft.

PRELIMINARY STUDIES

Much of the detail work on the new carrier was taken from the Fleet Carrier study: speed and endurance (12 000nm at 20 knots, 33 knots on trial) were the same and defensive battery consisted, in 1946, of twelve 5in/54 (rapid-firing single mounts) and sixteen (four per quadrant) of the new twin 3in/70. Protection was to consist of a 3in flight deck supplemented by a 1.5in deck one and one-half decks above the designed waterline, as well as by 1.5in STS spread from hangar deck to 8ft below water over about 700ft of length, closed at the ends by 1.5in STS bulkheads extending all the way up to the flight deck. The absence of hangar deck armor conflicted with wartime practice; presumably the designer assumed that the hull was so deep that any bomb whose fuze was initiated by the flight deck would have burst before it hit the armored fifth deck. The size of the flight deck was fixed by a requirement to stow 23 aircraft while yet leaving the 24th enough space to land. BuAer estimates

were based on a bomber sketch design (ADR 42) about 90ft long, with 116ft wing span (44 folded) which required 500ft to land and 400ft to take-off using a catapult. Allowing for the densest possible parking, about 75ft of flight deck length would be consumed by three bombers abreast; 24 bombers would require a flight deck about 1125ft long. Even fifteen would require 900ft.

All of this the ship designers were glad to provide; they were not happy, however, with the concept of the flush deck. 'To meet this characteristic would require locating of ship conning stations in sponsons and possibly also under the flight deck forward, with special provision for some means of conning the ship from an overall vantage point, such as from a telescopic structure, when working the ship in congested waters . . . Special means would have to be devised for discharge of exhaust gases to minimize interference with flight operations. In the CVB-X study, therefore, the conning station and uptakes are included in a small island. By locating this island just forward of the barriers, the landing area is not affected. The location of the island provides an unobstructed flight deck length for landing and take-off of 500ft . . . The advantages of the island warrant accepting this protrusion in way of the first part of the take-off run when unassisted by catapult.' Similar logic had eliminated the flush deck of the *Ranger* and a flush deck proposed for the *Yorktown* (CV 5). However, in 1945 the aviators were so much in the ascendant that the Bureau of Ships arguments against the flush deck were quickly rejected. All through the CVA 58 (and CVA 59) design periods the effort to keep the flight deck clear of obstructions caused problems, the worst being not the lack of vision to conn the ship by, but rather smoke disposal through funnels which had to tilt down for flight operations at high speed. It seems remarkable in retrospect that nowhere in the design correspondence on this subject, which is quite extensive, is there mention of Japanese practice with regard to flush flight decks,

which characterized most of their carriers.

In any case, as the ADR 42 design developed, it began to appear that some could in fact be stowed in a hangar of reasonable size thus relieving the pressure for so large a flight deck. For example, although it was estimated that a CVB-X intended to stow 24 aircraft on deck would have an overall length of 1190ft (1124 on the waterline), drydock considerations would probably limit her to a 1050ft flight deck (15 aircraft). Ultimately the flush-deck carrier project would incorporate a hangar with a 28ft clear height. By way of comparison, the wartime standard had been 17.5ft and carriers actually built since 1951 have 25ft clear hangar heights.

As an illustration of the importance of the flush deck, in 1946 several air Admirals proposed the conversion of an existing *Essex* class carrier to test the concept. Others, observing that a flush-deck carrier would not be able to accommodate the forest of wartime electronic gear, suggested the conversion or construction of specialized ships to this end; this was the origin of the *Northampton*. The flush deck exemplified the impact of the new ADR 42 bomber on the new carrier: for the first time in US (and possibly world) carrier design, a ship was designed specifically for a new class of aircraft. At the same time, the aircraft itself was being developed; the Bureau of Aeronautics pursued the ADR 42 design study specifically in order to guess the dimensions of the aircraft on which in turn, flight deck dimensions and catapult characteristics were to be based. This was very tricky, as aeronautics was in a period of very rapid development. A carrier design conference was convened by DCNO (Logistics), who was in charge of the Ship Characteristics Board, on 19 June 1946. It was unlikely that a ship would be ready before 1952, so that it was necessary for DCNO (Air) to estimate aircraft characteristics for the 1952-60 period. At this time it was decided that design would be funded under the FY 48 Budget, fo the year beginning 1 July 1947, and construction would begin in FY 49.

DESIGN CHARACTERISTICS

The Ship Characteristics Board produced draft Characteristics in February 1947 calling for an air group of 54 fighters (the new XF2H Banshee) and either 12 to 18 ADR 45A attack aircraft (57 000 lbs, four turbo-props, 750mile combat radius) or 12 ADR 42 (now listed at 89 000lbs, four augmented turbo-props, 2000nm radius); the fighters appear to have been accepted as bomber escorts far more than as a means of carrier self-protection. There were to be four flight-deck catapults, the forward pair 'capable of launching fully loaded aircraft of the largest size used on the ship. The remaining two catapults shall be capable of launching a 60 000 lb aircraft. Provision shall be made for simultaneous rapid positioning and launching of jet powered aircraft on each catapult without mutual interference and without disturbing landing arrangements.' There would be four deck edge elevators (at one time ramps were considered instead in view of the great weight of the aircraft to be lifted).

As in the 1946 fleet carrier (see *Warship 10*), the need for simultaneous catapult operations led to a kind of angled flight deck, with two catapults in conventional positions near the bow and two more on sponsons angled out to port and to starboard, where aircraft emerging from them would not interfere with those launched forward. The philosophy of such a deck is entirely different from that of a modern angled flight deck, in which the angled portion is there primarily to allow for a long landing run without interference from either parked aircraft or from aircraft sitting on the catapults. In the new big carrier, aircraft would land straight ahead from aft, as in Second World War carriers, and it would still be vital to interpose a barrier between the landing run and the aircraft parking area further forward. The emphasis, rather, was on quick launches, to get a strike

into the air as fast as possible, perhaps in part due to the limited endurance of the new jet aircraft.

The Board called for a 3in flight deck, 60lb STS hangar and protective decks (over the machinery), with 60lb STS on the side, from 8ft below the waterline up to the hangar deck, over the length of the hangar. A new feature was internal armour consisting of a 4in side and 60lb deck over the three armoured boxes housing magazines, gasoline and steering gear. In the course of detailed design, BuShips split the 3in flight-deck into a 2in flight-deck with a 1in gallery deck below it. It might well prove impossible to keep bombs entirely out of the ship but the Bureau felt that a big break in the flight-deck, which in this ship was also the strength deck, might well cause the ship to break up, unless there were some structure underneath to take the loads for a low-speed run out of the battle area. That was the gallery deck. A loss in direct bomb protection had to be accepted; 2in plus the separate 1in deck were equivalent to about 2.5in, but there was insufficient weight for more, even in a very large ship.

The major problem in the design was always arrangement. One Bureau of Ships memorandum observed that 'the interrelationship of the four catapults, four bomb elevators, and two special (nuclear) bomb magazines governed the arrangement to a considerable extent. The location of the catapults fixed the position of the bomb elevators which, assuming direct hoisting from below, located the special bomb magazines. With the after special bomb magazine pushed far into the stern, it became necessary to fit an underwate defense system relatively farther aft in the ship than has been done in recent carriers. The result was that the outboard shafting penetrated the system, necessitating the working of shaft alleys through and between the underwater defense system bulkheads.'

'The main magazines, located forward and aft, are intended primarily to contain aircraft ammunition. All the 3in and 5in

ship ammunition except the forward 5in ammunition is stowed in unprotected magazines. Since the ship's battery is located so far forward and aft it was considered impracticable to extend the heavily armored magazines to include ship ammunition or to enlarge the bomb magazines and carry long hoists to the mounts. It was felt that the character of the ship ammunition was such that we could risk a hit in that type of magazine.'

Ultimately the magazine problem was made even more complex by a decision to use powder (explosive) catapults, the charges of which required magazine stowage. The explosive charge catapult concept carried over to the *Forrestal* design, causing great problems until the advent of the steam catapult eliminated them.

OPERATIONAL EMPLOYMENT

At this time the Navy expected to operate its big carriers in task forces consisting of one flush-deck carrier, one modernized *Midway* and two modernized *Essexes*; one additional force with three *Essexes* was also planned. Each force would also include cruisers (including a command ship), one guided missile ship and destroyers and submarines for ASW screening and radar picket duties. Such a force would be extremely powerful. A January 1948 Navy internal study indicated that the flush-deck carrier would be able to accommodate 24 ADR 42 and F2H fighters; the *Midway,* 12 A2J (an abortive turboprop attack plane) and 43 ADR-54 (long range escort fighters); the *Essexes,* a total of 48 escorts (F9F or F2H), 48 interceptors (F4D, for fleet air defense) and 48 single-seat attack aircraft (A2D Skysharks). All of these aircraft together would be able to carry 456 000lbs of bombs or other ordnance; and even though this seemed impressive, it did not take into account the development of nuclear weapons easily portable by relatively small attack aircraft.

The Navy study went on to evaluate carrier task force performance (in a 1955 scenario) against likely Soviet defences, assuming that one task force would be deployed in the Eastern Mediterranean, one in the Western Pacific and two in US East Coast ports. Typical operating areas would include the Norwegian and Barents Seas and the Pacific, off the Soviet coast; it was shown that 'there is no spot within the USSR which cannot be reached from four such carrier task forces, suitably deployed . . . If 1955 targets were the same as 1947 targets and four such task forces were available to us, it would appear that the most effective and early assault would be that from two forces in the Barents Sea, one in the Norwegian Sea and one in the Mediterranean . . . The D-Day probable disposition for our carrier task forces would dictate a slightly different arrangement, such as one force in the Barents Sea, one in the North Sea, one in the Mediterranean and one in the Arabian Sea. This deployment fails to cover targets in Eastern Siberia but, as previously noted, the present USSR target system makes this an unproductive area for attack, only five targets of secondary importance being known to exist there . . .'

This kind of thinking could not fail to upset the Air Force, which had based its own power on a monopoly of the means for strategic attack against the primary potential enemy, the Soviet Union. It must have seemed to the Air Force that the Navy's ability to carry out a major strategic role depended on its ability to fly very large carrier aircraft as the ADR 42, and that such capability depended, as the Navy claimed, on the existence of a new class of flush-deck carriers. The Navy in turn claimed that a new carrier would be essential to the further development of carrier aviation, which was far more flexible than simple nuclear attack on Soviet internal targets. Moreover, the Second World War had shown that submarines might well cut the vital life line to the UK and thence to the main theatre of operations in Europe (it was not then believed that nuclear weapons would make long wars impossible). The Navy claimed that one of its more potent ASW measures would be mine and bomb attack on Soviet

submarine bases, and that the new carrier would be essential for such a mission. The echoes of these ideas are still with us, albeit in different form.

AUTHORIZATION AND CANCELLATION

The carrier was authorized as CVA 58, USS *United States*, under the FY 49 budget; the 'A' suffix was new and indicated 'attack,' although surely some thought 'atomic' more appropriate. It was ordered from Newport News and laid down on 19 April 1949. However, in the meanwhile the Air Force and its friends had been busy; the Air Force charged that the new carrier would merely duplicate its strategic bombing mission, at a cost of $500 million (the Navy claimed that cost would be $189 million). Construction was stopped on 23 April and the funds used instead to buy heavy bombers. The ensuing fight was one of the Navy's worst peacetime disasters and appeared to leave the Air Force triumphant. The big carrier, and its heavy bomber, were cancelled and new aircraft funds redirected towards aircraft which could fly off *Midway* and *Essex* class carriers: the chief heavy attack aircraft of the late 1950s and 1960s, the A3D or A-3, was designed under these constraints.

However, the idea of a big flush-deck aircraft carrier had not died completely. Even as CVA 58 was being cancelled, the Bureau of Ships began to study reduced versions, in the hope that a substantial reduction in the 66 850ton standard displacement would permit a revival of the project. Somewhat later, Senator Carl Vinson, the Navy's great friend, suggested that Congress was still disposed in favor of a new carrier but that it would have to be kept below 60 000tons. The result was the *Forrestal,* studies of which began in earnest (as 'CV Junior') in February 1950. The outbreak of the Korean War that June made defence funds readily available and so alleviated the interservice rivalry which had destroyed the *United States.* The ultimate result, of course, was not merely a reduced

CVA 58 although many CVA 58 features remained, and it is possible to see in all current US carriers a direct outgrowth of the original *United States* and so of Mitscher's concepts of 1945.

Indeed, the *Forrestal* began as a flush-deck carrier (with much the same flight-deck arrangement as the *United States*) and was actually laid down as such. Part of the Navy's urgency in her design and construction can be seen in the fact that the viability of the essential powder-driven catapult had by no means been proven when the new ship was designed to incorporate it; in fact it appears that the steam catapult arrived just in time, since there was no alternative capable of launching even heavily loaded jet fighters. Similarly, the modern angled deck was not incorporated in the initial design and the ship had to be modified while under construction. Given the extreme difficulty of disposing of smoke at high power *except* through a conventional funnel, the angled

deck must have been a very major factor in the success of the *Forrestal* design.

In one way the angled deck and island combination was a retreat. The catapult originally intended for the starboard sponson, and therefore originally clear of the other three, had to be moved to the port sponson, where it is mounted at an angle to the one already there, so that aircraft can be held on both catapults in readiness but not fired off simultaneously.

One theme runs through the *United States* design and indeed through the design of many large ships. Even though these ships seem so immense that surely they must be able to accommodate nearly anything, in fact their designs are very tight. For example, for all of her great size, the *United States* was actually less heavily armoured than was the *Midway*. Indeed, some magazines had to be unprotected although, on the other hand, total bomb stowage volume greatly exceeded that of earlier carriers, as

did gasoline stowage. It proved impossible to accommodate the gun battery originally desired, and even accommodation of enough elevators to feed the catapults continuously proved impossible. The original *Forrestal* characteristics actually asked for more (in some ways) in a smaller hull and the great surprise is that some sacrifices (eg in hangar height) sufficed to buy most of the Characteristics originally demanded.

ACKNOWLEDGEMENTS

I am, as always, grateful to the staff of the Federal Record Center (Suitland) and the Naval History Center (Operational Archives) for their invaluable assistance. Much BuShips material was made available through the courtesy of Mr Charles Wiseman, formerly of the US Navy Ship Engineering Center, and I am grateful to David Rosenberg, who has long studied US strategic (particularly naval) policy of the postwar period, for operational material.

CHARACTERISTICS

Displacement: 66 850 (std), 78 500 (full load)
Dimensions: 1030 (wl), 1090 (oa) x 130 (mld), 190 (over sponsons) x 34.5 (full load) ft
Machinery: 280 000 SHP = 33kts (four shafts; four main machinery rooms each containing two boilers and a turbine, with auxiliary rooms between these). All used 1200psi boilers (950°). Eight 2000kw ship service turbo-generators, plus four 1000kw emergency diesel generators
Armament: 8 single rapid-fire 5in/54in, 6 twin 3in/70 rapid-fire mounts. For a time twenty 20mm guns were provided for (weight only). Ammunition: 700 rounds per 5in, 1100 per 3in barrel. 2000 tons of aviation ordnance. The air group itself came to 1339 tons
Endurance: 12 000nm at 20kts
Complement: 4127

The US carrier *Constellation,* one of the six *Forrestal* class ships whose basic design was derived from the aborted *United States*
MoD, courtesy A Preston

THE 18-INCH GUN IN BRITISH MONITORS

BY I L BUXTON

The British 18in, BL Mk I gun was a product of Jacky Fisher's megalomania. The two 'large light cruisers' *Courageous* and *Glorious* planned for his Baltic project (in which a British fleet would support a Russian landing in Pomerania only 90 miles from Berlin) had been ordered in January 1915, each to carry two twin 15in gun turrets and have a speed of 32 knots. In March a third ship, *Furious,* was ordered to a generally similar shallow draft design but to be armed with two single 18in gun mountings. The Royal Gun Factory at Woolwich had drawn up a design for a 40 calibre 18in gun capable of firing a 1½ton projectile, while the EOC (Elswick Ordnance Company), Armstrong Whitworth's main Newcastle works, had prepared a conventional single turret mounting of the same general design as the twin 15in, which had just entered service in the battleship *Queen Elizabeth.*

The design performance of the 149ton[1] gun provided for a range of 30 000yds at 30° elevation with a 3320lb projectile and a muzzle velocity of 2300 ft/sec. This range was hardly greater than the 15in firing a 1920lb projectile at 2450 ft/sec, since manufacturing difficulties, as discussed by John Campbell in *Warship 11,* prevented any size larger than MD 45[2] being made, which would have produced better ballistics. The 630lb full-charge had to be made up of six 105lb part charges to ease handling.

Design and construction work on the two single 18in turrets and the three guns (one spare) progressed well during 1915, when it was known for security reasons as the 15in B. Two British companies manufactured heavy projectiles, Firth's and Hadfield's (both of Sheffield) and the latter was selected to prepare a design. In June 1915, they submitted a design of their 'Eron' pattern as a CPC (Common Pointed Cap) projectile. This had a 4crh (calibre radius of head), the then RN standard, and a bursting charge of 7.3% of the total weight. 500 such projectiles were ordered, followed in 1916 by 500 APC (Armour Piercing Cap) 4crh of Hadfield's 'Heclon' design with a 3.6% burster.

FURIOUS

Furious was launched on 15 August 1916, about the same time as Elswick were completing her guns. Each was taken by rail to EOC's proving ground at Ridsdale, 25 miles north-west of Newcastle, for proof firing. Trials of gun Register No2 began on 20 September, firing both full charges and supercharges. Trials of No3 gun included reduced charges, allowing muzzle velocity to be correlated with charge weight. The standard 630lb full charge produced on average a muzzle velocity of 2260 ft/sec, rather less than designed, the 705lb proof charge averaged 2450 ft/sec, the 420lb two-thirds charge 1750 ft/sec and the 315lb half charge 1470 ft/sec. In October a CPC projectile was tried in the butts against a 600lb (14.7in) Cammell Laird cemented armour plate. The plate was penetrated at a striking velocity of 1555 ft/sec, corresponding to a range of about 16 000 yards.

Meantime *Furious'* 'Y' turret had been installed (after turrets were installed before forward turrets to aid machinery and shafting alignment), together with No1 gun. Early in 1917, Admiral Beatty, now C-in-C of the Grand Fleet, had set up a committee to review the provision of aircraft for the fleet. By March, it was decided that *Furious* would be more valuable as a seaplane carrier than as a battlecruiser type, so plans were made to add a flying-off deck and hangar for seaplanes over the forecastle. Shipment of her 'A' turret and No 2 gun had not been completed, so there was now at least one single 18in turret available for fitting in another vessel. Charles Lillicrap, a young constructor who had designed the first British monitors in November 1914, was called in to examine the feasibility of installing the 18in turret in one of these vessels, presently armed with a Bethlehem-built twin 14in turret. The four 6150 ton ships, *Abercrombie, Havelock, Raglan*

and *Roberts,* had been completed in only seven months in mid 1915. Lillicrap's calculations, dated 21 March 1917, showed that replacing the turret with another would add about 440tons extra weight – technically feasible although considerable reconstruction would be necessary to accommodate the taller, larger diameter 18in turret.

This ambitious rearming plan was not proceeded with; instead two of the 18in guns were offered to Vice Admiral Reginald Bacon, in command at Dover. The Navy had been manning heavy artillery ashore near the Franco-Belgian border since 1915, so Bacon conceived the idea of installing the 18in guns at Westende, whence they could bombard the important German U-boat and destroyer base at Bruges. Although Westende was still in German hands, it was hoped that the forthcoming 'Third Ypres' offensive would enable the Allies to advance far enough in conjunction with a seaborne landing west of Ostende to capture the area. Bacon describes in detail, in his book *The*

Dover Patrol 1915-1917, how he planned to ship the guns and specially designed mountings across the Channel lashed to the bulges of monitors, for installation inside the Palace Hotel at Westende. But the offensive petered out in the Flanders mud in September, so plans to mount the guns had to be shelved.

MONITOR REARMAMENT
Bacon had already come up with an alternative plan to mount the 18in guns on board some of the 12in gun monitors, not in place of their twin turret forward, but as an addition on the forecastle deck abaft the funnel. The CD (Coast Defence) mounting which had been designed for land service could be installed without too much reconstruction if it was fitted on deck and trained permanently over the starboard beam, since no revolving turret or ammunition supply trunk was needed. The gun would be mounted as illustrated, capable of elevation up to 45° for maximum range, but trainable through a total arc of only

On board *Lord Clive* looking aft along the starboard side. The 18inch gun is at its maximum elevation of 45°

IWM

¹ This figure is given in Ordnance Board minutes and is believed to be the final figure rather than the estimated figure of 152.3 tons quoted in the 18in gun handbook (CB 830).

² MD was cordite modified to reduce bore erosion, 45 the diameter of the sticks in hundredths of an inch.

20°. Bacon's proposals included the following items:

(a) Strengthen and support the forecastle deck, and work in the front pivot girders and rear supporting girders

(b) Pocket this deck for a length of 24ft to allow for recoil at maximum elevation

(c) A camouflage of thin plating to represent armour in aircraft photographs

(d) A plain push-and-pull cylinder (elevating cylinder with trunnions vertical) for training through 20°

(e) A good windlass aft to work a stern anchor and chain aft, of the same size as the bower cable and anchor of the ships (4tons and 2¹/₈in diameter) together with chain locker

(f) The shell to be stowed on the upper deck, point up and 30° to the vertical, under the 1in forecastle deck, as a protection against bombs, and provided with suitable nose-caps (this presumably meant ballistic caps to give greater range)

(g) The cordite cases to be stowed on the forecastle deck, spaced apart to prevent one deflagrating the next; if possible in a water-jacket, steam-heated to keep up the temperature of the cordite in winter (to provide maximum and consistent range)

(h) Sufficient ammunition for the day's firing, about 60 rounds only, would be embarked. Such a stowage of ammunition should be far safer than the present monitors' magazine and shell-rooms

(i) The loading arrangements to be those as for the land mounting; two winches for hoisting shell only would be required in addition

(j) A pressure pipe from the present hydraulic system would be led to the gun

(k) None of the present armament to be disturbed

(l) Indicators from the present director to be taken to the gun, which would be laid by clinometer, much on the same principle as is now employed

Apart from (f) and (l), all these proposals were approved in September by Admiral Jellicoe, now First Sea Lord, himself a former Director of Naval Ordnance. It was considered easier to stow and transport the shells horizontally, while a second director was to be fitted on the foremast below the spotting top, but angled out to port where it could train out to sea on a ship anchored as a fixed aiming mark –necessary because the ships would be ten miles or more off the low-lying featureless Belgian Coast.

W H Gard, one of the Assistant Directors of Naval Construction, arranged for Lillicrap and a new assistant constructor, K H Watkins, to work up the detailed design, including alternative mounting positions and ballasting arrangements. The only place to fit the mounting without removing the 12in turret was abaft the funnel but, in order to provide adequate structural support beneath the mounting, it would need to be sited abaft the engine room. The huge trimming moment due to the concentrated load about 100ft aft of

1 An 18inch gun being shipped aboard *Lord Clive* at Portsmouth Dockyard on 7 September 1918

Cdr L F Robinson

2 A close up of the breech of *Lord Clive's* 18inch gun viewed from the right side of the mounting. The mechanism in the extreme left background is the training control and the raised platform is for the breechworker.

Cdr L F Robinson

midships would increase the draft aft to about 14ft, seriously reducing the freeboard to only about 4ft. Various proposals were examined to reduce the trim, including water ballast forward. The most satisfactory solution was found to be closing up watertight the after inboard bulge compartments, which were normally open to the sea. It was calculated that the resulting drafts would be 9ft 2½in forward and 11ft 10½in aft, with a displacement of about 6645 tons. The latter figure assumed that 645 tons was added to a basic condition of 6000 tons at a level draft of 10ft. This draft was the designed condition, no attempt having been made to check whether it represented the monitors' current condition. In fact two years' service had added several hundred tons to the monitors' weight, so they all had a trim by the stern of a foot or more. The result was that, as finally converted, the ship's drafts became 8ft 9in forward and 13ft 2in aft, corresponding to a displacement of 6850tons. Not only was freeboard aft now dangerously reduced, but the bulge was fully submerged, increasing the risk of a torpedo or

distance-controlled explosive motor boat riding over the bulge and exploding against the main hull proper. A heavy steel rail was built up on top of the bulge to prevent this happening.

THE 18IN CD MOUNTING
Meantime approval had been given to convert *Furious* fully to a seaplane carrier, by installing a flying-on deck aft. A third 18in gun would thus be available permitting three monitors to be converted. Orders went to Elswick on 23 September 1917 to construct three new mountings for delivery between March and May 1918. The mounting consisted of two massive side girders parallel to the barrel, tied together at each end, between which the gun carriage and slide was slung. At the forward end was a strong support and a pivot about which the gun could train in a limited arc. The gun would be loaded at the fixed angle of 10°, but actual firing would only be permitted between 22° and 45° in order to distribute the recoil forces fairly evenly between the forward and after supports. The maximum

firing loads (which included the dead load of the mounting) were estimated to be 460 tons force vertically and 675 tons horizontally on the forward support and 400 tons vertically on the sliding after support. 10° of training on either side of the mounting centre-line was achieved by a push-pull hydraulic cylinder – actually a gun elevating cylinder placed horizontally. Only the mounting itself trained, the shield being fixed to the deck. Hydraulically operated cranes, loading tray, rammer and breech mechanism were all provided to ease the physical effort by the gun's crew. The ammunition supply parties were not so fortunate as all movement had to be done by muscle power. The projectiles were to be stowed horizontally on the upper deck and moved by overhead transporter rail to the hatch in the forecastle deck through which they were to be lifted to the breech, while the cordite was to be transferred from the stowage tanks onto a small bogie running on rails, two one-sixth charges at a time. Total stowage was provided for 60 projectiles and 72 full charges (equivalent to 61 supercharges). By

cutting out the armoured gunhouse and all the elaborate ammunition working arrangements associated with a revolving mounting, the weight was reduced to 384tons, including the gun.

MONITOR CONVERSIONS
The actual ships to be converted to take the 18in gun were those with the three most senior commanding officers, *Lord Clive, Prince Eugene*

Transverse section of the 18inch mounting as fitted in the monitors

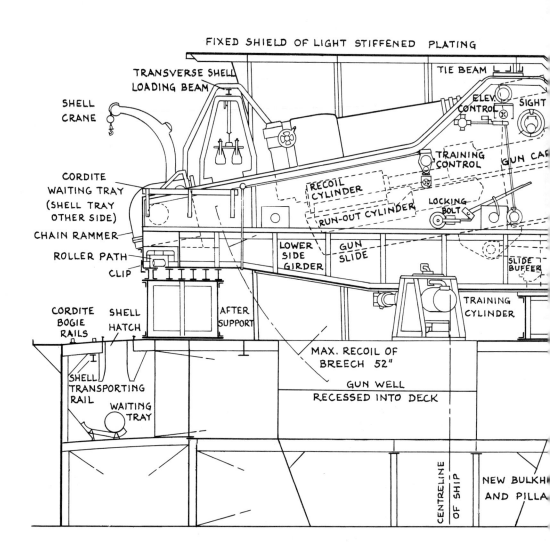

and *General Wolfe*. The plan was to take the first two vessels in hand at Portsmouth Dockyard in December 1917, fit the extra supports in January and ship the mounting in March. After trials, they would return to service in May, while the third vessel started her conversion. But delays in completing the mountings meant that work on the hulls of the first two vessels was finished in early April before the mountings were ready. Elswick had expected the trials of the first mounting to take place at the Proof and Experimental Establishment at Silloth on the Solway Firth at the end of January 1918, but they had underestimated the work involved and were plagued by labour shortages and strikes at sub-contractors. Although the first two guns had been sent to Portsmouth in January, it was not until May that the first mounting started trials. These were intended to prove in addition a new 8crh projectile and a supercharge to give longer range. The first trials revealed that the rammer motor was not powerful enough to ram the $1\frac{1}{2}$ton projectile fully into the gun. Eventually everything was working satisfactorily by 26 May and the mounting was despatched in pieces to Portsmouth where it arrived on

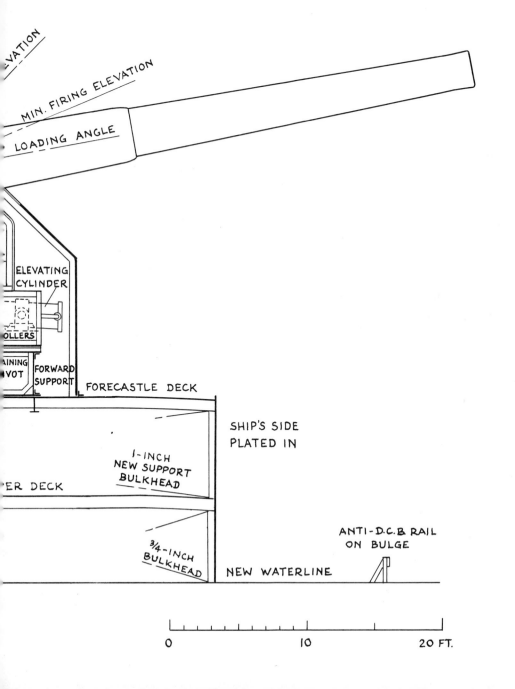

Profile and decks of *General Wolfe's* after 180ft.

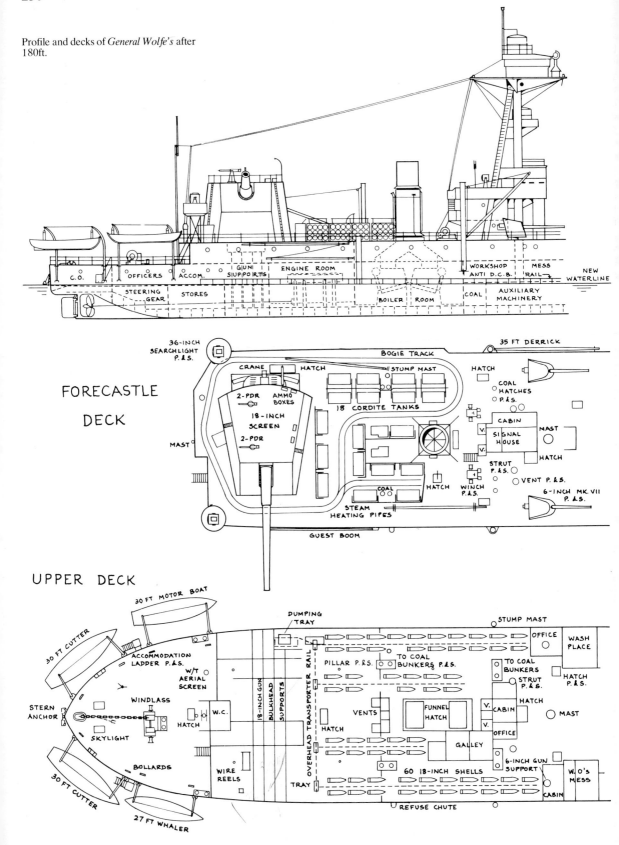

Profile (side view labels):
C.O. · OFFICERS · ACCOM. · GUN SUPPORTS · ENGINE ROOM · WORKSHOP · MESS · ANTI D.C.B. · RAIL · NEW WATERLINE
STEERING GEAR · STORES · BOILER ROOM · COAL · AUXILIARY MACHINERY

FORECASTLE DECK

36-INCH SEARCHLIGHT P. & S.
35 FT DERRICK
BOGIE TRACK
CRANE · HATCH · STUMP MAST · HATCH
COAL HATCHES P. & S.
2-PDR · AMMO BOXES
18-INCH SCREEN
2-PDR
18 CORDITE TANKS
MAST
CABIN · SIGNAL HOUSE · MAST · HATCH
STRUT P. & S.
VENT P. & S.
WINCH P. & S.
COAL · HATCH
6-INCH MK. VII P. & S.
STEAM HEATING PIPES
GUEST BOOM

UPPER DECK

30 FT MOTOR BOAT
DUMPING TRAY
STUMP MAST
OFFICE · WASH PLACE
30 FT CUTTER
ACCOMMODATION LADDER P. & S.
W/T AERIAL SCREEN
PILLAR P. & S. · TO COAL BUNKERS P. & S.
TO COAL BUNKERS
STRUT P. & S.
HATCH P. & S.
STERN ANCHOR
WINDLASS
W.C. · HATCH
18-INCH GUN BULKHEAD SUPPORTS
OVERHEAD TRANSPORTER RAIL
VENTS
FUNNEL HATCH
V. · CABIN
V. · OFFICE
HATCH · MAST
SKYLIGHT
HATCH
GALLEY
6-INCH GUN SUPPORT
BOLLARDS
WIRE REELS
TRAY
60 18-INCH SHELLS
W.O'S MESS
30 FT CUTTER
CABIN
27 FT WHALER
REFUSE CHUTE

20 June for erection in the third ship, *General Wolfe,* which had been taken in hand at Portsmouth Dockyard on 5 April. *Wolfe* was not yet ready to receive it, so it was not unly 9 July that the huge gun was actually lifted on board. After coaling and ammunitioning, she was ready for gun trials, which were carried out successfully off the Isle of Wight on 7 August.

Wolfe's appearance had substantially altered. The closing-in of the sides of the upper deck and the huge 18in gunshield gave her a much more businesslike appearance. Two 2pdr pompoms were perched on top of the shield, but otherwise her secondary armament was concentrated forward – two 6in BL Mk VII and two 3in high angle guns. Smaller changes included installing two 36in searchlights aft, a slim mainmast to support the wireless aerials, bow defence gear against mines, the 18 cordite stowage tanks, a new ammunition derrick for the 18in and a more substantial bridge structure. Internally the new armament necessitated many changes. The after half of the upper deck was given over to the 18in shell stowage and their transporters plus the extensive structural supports for the mounting. The supports, consisting mainly of partial transverse bulkheads of $\frac{1}{2}$ and 1in thickness, extended right down to the double bottom,

General Wolfe at Portsmouth ready to re-enter service in August 1918. Her 4½ft trim by the stern is readily apparent

232

cramping the officers' accommodation space on the main deck. The warrant officers were moved up to cabins on the upper deck, where the crew berthing was increased for the new complement of 278.

Clive returned to Portsmouth on 16 August 1918 for her missing gun, which was shipped on 7 September, trials being carried out hurriedly on 13 October. *Eugene* arrived at Portsmouth on 19 October moving into No14 dock for final modifications, but the war was over before she could receive her gun.

GUN PERFORMANCE

It was necessary to get every possible extra yard of range for bombardment purposes off the Belgian Coast, which was defended by German batteries of 15in calibre capable of ranging up to 52 000 yards. No fully accurate range tables exist in British records for the 18in gun as finally installed, so that it is

necessary to estimate performance figures from a variety of official and unofficial sources. These in turn are complicated by the fact that there are some eight possible maximum ranges for the gun: the combinations of two maximum elevations (30° and 45°), two charges (normal and super) and two projectiles (4 and 8 crh). Further, any actual firing ranges require calibration correction to a standard muzzle velocity, temperature, pressure, wind, etc. Most figures indicated in unpublished sources lie between 37 000 and 43 000yds; one published estimate of 60 000yds is far too high. A range table drawn up in 1916 (Included in CB1245, Public Record Office ADM 186/236) for the 4crh projectile with normal charge gives a range of 30 000 yards at an elevation of 30° 45′ with 2275 ft/sec muzzle velocity, but the figures for elevations above 15° are doubtful, being based on approximations, not measured ranges. Ordnance Board minute

B2535 of 7 January 1920 (PRO SUP 6/291) gives 35 000 yards for the 8crh with normal charge at 40° 39′ with 2250 ft/sec.

An 8crh HE (High Explosive) projectile had been designed late in 1917 for bombardment purposes which was 84¾ins long; there were also shrapnel designs. A 690lb supercharge had been provided in which one of the six, part charges was increased from 105 to 165lb. Such an increase gave a muzzle velocity about 150 ft/sec higher and range about 11% longer. The 8crh ranged about 10% further than the 4crh at maximum elevation, while 45° elevation gave about 15% greater range than 30°. The balance of evidence suggests that the maximum supercharge range with 8crh was between 40 500 and 40 500 yards, which leads to the figures given in the accompanying table for the nominal performance of a new gun (to nearest 100 yards).

Port broadside view of *General Wolfe* in November 1918
IWM

18in BL Mk I, 3320 lb Projectile, Cordite MD45				
Projectile	Charge (lbs)	MV (ft/sec)	Range at 30° (yds)	Range at 45° (yds)
4crh	630	2270	28 900	33 100
4crh	690	2420	31 400	36 100
8crh	630	2270	32 200	36 900
8crh	690	2420	35 000	40 500

Practical service range was rather less, since with gun wear, muzzle velocity soon dropped below 2250 ft/sec. The longest range used in the gun's few weeks active service was 36 000 yards which, allowing for wind and other ballistic corrections, would require an 8crh projectile with supercharge. Only eight shoots against the enemy were carried out by *Wolfe* and one by *Clive*, with a total of 85 rounds. These rounds were probably Hadfield's APC 4crh modified with ballistic caps, since only two HE 8crh had been delivered by the end of September, when stocks ashore and afloat amounted to 452 APC, 487 CPC and 2 HE. Both ships supported the Allied offensive of September 1918, taking as targets canal bridges inland from Ostende. Full details of these firings are given in *'Big Gun Monitors'**. Given better firing conditions allowing air spotting, and worthwhile targets, the 18in would have been a useful bombardment weapon, although of limited value against ships where the few guns mounted and slow rate of fire would have reduced the chances of a hit. Any hit would have caused massive damage, as the APC could penetrate about 18in of armour at 15 000yds.

The monitors were laid up soon after the Armistice, their 18in guns being removed at the end of 1920, and the guns used for experimental purposes as described by John Campbell in *Warship 11*. Some of the ammunition was used up in these trials, as by November 1929, stocks had fallen to 203 APC, 57 CPC, 96 HE, 92 shrapnel and 92 practice. One at least of the HE survives today, on display at Priddy's Hard Ordnance Museum, Portsmouth.

ACKNOWLEDGEMENT

I would like to thank John Campbell for his help over the years in unearthing and interpreting ordnance information.

Big Gun Monitors. The History of the Design, Construction and Operation of the Royal Navy's Monitors, by Ian Buxton. Published by World Ship Society/Trident Books, 12 Grand Parade, Tynemouth, Tyne & Wear. Price £9.95 (plus £1.00 postage & packing) or $22.50 (plus $2.50).

THE KING GEORGE V CLASS PART 4

BY ROBERT DUMAS

ANSON
1942 – June 1944. Admiralty intermediate disruptive type, colours 507A, B5, B6 and 507C.
March 1945 – early 1946. Admiralty standard type B with B20 panel and G45 over remainder of hull and upperworks (as in *King George V*)
Early 1946 – end 1946. Hull G10, superstructure G45
1946 onwards. Overall light grey.

HOWE
1942 – Decmber 1944. Admiralty intermediate disruptive type, colours 507A, B5, B6 and 507C. When docked in 1943 the patterns on port and starboard bow were modified.
December 1944 – September 1945. Modified Admiralty standard type with B20 hull and G45 superstructure.
September – December 1945. Admiralty standard Type B as *Anson*.
December 1945 - end 1946. Hull G10, superstructure G45.
End 1946 onwards. Overall light grey.

FATES
King George V. Decommissioned 4 December 1949 and placed in reserve. Sold to Arnott Young, 1957 and arrived Dalmuir for scrapping 20 January 1958.
Prince of Wales. Sunk by Japanese aircraft off Malaya 10 December 1941.

Duke of York. Decommissioned September 1951 and placed in reserve. Sold to Shipbreaking Industries, 1957 and arrived Faslane for scrapping 18 February, 1958.
Anson. Decommissioned September 1949 and placed in reserve. Sold to Metal Industries Ltd, 1957 and arrived Faslane for scrapping 17 December 1957.
Howe. Decommissioned at Devonport at end 1951 and placed in reserve. Sold to T W Ward, 1957 and arrived Inverkeithing for scrapping 2 June 1958.

SOURCES CONSULTED
Official plans held by the National Maritime Museum, Greenwich. Author's photograph collection. The very fine and complete collection of Mr Pierre Froger (Paris)
Ensign I, *King George V class Battleships,* by Alan Raven (Bivouac Books, London)
British Battleships and Aircraft Carriers, by H T Lenton (Macdonald, London)

The *Duke of York* on 1 March 1958 shortly
after her arrival at the Faslane yard of
Shipbreaking Industries for scrapping.

CPL W/12/004

236

KEY TO CAMOUFLAGE COLOURS

A. 507A/G10 (dark grey)
B. 507B/MS3 (medium grey/medium grey green)
C. 507C/G45 (light grey)
D. B5 (medium blue)
E. B6 (light blue)
F. MS4 (light grey/green)
G. PB10 (dark ultramarine blue)
H. MS2 (dark grey green)
I. B20 (medium blue)

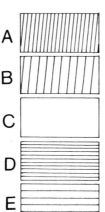

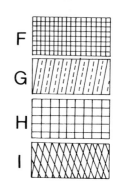

A
B
C
D
E
F
G
H
I

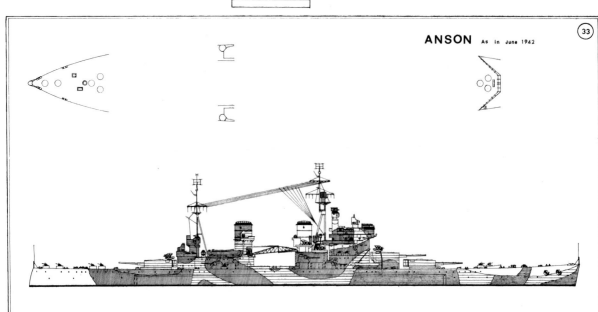

ANSON As in June 1942

33

ANSON As in June 1942

34

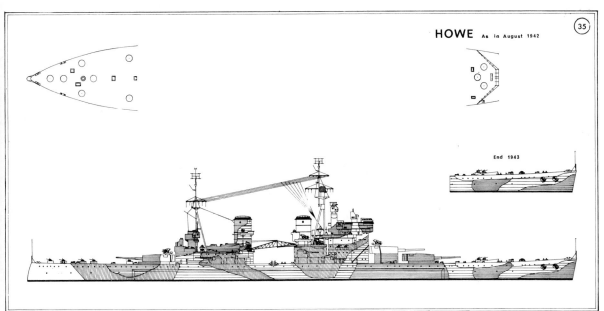

35

HOWE As in August 1942

End 1943

36

HOWE As in August 1942

End 1943

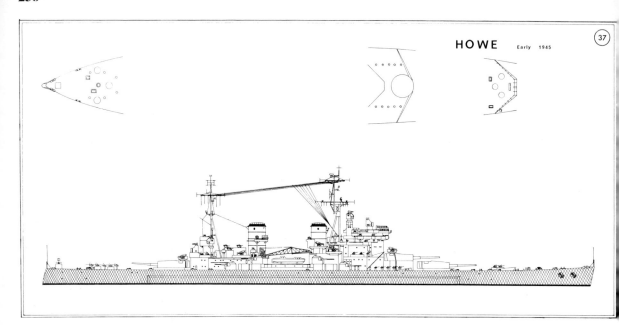

HOWE   Early 1945   ③⑦

Anson steams past the eastern coast of the
Shetland Islands on 16 May 1943, the
aircraft is a Wellington of Coastal
Command

NMM

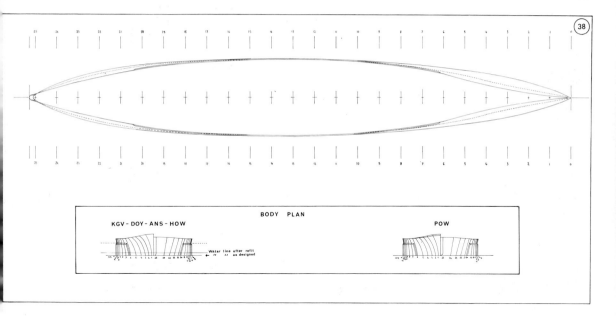

BODY PLAN

KGV - DOY - ANS - HOW

POW

Water line after refit
" " as designed

KEY TO DETAIL DRAWINGS

1. Aerial trunk
2. Loading derrick
3. Single 20mm Oerlikon mounting
4. Saluting gun
5. Twin 20mm Oerlikon mounting
6. 44in searchlight
7. 20in signal projector
8. Pompom director pedestals
9. Flag lockers
10. Foremast
11. Halyards
12. Quad pompom
13. HACS support
14. Pompom directors
15. Stowed position for head of crane
16. Forward boiler room ventilator
17. 8 barrelled pompom
18. Galley funnel
19. Aerial for Type 570
20. Crows nest
21. 13.7m (45ft) fast motor boat
22. 13.7m (45ft) motor launch
23. 7.6m (25ft) fast motor boat
24. 8.2m (27ft) whaler
25. 4.8m (16ft) fast motor dinghy
26. 4.2m (14ft) sailing dinghy
27. 9.75m (32ft) motor cutter
28. 10.9m (36ft) motor pinnace
29. Crane support
30. After boiler room ventilator
31. Admiral's sight
32. Aerial for Type 279
33. Aerial for FH 3 HF/DF
34. Aerial for Type 281
35. Lantern for Type 273 aerial
36. Aerial of Type 243 IFF for Type 279
37. Aerials for Type 91 TBS
38. Aerials for Type 86 TBS
39. Aerials for Type 87 TBS
40. Aerials for Type FV1 enemy raider transmission interception equipment
41. Aerial for Type 86M TBS
42. Aerial for Type 293
43. Aerial for Type 242 IFF for Type 293
44. Aerial for Type 242 IFF for Type 277
45. Aerial for Type 277
46. Aerials for 'Headache' equipment
47. Radio aerial
48. Aerial for Type 253 interrogator for Type 277
49. Aerial for Type 251 surface radar beacon
50. Aerial for Type 651
51. Aerial for Type 281B
52. Anemometer

Note: The numbers in brackets on the detail drawings refer to the numbers of the outboard profiles which have appeared in *Warship 9* to *12*. R on the drawings means a detail exclusive to a particular ship.

DETImage

DETAILS

No 1 platform

Starboard Side
KGV (1)
POW (6-7)

Starboard Side
KGV (2-3)
DOY (10)
HOW (20)

Starboard Side
DOY (11-12)

Top
KGV (1)
POW (6-7)

Top
KGV (2-3)
DOY (10)
HOW (20)

Starboard Side
HOW (18-19)
ANS (13-14)
POW (7)

then 4 (12)

5 (12)

3 then 4 (16-17)only

Top
ANS (15-16-17)

3 then 4 (16-17)only

Section of the tower

Front
KGV (1)
POW (6-7)

Port side
KGV (1)
POW (6-7)

Starboard Side
KGV (4-5)

Top
KGV (4-5)

(19) only

(19) only

Top
HOW (18-19)
ANS (13-14)
POW (7)

Signal platform

Top
DOY (8-9)

Starboard Side
HOW (21-22)

Top
HOW (21-22)

Modified signal platform

After side
All the ships

Top
DOY (11-12)

3 then 4 (13)
5 (12)

5 (12)
3 then 4 (12)

Starboard Side
ANS (15-16-17)

3 then 4 (16-17)

DOY (11) and (12)

ANS (15-16-17)

King George V entering Portland harbour
on 4 November 1946

CPL W/12/001

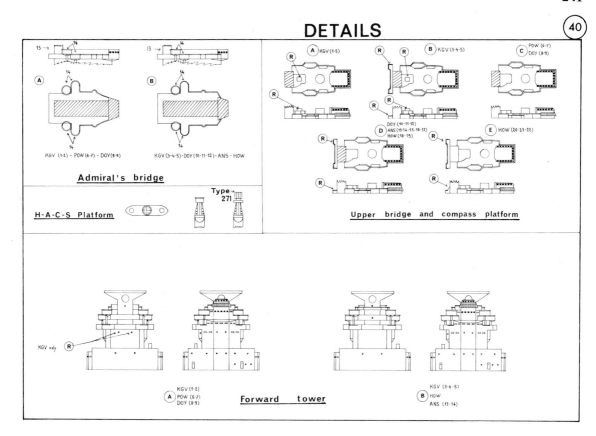

Admiral's bridge

H-A-C-S Platform

Type 271

Upper bridge and compass platform

KGV only R

KGV (1-2)
A POW (6-7)
DOY (8-9)

Forward tower

KGV (3-4-5)
B HOW
ANS (13-14)

DETATLS

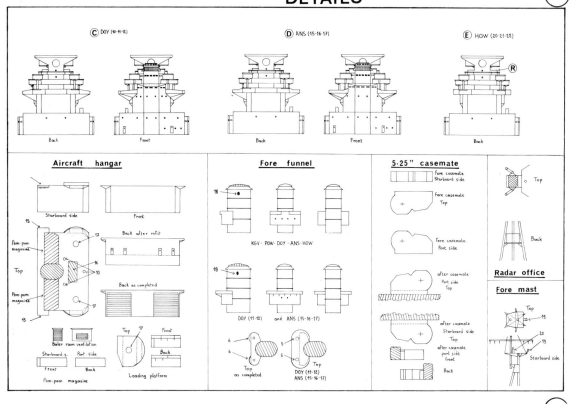

41

Ⓒ DOY (10-11-12) Ⓓ ANS (15-16-17) Ⓔ HOW (20-21-22)

Back Front Back Front Back

Aircraft hangar

Starboard side Front

Pom-pom magazine

Top

Back after refit

Back as completed

Pom-pom magazine

Boiler room ventilation

Starboard-s Port-side

Front Back

Pom-pom magazine

Top Front

Back

Loading platform

Fore funnel

KGV · POW · DOY · ANS · HOW

DOY (11-12) and ANS (15-16-17)

Top as completed

DOY (11-12) ANS (15-16-17)

Top

5·25" casemate

fore casemate Starboard side

fore casemate Top

fore casemate Port side

after casemate Port side Top

after casemate Starboard side Top

after casemate port side Front

Back

Top

Back

Radar office

Fore mast

Top

Starboard side

DETAILS

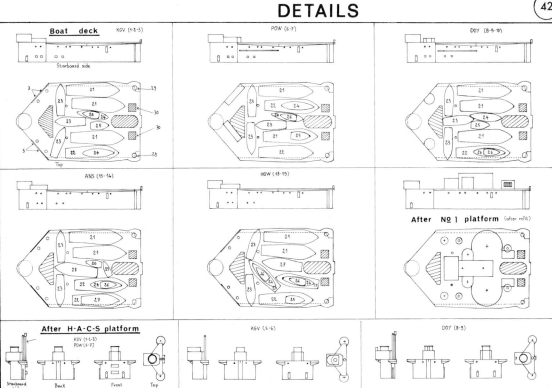

42

Boat deck KGV (1-2-3) POW (6-7) DOY (8-9-10)

Starboard side

Top

ANS (13-14) HOW (18-19)

After N̊ 1 platform (after refit)

After H-A-C-S platform

KGV (1-2-3) POW (6-7)

Starboard Side

Back Front Top

KGV (5-6)

DOY (8-9)

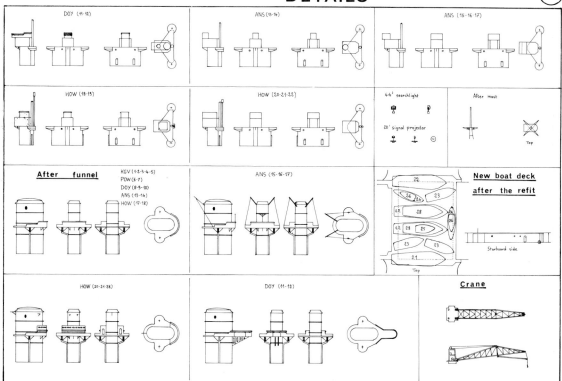

DETALLES

Viewed from the flight deck of an aircraft carrier (either *Implacable* or *Indefatigable*) the *Anson* steams out of harbour to take part in Home Fleet manoeuvres (Operation Dawn) during her last commission

CLP W/12/002

DETmore

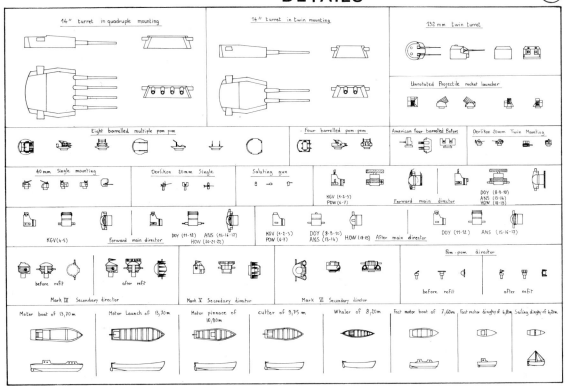

14" turret in quadruple mounting

14" turret in twin mounting

132 mm Twin Turret

Unrotated Projectile rocket launcher

Eight barrelled multiple pom pom

Four barrelled pom-pom

American four barrelled Bofors

Oerlikon 20mm Twin Mounting

40 mm Single mounting

Oerlikon 20mm Single

Saluting gun

KGV (1-2-3)
PDW (6-7)

Forward main director

DOY (8-9-10)
ANS (13-14)
HOW (18-19)

KGV (4-5)

Forward main director

DOY (11-12)   ANS (15-16-17)
HOW (20-21-22)

KGV (1-2-3)
PDW (6-7)

DOY (8-9-10)
ANS (13-14)   HOW (18-19)   After main director

DOY (11-12)   ANS (15-16-17)

before refit

after refit

Mark IV Secondary director

Mark V Secondary director

Mark VI Secondary director

Pom-pom director

before refit

after refit

Motor boat of 13,70m

Motor Launch of 13,70m

Motor pinnace of 10,30m

Cutter of 9,75 m

Whaler of 8,20m

Fast motor boat of 7,60m

Fast motor dinghy of 4,8m

Sailing dinghy of 4,20m

DETAILS

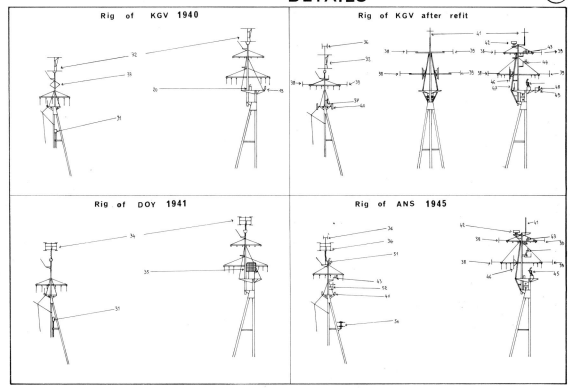

Anson leaving the Gareloch on 18 December 1957 at the beginning of her journey to Faslane to be broken-up

CPL W/12/003

1 *Howe* on the 26 May 1944; the same camouflage was carried by *Anson* and *King George V* but there were several subtle differences in the details of the pattern applied to each ship

MoD

2 *Anson* departs Malta for Portsmouth, 23 July 1946

A & J Pavia

3 Howe arrives at Inverkeithing for breaking-up 2 June 1958

T W Ward

1

A's and A's

Part of a fascinating series showing the final destruction of the *Wilkes-Barre* – fully described by Norman Friedman in *Modern Warship Design and Development,* published in October 1979 by Conway Maritime Press.

USN

THE END OF THE WILKES-BARRE from Thomas N Bernard Jr, New Orleans

Mr Sowinski's article on the *Wilkes-Barre* which appeared in *Warship 1,* January 1977, was most enlightening and informative. He claims that '. . . she cheated the razor blade factory; while being towed from Philadelphia to Orange, Texas, she foundered.' I think, however, you will see that this was not by accident but rather by design.

While on active duty with the US Navy, I served as gunnery officer on board the USS *Hawkins* (DD-873) and during our regular overhaul at Norfolk Naval Shipyard in late April 1972 I remember watching several harbour tugs manoeuvre what appeared to be a mothballed cruiser alongside a wharf not far from where we were moored. The next morning at officers' call our Chief Engineer told us that the mothballed ship was the *Wilkes-Barre* (CL-103). She was under the cognizance of the Naval Underwater Research Group who planned to tow her out to sea and sink her with an explosive device. She would finally lay to rest as an artificial reef. Our Chief Engineer made arrangements for the damage control assistant (DCA), myself and our respective working parties to go aboard *Wilkes-Barre* to remove any needed spare parts so long as their removal would not in any way compromise the ship's water-tight integrity. We were delighted with this opportunity since *Hawkins* was a 27 year old Second World War vintage destroyer and many parts were obsolete or long lead-time procurement items. This was of

particular concern to the engineers since they were constantly having trouble replacing worn out obsolete valves or fittings. Naturally, I was most interested in the 5in/38 dual-purpose gun mounts which were only slightly less modified versions of those on *Hawkins.* I must say that I was amazed at their excellent condition and state of preservation. Shortly after going on board, my Chief Gunners Mate came out of a hatch, with a smile from ear to ear, carrying a practically new set of wooden ram poles used for cleaning the gun barrels thus replacing the broken ones on board *Hawkins.* We were also able to remove several firing keys used on the trainer's side of the gun mount, which were not in stock in the Naval Supply System at that time.

Unfortunately we were only allowed one short visit to *Wilkes-Barre* and I am sure that given ample time we would have found a truck load of useful equipment. While my gunners mates were on their scavenger hunt, I roamed around the ship being careful not to step on the numerous strain gauges which the Naval Underwater Research Group had placed on the deck and bulkheads to monitor the final moments of *Wilkes-Barre.* I started aft, at the hangar deck where the large air-search radar antenna was tied down to the deck. In that same area there were numerous boatswain's lockers neatly stacked with life rafts and kapok jackets. As I worked my way forward I was impressed with the overall good condition of the various spaces. There were complete DC (C & R) lockers fully

equipped and practically untouched. Radio central was immense, with large transmitters and receivers of the vacuum tube era. Regretfully, I did not make it to the bridge since my time was running out but on my way back to the quarterdeck I passed through the Chief's quarters; and to show you that some aspects of naval life never change, there against the bulkhead was the CPO coffee pot, probably in working order and ready for service!

Mr Bernard also sent a press cutting from the *Virginian Pilot* for Sunday, 14 May 1972 which states that *Wilkes-Barre* 'broke apart and sank Friday in about 290ft of water 13 miles out in the Atlantic Ocean after Navy technicians set off explosives . . . in a series of damage control tests . . . The *Wilkes-Barre* was not supposed to go down until Saturday, when newsmen and photographers were to shuttle from shore to watch the end of her seagoing life and conversion to an artificial fishing reef. The damage caused by the explosives proved fatal sooner than expected.

'Although most of the ship was on the bottom the bow section was still above the waves Saturday. A spokesman at the Key West Naval Base said divers would plant more explosives and sink the bow section to make sure it is not a menace to navigation.'

A's and A's

The 'Tribal' class frigate *Eskimo*
C & S Taylor

JAPANESE SUBMARINES

Mr Pierre Hervieux has forwarded the following corrections to his article on Japanese B type submarines published in *Warship 7* and *8*. The corrections are based on new information recently received by the author from Japanese sources.

I 15 Sunk 10.11.42 by US destroyer minesweeper *Southard,* off Guadalcanal
I 19 Sunk 25.11.43 by US destroyer *Radford,* off Tarawa
I 23 Last heard of on 14.2.42, lost accidentally or sunk by US submarine *Tautog* off Oahu, 26.2.42(?)
I 25 Last heard of 24.8.42, sunk by ship or plane which was not credited for the sinking, off Espiritu Santo (the submarine sunk by US destroyer *Ellet* on 3.9.43 was *I 20*)
I 26 Sunk 24.10.44 by US destroyer scout *R M Rowell* 70 miles east of Surigao Strait
I 31 Sunk 13.6.43 by US destroyer *Frazier,* off Kisker
I 32 Sunk by PC (not SC) 1135
I 40 Lost between 29.11 and 3.12.43 off Gilbert Islands cause unknown
I 41 Sunk 28.11.44 by US destroyers *Pringle, Waller, Saufley* and *Renshaw* and aircraft in Ormoc Bay
I 44 Sunk 29.4.45 by aircraft from US escort carrier *Tulagi,* south east of Okinawa

I 54 Sunk 28.10.44 by US destroyers *Helm* and *Gridley,* off Leyte

In addition to the above Mr Hervieux received information from an American source that the US submarine *Snook* (SS279) was sunk by the *I 56* on 14 April 1945. This is not confirmed by the Japanese but as *I 56* was herself sunk only four days later she may not have reported her success due to the maintaining of radio silence during the remainder of her patrol.

TRIBAL CLASS FRIGATES from I A Sturton, Southampton

Peter Hodges's conjectures on the speed of the *Tribals* and in particular, the impossibility of them achieving the 28 or 30 knots quoted in reference books, are confirmed in the authoritative paper by M K Purvis, 'Post-War RN Frigate and Guided Missile Destroyer Design 1944-69', Trans RINA, Vol 116 pp 189-222 (1974). According to this, steam alone gives up to 20 knots, which the gas turbine boosts to exceed 24 knots. As regards hull form, there was something novel, although not to produce a high speed from low SHP. In the discussions after the paper, D K

Brown stated that the gas turbine boost concept led to a new approach; the prismatic coefficient was chosen to give good endurance at 18-20 knots and the full speed of about 24 knots was obtained by brute force!

The paper and discussion also contain a restrained but informative debate on the various virtues and defects of lattice and plated masts, steel and aluminium superstructures and other points of interest.

BLYSCAWICA from D K Brown, Bath

Since Mr Kolesnik takes my name in support of his trial data for the destroyers *Blyskawica* and *Grom* (*Warship* 4) I feel some corrections are necessary. First, however, I must apologise for the omission of a square root sign in the formula for minimum depth of water in my article in *Warship* 3 ('Speed on Trial'). The formula should read 5/3 x draught x speed $\sqrt{\text{length}}$. With this correction the minimum depth for *Blyskawica* and *Grom* at full speed is 36 fathoms, not the 24 fathoms of the Talland mile. Put another way, 24 knots is the highest speed obtainable for reliable results with a ship of that size on the Talland course. The difference is not large

and would not have had operational significance but it would make the trial worthless as an aid to new design.

Using Rota's approximate corrections (Trans INA, 1900) we have:

Speed Recorded (knots)	Corrected to deep water
15	15
22.8	22.8
27.11	27.5
28.7	29.1
31.6	32
32.8	33.4
34.7	35.3
36.5	36.4
38.9	38.4

The effect is best seen by plotting SHP/V to base V for both recorded and corrected speeds when a prominent bulge will be seen in the uncorrected curve at about 35 knots.

The two forward twin 4inch Mk XIX mountings of the destroyer *Blyskawica* as they appear today

Muzeum Marynarki Wojennej, Gdynia

P49

In 1915 the need arose for a large number of vessels for general escort, patrol and anti-submarine work. These functions were normally allotted to the destroyer flotillas but destroyers were limited in number and badly needed for other duties, besides being rather sophisticated for such mundane work. Among the vessels designed to relieve the destroyers of these tasks were the *P* – or Patrol – boats of which 64 were built during 1915-18. The requirements of the design were: that they be economical to both build and operate; have sufficient speed to deal with U-boats but no more; a shallow draught; a low silhouette similar to that of a steam submarine; the minimum possible size and of simple construction; and to allow the use of non-specialist shipbuilders – in all a standard wartime concept of cheap mass production vessels.

The resulting ships proved successful in service except that, although very seaworthy,

their low freeboard and superstructure made them extremely wet vessels – normally most of the guardrails and awning frames were rigged with canvas screens to give some protection from the weather. As completed the early units carried two depth charges in traps (virtually a box enclosing the depth charge and its release gear) at the stern but subsequently stowage was increased to four, then six and finally 30 or more which entailed removing the fixed torpedo tubes. They were also designed to carry a second 4inch gun (positioned about halfway between the pom-pom and the torpedo tubes) but this was omitted from all of the class except *P52*. The hull was constructed entirely of mild steel except for the stem plate which was of hardened steel for use in ramming surfaced submarines.

Twenty of the original class were modified on the stocks to *PC* boats – submarine decoy vessels disguised to look like small merchant

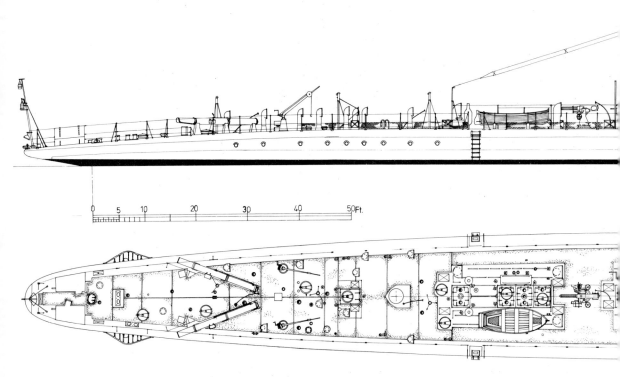

0 5 10 20 30 40 50 Ft.

ships. They proved very successful, sinking four U-boats compared with only one sunk by a P-boat. The value of the group cannot however be judged by sinkings alone and there can be no doubt that their availability assisted greatly in the protection of coastal waters and easing the demands made on fleet destroyers. Nevertheless, they were a wartime expedient and apart from a few which were retained into the 1930s for minor and experimental duties the majority were scrapped during the early 1920s.

The drawing, which is based on the official as-fitted plans held by the National Maritime Museum, shows *P49* as completed. This vessel was ordered from R Thompson in March 1916 and launched on 19 April 1917. She served at Dover until the end of 1918 and was then placed in reserve: she was sold for breaking up in January 1923.

PARTICULARS OF P49 AS COMPLETED

Displacement:	613 tons
Length:	230ft pp, 244ft 6in (oa)
Beam:	23ft 9in
Draught:	8ft (8ft 4½in to propeller tip) at load water line
Armament:	1 – 4inch QF MkIV gun, single PIX mounting (50 Common, 50 Lyddite and 4 practice shells)
	1 – 2pdr pom-pom MkI, single MkII mounting
	2 – 14inch fixed torpedo tubes (2 torpedoes)
	2 – depth charge traps (4 depth charges)
Searchlight:	One 20inch mounted on charthouse roof
Boats:	4 – 20ft collapsible Berthon boats
	1 – 13ft 6in dinghy
Anchors:	1 – 12cwt stockless (port bower), 1 – 15 cwt stockless (starboard bower) 1 – kedge anchor
Machinery:	2 shaft geared steam turbines, two boilers, 3500 SHP = 20 knots 98 tons oil fuel (100% capacity), 93 tons oil fuel (95% capacity)
Complement:	50 – 54

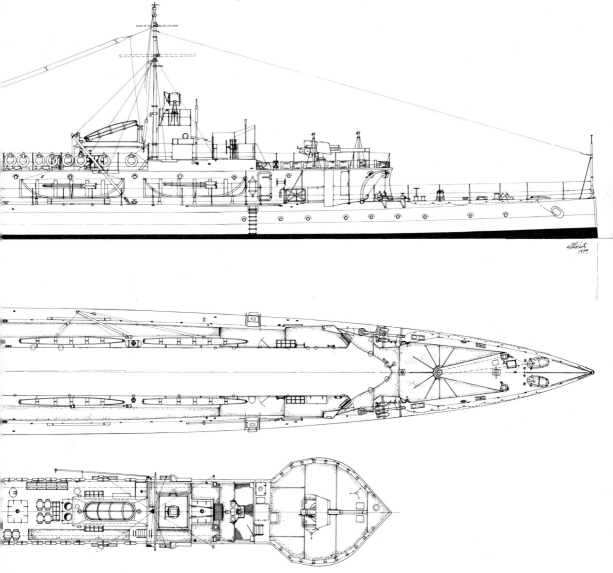

U48

GERMANY'S TOP SCORING SUBMARINE

BY PIERRE HERVIEUX

Some of the officers and crew of the *U48*
Drüppel

Among the submarines that served in the Second World War that which achieved the highest score of sinkings was the German *U48*, which accounted for one British sloop and 54 merchant vessels. These figures become all the more remarkable when it is realised that these sinkings were made in the space of less than two years, between September 1939 and June 1941, and despite torpedo defects which hampered operations in September 1939 and April 1940. When new 'boats' became available, *U48* was reduced to the role of a training submarine and her operational career came to an end; she was scuttled at Neustadt on 3 May 1945.

The *U48* was a Type VIIB boat, built by Germania Werft at Kiel and launched on 8 March 1939. The Type VIIB was a slightly enlarged Type VIIA, with saddle tanks modified to improve seaworthiness, increased oil fuel stowage for greater endurance, and more powerful diesel engines for increased surface speed. The boats belonging to this type were *U45* to *U55*, *U73* to *U76*, *U83* to *U87* and U99 to *U102*. The *U48* first commissioned in April 1939 and during her subsequent operational career was commanded by three captains, Herbert Schultze, Hans Rösing and Heinrich Bleichrodt. Shortly before the outbreak of war she was sent out, with other U-boats, by the German Naval Staff to take up a waiting position in the North Atlantic. Under the Command of Herbert Schultze she sailed from Kiel on 19 August 1939 as part of the 7th U-boat flotilla which included four other submarines. Nine other U-boats were sent out from Wilhelmshaven on the same day.

The *U48* began war operations west of the Bay of Biscay on 3 September and two days later she sank her first ship, the British cargo vessel *Royal Sceptre*. She was recalled on 7 September and on her way back to Germany accounted for two more ships. In October 1939 she was again at sea in the North Atlantic where she attacked several convoys and sank 5 more vessels totalling 37 153 tons. She returned to Kiel on 25 October where Captain Schultze declared that 5 torpedo failures had prevented even greater success.

At the end of November she was stationed off the Orkneys, in support of fleet operations, and sank the Swedish tanker *Gustafe Reuter.* A month later she had shifted south to the English Channel where she accounted for four merchantmen totalling 25 618 tons. In February she returned to the North Atlantic and on her way out laid mines off Weymouth. West of the channel she attempted to locate a British force comprising the carrier *Ark Royal,* battlecruiser *Renown* and the cruiser *Exeter* but neither this nor her mines achieved successes. She was however able to add a further four merchant ships, totalling 31 526 tons, to her score.

In April 1940, during the Norwegian campaign, *U48* was stationed off the Shetlands but despite obtaining favourable attack opportunities the operation was a total failure due to defects in the depth keeping mechanisms and magnetic fuzes of her torpedoes. For example on 11 April, west of Trondheim, Captain Schultze twice launched salvos of three torpedoes at a British heavy cruiser. The first at 12.30 (German time) and the second at 21.15 but in both cases the torpedoes detonated prematurely – probably due to the magnetic fuzing. The British heavy cruisers then operating in the area were *Devonshire, Berwick* and *York.* Similar events occurred on 14 April when *U48* fired on the battleship *Warspite* as she left Vestfjord.

At the end of May 1940 Captain Schultze was relieved by Hans Rösing and *U48s* first operation under her new commander took her in search of the Atlantic convoy US3, between 12 and 15 June. The convoy was not sighted, and reached the Clyde safely on 16 June, but during the remainder of the cruise Rösing sank seven ships, totalling 31 511 tons, and damaged an eighth. It was August 1940 before *U48* returned to the North Atlantic and again she failed to contact her initial target, an HX convoy, for which she searched

from the 13 to 16 August. She did however attack and sink five vessels, totalling 29 169 tons, before returning home.

In the following month her third commander, Captain Bleichrodt, took over from Rösing and she sailed once more for the North Atlantic where she attacked several independent merchantmen and convoys SC3 and HX72. During this patrol she sank the British sloop *Dundee* and seven merchant vessels, totalling 35 138 tons, and damaged another merchant vessel of 5136 tons. Another seven totalling 43 106 tons were sunk in her next operation, in October, although her first attempt to attack a convoy, off Rockall on the 9th, was a failure. Two days later she sank three ships from convoy HX75 then, on the 17th, two more from convoy SC7, before being driven off by flying-boats. On the 18th she sank an independent and on the following day one ship, previously disabled by *U47* (Captain Prien) from convoy HX79.

At the end of January 1941, *U48,* once again under the command of Captain Herbert Schultze, was operating west of the North Channel and Ireland. She sank two ships, the first an independent, on 1 February, and the second a straggler from convoy SLS 64S, on 24 February. Between these two sinkings she searched for convoy OB287, which she was ordered to attack on 19 February, but as the reported position, which came from an Fw 200 reconnaissance aircraft, was inexact she could not find the target.

On 21 March 1941 she was deployed against a homeward bound convoy west of southern Ireland but achieved no success. Four days later, she was south of Iceland where it was intended that she should operate in conjunction with air reconnaissance on convoys. The aircraft only located single ships, however, and most of these were directly attacked by the Fw 200s. On the 29 March, *U48* sighted the homeward bound convoy HX115 and sank four of its ships, totalling 17 299 tons.

On 24 May she was patrolling the western sector of the Bay of Biscay,

as a precautionary measure, to meet the *Bismarck.* Early in June she attacked several independent ships and sank four of them, totalling 27 716 tons, and also sank one vessel of 10 746 tons from a convoy.

On the 22 June 1941, *U48* returned to Kiel after her twelfth and final patrol into enemy waters. On these missions, under the command of Captain Schultze (8 patrols, 28 ships sunk, 202 days at sea) between September 1939 and April 1940 and again between January and June 1941, Captain Rösing (2 patrols, 12 ships sunk) between June and August 1940 and Captain Bleichrodt (2 patrols, 15 ships, including one sloop, sunk) during September/October 1940, 54 merchant vessels totalling 322 292 tons had been sunk, one sloop of 1060 tons sunk and two merchantmen, totalling 11 024 tons damaged. The *U48* was undoubtedly the most successful U-boat of the Second World War.

LIST OF VESSELS SUNK BY U48

1 5.9.39 (1400hrs) the British cargo ship *Royal Sceptre* (1939, 4853 tons) by torpedo and gunfire, 46°23N/14°59W

2 8.9.39 (0744hrs) the British cargo ship *Winkleigh* (1927, 5055 tons) torpedoed, 48°06N/18°12W

3 11.9.39 (1457hrs) the British cargo ship *Firby* (1926, 4869 tons) torpedoes and gunfire, 59°40N, 13°50W

4 12.10.39 (1930hrs) the French tanker *Emile Miguet* (1937, 14 115 tons) from convoy KJ25, by gunfire, 50°15N/14°50W

5 12.10.39 (2300hrs) the British cargo ship *Heronspool* (1929, 5202 tons) from convoy OB175, torpedoed, 50°13N/14°48W

6 13.10.39 (0855hrs) the French cargo ship *Louisiane* (1905, 6903 tons) from convoy OA17, by gunfire, 50°14N/15°02W

7 14.10.39 (1224hrs) the British cargo ship *Sneaton,* sailing independently, (1925, 3677 tons) torpedoes and gunfire, 49°05N/13°05W

8 17.10.39, the British cargo ship *Clan Chisholm* (1937, 7256 tons) from convoy HG3, torpedoes, 45°..N/15°..W

9 27.11.39 (0055hrs) the Swedish tanker *Gustafe Reuter* (1928, 6336 tons) torpedoed, 14 miles west north west of Fair Island

10 8.12.39, the British cargo ship *Brandon* (1917, 6668 tons) from convoy OB48), torpedoed, 50°28N/08°28W

11 9.12.39 (0630hrs) the British tanker *San Alberto* (1935, 7397 tons) from convoy OB48, torpedoed, 49°20N/09°45W

12 15.12.39 (1630hrs) the Greek cargo ship *Germaine* (1911, 5217 tons) torpedoed, 51°00N/12°18W

13 10.2.40 (1835hrs) the Dutch cargo ship *Burgerdijk* (1921, 6853 tons) torpedoed, 49°45N/06°30W

14 14.2.40 (1652hrs) the British cargo ship *Sultan Star* (1930, 12 306 tons) torpedoed, 48°54N/10°03W

15 15.2.40 (1315hrs) the Dutch tanker *Den Haag* (1925, 8971 tons), torpedoed, 48°02N/08°26W

16 17.2.40 (2040hrs) the Finnish cargo ship *Wilja* (1914, 3396 tons) torpedoed, 49°00N/06°33W

17 5.6.40, the British cargo ship *Stancor* (1904, 798 tons) by gunfire, 58°48 N/08°45W

18 6.6.40, the British cargo ship *Frances Massey* (1927, 4212 tons) torpedoed, 55°33N/08°26W

19 7.6.40, the British cargo ship *Eros* (1936, 5888 tons) torpedoes *and only damaged* 55°33N/08°26W

20 10.6.40 the Greek cargo ship *Violando N Goulandris* (1919, 3598 tons) torpedoed, 44°04N/12°30W

21 19.6.40, the Norwegian cargo ship *Tudor* (1930, 6607 tons) torpedoed, 45°10N/11°50W

22 19.6.40, the British cargo ship *Baron Loudoun* (1925, 3164 tons) torpedoed, 45°..N/11°21W

23 19.6.40 the British cargo ship *British Monarch* (1923, 5661 tons) torpedoed, 45°..N/11°21W

24 20.6.40, the Dutch tanker *Moerdrecht* (1930, 7493 tons) from convoy HX49s, torpedoed, 43°34N/14°20W

25 16.8.40, the Swedish cargo ship *Hedrun* (1920, 2325 tons) torpedoes 57°10N/16°37W

26 18.8.40, the Belgian passenger ship *Ville De Gand* (1920, 7590 tons) torpedoed, 55°28N/15°10W

27 24.8.40, the British tanker *La Brea* (1916, 666 tons) torpedoed, 57°24N/11°21W

28 25.8.40, the British tanker *Athelcrest* (1940, 6825 tons) from convoy HX65A torpedoed, 58°24N/11°25W

29 25.8.40 the British cargo ship *Empire Merlin* (1919, 5763 tons) from convoy HX65A, torpedoed, 58°30N/10°15W

30 15.9.40, the Greek cargo ship *Alexandros* (1906, 4343 tons) from convoy SC3, torpedoed, 56°50N/15°04W

31 15.9.40, the British sloop HMS *Dundee* (1932, 1060 tons) from convoy SC3, torpedoed, 56°45N/14°14W

32 15.9.40, the British cargo ship *Empire Volunteer* (1921, 5319 tons) from convoy SC3, torpedoed, 56°43N/15°17W

33 15.9.40, the British cargo ship *Kenordoc* (1926, 1789 tons)

from convoy SC3, torpedoed, 57°42N/15°02W
34 17.9.49, the British passenger ship *City of Benares* (1936, 11081 tons) torpedoed, 56°43N/21°15W
35 17.9.40, the British cargo ship *Marina* (1935, 5088 tons) torpedoed, 56°46N/21°15W
36 18.9.40, the British cargo ship *Magdalena* (1923, 3118 tons) torpedoed, 57°20N/20°16W
37 21.9.40, the British cargo ship *Blairangus* (1930, 4409 tons), from convoy HX72, torpedoed 55°18N/22°21W
38 21.9.40, the British cargo ship *Broompark* (1939, 5136 tons) from convoy HX72, torpedoed *and only damaged*, 55°08N/18°30W
39 11.10.40, the Norwegian cargo ship *Brandanger* (1926, 4624 tons) fron convoy HX75, torpedoed, 57°10N/17°W
40 11.10.40, the British cargo ship *Port Gisborne* (1927, 8390 tons) from convoy HX75, torpedoed, 56°38N/16°40W
41 11.10.40, the Norwegian tanker *Davanger* (1922, 7102 tons) from convoy HX75, torpedoed, 57°..N/19°10W
42 17.10.40 (0400 hrs) the British tanker *Languedoc* (1937, 9512 tons) from convoy SC7, torpedoed, 59°14N/17°51W
43 17.10.40 (0400hrs) the British cargo ship *Scoresby* (1923, 3843 tons) from convoy SC7, torpedoed, 59°14N/17°51W
44 18.10.40, the British cargo ship *Sandsend* (1925, 3612 tons) torpedoed, 58°12N/21°29W
45 19.10.40 (2322hrs) the British tanker *Shirak* (1926, 6023 tons) from convoy HX79, torpedoed 57°00N/16°53W (this tanker had been torpedoed and damaged by *U47* at 2229hrs)
46 1.2.41, the Greek cargo ship *Nicolaos Angelos* (1912, 4351 tons) torpedoed, 59°..N/17°..W
47 24.2.41, the British cargo ship *Nailsea Lass* (1917, 4289 tons) torpedoed, 60 miles south west of Fastnet.
48 29.3.41, the British cargo ship *Germanic* (1936, 5352 tons) torpedoed, 61°18N/22°05W
49 29.3.41, the Belgian cargo ship *Limbourg* (1938, 2483 tons) torpedoed, 61°18N/22°05W
50 29.3.41, the British cargo ship *Eastlea* (1924, 4267 tons) torpedoed, exact position unknown
51 29.3.41, the British cargo ship *Hylton* (1937, 5197 tons) torpedoed, 60°20N/18°10W
52 2.4.41, the British tanker *Beaverdale* (1928, 9957 tons) torpedoed, 60°50N/29°19N
53 2.6.41, the British tanker *Inversuir* (1938, 9456 tons) torpedoed and gunfire, 48°28N/28°20W
54 4.6.41, the British tanker *Wellfield* (1924, 6054 tons) torpedoed, 48°34N/31°34W
55 6.6.41, the British cargo ship *Tregarthen* (1936, 5201 tons) torpedoed, 46°17N/36°20W
56 8.6.41, the Dutch tanker *Pendrecht* (1939, 10746 tons) from convoy OB329D, torpedoed, 45°18N/36°40W
57 12.6.41, the British cargo ship *Empire Dew* (1941, 7005 tons) torpedoed, 51°09N/30°16W

The top scoring submarine of the second world war – the *U48*
Drüppel

1

2

1 The battleship *Warspite* (in July 1937) which was unsuccessfully attacked off Vestfjord by *U48* in April 1940
Wright & Logan

2 The sloop *Milford* whose sister ship, *Dundee,* was sunk by *U48* while escorting the Atlantic convoy SC3 in September 1940
Wright & Logan

3 The type VIIB U-boat, *U54,* fitting-out at Krupp's Germania Yard, Kiel. Her career was very different from that of her sister *U48*, as she was sunk by the British submarine *Salmon* in April 1940 on her first operational patrol
Drüppel

3

PARTICULARS OF TYPE VIIB U-BOATS

Length:	218ft 3in, 66.52m (oa)
Beam:	20ft 3in, 6.17m
Draught:	15ft 6in, 4.72m
Displacement:	753 tons (surface), 857 tons (submerged)
Machinery:	2 shaft diesel/electric motors, 2800 BHP = 17.25 knots (surface)/750 HP = 8 knots (submerged)
Oil Fuel:	108 tons
Endurance:	6500 miles at 12 knots (surface) 80 miles at 4 knots (submerged)
Gun armament:	One 8.8cm (3.46in) One 2cm (0.79in) AA. AA armament was later increased to one 3.7cm (1.45in) and two (2x1) 2cm and the 8.8cm gun was removed.
Torpedo armament:	Five 53.3cm (21in) torpedo tubes, four forward and one aft, Twelve torpedoes or 14 mines.
Complement:	44

1 One of the later Type VIIB vessels, the *U74*. She was launched in July 1940 and sunk by aircraft and the destroyers *Wishart* and *Wrestler* in the Mediterranean in May 1942.
Drüppel

2 The *U51*, another Type VIIB, was sunk by the British submarine *Cachalot* in the Bay of Biscay in August 1940
Drüppel

Warship Pictorial
GUNS OF THE IRONCLADS

The introduction of the ironclad brought with it a revolution in naval ordnance in which gun design developed so rapidly that new ships quickly became obsolete due to their vulnerability to weapons which were growing in size year by year. During the early stage of this development the British adopted the Armstrong breech-loader but its unsatisfactory nature soon led to its abandonment in favour of the heavy muzzle-loading rifle (MLR). These latter, developed initially along a comparatively logical path, starting in 1864 with the 6inch, 64cwt and ending in 1875 with the 12.5 inch, 38 ton. This period was followed by a brief excursion into the unsatisfactory 'monster' muzzle-loader, in the shape of the 16inch 80ton MLR, and then settled into a new path of development with the re-introduction of the breech-loading gun.

The photographs here serve to illustrate the initial period of development and cover mainly the MLR models, all but three of which (the 6inch, 8inch and 12.5inch) are shown.

1 At the end of the 1850s, after a long series of trials and experiments with a variety of rifled and smooth-bore guns, it was decided to rearm the British Fleet with Armstrong breech-loaders. The largest of these weapons, the 7inch, 110pdr, illustrated here, was introduced in 1861 as a replacement for the 68pdr smooth-bore. It was not successful as it was prone to accidents (due mainly to the fact that there was no certain method of ensuring that the breech piece was securely clamped) and an inefficient armour-piercer, compared with contemporary muzzle-loaders of modern design. It was phased out towards the latter half of the 1860s together with the 40pdr BL, a gun of similar length but slimmer proportions but the smaller Armstrong BL guns, the 20, 12, 9 and 6pdrs, which were comparatively safe, remained in service for several years eventually being superceded by the quick-firing gun.

NMM

2 A very early view of an Armstrong 110pdr BL on a wooden slide carriage. This mounting was only one stage removed from the old truck carriage; the trucks having been replaced by wooden blocks which ran on a metal faced wooden platform or 'slide'. Recoil was taken-up partly by the standard block and tackle and partly by a pair of compressors (the left compressor – a 'vice like' clamp – can be seen fixed to the rear block at the lower side of the carriage); run-out was assisted by small metal rollers at the ends of the carriage, which were lowered for the purpose. The slide carriage (which in simple form had been in use for many years) was introduced to give easier training with heavy weapons, the forward end being pivoted at the gunport while the rear end ran on a metal track in the deck. Metal tracks were also used to manoeuvre the guns about the deck, either to another gunport or a stowed position on the centre line, using various pivot points – both tracks and a pivot (in the deck directly below the breech) are visible in this photograph. Pivot holes and rollers were fitted at both ends of the slide which was moved about the deck by means of tackles and handspikes.

NMM

3 A view, looking aft, on board the five-masted broadside ironclad *Minotaur* during the late 1860s. The gun in the left foreground is an early model of the 7inch MLR (muzzle-loading rifle) mounted on a wrought iron slide carriage known as the RCD(Royal Carriage Department). Adopted in 1964 the RCD was of similar design to the wooden types that it replaced but incorporated several refinements of operation including the Armstrong plate compressor.

CPL W/12/005

4 A 9inch MLR mounted on an RCD carriage in the upper battery of the central battery ironclad *Iron Duke* (completed in January 1871). The lever on the side of the carriage operated the plate compressor, which had to be released to allow the gun to be run out. The compressor consisted of a number of flat metal plates, fitted along the middle line of the slide, between which ran metal strips attached to the gun carriage; by compressing this assembly sufficient friction was created to absorb the energy of recoil. The disc carrying the two arms (visible just behind the compressor lever) is the elevating drum which carried a pinion to drive the toothed arc attached to the side of the gun barrel. The arm protruding vertically just behind the drum is the elevating handle which could be taken out and moved forward or back around the pinion as the gun was elevated or depressed. The gear at the rear end of the slide is for running the gun in by hand.

NMM

3

3 Captain Scott's naval gun carriage and slide, 1871. This mounting was an improved version of the RCD carriage named after its inventor Captain, later Admiral, Scott. The carriage was shallower than in the RCD and the slide raised further from the deck, while the compressors were fitted to the sides of the slide instead of at its middle. The latter were known as bow-compressors due to the means of clamping, which was by a curved metal frame and a screw rather like a G-clamp. The screw was attached to the notched metal wheel visible here just below and behind the trunnion. Note also the provision of training gear in the form of pinion operating in a toothed rack fitted in the deck.

NMM

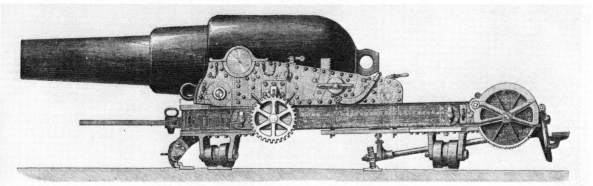

6 The maindeck battery of the central battery ironclad *Sultan* (completed October 1871) showing four of the eight 10inch, 18ton, MLR which she carried. The 18 ton gun, introduced in 1868, fired a 400lb shell (compared with 250lb in the 9inch, 12 ton, and 115lb in the 7inch, 6½ ton, MLRs) and could penetrate almost 13 inches of wrought iron at the muzzle. The mounting is a Scott's carriage, the outer plate of the right compressor being clearly visible on the side of the slide. Although described as an iron carriage it is interesting to note that the trunnion supports for these particular weapons, are constructed of wood although the fittings and, of course, the slide are metal.

NMM

7 The aftermost 11inch, 25 ton, MLR of *HMS Temeraire,* one of the most unusual of the early ironclads. Basically she was a central battery ship but she carried two of her guns in barbettes and was also the largest brig rigged vessel ever built. The barbette guns were, however, carried on disappearing mountings, originally developed for land service, in which the gun was raised by hydraulic power to its firing position and, having been discharged, was lowered behind the protection of its armoured wall for reloading. The whole process had a certain sinister air which comes over well in a description by Admiral Ballard in *The Mariner's Mirror* of July 1943, '. . . the . . . mechanism worked without a hitch and almost without a sound. It was interesting to watch from an outside observer's standpoint. At first nothing was to be seen but its surrounding parapet about 3ft high. Then quite silently, except for a faint hissing, the gun would suddenly appear, coming up from inside and swinging round simultaneously towards the target, in a fashion rather suggesting of an elephant getting on its legs and turning to make a charge. It checked and steadied, while the gun-layer passed the degrees of elevation, and got the reply 'Elevation correct'. A momentary pause followed and then came the full toned bellow of an old fashioned muzzle-loader using pebble powder, as it sent the shell away – easily seen in flight when clear of an immense rolling cloud of white smoke – while the hydraulic buffers in the raising mechanism checked the recoil. And almost immediately the gun was turning back and sinking down all in a combined movement to the loading position. In a few seconds it had totally disappeared.'

NMM

8 An early photograph, taken on the upper deck of the turret ship *Monarch* (completed June 1869), showing her two twin turrets. The *Monarch* was the first ship to mount the 12inch, 25 ton, MLR which fired a 600lb Palliser shell and a 495lb common shell. Apart from training being automatically provided by the steam powered turret, the design of the mountings for each gun was generally similar to that of the standard slide carriage, elevation and loading still being carried out by hand. The turrets were 26ft in diameter and protected by 8inch and 10inch thick wrought iron plates.

CPL W/12/006

6

7

8

9 The forward turrent of *Monarch*'s ill-fated contemporary, HMS *Captain,* completed in January 1870 and lost nine months later when she capsized in a gale in the Bay of Biscay. She carried the same main armament as the *Monarch* except that her turrets were of different design being slightly smaller in diameter and having elevation arrangements which entailed raising and lowering the entire gun carrriage and slide rather than just swivelling the guns on their trunnions.

CPL W/12/007

10 The single 12inch, 25 ton, MLR gun of the armoured ram *Hotspur* (completed November 1871), the only British warship with a fixed turret. The mounting is a standard broadside slide carriage but the deck

on which it stands is in fact a turntable within a fixed armoured gunhouse. The gunhouse had four ports and the turntable was rotated to bring the gun into position at the desired port where the carriage could then train to cover an arc of approximately 60°. Note the shell, ready for loading, hanging just inside the port and the ramming and sponging staffs laying on the deck beside the mounting.

NMM

11 A view of the rear of *Hotspur's* 12inch gun mounting showing the elevating, run in and training gear. The turntable has been rotated to a position where the gun is not in line with a port.

NMM

9

13

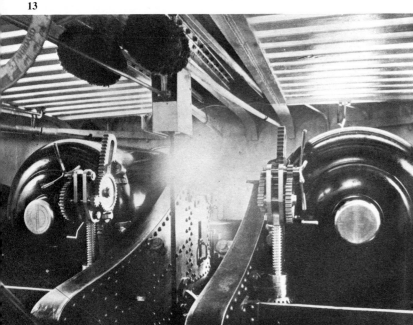

12 The forward turret and superstructure of the first sea-going 'mastless' turret ship – HMS *Devastation* (completed April 1873). This and the second turret aft, were 30ft 6inches in diameter and protected by 10inch and 14inch wrought iron plates. When the ship was modernised during 1890-93 the original guns were replaced with modern 10inch breech loaders.

CLP W/12/008

13 A photograph taken in the interior of one of *Devastation's* turrets showing two of her 12inch, 35 ton, MLRs. This gun fired a 700lb Palliser and a 618lb common shell and, with the former projectile, could penetrate almost 16 inches of wrought iron at the muzzle. The carriages, although having a more modern and cleaner appearance, were still hand operated slide designs with compressors for recoil damping. However one of the turrets in *Devastation's* sister ship, the *Thunderer*, was equipped with experimental hydraulic loading thus initiating a general trend towards the adoption of power operation in future heavy gun mountings. Note the turret training indicator (top left hand corner), the absence of cascabel rings on the rear of the guns and the complex elevation gearing (necessitated mainly by the heavy weights to be moved).

NMM

FRIGATE DESIGN
IN THE 18th CENTURY
PART 3
BY ROBERT GARDINER

Eighteenth century English ship design was probably at its best during the 1750s and 1760s (as outlined in Part 2 of this article in *Warship* 10) and it is perhaps more than historical accident that these ships made the Seven Years War one of the most brilliantly successful in the history of the sailing navy. The design pre-eminence of this period was the work of one man, Sir Thomas Slade, who is principally remembered as the designer of the *Victory* (an unusually fast First Rate, and a favourite flagship for half a century). However, his design for a 74 gun ship was so highly regarded that examples were still being added to the class a decade after his death in 1771. Nor did his successors in the office of Surveyor, Sir John Williams and Sir Edward Hunt, show any great originality in frigate design and neither the *Amazon* nor the *Active* classes were radically different from Slade's *Niger* class in overall specification, although Hunt's *Andromeda* class was an attempt at a longer, finer-lined '32' (see Table 1).

These – and indeed all frigates designed by Williams and Hunt – showed some resemblance to *L'Abenakise,* but this reflected a deference to Slade's *Lowestoffe* and *Mermaid* designs rather than to the French prize herself. None of the Williams or Hunt designs quite matched the all-round sailing

qualities of Slade's ships and the principal contribution of these two Surveyors to frigate development was the introduction of 18pdr armament, fractionally before such ships became standard in the navies of France and Spain. Williams' *Flora* and Hunt's *Perseverance* classes were practically identical 36 gun designs and both built broadly similar 38 gun ships. All were sturdily built, powerful ships but none of them was particularly fast under sail.

This initiative in the introduction of a larger calibre armament was contrary to the usual Royal Navy policy of responding to technical improvements in opposing navies and was even more unusual in that the suggestion came from the Navy Board. This reflected the Navy Boards' re-assertion of control over ship design and the Admiralty-inspired experiments of the 1760s were forgotten. Certainly no radically new hull form was tried out during the period of the American War but this may have been a result of the acute shortages in resources during a war which stretched the Royal Navy more than any other in the eighteenth century. The English ship design of this period, although perfectly competent, was somewhat second-hand and lacked the genius of the previous generation. Not surprisingly, it was during this war

that the idea of French superiority began to take hold and in many ways the generalisations about the characteristics of English frigates outlined in the previous part of this article apply more precisely to the ships of the 1770s and 1780s. To recap, these were:
1) Robust construction
2) Emphasis on all-round seakeeping abilities, particularly in heavy weather
3) High reserve of stability, to give a steady gun-platform and to enable sail to be carried in all weathers
4) Weatherliness
5) Reasonable average speed on all points of sailing
6) Heavier armament for given dimensions than French frigates

Owing to a change in the system of keeping records, documentation for French captures between 1778 and 1783 is not as full as for earlier periods. Nevertheless, surviving surveys (*Monsieur, Licorne, Pallas,* for example) indicate that the French style of construction had not changed and historical evidence points to no alterations in French design policy before the reorganisation of 1786. Therefore, it is possible to summarise the characteristics of French frigates as follows:
1) Light construction
2) A very high speed in optimum conditions – usually on one point of sailing

3) Less stability at large angles of heel; therefore less able to carry canvas in high winds, but able to 'ghost' in light conditions
4) Relatively leewardly
5) Preference for lighter conditions
6) Lower firepower than English ships of similar size

WEIGHT BREAKDOWNS
The consistency of these emphases suggests a conscious design policy and this suggestion could be quantified with some typical weight breakdowns. Since weights were not fully calculated on a regular basis until after 1800 these are virtually unobtainable from official sources but the accompanying figures are based on treatises of naval architecture, with those for *Pearl* based on calculation and an official bill of lading.

The principal comparison, between the French *Renommée* and the English *Pearl* shows ships of similar dimensions (and hence tons burthen) but the far heavier construction of English ships is emphasised by the difference in actual displacement. Even so, a greater proportion of this larger displacement is devoted to the hull in *Pearl,* although the particular requirements of English cruiser design can also be seen in the higher percentages of displacement devoted to armament and top hamper. On gun decks of virtually the same length, *Renommée* carried 26 x 8pdrs while *Pearl* mounted 26 x 12pdrs and stowed about twice the ammunition. In fact, at the time these figures were compiled *Pearl* was stored for 3 months with 70 rounds of balls and 10 of grape per gun (plus 3 rounds of double headed dismantling shot per 12pdr) whereas a full establishment for a 6 month cruise was 100 rounds of ball per gun; So English frigates were obviously expected to stow far more ammunition than their French counterparts.

The heavier top-hamper reflects the traditional Royal Navy concern with all-weather performance. English frigates were expected not only to stay at sea but also to be able to carry sail in heavy weather, and accordingly required sturdy masts, yards and rigging. When the considerably more substantial ground tackle is taken into consideration it seems clear that English frigates were designed to be independent of shelter in most conditions.

In French frigates a higher percentage of displacement was given over to stores, provisions and other consumable items. During the course of a lengthy cruise this would produce considerable reductions in displacement and alterations to the trim of the vessel, with possible adverse affects on stability and sailing performance. French hull design, with its emphasis on the optimum, did not respond well to these significant alterations to the water-lines as stores were consumed and the only effective answer was to limit cruises to relatively short periods where the changes would be less radical.

The figures for the later French 18pdr armed *Embuscade* and the standard English 38-gun frigates (later re-rated 46s) of the Napoleonic Wars serve only as a general check, since cruiser design changed in many details towards the end of the century. Nevertheless, the hull, armament, top-hamper and ground tackle still consume greater percentages of displacement in the English vessels.

STRATEGIC CONSIDERATIONS
These strikingly different design parameters are interesting in their own right – if only to counter the common belief that naval architecture in this period was a hit-or-miss affair – but they also offer insights into the strategic and tactical thinking of the two navies. To understand the French attitude it is important to remember that after the massive defeats of Barfleur and La Hogue in 1692 the French Navy could never again assume it would enter any war against the Royal Navy with numerical superiority, and any advantage of numbers due to alliances or strategy was too short lived – or too uncertain – to affect the basic premise. The only answer to larger numbers is better ships and the French navy, like the German navy in the 1930s or the Russian in the 1960s, was forced into an attempt to get more from

Ambuscade, an *Amazon* class frigate launched in 1773. This is one of a series of paintings of models undertaken for George III.

Science Museum

contemporary technology on the ship-for-ship basis than their opponents. In the battle-line, this meant the introduction of the 80-gun ship, designed to overpower British 74s, and for cruising ships it produced a distinct preference for speed, at the expense of seaworthiness.

Because of its superior numbers, the English Fleet could usually expect to dominate the strategic situation merely by being at sea and could protect its freedom to use the seas by offering battle whenever the opportunity arose. Knowing that the English would always attempt to control the sea-lanes, French strategists evolved a theory that the smaller French fleet should be used in support of specific objectives, and on particular missions, where they might achieve local superiority. There was never any question of permanently denying the use of the sea to the enemy and consequently the French fleet was not expected to undertake lengthy cruises to no particular purpose.

The inferiority of her battlefleets also forced France into a reliance on

AMBUSCADE,
5.ᵗʰRate 32 Guns.

the 'guerre de course'. England had the largest merchant fleet in the world and as a trading country was particularly vulnerable to attacks on her commerce. Privateering was metamorphosized from a form of licenced piracy into a powerful weapon of national policy, and this policy also left its mark on the design of cruising ships for the French navy. Whereas English frigates were ideally suited for their trade-protection role by their sea-worthiness, range of independent action and relatively heavy armament, French frigates were predators par excellent – fast and lightly built, they were ideal for the pursuit and rapid capture of merchantmen and in theory even ships in convoy would be vulnerable since the slower English escort could be out-manoeuvred and the luckless merchantman snapped up. The lighter scantling and armament would not be a disadvantage since they were not expected to take on the escort: according to the theory British seapower would not be shaken by the loss of one warship but could be undermined by sustained economic damage to

commerce, an extreme example of the doctrine of the 'specific objective'.

In these circumstances, although French frigates could make long cruises, it is obvious that neither lengthy convoy duty nor detached patrolling would be necessary. This explains why so many English surveys of French prizes complain of the lack of 'conveniences' – the platforms, storerooms, cabin divisions and fittings that would tend to make life slightly easier for the crew and assist in the maintenance of gear during long periods away from dockyard services. Indeed, the lower ammunition stowage, and a hull form that often made French frigates wet, lively and uncomfortable cruisers, implies that lengthy cruising was not a primary requirement.

The English stress on seakeeping and independence is in direct contrast. Convoys and patrols implied months at sea but even duty with the battlefleet in a sea-control role would require frigates to carry out their duties in all weathers and over long periods. To the roles of

trade-protection and fleet scout was added the tedious and exacting duty of close-blockade, introduced by Admiral Hawke in the Seven Years War and adopted thereafter whenever strategically possible. The introduction into the Royal Navy of close-blockade and the frigate-form is virtually simultaneous, which is one of the accidents of history that seems to be more than mere coincidence. Certainly the old two-decker 24 and 44 gun ships did not have the seakeeping abilities of the new frigates and did not have the freeboard for their guns – since the French ports were usually on the lee shore, freeboard was of paramount importance if the inshore elements of the blockading squadron were to be able to defend themselves, or to attack opportune targets.

TACTICAL CONSIDERATIONS

Because of the doctrine of the 'mission' it was perfectly possible for a French fleet commander to refuse battle without loss of honour, if a set-piece engagement might interfere with his achieving his ultimate objective. This attitude

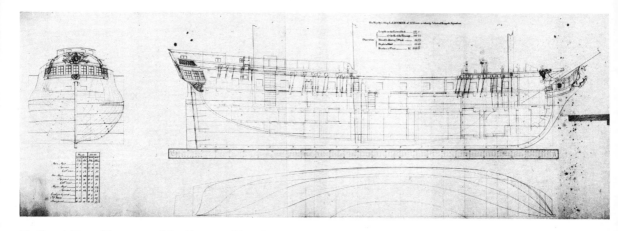

The French frigate *Licorne,* one of the ships for which a survey has survived. This ship was launched at Brest in 1755 so really belongs to the earlier generation, but other surveys (such as *Pallas,* built in 1778) suggest that the French style of construction had not altered.

By courtesy of the NMM

extended to single-ship engagements and the speed of French frigates could enable their captain to offer or refuse battle, since in most circumstances they could choose the frigates' best point of sailing in order to escape. That they were unweatherly would not matter unless forced by coastline or other enemy ships into a disadvantageous point of sailing.

The French Navy was tactically more sophisticated than its principal opponent, which was forced into attack whenever possible by its strategic intentions to retain control of the sea. The essence of offensive tactics under sail was to take the 'weather-gage' because the ship or squadron to windward could sail down and force battle upon even a reluctant enemy. Faced with an opponent that could be relied upon to attack – and from the windward gage – the French devised a series of elaborate tactical manoeuvres to counter the apparent advantages of the weather-gage. For example, if the battle-line was broken, it was easier for the leeward line to fall away downwind and reform, and damaged ships would drift to leeward away from the enemy which was to windward. The weather-line, on the other hand, would probably have to approach at an oblique angle being exposed to

raking fire to which little return could be made, and damaged ships would tend to drift down onto the enemy line (Figure 1).

This sophistication also applied to French single-ship tactics, where again the lee-gage was seen as no disadvantage. In general terms, it seems that French frigate captains expected to manoeuvre their faster and more lightly-built ships to victory, whereas the sole concern of the Royal Navy was to close to 'half-pistol' range and hammer the enemy into submission, a tactic which suited their robust construction and heavier armament. Under most conditions the windward ship would be heeling towards its enemy, so that the guns would need to be carried further from the water, and the greater freeboard of English frigates' upperdeck gunports is an indication of their firm commitment to weather-gage (ie offensive) tactics.

This introduces the frequently expressed ascertion that while the French, firing on the 'up roll', aimed at the rigging to disable and out-manoeuvre, the English aimed on the 'down roll' at the hull to destroy enemy fire-power and induce surrender. It will be obvious that destruction of the enemy top-hamper might assist a reluctant ship or squadron to escape, if the strategic dogma of the 'mission' required it, or might allow a French frigate to dictate a single-ship action, but in anything but a flat calm the heeling away of the leeward ship would make it difficult to fire at anything except the opponents' rigging (Figure 2). This

naturally applied in reverse: firing on the 'up roll' or 'down roll' was difficult to achieve in practise and merely formalised the natural tendency of gunnery in the tactical circumstances preferred by the two navies.

STAFF REQUIREMENTS

Although the details of frigate design altered significantly in later periods, a French report of 1832 suggests that the same staff requirements were operative. This report into the alleged *inferiority* of French ships summarises the usual criticisms, most important of which is that 'their forms soon alter, as the effects of breaking, occasioned by the excess of weights, by deficiency of support [ie lines too fine] . . .'. This could have been written in the 1750s, but the report goes on (mentioning the adverse effects on sailing qualities of changes in displacement caused by the consumption of stores) to stress the superiority of the English in 'setting-up'; that is, in the ballasting, trimming and 'tuning' of the masts and rigging to get the best performance from a ship. The report points out that not only are some of the fastest ships in the Royal Navy French prizes but that they sail better than they ever did in the French service. The Sailing Quality Reports first established in the 1740s would build up a permanent record of ship's sailing abilities so that officers would only have to start from scratch with completely new classes, but ultimately the superiority could only be a matter of greater sea

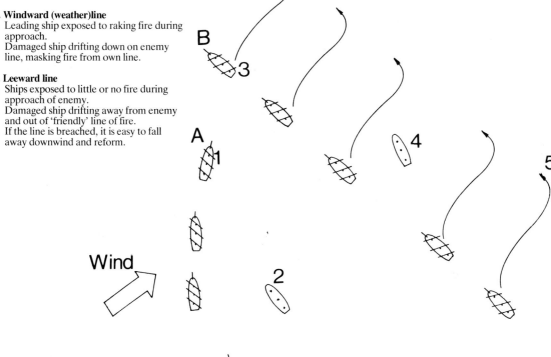

Fig 1: LEE GAGE TACTICS

A. Windward (weather)line
1. Leading ship exposed to raking fire during approach.
2. Damaged ship drifting down on enemy line, masking fire from own line.

B. Leeward line
3. Ships exposed to little or no fire during approach of enemy.
4. Damaged ship drifting away from enemy and out of 'friendly' line of fire.
5. If the line is breached, it is easy to fall away downwind and reform.

FIG 2: LEE GAGE GUNNERY

A. Windward ship
a. Windward ship requires greater even-keel freeboard (note tendency to fire into hull of opponent)

B. Leeward ship
b. Leeward ship requires less freeboard (note tendency to fire into rigging of opponent)

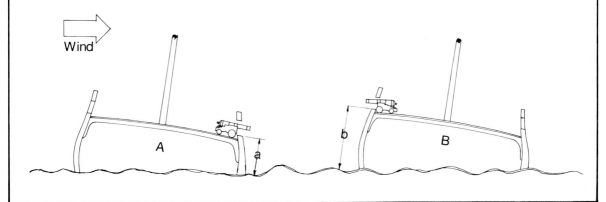

TABLE 1: PARTICULARS OF ENGLISH FRIGATE CLASSES 1773-1785

AMAZON class, 32 guns, 18 vessels

Armament:	As *Southampton* (*Warship* 10, p 82)				
	Gundeck length	**Keel length for tonnage**	**Extreme breadth**	**Depth in hold**	**Tonnage**
Design dimensions:	126ft	104ft	35ft	12ft 2in	678
Designer:	Sir John Williams				

ACTIVE class, 32 guns, 8 vessels

Armament:	As *Southampton*				
	Gundeck length	**Keel length for tonnage**	**Extreme breadth**	**Depth in hold**	**Tonnage**
Design dimensions:	126ft	103ft 9 $^5/_8$in	35ft 4in	12ft 2in	685
Designer:	Sir Edward Hunt				

ANDROMEDA class, 32 guns, 6 vessels

Armament:	As *Southampton*				
	Gundeck length	**Keel length for tonnage**	**Extreme breadth**	**Depth in hold**	**Tonnage**
Design dimensions:	129ft	107ft	35ft 4in	12ft 10in	710
Designer:	Sir Edward Hunt				

FLORA class, 36 guns, 4 vessels

Armament:	26 x 18pdrs on upper deck, 6 x 9 pdrs on quarterdeck, 4 x 9 pdrs on forecastle (as designed). Carronades added later.				
	Gundeck length	**Keel length for tonnage**	**Extreme breadth**	**Depth in hold**	**Tonnage**
Design dimensions:	137ft	113ft 1in	38ft	13ft 3in	869
Designer:	Sir John Williams				

PERSEVERANCE class, 36 guns, 4 vessels

Armament:	As *Flora*				
	Gundeck length	**Keel length for tonnage**	**Extreme breadth**	**Depth in hold**	**Tonnage**
Design dimensions:	137ft	113ft 5½in	38ft	13ft 5in	871
Designer:	Sir Edward Hunt				

MINERVA class, 38 guns, 4 vessels

Armament:	28 x 18pdrs on upper deck, 6 x 9pdrs on quarterdeck, 4 x 9pdrs on forecastle (as designed). Carronades added before completion				
	Gundeck length	**Keel length for tonnage**	**Extreme breadth**	**Depth in hold**	**Tonnage**
Design dimensions:	141ft	117ft $^3/_8$in	38ft 10in	13ft 9in	939
Designer:	Sir Edward Hunt				

LATONA, 38 guns, 1 vessel

Armament:	As *Minerva*				
	Gundeck length	**Keel length for tonnage**	**Extreme breadth**	**Depth in hold**	**Tonnage**
Design dimensions:	141ft	116ft 7in	38ft 10in	13ft 6in	933
Designer:	Sir John Williams				

experience – the navy which controlled the sea has to spend considerable time at sea.

The consistency in English cruiser design is even more impressive. As late as 1924 the Admiral of the Fleet, Sir Doveton Sturdee, wrote a paper for the Institution of Naval Architects in which he outlined, in order of importance, the requirements for a British cruiser. The following is an exact quotation:
1) Sea-keeping is probably the most important, also to carry the guns at such a height and manner that they can be used effectively in most weathers
2) Steadiness of [gun] platform
3) A good radius of action is essential
4) A higher maximum speed than that of possible enemy battleships [not, it should be noted, of other enemy cruisers]
5) Good offensive power
The needs of a trading country with a large overseas empire had not changed in two centuries. These five characteristics, in exactly the same order, could easily form the staff requirements for an eighteenth century English frigate.

CONCLUSIONS

While this series of articles was principally aimed at dispelling the myth of French design superiority in the age of sail, it has only proved that different needs produce different designs. Although lacking a framework of theory, eighteenth century naval architecture was far more sophisticated than is usually believed and was capable of responding to specific requirements. In this context it was not radically different from the modern profession; even today the starting point is usually the 'previously successful ship' and a naval designer is still required to balance mutually contradictory requirements in the search for an ideal ship. Therefore, it is perfectly valid to apply the same criteria and the same techniques of analysis, to sailing warships as to their powered decendants.

TABLE 2. TYPICAL WEIGHT BREAKDOWNS

	French *Renommée* 1744, 30 guns 669 tons burthen		English *Pearl,* 1762, 32 guns, 683 tons burthen		French *Embuscade,* 1789, 40 guns, 906 tons burthen		English *Leda* class, 1800-30 46 guns, 1070 tons burthen	
	Tons	%	Tons	%	Tons	%	Tons	%
HULL	350.69	48.13	516.40	52.32	569.31	50.25	795.15	54.25
Guns	37.15		42.95		66.65		80.35	
Shot	7.33		14.40		14.00		45.50	
Powder	3.61		6.80		6.00		11.95	
Gunner's Stores	3.55		9.30		**+		12.55	
ARMAMENT	51.64	7.09	73.45	7.44	86.65	7.65	150.35	10.26
Spars	20.00		29.60		?		47.80	
Rigging	11.53		22.60		?		31.40	
Sails	4.00		6.35		?		6.05	
TOP HAMPER	35.53	4.88	58.55	5.93	64.95	5.73	85.25	5.82
Cables	12.22		24.90		34.00		39.15	
Anchors	4.78		7.35		5.00		10.05	
GROUND TACKLE	17.00	2.33	32.25	3.27	39.00	3.44	49.20	3.36
BOATS	3.30	0.45	2.95	0.30	6.00	0.53	8.80	0.60
Sea Stores	5.52		21.50		36.00		31.00	
Water	50.00		42.75		77.00		110.00	
Provisions	93.00		67.85		108.00		69.20	
Fuel	*		18.20		15.00		32.00	
STOWAGE	148.52	20.38	150.30	15.23	236.00	20.83	242.20	16.53
MEN AND EFFECTS	22.00	3.02	23.05	2.34	(22.00)***	1.94	27.15	1.85
Iron	?		50.00		69.00		?	
Shingle	?		80.00		40.00		?	
BALLAST	100.00	13.72	130.00	13.17	109.00	9.62	107.5	7.33
TOTAL	728.68		986.95		1132.95		1465.60	

* 'Provision' total includes fuel
** 'Guns' total includes Gunners Stores
*** Estimated

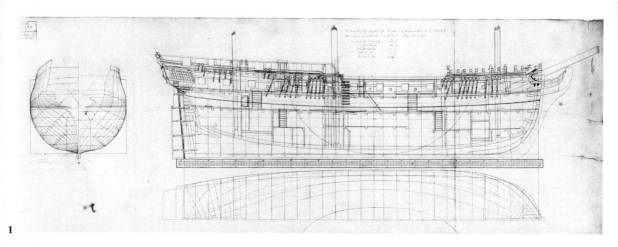

1

1 *Andromeda,* the name-ship of a small class of
enlarged '32's designed by Sir Edward Hunt.
By courtesy of the NMM

2 The 38 gun *Latona,* designed by Sir John
Williams. This design draught shows that the
quarterdeck and forecastle armament was
originally intended to be 6pdrs.
By courtesy of the NMM

3 An 'as fitted' draught of the 36 gun *Flora,*
redrawn from Admiralty originals. All the
frigates of this generation have generally
similar lines, although Hunt's designs are
slightly sharper.

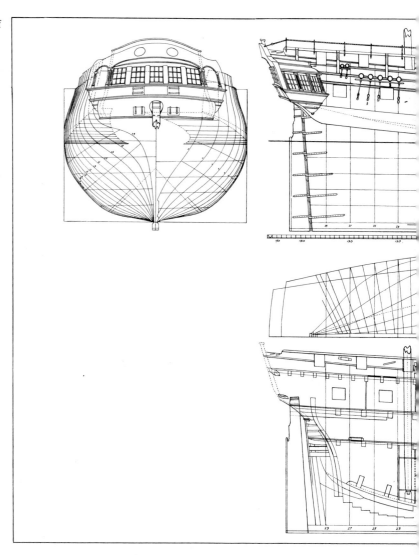

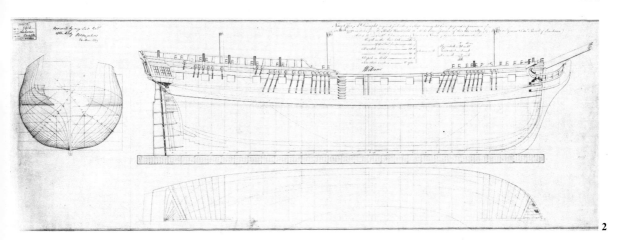

2

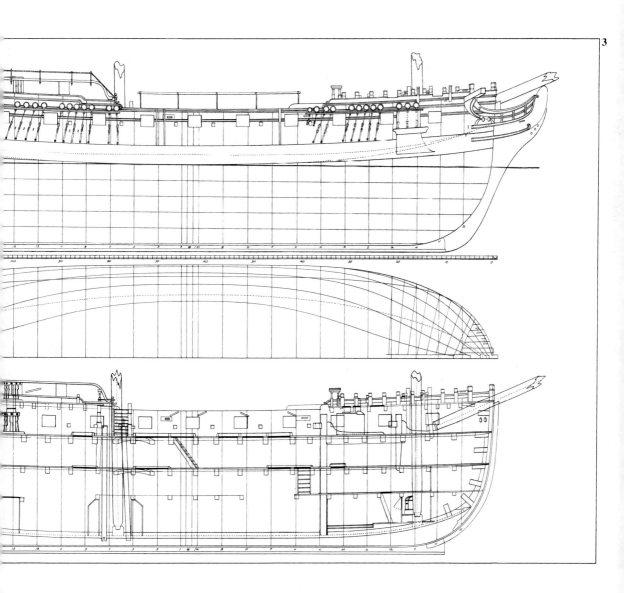

3

BRITISH SUPER-HEAVY GUNS PART 4

BY N J M CAMPBELL

The nine 16inch Mk I guns of the battleship *Nelson* in 1940. Note the UP mountings on the roofs of B and X turrets.

IWM

16IN MARK I

The history of this gun goes back to January 1921 when it was determined that the proposed battlecruisers of the *G3* type could not take a larger gun if they were to be able to use the drydocks at Rosyth, unless protection and/or speed were reduced or only 6 guns were accepted for the main armament. There was no time to experiment with alternative constructions and the first two guns were ordered from Elswick on 22 August 1921. The bulk orders for the *G3's* guns were placed on 25 October 1921, 13 going to Elswick, 9 to Beardmore and 14 to Vickers, who were also to make one to a special design. These orders except for that of August 1921, were cancelled with the *G3's*, and fresh orders were placed for the *Nelson* and *Rodney's* guns, Nos 3-10 being ordered from Elswick, Nos 11-18 from Vickers, and Nos 19-23 from Beardmore, all on 11 December, 1922, while Nos 24-29 were ordered from Woolwich two days later. One of the 18in Mark I guns had been relined to 16in, as previously noted, and also one of five Army 18in howitzers to be used for relatively low velocity trials such as those for the APC shells.

The construction resembled that of the proposed wire wound 18in/45 but the gun was relatively heavier. There was an inner A tube with a taper fit in the A tube and 2 rear locating shoulders. Next came a taper wound wire layer and over this the B tube and overlapping jacket. There was the usual breech ring over the jacket, breech bush located in the A tube, into which the breech block screwed, and a shrunk collar on the rear of the A tube. The Welin breech block was actuated by the American Asbury roller cam mechanism for which Vickers had acquired the rights. No 1 gun was completed in March 1924 and No 2 followed in July but trouble was soon apparent. A light 2048lb projectile had been chosen, of proportionately the same weight as the 18in/45 and the experimental 1688lb 15in, and with a charge of 550lb of oval MD Cordite it was intended that the new gun (80°F) muzzle velocity should be

2715ft/sec. In March 1925 2670ft/sec was attained with a 525lb charge but wear was rapid with a loss of 1.5ft/sec per round, and the probable life was at most 180 efc (equivalent full charges), too low for the British, though acceptable in some navies. Also accuracy was not very good and the rifling was damaged by the hammering of the short bodied, long headed projectile so that stripping occurred. These troubles were cured by reducing the muzzle velocity to 2575ft/sec which, as will be seen, was later slightly increased, and the rifling was also improved on relining.

The first three service guns, Nos 3,4 and 24 were completed with a chamber 118.5in long but later guns had a chamber of different form and 125.5in long. As the three short chamber guns were in *Nelson's* A' turret until February 1945, the nominal shell ramming distance was 7in less in this turret than in the others. The replacement of the 2048lb shell by one of 2250lb was considered and No 2 gun was relined in 1928-1929 with improved rifling and a chamber of 30 011 cu in instead of the standard 35 205 cu in. It was thought that a 506lb charge of solventless cordite, SC381, would give an MV of 2575ft/sec with the 2250lb shell in this gun and a range of about 40 500yds at 40° elevation but financial stringencies prevented any change.

Details were as follows:

Weight (including breech mechanism): 108 tons
Weight (less breech mechanism): 106 tons
Length (oa): 61ft 10.2in – 742.2in
Length (bore): 45 cal – 720in
Diameter: 65in max, 27in at muzzle
Chamber size: 125.5 x 19.9in (except Nos 3, 4, 24 – 118.5in long), volume 35 305 cu in.
Rifling: Mark I 586.964in (except Nos 3, 4, 24 – 592.4in), uniform twist 1 in 30, 96 grooves, polygroove plain section 0.124 x 0.349in, lands 0.1745in; Mark II 588.95in, uniform twist 1 in 30, 80 grooves, polygroove plain section 0.135 x 0.377in, lands 0.2513 in
Centre of gravity: 245.4in from breech face (unloaded)
Projectile weight: 2048lb

Charge: 498lb MD45 (6 x 83lb) (later 495 SC280 (6 x 82½lb))
Muzzle velocity: 2586ft/sec (with Mark II rifling 2614ft/sec)
Design pressure: 20 tons/sq in (with Mark II rifling about 21.3)

As completed both *Nelson* and *Rodney* had Mark I rifling in all their guns but *Nelson* had 'B' and 'X' turrets changed to guns with Mark II rifling in May 1944, while 'A' turret did not receive these until March 1945.

In *Rodney* 'B' turret changed to two guns with Mk II, and one with Mk I rifling in December 1937, while 'X' had three new guns with Mk I rifling in September 1938 and 'A' three with Mk II rifling in February 1942. This mixing was less serious than it might seem as the muzzle velocities tended to become similar as the guns wore. The triple mountings in *Nelson* and *Rodney* allowed 40° elevation giving a range, calculated for an MV of 2525ft/sec, of 38 400yds or about 39 900 at 2600ft/sec. The estimated life was about 250 efc and the intended rate of fire 2 rounds per gun per minute but the shell room arrangements and also the mountings gave a good deal of trouble originally. As a result the full salvo per minute rate for single ship practices from 1928 to 1933 showed a yearly average of 1.90 to 1.53 compared with 2.28 to 1.93 for 15in gun ships.

Unless bombardment was intended only APC shell was carried, this having a 6/∞ crh head and a length of 66.23in. The burster was 2⅓% of the projectile weight and, unlike most other heavy British APC shells, block TNT was used. During World War II 'K' shell containing dyes for colouring the shell splashes was introduced and these weighed up to 2059lb 5oz. The longest HE shell had a maximum length of 75.94in.

In conclusion it may be said that the 16in Mark I was a good gun which would have been better if the unfortunate decision to use a light shell had not been taken. It was the last British heavy gun to be built with wire winding.

16IN MARK II AND III

The sole difference between these

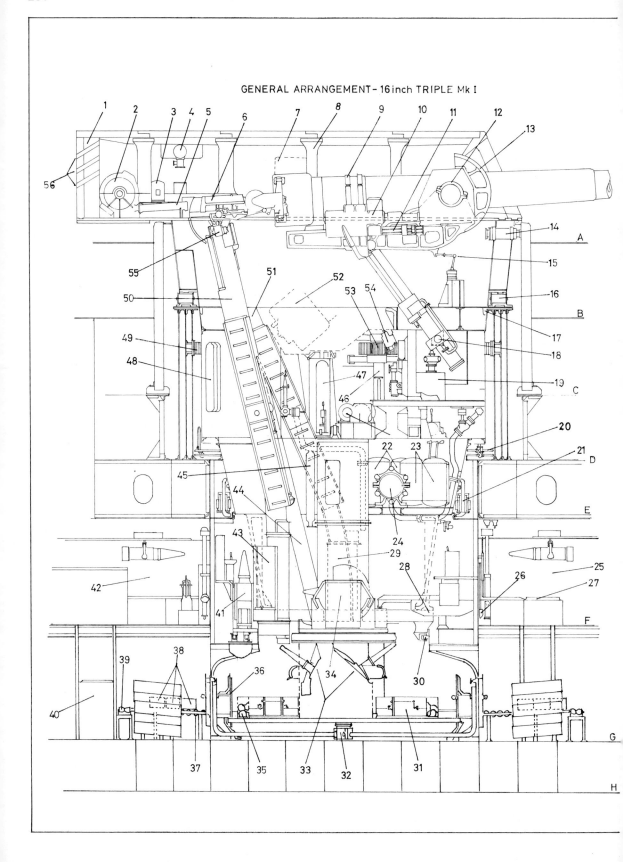

GENERAL ARRANGEMENT – 16 inch TRIPLE Mk I

GENERAL ARRANGEMENT – 16inch
Triple Mk I
1. Counterbalance weight
2. Rammer engine casing
3. 'Churn' levers
4. Rangefinder
5. Telescopic rammer tube casing
6. Tilting tray
7. Position of breech at full depression (−3°)
8. Gunhouse roof support pillar
9. Rear collars
10. Recoil cylinder
11. Sliding pipes for hydraulics, air blast and wash-out squirt to breech
12. Trunnion cap
13. Mantlet plate
14. Locking bolt
15. 'Walking' pipes to elevating structure
16. Training base roller
17. Turret clip
18. Elevating cylinder trunnion
19. Exhaust tank
20. Steam heating pipes
21. Cable winding gear
22. Turret drenching tanks
23. Hydraulic accumulator
24. Watertight door
25. Shell room ('X' turret')
26. Watertight door
27. Shell room rammer tray
28. Pivoting tray
29. Revolving shell scuttle
30. Trunk guide roller
31. Cordite swinging tray
32. Central pivot
33. Cordite tilting hoppers
34. Shell bogie (in horizontal position)
35. Cordite rammer engine
36. Flash door
37. Cordite roller-conveyor
38. Triple cordite charges
39. Athwartships cordite roller-conveyor
40. Cordite stowage bay
41. Shell bogie (tilted upright)
42. Shell room ('A' turret)
43. Revolving shell scuttle
44. Cordite hoist trunk
45. Wash-out squirt air bottles
46. Training drive shaft
47. Shell striking down trunk
48. Air blast bottles
49. Training rack
50. Centre gun shell hoist trunk
51. Left gun shell hoist trunk
52. Breech in full recoil at maximum elevation (+40°)
53. Drive pinion and twin training pinion
54. Elevation buffer stop
55. Tilting engine
56. Gunhouse vents

A. Upper (fo'c'sle) deck
B. Main deck
C. Middle deck
D. Beam line
E. Lower deck
F. Platform deck
G. Inner bottom
H. Outer bottom

Drawing by Peter Hodges from his forthcoming book *The Big Gun: Battleship Main Armament 1860-1945* to be published in 1980 by Conway Maritime Press.

Marks was that II had 3 rear and 2 forward shoulders where the jacket was located on the A tube, and III had 2 rear and 3 forward. The design went back to 1935 and was in most respects an enlarged version of the 14in Mark VII, to be mounted in the *King George V* class battleships, and the 15in Mark II which was never made. Alternative designs with 16in guns were considered for the *King George V* class but it was not until the battleships *Lion* and *Temeraire* of the 1938 programme that ships with 16in guns were again laid down. The first gun, No 30, was ordered from Woolwich on 31 January 1938, and was followed by Nos 31 to 39, ordered from Royal Ordnance Factory, Dalmuir on 16 September 1938, and by Nos 40 to 57 from Vickers Armstrongs, Elswick, on 23 September 1938. The *Lion* and *Temeraire*, laid down respectively on 4 July 1939 and 1 June 1939, would each have had nine guns, as would their sister ships *Conqueror* and *Thunderer* of the 1939 programme. All four ships were suspended, to be cancelled later during the Second World War, and the gun orders were reduced to Nos 30 to 35 and 40 to 42. Of these No 30 and 40 to 42 were Mark II and Nos 31 to 35 Mark III. Only Nos 30, 31, 32 and 40 were completed.

For preliminary trials it was determined in August 1935 that a standard 16in Mark I would give the desired performance with a 2375lb projectile, an MV of 2475ft/sec at 70°F and a pressure of 20 tons/sq in with a 524lb charge of SC320, but the construction of the new 16in was very different to that of the former gun. In the Mark II and III there was an inner A tube with a 1 in 500 taper on the radius throughout, an A tube and jacket with a rectangular breech ring, a breech bush taking the Welin screw breech block and located in the A tube, and a shrunk collar on the A tube. The two locating shoulders for the inner A tube were 555 and 571in from the muzzle. An Asbury roller cam breech mechanism was used and balancing weights were fitted to the breech ring to bring the centre of gravity near the breech end. This construction needed a heavy A tube and the forging weighed about 64 tons, the largest British gun forging, with a finished weight of 44½ tons. The design was slightly modified in 1939 to permit a loose liner type of inner A tube to be used subsequently if desired. As noted above this construction was similar to that of the 14in Mark VII and both guns were mounted in a cylindrical cradle instead of the previous saddle and slide. This feature and also the type of construction date back to the experimental 12in/50cal Mark XIV completed in 1933.

Details of the 16in Mark II and III were as follows:
Weight (including breech mechanism): 118 tons 14cwt 84lb (with balance weights 131 tons 1cwt 84lb)
Weight (less breech mechanism): 116 tons 1cwt 84lb
Length (oa): 61ft 11.3in – 743.3in
Length (bore): 45 cal – 720in
Diameter: 52in over jacket, 24in at muzzle
Chamber size: 129.4 x 19.0in,

volume 34 022 cu in

Rifling: 583.47in long, uniform twist 1 in 30, 80 grooves, polygroove plain section 0.131 x 0.377in, lands 0.2513in

Centre of gravity: 226.24in from breech face with breech mechanism; (with balance weights 208.9in)

Projectile weight: 2375lb APC 2048lb HE – this latter was shorter than the original HE for 16in Mark I guns, and was to be used by Mark I, II and III guns.

Charge: Estimated 520lb SC350 in sixths

Muzzle velocity: 2475ft/sec at 70°F (probably about 2485ft/sec at 80°F, with 2048lb shell about 2600ft/sec)

Design pressure: 20.5 tons/sq in

The triple mountings, of different design to those in the *Nelson* class, would have allowed 40° elevation. Range tables were never issued but, at 2400ft/sec, between 38 000 and 39 000 yards would have been reached. Shells were limited to 73in length by the mounting and, with a 6/12 crh head, the APC shell came within less than half an inch of this. The burster was 2½% of the total shell weight and 70/30 shellite was used. The design was a scaled up 14in and was expected to pierce 14in armour where the 14in shell would pierce 12in. The specification called for piercing 14in carburised and hardened armour at 30° to the normal and at striking velocities of 1770 and 2100ft/sec equivalent to 16 000 and 7000 yards.

The redesigned *Lion* and *Temeraire,* which it was proposed to lay down after the War, would not have had these guns but the 16in Mark IV, though the two Mark IIIs Nos 31 and 32 were to be altered for trials as related below.

16IN MARK IV

This, the last British naval heavy gun to be designed and dating from 1944-1945, was 45 calibres in bore length with a minimum new gun muzzle velocity of 2450ft/sec at 70°F. Otherwise it was a new departure with a loose barrel, a design pressure of 24 tons/sq in and it was to be flashless with the suitable propellant. The breech block was to open upwards and the weight of the projectile, which was

limited to 78in length, was to be determined by the best CP – that is the base fuzed HE – shell that could be designed within this length. Such a bombardment shell was expected to cause the maximum damage against light armour up to 3in thick. The APC shell, which now took second place, was to be of the same weight as the CP with the best possible performance against deck armour combined with a reasonable performance against heavy side armour. The 24ton design pressure would not normally have been reached, but would have allowed light shells to be fired at very high velocity; clearly this requirement came from the employment of some of the German heavy guns in this manner when firing across the Channel.

The redesigned *Lion* and *Temeraire* were each to have nine 16in guns in three triple turrets and new mountings were to be designed with a loading cycle of 20 seconds instead of the usual 30. The upward opening breech block was a feature of the *Richelieu's* 15in quadruple turrets and it would presumably have opened as the guns ran out after recoil as in the *Richelieu.* 'One shot' ramming was to be employed, it would seem with coaxial rammers as in the British 8in cruisers.

For preliminary trials, one of the 16in Mark IIIs, No 31, was relined with a 27 000 cu in chamber for use with flashless propellant and an auto-frettaged loose barrel was ordered for No 32, though this conversion could not have been used at anywhere near the designed pressure.

The *Lion* and *Temeraire* were cancelled and all this work on the gun and mounting was abandoned.

Details are given of a Vickers Armstrong design, dated 6 July 1945, though this may well not have been the final design.

Weight (including breech mechanism): 117 tons 17cwt

Length (oa): 61ft 11.3in – 743.3in

Length (bore): 45 cal – 720.1in

Diameter: 52in over jacket, 25in muzzle swell, 24in minimum

Chamber size: 113.4 x ?17.9in, volume 26 000 cu in

Charge: 610lb (approx) flashless

Design pressure: 24 tons/sq in

The loose barrel weighed 35 tons 2cwt, had an 0.01in taper on the diameter and was to be auto-frettaged at 32 tons/sq in in order to obtain a yield point of 45 tons/sq in. This corresponded to the inner A tube and was easily the largest of British design. The A tube ended 188in from the muzzle, and there was a jacket, breech ring and removable breech bush weighing 1 ton 5cwt 28lb. Rifling details remained to be decided.

This remarkable, if unbuilt, design concludes the story of very large British naval guns. Extreme performance was not aimed at in normal service, at least latterly, and attention was concentrated on reasonably long life, regularity and accuracy. There seems little doubt however that the two latter qualities could have been retained with a higher performance if a tubular grain propellant had been used instead of cord.

Technical Topics

ROUGHNESS AND FOULING

BY D K BROWN

In almost all the seas of the world marine life, both animal and vegetable, will grow on the sides of ships and marine structures which are close to the surface. In the case of ships this growth will add considerably to the power required to drive the ship through the water. Something like one-sixth of the Royal Navy's current fuel bill goes in overcoming the effects of fouling.

COPPER BOTTOMS

Fouling is an age old problem which was first tackled with success at the end of the Seven Years War when, in 1761, the Navy Board had the frigate *Alarm* sheathed with copper. At the end of a two year voyage, there was little visible fouling but another problem was manifest. When two dissimilar metals are connected together in sea water they form a weak electric battery and one of the metals will be corroded severely. In the case of *Alarm,* it was the iron bolts holding the frames to the planking which suffered. From 1775 onwards great efforts were made to eliminate the corrosion problem and by 1779 an enormous, and successful, operation to apply copper sheathing to the whole fleet was in hand (Ref 1). During the American War of Independence the sheathed British

fleet enjoyed a considerable speed advantage over their enemies which went far to offset their numerical disadvantage. In particular, Rodney attributed much of his success in capturing 6 Spanish ships of the line off Gibraltar in 1780 to the speed of his copper bottomed ships.

It was an expensive process and not without problems. The thin copper sheets were easily torn off, allowing fouling to grow rapidly on the bare patches. The French, affected by the blockade during the Napoleonic wars, tried to economise by using thinner copper, and in consequence, suffered an even more rapid deterioration in sailing qualities.

Copper has to dissolve before it is effective in poisoning marine growths. Both the rate at which the copper wastes away and its effectiveness in killing fouling are very sensitive to impurities in the metal and attempts to increase the life of the copper usually made it useless as an anti-fouling coating. A spectacular failure of this nature was when Humphrey Davey applied blocks of zinc to the copper sheathed hull of the frigate *Samarang* in the 1820s. The idea was that the zinc would corrode in preference to the copper, so protecting it. While, in this sense,

the experiment was a success in that it prevented the copper from dissolving, the copper then failed to kill the growth of fouling.

The electro-chemical corrosion of iron when placed close to copper caused many problems to the early paddle steamers; *Elfin, Penelope* and *Geyser* all reported rapid damage to the iron frame of their paddle wheels.

The introduction of the iron hulled ship made the problem much worse. Obviously, a copper sheath could not be fastened directly to the iron hull as this would cause immediate and severe corrosion. During the latter half of the nineteenth century a few ships, intended for tropical waters where fouling is most severe, were given a watertight wood skin over the iron hull and the wood then sheathed with copper. This expensive treatment was indicative of the lack of success in developing anti-fouling paints.

ANTI-FOULING PAINT

The normal paint used underwater on iron hulls was red lead and this, if applied properly, was successful in protecting the iron from corrosion but was ineffective against fouling. Ships in home waters required docking every twelve months and even in this time their hulls would be covered with small shells and 'grass'. Vessels sailing to the Mediterranean or Black Sea needed docking every six months, while in the Indian Ocean four monthly dockings were necessary unless the ship spent some time in fresh water.

The chief engineer of the East India Company at Bombay, A Cursetjee, reported that he removed barnacles 12in thick and 18in long from the *Indus*. The P & O liner *Pekin* left England in February 1847 and was docked in Bombay that October. Her captain said 'I can compare her to nothing else than a half tide rock. The barnacles were 9in long, the second strata being complete, with a feathery coral formation sprouting from cluster to cluster. The *Pekin,* though a fast ship had her speed reduced by the fouling to six and a half knots per hour.'

Many inventors tried to develop

paints which would either poison the fouling or were so slippery that fouling could not get a grip. Successes were frequently claimed, since the rate of fouling varies dramatically with the temperature and salinity of the water and even unprotected surfaces can sometimes remain free for considerable periods. Such 'successes' were always followed by disappointments. The Royal Navy was among the leaders in the research work. W J Hay, chemist and lecturer at the RN College, Portsmouth, set up a laboratory which was to achieve fame as the Central Dockyard Laboratory, now part of the Admiralty Marine Technology Establishment. Hay's successors still produce some of the most successful anti-fouling paints.

Hay used an oxide of copper carried in linseed oil which was applied to HMS *Rocket* in May 1845, to the Royal Yacht *Fairy* in September of the same year and to the *Undine* in May 1847. In

October 1847, Portsmouth Dockyard reported '. . . we found the starboard side, which had been prepared with red lead, very foul with grassy weeds and slime, under which a thick coat of oxide had generated, whilst the port side which was prepared with Mr Hay's composition was perfectly clean.'

A fourth trial in which the unique, iron sailing ship HMS *Recruit* had one side coated with Hay's composition gave a similar result. However, the continued use of copper sheathing suggests that Hay's composition had its limitations. Indeed, one rival claimed that it was a good manure, encouraging the rapid growth of weed.

Probably the first really successful anti-fouling paint was developed by Captain Rahtjen in 1860 (Ref 2) using mercury oxide and arsenic – toxic to barnacles and men alike. A number of well known marine paint firms began as agents for Rahtjen's paint.

The *Torquay*, pictured here in 1973, was one of four frigates employed in a series of experimental speed trials in the early 1960s to obtain data on the effectiveness of anti-fouling paint.

C & S Taylor

POST WAR DEVELOPMENT

The Royal Navy used proprietary materials until the end of the Second World War when Pocoptic, based on US research and manufactured in Portsmouth Dockyard, was introduced. In 1959 the current RN anti-fouling paint (161P), developed in the Central Dockyard Laboratory and made in Portsmouth Dockyard, came into service.

During the early 1960s the Admiralty Experiment Works carried out a series of repeated speed trials on four frigates over periods of up to two years out of dock in the North Atlantic area. A limited amount of further information was obtained from two other ships operating in the Persian Gulf. Details of the ships and trials are summarised below.

The results of trials such as there are bound to show a considerable scatter but a reasonable interpretation of the results is to assume that the frictional resistance

Ship	Hull construction	A/F paint	No of trials	Time out of dock (days)	Age of ship at start (months)
Venus	Riveted	161P	5	676	226
Urchin	Riveted	Pocoptic	3	273	222
Torquay	Welded	161P	5	790	100
Tenby	Welded	161P	5	566	87
Nubian	Welded	161P	2	337	57
Erskine	Welded	161P	2	299	63

of the ship increases by $\frac{1}{8}$% per day for ships coated with 161P in Atlantic waters and by $\frac{1}{4}$% per day in the Persian Gulf. Results from *Urchin* were complicated by damage to the propellers but it would seem that her older Pocoptic paint fouled at about twice the rate of 161P.

It is likely that some of the increase in power was due to fouling on the propeller blades. Roughening of the surface of the hull of a ship or the propeller blades can arise from causes other than fouling. These include:

1. During building as a consequence of: plate roughness, rough welds, poor surface preparation, poor paint application or the use of paint with a rough surface.

2. In service due to: damage to the paint, corrosion, poor application of later paint coats (eg paint runs), application over dirt or incompletely removed fouling.

Based on work by Lackenby, it can be shown that a mean roughness of 100 microns (1000 microns = 1 millimetre) adds 5% to the power requirements and hence to the fuel consumption of a frigate. Even the slimy deposit (di-atom slime) found on the surface of ships with no visible fouling can have an equivalent roughness of as much as 600 microns (30% on the fuel bill).

CONCLUSION

It is very difficult to use the limited data on the speed trials of nineteenth century copper sheathed ships to estimate the rate of fouling. The best estimate, perhaps little more than a guess, is that fouling, other than slime, was prevented for about a year. After that the copper would develop the familiar green patina which, being insoluble, would reduce the effectiveness of the sheath as an anti-fouling treatment. Fouling and the attendant increase in drag would then develop at about the same rate as with older paints ($\frac{1}{4}$% per day). Since British ships in the Napoleonic wars spent years at sea on blockade duty, their bottoms must have become very foul, and this alone would account for the few verified cases of French ships, straight out of dock, being faster than those of the RN. One year's fouling at $\frac{1}{4}$% per day would reduce the speed of a sailing battleship by 1-1$\frac{1}{2}$ knots.

For a typical modern gas turbine destroyer with an interval of two years between dockings, the average increase in power over that time, due to fouling, will be 50% of that due to the frictional resistance of a smooth hull. The frictional resistance accounts for about half the average drag of the hull, the rest being due to wave making. This added resistance due to fouling adds about 20% to the annual fuel consumption of 7500 tonnes. With fuel prices of about £51/tonne (1976 prices), the direct cost of fouling to the destroyer is £73 000. However, some 40% of all the fuel used by the RN is taken on at sea from RFAs and it is correct accountancy to add the cost of the tanker fleet to the price of fuel. This would double the cost of fouling.

In total, the annual cost of roughness and fouling to the Royal Navy is about £4million. In war, the barnacle and green weed can slow a fleet sufficiently to lose a battle. The waste of energy associated with fouling has led to a world wide interest in anti-fouling measures. Underwater scrubbing can give a temporary improvement but, as Dr Betty Moss has said, it is rather like mowing a lawn, the scrubbing

In 1976 the resistance to propulsion caused by fouling on a destroyer hull added £73 000 to the ships annual fuel bill. This figure can moreover be doubled if account is taken of the additional cost of more frequent refuelling at sea. In this photograph a *County* class destroyer is about to begin (or has completed) refuelling from an RFA of the *Rover* class *MoD*

merely promoting an even more luxurious secondary growth.

A much more intriguing development, by a British firm, is the Self Polishing Co-Polymer, a paint which is polished and actually gets smoother as water flows past it as well as releasing toxin over a long period of time.

REFERENCES

1 'The Introduction of Copper Sheathing into the RN, 1779-1786', by R J B Knight, *The Mariner's Mirror*
2 *Anti Fouling,* by I Lunn, 1974
3 *Fouling and Economic Ship Performance,* by D K Brown, 5th Inter Naval Corrosion Conference, 1976

Warship Photograph Service

As part of the service to readers WARSHIP has come to a special arrangement with the Popperfoto/Conway Picture Libraries to make available any of their photographs used in the journal. These are credited 'CPL' after the captions and include a reference number for ordering prints. Please note that no other photos from these libraries are available to the general public, and that only two sizes of prints can be supplied.

This offer stands until further notice, although this advertisement may not appear in every issue.

RATES (per print, post free)

	UK	plus 8% VAT
A. Full plate, 6″ x 8″ (162 x 203mm)	£0.50p	4p
B. Continental postcard, 4″ x 6″ (102 x 162mm)	£0.12p	1p

OVERSEAS RATES (VAT does not apply, includes airmail postage to Europe or airmail printed paper rate elsewhere)

	US & Canada	Australia & NZ	Germany	France
A.	$2.00	$1.65	DM3.50	Fr 15
B.	$0.50	$0.45	DM1.00	Fr 4

Other rates on application

ORDERING

When ordering please quote your name and address in block capitals, the number, size (A or B), and reference numbers of the prints required. Payment by cheque, postal or International Money Order, crossed and made payable to Conway Maritime Press Ltd, and endorsed 'A/C Payee'.